www.wadsworth.com

www.wadsworth.com is the World Wide Web site for Thomson Wadsworth and is your direct source to dozens of online resources.

At *www.wadsworth.com* you can find out about supplements, demonstration software, and student resources. You can also send email to many of our authors and preview new publications and exciting new technologies.

www.wadsworth.com
Changing the way the world learns®

THE POLITICS OF POWER

A Critical Introduction to American Government

FIFTH EDITION

IRA KATZNELSON
Columbia University

MARK KESSELMAN
Columbia University

ALAN DRAPER
St. Lawrence University

THOMSON ™
WADSWORTH

Australia • Canada • Mexico • Singapore • Spain
United Kingdom • United States

THOMSON

★ ™

WADSWORTH

Publisher: *Clark Baxter*
Executive Editor: *David Tatom*
Developmental Editor: *Stacey Sims*
Assistant Editor: *Rebecca Green*
Technology Project Manager: *Michelle Vardeman*
Marketing Manager: *Janise Fry*
Marketing Assistant: *Teresa Jessen*
Marketing Communications Manager:
    Kelley McAllister
Project Manager, Editorial Production:
    Candace Chen
Art Director: *Maria Epes*

Print Buyer: *Rebecca Cross*
Permissions Editor: *Sarah Harkrader*
Production Service: *Sara Dovre Wudali, Buuji, Inc.*
Photo Researcher: *Myrna Engler*
Copy Editor: *Kristina McComas*
Illustrator: *Cadmus*
Cover Designer: *Brian Salisbury*
Cover Image: *Alley in Washington Slum*
    © Corbis
Compositor: *Cadmus*
Cover/Text Printer: *Transcontinental*
    Printing/Louiseville

Printed in Canada
2 3 4 5 6 7 09 08 07 06 05

For more information about our products,
contact us at:
**Thomson Learning Academic
Resource Center
1-800-423-0563**

For permission to use material from this text
or product, submit a request online at
http://www.thomsonrights.com.
Any additional questions about permissions
can be submitted by email to
thomsonrights@thomson.com.

Library of Congress Control Number: 2004117038

ISBN 0-534-60179-0

**Thomson Higher Education
10 Davis Drive
Belmont, CA 94002-3098
USA**

Asia (including India)
Thomson Learning
5 Shenton Way
#01-01 UIC Building
Singapore 068808

Australia/New Zealand
Thomson Learning Australia
102 Dodds Street
Southbank, Victoria 3006
Australia

Canada
Thomson Nelson
1120 Birchmount Road
Toronto, Ontario M1K 5G4
Canada

UK/Europe/Middle East/Africa
Thomson Learning
High Holborn House
50–51 Bedford Row
London WC1R 4LR
United Kingdom

Latin America
Thomson Learning
Seneca, 53
Colonia Polanco
11560 Mexico
D.F. Mexico

Spain (including Portugal)
Thomson Paraninfo
Calle Magallanes, 25
28015 Madrid, Spain

To Robert and Clarice Draper,
and in memory of
Ephraim and Sylvia Katznelson,
and in memory of
Paul and Anne Kesselman

———————————◼———————————

BRIEF CONTENTS

CONTENTS

CONTENTS

An entire political generation passed between the publication of the third edition of *The Politics of Power* in 1987, when George H.W. Bush was vice president of the United States, and the fourth edition that came out in 2002, when his son George W. Bush was president. We are glad that readers did not have to wait nearly so long between publication dates for this, the fifth edition of *The Politics of Power*.

The world and American politics have changed in important, fascinating, and often troubling ways since 2002. *The Politics of Power* continues to change with it. The chapters have been revised to keep track of new scholarship and updated to keep abreast of recent events. In addition, the structure of the book continues to be renovated and even expanded. Chapter 4, which previously covered social movements, is now devoted to new material, a description and analysis of American public opinion. Chapter 11 is an entirely new chapter that examines economic policy. By adding this chapter, we now provide a coherent cluster of chapters analyzing foreign, social, and economic policy. We believe these changes and additions provide students with a more thorough and comprehensive account of American politics than previous editions.

While *The Politics of Power* has been altered and extended, its aim remains the same: to introduce students to a critical perspective on American politics by highlighting how political conflicts, institutions, and processes are influenced by deep inequalities generated by the country's political economy. The text underscores the mutually supportive but uneasy relationship joining American democracy and American capitalism. We try to clarify this multifaceted association in the hope that our perspective and analytic framework will provoke thought and discussion. In so doing, we aim to assist students in developing not only their own approaches to the study of American politics but also their role as citizens.

Following the Introduction, which provides a theoretical framework that analyzes key issues in democratic theory, the book divides into four parts. Part I explores ties linking economics and politics. Economic power, which is based upon ownership and control of capital, has an impact upon political power, influencing who gets what, where, and how in society. Part II examines the political participation of citizens, looking at the views citizens hold and the ways in which they promote them. Part III investigates the federal government's executive, legislative, and judicial institutions. Part IV turns to how social, economic, and foreign policies have been shaped by the economy, political participation, and political institutions. It also reviews the impact these policies have had on American political and social life. The Conclusion reviews the main points developed in the text and points to future directions in American politics. Throughout, we have tried to be direct without being simplistic, engaging without being flippant, and critical without being cynical. We will be pleased if our discussions animate students new to the study of American politics, engage more advanced students, and challenge professors who assign the book.

We continue to be assisted by numerous people. Librarians at Columbia and St. Lawrence Universities were enormously helpful in locating difficult sources and information. We are most grateful for the fine help of colleagues who reviewed individual chapters or the entire manuscript: Charles Dannehl, Bradley University; Russ Dondero, Pacific University; Michael E. Good, California State University, Hayward; and James A. Norris, Texas A&M International University. Their advice improved the book's argument and presentation. In addition we were supported by friends and family who offered encouragement and diversion. Ira Katznelson and Mark Kesselman recognize the help they received from students and colleagues at Columbia University, while Alan Draper gives thanks to Pat Ellis and his children, Sam and Rachel, for their warmth and patience. Collectively, we appreciate and want to acknowledge the professionalism of our editors and other staff at Thomson Wadsworth and the other firms that helped publish our book: David Tatom, Executive Editor; Stacey Sims, Developmental Editor; Rebecca Green, Editorial Assistant; Candace Chen, Project Manager; Sara Dovre Wudali, Service Project Editor, Buuji, Inc.; Kristina McComas, Copyeditor; and Mary Dissinger, Account Manager, Cadmus Professional Communications.

DEMOCRACY'S CHALLENGE

It took three years to build at a cost of $7.5 million dollars—the equivalent of about $400 million today. It was almost 900 feet long—three football fields put end to end—weighed about 46,000 tons, and was 175 feet high from its keel to the top. Its owners said it was unsinkable. When it left the dock, the *Titanic* was the biggest, fastest, most luxurious ocean liner ever constructed.

The *Titanic* set sail on its maiden voyage from Liverpool bound for New York on April 10, 1912. On board were 2228 people, as were 40,000 fresh eggs, 12,000 dinner plates, 6,000 tablecloths, and 1,000 finger bowls. As the boat cruised toward New York, first-class passengers spent their days swimming in a pool, exercising in a gymnasium, relaxing in a reading room, or exchanging pleasantries in a lounge reserved for them. In the evening they enjoyed elegant parties, drank fine wine, and ate sumptuous meals before retiring to their spacious staterooms. Many of the first-class passengers on board were familiar names from High Society, such as John Jacob Astor IV, whose grandfather struck it rich in lumber and real estate; and George Widener, whose family made its fortune in streetcars; as well as members of British nobility, such as the Countess of Rothes and Sir Cosmo Duff Gordon.

Passengers in third class did not have it as good. But their accommodations were better than on any other ocean liner. Families in third class were crowded into small rooms, which could barely accommodate two bunk beds and a toilet. Single men and women were housed in separate, congested, unpleasant holds below on opposite ends of the ship. There were only two bathtubs for use by the 700 passengers in third class. In addition, they were restricted from moving about the ship and from using the amenities reserved for first-class passengers. Many brought food for the duration of the trip across the ocean because they could not afford to dine on board. The price of the ticket had exhausted their savings. Unlike the Anglo-American aristocracy in first class, many third-class passengers were non-British immigrants from such distant places as Poland, Italy, and Russia. They were fleeing persecution and poverty in the countries from which they had come in hopes of finding freedom and prosperity in America.

As the ship crossed the Atlantic, everything appeared calm. The Titanic had made good progress. Anxious to gain a competitive edge in the

An ad announcing the maiden voyage of the *Titanic*.

ruthlessly competitive steamship business—then the only means of cross-Atlantic travel—the owners of the *Titanic* instructed the captain to increase the ship's speed. Dismissing the risks involved, the owners hoped to break the record for cross-Atlantic travel and arrive in New York a day early. This would attract even more publicity for the ship's arrival and humble the competition. With its engines at full throttle, the *Titanic* entered treacherous waters off Newfoundland. Then disaster struck. An iceberg tore a 200 foot hole along the ship's hull. The *Titanic* began to sink. Bedlam broke out on board. While the *Titanic* was equipped with all sorts of luxurious facilities, the owners had outfitted the ship with only enough lifeboats to evacuate half the passengers. When the *Titanic* began to sink, the ship's owners ordered that first-class passengers be evacuated first. Meanwhile, third-class passengers trying to reach the lifeboats sometimes found the doors to the deck locked or blocked. Those fortunate enough to reach the deck found that first-class passengers were given priority on the lifeboats and that there were not enough boats to rescue everyone. In the end, two-thirds of the first-class passengers were saved. The results of that tragic night were quite different, however, for the passengers in steerage: Two-thirds of them froze to death in the icy waters of the Atlantic. Just as class influenced how people lived on board ship, so it influenced who would die.

There are many ways in which the tale of the *Titanic* offers a powerful metaphor for key features of American society and politics even today. The

United States is the most powerful, richest, and strongest nation in the world. It is the biggest, fastest, most luxurious ocean liner around. Like the *Titanic*, it is also characterized by massive disparities in wealth and income that separate first- and third-class passengers. The average income of the top quintile (one-fifth) has grown since 1977, while that of the bottom quintile actually has shrunk. In 2000, the average income for families in the top 20 percent of the income distribution was $141,621. That was more than 12 times the average income of the poorest 20 percent, which was only $10,188. Americans may all be passengers on the same ship, but they have very different experiences of the journey based upon their class position. Citizens who are in the top quintile of the income distribution and can afford first-class tickets have bigger homes, drive nicer cars, live in finer neighborhoods, and send their children to better schools than citizens who can only afford third-class tickets.

Not only does inequality affect which Americans live better in terms of access to the good things in life, but, just as on the *Titanic*, it influences who lives at all. Membership in a higher social class reduces the risk of heart attack, diabetes, infectious disease, arthritis, and some cancers, and is a more powerful predictor of health and mortality than genetics, exposure to carcinogens, and smoking.[1] Wealthier citizens can afford good medical care, while those who are poor often have to take their chances in the open seas and hope for the best.

Regrettably, there is another system of inequality that overlaps that of class. First- and third-class passengers are distinguished today by the color of their skin as much as by the size of their wallet. Whites earn more, are more fully employed, are more educated, are less victimized by crime, and live longer than minorities. An example of how people are treated differently depending upon their class and race occurred during the anthrax scare following the September 11, 2001, terrorist attacks on the Pentagon and World Trade Center. When a letter containing the deadly bacteria anthrax was discovered in a congressional office, every precaution was taken to protect the mostly white and educated staff members who worked there. The office was quickly quarantined and congressional aides were tested for exposure. But no such preventative measures were taken at the mail-sorting facility, employing mostly black workers, through which the lethal letter passed. The Postal Service did not begin to take protective measures until some postal workers became ill, with two eventually dying from the deadly bacteria.

The long arm of racial and class inequality even reaches into the voting booth, affecting whose vote is tallied. A congressional study found that minority and poor voters were three times more likely to have their vote voided in the 2000 presidential election than ballots cast by affluent whites. Voters in minority precincts, which tended to be poorer, used older voting

---

[1] *New York Times*, June 1, 1999.

machines that failed to record accurately how citizens cast their ballots because the county could not afford more modern, accurate models.[2]

The example of the *Titanic* even extends beyond how class and racial inequalities shape and distort the quality of life. The opulence on board ship while the owners skimped on lifeboats is all too reminiscent of the immense resources society devotes to satisfying extravagant consumer desires while investments in the public sector, such as schools, the environment, and the safety net, are underfunded. For example, the American welfare state does not provide enough lifeboats to those who need medical care, child care, or income support. The private affluence on board ship is at odds with inadequate public provision in the event of a personal emergency or broader social catastrophe.

Finally, the degree to which businesses put profits above other values is eerily similar to the way the owners of the *Titanic* recklessly endangered the lives of their passengers. The tragedy that occurred off the Newfoundland coast was in part due to the fact that the *Titanic's* owners were intent on arriving early in order to gain favorable publicity and overshadow the competition. Regrettably, there are all too many examples of corporations seeking profits at the expense of their customers' welfare. Recent and notorious examples include Firestone tires that explode, Ford cars that roll over, and Phillip Morris cigarettes that cause cancer.

DEMOCRACY AND CAPITALISM

Although powerful, the *Titanic* as a metaphor breaks down at a crucial point. The United States is a democracy, the world's oldest. The *Titanic* was not. The captain of the *Titanic* was accountable to the owners who employed him; the passengers did not elect him. By contrast, all adult American citizens today (with the exception of prisoners and some ex-felons) have the right to vote. Democrats and Republicans, as well as a host of minor political parties, compete actively to win the support of the electorate. Organized groups lobby to defend the interests of their members. Few countries allow as much freedom to engage in political debate. Citizens can mobilize to make demands others find uncomfortable. Newspapers and television provide regular reports of government activities, debate the wisdom of public policies, and expose wrongdoing by high government officials, including presidents. Perhaps more than ever, the American political system is a global beacon. When young people, at great risk, fought for democracy in China in 1989, they raised a model of the Statue of Liberty in Beijing's main square. More political refugees fleeing oppressive conditions seek asylum in the United States than anywhere else. Compared to other countries, public

---

[2] *New York Times*, July 9, 2001.

authorities are accessible and responsive. Their rule is not arbitrary. Citizens are protected by rights and by laws that prevent public authorities from acting in arbitrary ways. Government is accountable to the people, who are invited into the political process as participants. In the last resort, the people are sovereign.

Without citizen rights, lawful procedures, and political institutions that are responsive and accountable, no meaningful democracy is possible. Yet even if the rules of democracy are completely enforced, democracy cannot be judged only by its formal rules. What happens when we combine the democratic features of American government with deep inequalities? To what degree does the unequal distribution of wealth and life prospects between first-class passengers and those in steerage affect their ability to influence public policy? To what extent is popular sovereignty possible in a society characterized by large inequalities of resources? In the pages that follow, we show both how American democracy is distorted by vast economic and political inequalities and how democratic institutions make it possible for ordinary citizens to effect change.

Our starting point is the special status possessed by the country's major business firms. Those who own the means to produce goods and services have disproportionate power not only because they have more money and the ability to secure access and influence but also because governments must act in ways that promote the prosperity of the private economy, the country's great engine of wealth and employment. The well-being of everyone in terms of jobs and income depends on the investment decisions and the profits of private firms, and corporate executives decide the "nation's industrial technology, the pattern of work organization, location of industry, market structure, resource allocation, and, of course, executive compensation and status." As a result, the political economist Charles Lindblom shrewdly observed, "business leaders thus become a kind of public official and exercise what, on a broad view of their role, are public functions."[3] The leaders of the private economy cannot be ordered to invest or perform effectively. They have to be prompted and persuaded to do so. Public policies concerned with taxation, trade, and regulation, among other matters, are the instruments the government utilizes to achieve this goal.

Business thus commands a privileged position in public life. "In the eyes of government officials," Lindblom notes, "businessmen do not appear simply as the representatives of a special interest, as representatives of interest groups do. They appear as functionaries performing functions that government officials regard as indispensable."[4] Business leaders in general, but especially the leaders of major corporate firms, have a double advantage in the country's democracy. With more money, they can afford to hire lobbyists,

---

[3] Charles E. Lindblom, *Politics and Markets: The World's Political-Economic Systems* (New York: Basic Books, 1977), pp. 171, 172.

[4] Ibid., p. 175.

contribute to campaigns, create organizations, gain access to decision makers, and thereby influence debates about public policy. Even more importantly, by holding a key structural position—the jobs and income of many Americans depend upon corporate investment strategies and decisions— they become key partners of government in what might be called a corporate complex.

One consequence of this close relationship is that, although the Constitution provides ample protection for expressing the most unpopular opinions, many political views are, in fact, not adequately represented in public debate. Key issues of manifest public significance, such as what to produce, where to produce it, how to produce it, and what to do with the resources generated by production, are decided privately, with little public discussion. The result is a public sphere more limited than the cacophony of debate might suggest. The principle of majority rule, the very centerpiece of representative democracy, thus applies to a confined range of questions. The most important issues that affect the welfare of citizens are sometimes not even considered but are decided outside of democratic politics in corporate boardrooms, outside the reach of majority rule.

It is impossible to understand the politics of power, and powerlessness, in the United States without attention to the way democracy and inequality intertwine to affect virtually every aspect of American life, including the place of race and gender, the quality of city neighborhoods, the provision of services, and political choices made by government officials and citizens. These are the issues we place front and center in this critical introduction to American government. We wrote this book to highlight both the remarkable aspects of political democracy and the recurring problems that distort it, such as inequalities rooted in class, gender, and race that make the country's political system less democratic than it might be. We define democracy not only in terms of its formal rules but also by the more demanding yardstick of whether all citizens have relatively equal chances to influence and control the making of decisions that affect them.

Although formal, legal, democratic procedures and institutions are essential to this standard of democracy, they do not guarantee it. Just as the quality of democracy may be compromised when power is concentrated in the hands of a single elite combining economic with political power, it also may be diminished when many key issues are not considered appropriate for public discussion and when public policies are influenced by social inequalities.

STANDARDS OF DEMOCRACY

Efforts to assess American democracy in the face of these features have produced some of the best work on American politics. For example, in 1961, political scientist Robert Dahl published a brilliant and influential study of politics in New Haven, Connecticut. By commonly accepted standards, he argued, the city was a democracy, since virtually all of its adult citizens were legally entitled to vote and their votes were honestly counted. In New Haven, Dahl found that "two political parties contest elections, offer rival slates of candidates, and thus present the voters with at least some outward show of choice." Although the city's residents were legally equal at the ballot box, they were substantively unequal. Economic inequality in New Haven contrasted sharply with its formal political equality. Less than one-sixteenth of the taxpayers owned one-third of the city's property. In the wealthiest ward, 1 family out of 4 had an income three times the city average; the majority of the families in the poorest ward earned under $2,000 per year. Only 1 out of 30 adults in the poorest ward had attended college, in contrast to nearly half of those in the richest ward.[5]

Is the combination of legal equality and class inequality democratic? Dahl put the question this way: "In a system where nearly every adult may vote but where knowledge, wealth, social position, access to officials, and other resources are unequally distributed, who actually governs? . . . How does a 'democratic' system work amid inequality of resources?"[6] He placed quotation marks around the term *democratic* because its meaning in this situation is unclear. Should a democratic system be measured only by legal standards of equality, such as fair and open election procedures, or should it be measured by substantive standards, according to the control and distribution of resources? What, in short, is the relationship of capitalism and democracy?

In his study of New Haven, Dahl argued that, rather than one elite group making political decisions, different groups determined policy in different issue areas, such as urban renewal, public education, and the nomination of candidates for office. In each area, however, there was a wide disparity between the ability of politically and economically powerful people and that of average citizens to make decisions. As a result of such disparities, Dahl noted, New Haven was "a long way from achieving the goal of political equality advocated by the philosophers of democracy and incorporated into the creed of democracy and equality practically every American professes to uphold." Nevertheless, he concluded that "New Haven is an example of a democratic system, warts and all," because it met key procedural tests denied to the majority of humankind.[7] Not only could the city's citizens vote but also they had a choice between candidates in elections that were conducted honestly and freely.

The United States clearly is a democracy, warts and all. We prefer, however, a higher standard. We recognize and cherish the procedures essential to democracy at the same time we insist on a reckoning with the extent, character, and effects of inequality. Broadly, from this perspective, we distinguish

---

[5] Robert Dahl, *Who Governs? Democracy and Power in an American City* (New Haven, CT: Yale University Press, 1961), pp. 3–4.

[6] Ibid., pp. 1, 3.

[7] Ibid., pp. 86, 311.

three aspects of democracy. The first stresses popular participation in decision making; the second, the representation of interests; and the third, the reduction of advantages based on class, race, and gender.

Citizen participation in decision making traditionally has been regarded as a centerpiece of democracy. In the famous view of 18th-century French political theorist Jean Jacques Rousseau, when citizens exercise control by participating in making decisions, they subjectively feel like active citizens and thus develop loyalty to their society. In addition, by participating, citizens learn how to do so effectively. As social theorist Carole Pateman put it in her interpretation of Rousseau's *The Social Contract*, "the more the individual citizen participates, the better he is able to do so. . . . He learns to be a public as well as a private citizen."[8]

Direct participation is much easier to achieve in small groups and settings, like New England town meetings, than in society as a whole, especially one as large and complex as that of the United States. Hence, the first key standard of democracy with regard to participation concerns the ability and propensity of citizens to participate in politics via elections and also through various channels of influence like political parties, interest groups, and social movements.

A second standard concerns the concept of political representation. Since, as citizens, we cannot all participate simultaneously in making political decisions, we depend on having our preferences and interests literally "re-presented" by others inside the political process, as is done in Congress. Four dimensions of representative democracy provide us with a useful yardstick against which to test present realities. The first is *procedures*. It is essential in a democracy that individuals and groups be able to make their views known and to fairly select their leaders and public officials. In this regard, civil liberties and civil rights are essential. Freedom of speech, freedom of assembly, freedom of the press, and the absence of discriminatory barriers to participation are the basic hallmarks of procedural representation. When these procedural guarantees are suppressed, it is extraordinarily difficult for people to formulate and express their interests.

A second dimension of representation concerns *personnel*. Those who govern should reflect the characteristics of class, race, ethnicity, sex, and geography of those they formally represent. The demographic representativeness of those who make political decisions is important not to fulfill abstract numerical quotas of representation. Rather, the personnel dimension of representation is important because the more demographically representative a political system is, the more likely it is that the interests of different types of citizens will be adequately and substantively represented. Group members are much more likely than others to vigorously represent their own interests. It is not surprising, therefore, that workers represented by unions earn better

---

[8] Carole Pateman, *Participation and Democratic Theory* (Cambridge, England: Cambridge University Press, 1970), p. 25.

wages than when workers' wages are entrusted to the discretion of their employers; nor is it surprising that minorities receive more city services when they sit on the city council than when they are absent. "Descriptive representation," (the degree to which the social backgrounds of the representatives reflect the people they represent) contributes to "substantive representation" (more effective representation).[9]

The third dimension of political representation is *responsiveness*. Representatives must be aware of, and responsive to, their constituents' concerns. In this respect, ordinary citizens often find it much more difficult than the most privileged to achieve representation of their interests, since those with more resources tend to perceive and promote their interests more accurately and effectively than others do. Thus, representation concerns not only *who* rules but also the *uses* to which power is put by those who rule. The first two dimensions of representation—procedures and personnel—refer to the first of these two issues. But the dimension of responsiveness asks how representatives see the interests of their constituents and how they act on behalf of these interests. To satisfy the requirements of representative democracy, those who formally represent the population must use the power conferred by their positions to promote the interests of the citizens they represent.

But even where the first three dimensions of representation are satisfied, political democracy cannot be said to be entirely in operation. The last dimension that must be realized is *effectiveness*—the ability of representatives to produce the results they desire. A system cannot be democratically representative if effectiveness is distributed unequally among representatives. Thus, representative democracy can be said to have been achieved only when all four dimensions of representation are satisfied: when leaders are selected by regular procedures that are open to all people and all groups have relatively equal access to the political system; when representatives reflect the composition of the population as a whole; when they are conscious of and responsive to their constituents' interests; and when they can act effectively on behalf of those interests.

Unlike a purely procedural approach to democracy, this standard of representative democracy does not simply endorse present practices as democratic when they meet a procedural test. Rather, it allows us to measure the degree of representative democracy that exists. Conversely, it shows us how much needs to be done to achieve a fully representative democracy. For example, the right to free speech is precious. But it becomes distorted when those who own the media can use it to express their views to millions while most Americans lack the means to disseminate their opinions to even a few. Political rights, such as the right to vote, are an essential part of any democracy. But these rights are undermined when candidates pander to the rich who can provide them with campaign contributions that ordinary citizens cannot

---

[9] Hanna Fenichel Pitkin, *The Concept of Representation* (Berkeley: University of California Press, 1967).

afford. Civil liberties are to be cherished. But these are perverted when some people can afford to hire expensive lawyers to take advantage of these rights while others can only afford overworked and understaffed court-appointed attorneys to defend them. The point of all these examples is that procedural rights are important, but not enough. Substantive democracy takes us beyond these limits and is the best available standard to test the democratic content of existing political institutions and processes. It represents a demanding, yet realistic yardstick to measure the extent of democracy in America. Sadly, when we apply this yardstick, we find that America does not measure up in many key respects.

Nevertheless, even our more demanding standard by which to assess democracy is too limited. For it does not address the basic dilemma posed earlier in the chapter: In Dahl's words, "How does a 'democratic' system work amid inequality of resources?"

The answer to this question is that the two systems may coexist in varied and changing ways, as they have in much of the West for more than the past century. Even as this duality is a fact of life, however, its character and content have been, and continue to be, contested. It is clear that high degrees of inequality stand as a barrier to achievement of the fullest degree of democracy, of what we designate here as substantive democracy—a situation in which all citizens have relatively equal chances to influence the making of decisions that affect them. Indeed, the limits of procedural democracy help perpetuate the idea that what exists is democratic and therefore does not need reform. The more demanding, more critical standard of substantive democracy is based not only on the various political dimensions of representation but also on social equality.

POLITICAL CHANGE

The interplay of these dimensions of democracy with inequality raises pressing questions about political life not only in the United States and industrial societies in Western Europe, but also in Russia and other former Communist countries, in Latin American nations that have moved from authoritarian rule to democracy, and in post-apartheid South Africa—indeed, in most of the world. Many of the most significant questions of social theory and political philosophy in the past century have concerned the tension inherent in societies that are simultaneously capitalist and democratic. Even when these issues are not openly on the agenda, the relationship between the inequalities generated by the routine operation of the market economy and the equal rights and responsibilities of citizens in a democratic polity shape major features of political life.

These questions are not new. The particular conditions in which they are being probed and explored in American politics, however, have changed enormously in the past two generations. Four changes are of critical significance that force us to reassess American politics anew.

1. THE UNITED STATES IS THE LONE SUPERPOWER IN A MORE INTERCONNECTED WORLD.   The end of the Cold War in 1989 left the United States as the only superpower in the world. Its military power is unrivaled. It has the most technologically sophisticated, best-equipped military in the world, bar none. The United States spends more on defense than the next 15 highest spending nations *combined.* And its presence is global. Hundreds of thousands of American troops equipped with the most advanced weaponry are stationed in over 61 military bases in 19 countries, with American military personnel deployed in another 800 smaller installations across the globe.

The biggest and most powerful military helps serve and protect the biggest and most powerful economy in the world. The United States is the largest national market, home to more of the biggest, most profitable corporations than any other country. Although it contains only 4.65 percent of the world's population, the U.S. economy accounts for 32.9 percent of global Gross Domestic Product (GDP), and the American dollar continues to be the international medium of exchange, the currency in which the rest of the world does business. American corporations, such as IBM, Coca-Cola, and General Motors are as ubiquitous overseas as American military personnel.

Its military and economic power combine to give the United States extraordinary influence in international affairs. There are few significant places or issues around the world where the United States does not project its power, from sending humanitarian aid to Africa to negotiating trade agreements with China, from mediating the Arab–Israeli conflict to sending troops to Iraq, from signing defense treaties with Europe to fighting drug smugglers in South America. Yet even as the United States outdistances all other rivals, it is still vulnerable as was evident by the successful terrorist attack on the World Trade Center and Pentagon in 2001. The world has become a more complicated stage. There are now more countries with more weapons of mass destruction that can cause vast damage than ever before. Small conflicts now have a greater chance of escalating into larger ones that draw surrounding countries into the turmoil. The threat of terrorism remains and continues to haunt American society. And our economy is now more integrated with the rest of the world, subject to market changes that occur beyond our borders and over which we have little control. As the world has become more interdependent, domestic politics is less insulated by what happens beyond our borders. Throughout American history, the country has been shaped by war and trade, but the scope and velocity of today's movements of people, ideas, money, goods, and weapons across borders are unprecedented. Greater global interdependence increases our power and our vulnerability at one and the same time.

2. MONEY HAS BECOME VASTLY MORE IMPORTANT TO POLITICAL DEBATE AND OUTCOMES.   "Indisputably," one veteran Washington journalist writes, "the greatest change in Washington over the past twenty-five years . . . has been in the preoccupation with money. . . . The culture of money dominates

Washington as never before."[10] Politicians spend more time raising more money than ever before. They must win the first election for dollars, for campaign contributions, before they can advance to the next election for votes. Running for office is increasingly reserved for those with money or those who know people who have it. In 2000, about $2.9 billion was spent by parties, candidates, and interest groups on congressional and presidential races. In 2004, after campaign finance reform that was supposed to reduce the flow of money into federal elections, more than $3.9 billion was spent—one-third more than just four years before.

The culture of money has not only infected elections but has upped the ante for other forms of political activity. Lobbying public officials is a billion-dollar industry. The price of gaining access to and influence with lawmakers is rising. In addition, legal expenses are increasing as more groups are going to court to challenge government policies and decisions. Finally, the expense of funding organizations with which to coordinate lobbying and court cases is increasing, as overhead, research, and labor costs go up. In other words, you have to pay to play, and the price is getting steeper all the time.

The culture of money has even seeped into the way ordinary citizens behave politically. According to Harvard political scientist Robert Putnam, citizens are now more likely to substitute their money for their time when it comes to participating in politics. Citizens now perform their civic duty by contributing money as opposed to working on a campaign or writing a letter to their representative. Politics has become a spectator sport, in Putnam's terms, in which people prefer to pay the professionals to play instead of participating themselves.[11]

3. POLITICS HAS BECOME MORE POLARIZED IN TERMS DEFINED BY THE INTERPLAY OF PARTY, CLASS, RACE, AND REGION. Commenting on the differences between politics today and politics from a quarter of a century ago, one Washington insider told journalist Elizabeth Drew, "Everything is much more personal, much more partisan, and much more confrontational—and ideological."[12] For a very long time, one of the standard truisms of American politics was that the country's political parties were broad tents, covering a wide array of groups and interests. During the period spanning the 1910s to the early 1960s, for example, the Democratic Party housed liberal and progressive politicians who supported unions, civil rights, and social equality. It also sheltered the country's leading segregationist politicians from the South, where Jim Crow defined the law of the land. The Republican Party, likewise, was quite heterogeneous, including internationally minded,

---

[10] Elizabeth Drew, *The Corruption of American Politics: What Went Wrong and Why* (Woodstock, NY: Overlook Press, 2000), p. 61.

[11] Robert D. Putnam, *Bowling Alone: The Collapse and Revival of American Community* (New York: Cambridge University Press, 2000), p. 41.

[12] Quoted in Drew, *The Corruption of American Politics*, p. 35.

relatively liberal members and isolationist, more conservative party leaders. But conservative Democrats and moderate Republicans are endangered political species today. In Congress, liberals are grouped almost exclusively in the Democratic Party and conservatives, in the main, in the Republican Party. Differences *within* the parties are getting smaller at the same time differences *between* the parties are getting larger. The result is more partisan combat, less civility, more party unity, and less willingness to compromise.

The most significant cause of these developments has been the partisan realignment of the South. While the South was once solidly Democratic in its voting patterns, today it usually votes Republican in national elections and, increasingly, in local contests as well. The realignment of the South—a region whose population continues to grow—from a Democratic to a Republican stronghold has erased what was once a Democratic majority into parity between the parties, if not a Republican advantage. The realignment of the South has been the source of Republican resurgence and a strong conservative tilt in national politics.

4. *AMERICANS DEMONSTRATE A STRONGER BELIEF IN THE VIRTUE OF MARKETS.* The last two changes—the increased power of money in politics and the resurgence of the Republican Party due to partisan change in the South—are both cause and consequence of yet another large transformation in American politics. The election of Ronald Reagan as president in 1980 signaled the triumph of a more conservative ideology. Four years before the election, Robert Bartley, then in charge of the editorial page of the politically conservative *Wall Street Journal,* observed that liberalism as an "establishment . . . has ordered our political and intellectual lives for the past two generations." He predicted that "over the next few years we will see an increasing challenge to the very heart of liberal . . . thinking."[13] The new ideology he and other conservative intellectuals advocated as a distinctly minority position at the time was thought to be well outside the political mainstream. It held that government should do less, not more; that government should be smaller, not bigger; that more decisions should be left to the marketplace, not elected officials; and that society should provide more opportunity, not more equality. Just four years later President Reagan, drawing on the ideas of a new generation of conservative intellectuals promoting these ideas, began to implement this design for a more modest government and more reliance on the marketplace. As a result of the Reagan revolution, conservatives now set the main terms of public debate. The political center shifted to the right. Democrats, such as former President Bill Clinton, now were obliged to justify their policies by invoking the virtues of smaller government, balanced budgets, and the marketplace. President George W. Bush and the Republican

---

[13] Robert L. Bartley, "Liberalism 1976: A Conservative Critique" (paper prepared for the Conference on the Relevance of Liberalism, Columbia University Research Institute on International Change, New York, January 1976).

Party were able to invoke these ideas—with a large dose of patriotism thrown in following the 2001 terrorist attacks on the Pentagon and World Trade Center—in order to gain control over all three branches of government following the 2002 and 2004 elections.

CONCLUSION

The tension between democracy and capitalism, the manner in which formal, legal equality and real, substantive inequality interact, is the subject of this book. Capturing how democracy and capitalism shape the politics of such a large and complex country as the United States is an ambitious task. "I am large, I am multitudes," Walt Whitman wrote in his epic poem, *Song of Myself*, about America. So it is. Here is our plan in trying to make sense of this individualistic, tolerant, assertive, open, naive, and sometimes ruthless superpower: In Chapters 2 and 3, we consider the close relationship between the national government and the country's capitalist economy. In Chapters 4 and 5, we discuss public opinion and political participation. These chapters describe how political preferences are formed and transmitted to policymakers. In Chapters 6, 7, and 8, we address the interplay of political economy, political culture, and participation in the institutional settings of the presidency, Congress, and courts. In Chapters 9, 10, and 11, we assess the public policy outcomes produced by this process in foreign, domestic, and economic policy, respectively. Finally, in our conclusion, Chapter 12, we review the main points of the text and discuss possible futures for American politics and society.

AMERICAN POLITICAL ECONOMY

In the 1960s, Flint, Michigan, was a prosperous city. The town was built around automaker General Motors (GM), the world's largest corporation. GM employed over 40,000 workers in Flint, and the roads in town bore such names as Chevrolet Highway and Buick Freeway—an indication of Flint's connection to two of GM's automotive divisions. Work in the auto plants throughout the city was hard, but the union, the United Automobile Workers (UAW), helped to ensure that workers were rewarded for their efforts.[1] In 1969, average earnings in Genesee County, where Flint is located, were roughly $2,000 above those in the rest of Michigan, and $7,000 higher than average income throughout the United States.[2] Unemployment was low and poverty was negligible. In one of the first quality-of-urban-life surveys ever conducted, Flint ranked 18th out of 66 medium-sized cities.

Michael Moore, who grew up in Flint, left home in the 1970s to pursue a career in journalism and filmmaking. When he returned to Flint years later, he found a city on its knees. In 1980, Flint led the nation's cities in joblessness, with an unemployment rate of 20.7 percent, causing Moore to dub his hometown "the unemployment capital of America." Throughout the 1980s, Flint's unemployment rate remained twice as high as it was in the rest of Michigan. Nor did the picture improve much in ensuing years. In the 1990s, private-sector employment declined in Flint, even as it grew in the rest of the state. In 2002, Flint was among the ten worst metropolitan areas in terms of jobs lost, losing 3.3 percent of its jobs that year.

As jobs disappeared, so did people. Flint's population fell from 190,000 in 1970 to 125,000 in 2000. Depopulation left its mark on Flint, as once-proud, stable neighborhoods were defaced by abandoned buildings and dilapidated housing. Public services declined. Earnings fell. By 2000, almost a quarter of the families in Flint had income levels below the poverty line. Aggregate real earnings slumped 9 percent between 1969 and 1993. With

---

[1] Good accounts of Flint can be gleaned from Ronald Edsforth, *Class Conflict and Cultural Consensus: The Making of a Mass Consumer Society in Flint, Michigan* (New Brusnwick, NJ: Rutgers University Press, 1987); Ben Hamper, *Rivethead: Tales from the Assembly Line* (New York: Warner Books, 1991); and Steven P. Dandaneau, *A Town Abandoned: Flint, Michigan Confronts Deindustrialization* (Albany: State University of New York Press, 1996).

[2] Don Pemberton and Robert Schnorbus, *Genesee County and the Transformation of the Auto Industry* (Chicago: Federal Reserve Bank of Chicago, 1996).

AP/Wide World Photos

GM workers in Flint line up to file unemployment claims at their union local.

considerable understatement, a 1996 Federal Reserve Bank of Chicago study reported, "From a peak in 1977 to 1993, average real wage gains per job in Genesee fell by \$9,500 (about 28%), a significant decline in a community's standard of living over a sixteen year period."[3]

Efforts to revive the city failed. A luxury hotel opened in 1979 but declared bankruptcy in 1991. An \$80 million theme park extolling the virtues of automobiles opened in 1984 but filed for bankruptcy within two years. Two major retail projects that were supposed to spark Flint's revival also failed. All of these indignities—poverty, unemployment, bankruptcies, crime, and urban decay—combined to earn Flint last place in *Money Magazine*'s quality-of-life survey of 300 cities.[4] By 2002, the city of Flint's financial situation had become so desperate that the State of Michigan declared a financial emergency. Elected city officials were stripped of their power, and Flint became the largest municipality ever run by the state.

The origin of Flint's decline can be summed up in two words: General Motors.[5] Beginning in the 1980s, GM decided to disinvest, closing factories and moving product lines out of the city. GM closed plants in Flint, not out

---

[3] Ibid., p. 9.

[4] George F. Lord and Albert C. Price, "Growth Ideology in a Period of Decline: Deindustrialization and Restructuring, Flint Style," *Social Problems* 39, no. 2 (May 1992): 155–69.

[5] *New York Times*, July 10, 2002.

of malevolence but because its share of the U.S. auto market had declined from 46 percent in 1980 to just 28 percent by 2002. GM lost market share because it responded too late to the challenge of more efficient cars imported from Japan, experienced turmoil within the ranks of its board of directors, had the worst labor relations of any of the Big Three car companies, had greater administrative overhead than any of its competitors, and pursued an expensive and failed strategy of replacing workers with robots. GM employees absorbed the costs of GM mistakes. In 1983, GM merged its Buick and Fisher Body divisions, reducing employment in the two plants by 3,600 people. In 1986, GM announced it was closing 11 plants nationwide, affecting another 29,000 auto workers. Two of the plants slated for closure, employing over 7,000 workers, were located in Flint. A year later, GM shuttered Fisher Body plants 1 and 2, which had a special place in labor history. Exactly 50 years earlier, in 1937, during the height of the Great Depression, which had thrown millions out of work, autoworkers occupied the factories to force GM to accept their right to join the fledgling United Auto Workers (UAW) union. This historic sit-down strike contributed to the rise of industrial unionism and the Congress of Industrial Organizations (CIO) in the 1930s. But in 1987, the plants were closed, and another 3,000 autoworkers were left unemployed. The 1990s brought Flint no relief from plant closures. From a peak of 80,000 GM workers employed in Flint in 1970, only 15,000 were left by 2002. As plants shut down, Flint collapsed around them.

When Michael Moore decided to make a film about Flint, he went looking for the person whose decisions were key in producing the tragedy afflicting his beloved hometown. He did not go looking for the mayor of Flint or the city council. Nor did he go looking for the governor of Michigan or any other public official. Instead, he went looking for Roger Smith, the Chairman and Chief Executive Officer of General Motors. Moore believed that decisions made by General Motors had more consequences for the city than any action taken by any public official. Moore's film, *Roger & Me*, released in 1990, provides a graphic and tragicomic description of how Flint's dependence on its corporate sponsor led to the city's ruin and describes Moore's futile attempt to impress on Roger Smith the tragic consequences that GM's plant closures had on Flint and its citizens.[6]

But Roger Smith's decision to close plants in Flint was not the result of venality or callousness on his part. GM's decisions were dictated more by the imperatives of profit seeking in a capitalist economy than by the moral character of management. The costs that GM's decisions imposed on Flint were invisible from the perspective of GM's balance sheet. They were an unfortunate, unintended byproduct of management's attempt to maximize earnings. The movie ends with Roger Smith presiding at a lavish Christmas

---

[6] Ronald Edsforth, "Review of Roger & Me," *American Historical Review* 96 (October 1991): 1145–47.

celebration in Detroit, while Moore is back in Flint filming the sheriff evict-
ing another family from its home during the holiday season.[7]

The manner in which GM held the fate of Flint in its hands illuminates
basic features of capitalist democracy and the way power is exercised in the
United States. The impact that private firms like General Motors have on the
general welfare and the demands that citizens make on government are connected to each other. Part 1 of *The Politics of Power* examines the interaction
between the economy and government. Chapter 2 highlights the impact that
corporations, such as General Motors, have on politics. Chapter 3 provides a
short history of the American political economy. It describes the sometimes
tense, sometimes smooth relationship between political and economic
power.

---

[7] Ronald Edsforth, "Review of Roger & Me," *American Historical Review* 96 (October 1991):
1145–47.

GOVERNMENT, THE ECONOMY, AND THE POLITICS OF POWER

Because large corporations exercise enormous power over workers and communities, we suggest that our economic system—that is, capitalism—can be considered a form of *private government*. It is *private* in the sense that those who own and control capital—the financial resources and factories, machines, offices, and raw materials used to produce commodities for sale—are not elected by the public through democratic procedures. Key economic decisions, notably what, where, and how to produce, are made privately, without public debate. However, this system resembles *government* in the sense that corporate policies have profound consequences for all citizens. More than almost any action taken by government, people's lives and their communities are affected greatly by the decisions that private corporations make.

The private power that enables corporations to make decisions that influence the economy and our common welfare give them unique political leverage. But corporations are far from all-powerful. They must compete with each other in the economic and political marketplace. In addition, they must contend with other groups who represent alternative views and interests. The results of these struggles for political power are contingent and open, despite the advantage to business that ownership and control of the means of production confers.

This chapter will first review the rights and privileges that business enjoys by virtue of its control of the means of production. This gives business a built-in, structural advantage in the political system. Next, we describe the economy as divided between a competitive sector of countless small businesses that orbit around and depend upon the corporate sector, which includes a much smaller number of large, diversified, global corporations. These corporations are owned and controlled by a small group of stockholders and executives who make corporate policies, which have implications for all of us, and reap the lion's share of the profits. They constitute America's private government. Finally, the chapter proceeds to review changes in the structure of corporate management, the occupational order, the sources of cohesion and conflict within the capitalist class, and the distinctive form of American capitalism.

THE SYSTEM OF CAPITALISM

Capitalism is commonly defined as a system in which production is privately controlled and carried on for sale or profit rather than directly for consumption and use. Those who own and control capital set the process in motion by hiring workers to carry out the actual work. Their aim in doing so is to make a profit, which can be used for further investment and the accumulation of additional profits. Firms compete with each other for profits. This is the source of capitalism's dynamism, as the competitive drive for profits requires firms to constantly improve efficiency, invent new technology, and explore new markets. But the dynamism of capitalism, its revolutionary thrust, is also the source of its instability. Supply and demand is not coordinated. Investment, production, and consumption fail to equilibrate. Consequently, business cycles occur in which periods of economic growth, measured by output, employment, and profits, are followed by periods of economic contraction in which production declines, unemployment increases, and bankruptcies rise.[1] The business cycle, the alternation of boom and bust, is a universal characteristic of capitalism, exemplified most recently by the stock market bubble of the 1990s and its collapse in 2000. Capitalist economies oscillate between such swings of expansion and contraction, with each period pregnant with the conditions that will produce its opposite. Just as a recession sets the stage for a new period of profitable investment and economic growth by weeding out inefficient firms, expansion creates the conditions for contraction by its tendency to promote inflation and overproduction.

In capitalist economies, a small proportion of the people live off the income they receive from owning a business. Most people, however, earn their living by working for others—by selling their labor to employers in return for wages.

Unlike feudalism, where peasants were tied to a lord's domain, capitalism allowed workers the freedom to contract for work with any employer. But this freedom obscured a lack of alternatives. Unless workers put their labor up for sale and hired themselves out to employers, they could not sustain themselves. As Adam Smith, a 19th-century economist who was a passionate advocate of capitalism, acknowledged, "Many workmen could not subsist a week, few could subsist a month, and scarce any subsist a year without employment."[2]

---

[1] Of course, the major alternative to capitalist production in modern times, the command or socialist economies found in the Soviet Union and its allies in the 20th century, proved even more unstable. Only Cuba continues to organize its economy in this fashion. This is not to claim that radical, desirable, and feasible alternatives to capitalist production cannot be devised. But none has yet proved itself by the test of history.

[2] Smith is quoted in Robert L. Heilbroner, *The Nature and Logic of Capitalism* (New York: Norton, 1985).

Not only is wage labor a characteristic feature of a capitalist society, but relations within the workplace and the economy as a whole are highly undemocratic. Employers have the right to hire and fire, to set wages and salaries, to determine what jobs workers do, and to tell them how to do it.

For example, consider the simple case of going to the bathroom. Students think nothing of leaving class to go to the bathroom. Imagine the outcry if faculty announced that no one could leave class to answer nature's call and that violators would be penalized with reduced grades or even dismissal from the course. Yet, these restrictions prevail in many workplaces. No federal law exists that allows workers to take a bathroom break. Management can require permission to go to the bathroom, restrict the number of bathroom trips employees make, regulate their duration, specify when they will occur, and penalize workers for violating these rules.[3]

Employers, of course, make more important decisions than regulating workers' trips to the john. Those who own and control companies decide what to produce, where to produce, and how to produce it. They organize the process of production and set the rules within the workplace. It is often claimed that this workplace despotism is the price that must be paid to achieve maximum efficiency. However, there is compelling evidence that democratic relations in the workplace would not only provide benefits to workers but to society as well through increased productivity.[4]

The ultimate consequence of this situation, in which workers produce commodities at capitalists' direction, is a society whose core sector is exploitative and undemocratic. This harsh fact is rarely noted. It is only at unusual moments, like the demise of Flint, which Michael Moore captured so vividly in *Roger & Me*, that the authoritarian and exploitative character of capitalism becomes transparent and exposed. Much of the time, it appears to most people as the only possible way to organize an economy and as the product of free choice.

Of course some people argue that capitalists, far from being powerful, are themselves slaves to the marketplace. The consumer is king, not the capitalist. If capitalists do not produce what the public wants, their business will fail. A consumer democracy rules. But there are several problems with this argument.

First, the marketplace is not a democracy where everyone has an equal vote. In the political arena, for example, one person is entitled to one vote. In the marketplace, on the other hand, one dollar equals one vote, permitting

---

[3] Marc Linder and Ingrid Nygaard, *Void Where Prohibited: Rest Breaks and the Right to Urinate on Company Time* (Ithaca, NY: Cornell University Press, 1998).

[4] See, for example, Samuel Bowles, Herbert Gintis, and Bo Gustafsson, eds., *Markets and Democracy: Participation, Accountability and Efficiency* (New York: Cambridge University Press, 1993); Jon Elster and Karl Ove Moene, eds., *Alternatives to Capitalism* (Cambridge, England: Cambridge University Press, 1989); and Robert B. Reich, *The Work of Nations: Preparing Ourselves for 21st Century Capitalism* (New York: Vintage Books, 1992), pt. 3.

the affluent to cast more votes than the poor. Consumer democracy violates the principle of political equality where each citizen has one vote, replacing it with a new principle where votes are distributed according to the size of each citizen's wallet. Second, consumers may register their preferences regarding specific products on the market, but they do not vote on where or how such products are made. Such decisions are made behind the backs of consumers, without their input, in corporate boardrooms. Finally, business spends enormous amounts of money on advertising and marketing to shape consumer preferences. Consumers enjoy the illusion of democratic choice in a marketplace that is contrived and manipulated.

The marketplace is not a consumer democracy. To the contrary, capitalists have extraordinary influence over the entire political economy. The day-to-day strategic decisions that capitalists make affect the fate of local communities like Flint, entire regions, and the whole nation. Such strategic decisions include whether to invest, where to invest, what to invest in, and how to organize production. These decisions, which have extensive consequences for society, are the prerogative of capitalists because they own and control the means of production. A fuller picture of capitalism as a system of private government can be gained by analyzing the rights conferred on capitalists by their control over capital.

WHETHER TO INVEST

Investment decisions by giant corporations determine the level of production and are made on the basis of what promises to fetch the highest profit. Whole communities can be affected by capitalist investment decisions, as Flint discovered to its dismay when GM decided to disinvest from the city. When investment lags, then production lags, wages stagnate, and workers are unable to find jobs. When investment booms, then production booms, jobs are plentiful, and wages rise as employers compete for workers.

A consequence of this process that has profound political implications is that citizens tend to identify their individual welfare with the welfare of capitalism. This helps explain the widespread support for capitalism in the United States. In addition to the intensive propaganda on behalf of capitalism generated by schools, businesses, political parties, the media, and other institutions, there is a rational basis for pro-capitalist beliefs. Capitalism is the goose that lays the golden eggs, on which the livelihood of workers depends. Society's dependence on business to generate jobs and prosperity makes plausible the arguments of business representatives that their specific interests are the interests of the wider society; that high profits for business are necessary for the rest of society to enjoy more investment, more jobs, and higher wages. This situation creates a terrible paradox for workers. Their jobs depend on the profitability of their firm, which, perversely, depends on workers' own exploitation. As one autoworker wrote to his union with some irony: "Believe me—we know how hard it is to make a profit—we spend 50 to 60 hours a week at the company, working to make a profit for our employers."[5] Workers in Flint recognized the awful horns of this dilemma when, in the midst of the crisis afflicting them, they joked in an often repeated phrase, "The only thing worse than working for General Motors is not working for General Motors."

This does not mean that citizens do not perceive conflicts between their interests and those of the companies where they are employed. Again, workers in Flint hardly needed to be reminded that GM sacrificed their jobs because of its declining competitive position. Nor does widespread support for capitalism mean that workers and other citizens do not struggle against specific features of capitalist domination. Environmental activists protest industrial pollution and demand stricter environmental controls on business. Voters elect candidates who stretch the boundaries of reform and oppose corporate power. Tenants organize rent strikes demanding that landlords maintain their buildings. Women demand an end to sexual discrimination inside and outside the workplace, and unions seek to improve working conditions, which employers resist fiercely.

In fact, Americans tend to support capitalist values, such as individualism and minimum state interference, mostly in the abstract. When questioned as to their support for specific government programs to assist the poor, help the sick, and feed the hungry, Americans tend to express broad approval for such activities. Political scientist Elizabeth Sanders writes that "whatever their reservations about government power," non-elite Americans "have shared a powerful belief in community, collective action, and the government's responsibility to remedy market 'defects.'"[6] Even during the heyday of conservatism in the 1980s, when Republican presidents were regularly denouncing the sins of big government, the public continued to support social programs by large and stable majorities.[7] Similarly, when President George W. Bush criticized environmental regulation as costly to business, a firestorm of protest forced him to move stealthily in this area.

WHERE TO INVEST

In a capitalist system, corporate leaders are free to decide where to locate their facilities. These decisions are made on the basis of which location will minimize production costs and maximize sales. Such factors as proximity to suppliers, raw materials, and markets are taken into account when corporations consider where to invest. Corporations also take into account whether the local community is sympathetic to their needs. States and local

---

[5] Kim Moody, *Workers in a Lean World: Unions in the International Economy* (New York: Verso Press, 1999), p. 12.

[6] Elizabeth Sanders, *Roots of Reform: Farmers, Workers, and the American State, 1877–1917* (Chicago: University of Chicago Press, 1999), p. 387.

[7] Thomas Ferguson and Joel Rogers, "The Myth of America's Turn to the Right," *Atlantic Magazine*, May 1986, 43–53.

governments compete with each other by offering concessions to attract investment and the jobs it brings. They fear that, if they do not prostitute themselves in an attempt to lure capital, then another state or community will. States and local communities woo business with special tax incentives, loans, anti-union laws, and weak environmental regulations.[8] For example, in 1993, Alabama offered $300 million in incentives to attract a small Mercedes car factory that would employ only 1,500 people, in effect paying $200,000 for each job. Not to be outdone, Mississippi offered even more incentives when it courted the Nissan Corporation in 2001. The Magnolia State offered $400 million in spending and tax rebates to attract a car factory that would employ 4,000 people and build about 250,000 vehicles every year. In a special one-day session, the Mississippi legislature passed a bill granting a variety of privileges to the project, including $80 million in job training for Nissan workers; $17 million for buildings; $60 million for new, improved roads; a $5,000 per worker tax credit; a rollback of county property taxes; and use of the state's power of eminent domain to acquire and move homeowners off the 1,500 acre site Nissan wanted.[9]

Ironically, such financial incentives are rarely the deciding factor in plant location decisions. Indeed, rather than contributing to a region's economy, low tax rates and abatements on property taxes may actually retard it. Tax revenue lost due to such incentives offered to corporations could leave a community without enough money to support basic services and amenities that make an area attractive. After an exhaustive analysis of these incentives, political scientist Peter Eisinger concluded, "The positive effects of such incentives have not been established incontrovertibly, and there are even potentially perverse effects."[10]

Corporations also consider the characteristics of the local workforce when they decide where to invest. Companies search for areas where workers will accept low wages or are hostile to unions. Corporations may force workers to compete with each other in the same way they play one state against another. In 1991, GM announced it would close an assembly plant in either Ypsilanti, Michigan, or Arlington, Texas. GM chose to close the Ypsilanti assembly plant despite its cost advantage over the Arlington site because its workforce had a reputation for militance and offered fewer concessions. In contrast, the union local in Arlington promised GM—in defiance of the United Auto Workers' national leadership—that it would run three daily shifts, instead of the normal two, if the company kept the plant open.[11]

---

[8] This section draws heavily from Peter Eisinger, *The Rise of the Entrepreneurial State: State and Local Economic Development Policy in the United States* (Madison: University of Wisconsin Press, 1988), pp. 128–73. See also James C. Cobb, *The Selling of the South: The Southern Crusade for Industrial Development, 1936–1980* (Baton Rouge: Louisiana State University Press, 1982), pp. 229–54.

[9] *New York Times*, September 10, 2001.

[10] Eisinger, *Rise of the Entrepreneurial State*, p. 224.

[11] *New York Times*, September 7, 1992.

Finally, corporations are increasingly likely to invest abroad, beyond American borders. For example, from 1920 through 1950, the textile industry moved from New England to the South, which offered special tax incentives, lower wages, and an anti-union climate to firms that relocated. But in a trend beginning in the 1960s and continuing to the present, those same firms left the South to invest in Third World countries like Bangladesh, Mexico, and the Dominican Republic that offered still lower wages, more subsidies, and a more anti-union climate than southern states could offer.

WHAT TO INVEST IN

Investment decisions by giant corporations also determine the kinds of goods available in society. Corporations make these decisions according to what is most profitable to produce and not what society needs. For example, pharmaceutical companies fund research they believe will be profitable. Consequently, little research is done to find cures for rare diseases or to combat epidemics that afflict vast numbers of people in poor regions of the world. For example, researchers accidentally found the cure for sleeping sickness, a fatal disease prevalent in Africa. But it became unprofitable to produce the antidote because so few people who suffered from the disease in Africa could afford to buy it. However, the patent holder resumed production when it was discovered that the medicine could prevent the growth of facial hair on women. It was then marketed as a cosmetic to women in the West as opposed to a lifesaving drug in Africa.[12]

Talent and money are diverted to develop drugs that have commercial as opposed to medical value. One study found that two-thirds of the new drugs approved from 1998 to 2000 were modified versions of existing drugs that did not provide significant benefits over those already on the market.[13] They had virtually the same ingredients as previously approved drugs. The development of profitable "copycat" drugs hardly qualifies as a medical breakthrough, compared to medical and scientific research that could be done in more pressing and life-threatening fields.[14] Of course, drug companies claim that they need to charge high prices in order to finance research for new drugs to cure diseases. But, in fact, 42 percent of all health research and development is paid for by the federal government's National Institute of Health. Not only do taxpayers pay a substantial share of the costs involved in research and development, but the drug companies spend more on marketing than they do searching for new drugs. In 1999, GlaxoSmithKline spent 37 percent on marketing and administration and only 14 percent

---

[12] John McMillan, *Reinventing the Bazaar: A Natural History of Markets* (New York: Norton, 2002), p. 28.

[13] *New York Times*, May 29, 2002.

[14] Jennifer Washburn, "Undue Influence," *The American Prospect* (August 13, 2001), p. 20.

on research. Pharmacia, another drug company, spent more than twice as much of its revenue on marketing and administration than it did on medical research.[15]

How Production Is Organized

New recruits for work at the Springfield, Arkansas, poultry plant receive orientation in a classroom that contains a prominently displayed sign: "Democracies depend on the political participation of its citizens, but not in the workplace." The sign is printed in Spanish and English, "but the message is clear in any language."[16] Unlike the rules of political equality that pertain in the political arena, in a capitalist society the workplace is not organized democratically. Private managers decide who will be hired, fired, and promoted; what kind of technology will be utilized; and how the process of production will be organized. Workers are paid to take orders, not take initiative. The British historian R. H. Tawney put it this way: "[T]he man who employs, governs, to the extent of the number of men employed. He has jurisdiction over them. He occupies what is really a public office. He has power, not of pit and gallows . . . but of overtime and short-time, full bellies and empty bellies, health and sickness. . . ."[17] The difference between capitalist and command economies may be less than we think. In market economies, firms do not have to take orders from central planners. But the command economy is internalized *within* each firm, as workers have to take orders from managers.[18]

Control of the process of production is crucial to management because profits depend, in part, on how efficiently labor can be put to work. But capitalists have a difficult time translating their formal control over the labor process into actual control of the shop floor or office. While management views the issue of the pace of work through the lens of productivity and production costs, workers perceive it as an issue of health and endurance. Consequently, workers have devised various strategies to resist capitalist efforts to maximize how long and how hard they work. For example, workers have used their political power as citizens to limit the length of the workday and to press for the passage of laws that require employers to meet health and safety standards at work. Workers have also limited the power that management exercises over the labor process through collective bargaining agreements between employers and unions. Such agreements often include work rules that restrict management's otherwise unlimited power

---

[15] McMillan, *Reinventing the Bazaar*, p. 29.

[16] Steve Striffler, "Inside a Poultry Processing Plant: An Ethnographic Portrait," *Labor History* 43, no. 3 (2002): 306.

[17] Tawney is quoted in Heilbroner, *The Nature and Logic of Capitalism*, p. 100.

[18] Charles Lindblom, *The Market System: What It Is, How It Works and What to Make of It* (New Haven, CT: Yale University Press, 2001), p. 78.

on the shop floor and in offices.[19] Workers have also used informal means to limit employers' power. Workers may restrict output by setting their own standard of what constitutes a fair day's work, as opposed to what management might consider an appropriate level of effort.[20] But in recent years, unions have grown weaker, and enforcement of legal standards has become lax. The result, according to two labor experts, is that private employers in the United States "have more authority in deciding how to treat their workers than do employers in other advanced countries."[21]

THE MOBILIZATION OF BIAS

Corporate decisions on how much to invest, where to invest, what to invest in, and how to organize production affect the entire society. As political economist Charles Lindblom pointed out, "Because public functions in the market [capitalist] system rest in the hands of businessmen, it follows that jobs, prices, production, growth, the standard of living, and the economic security of everyone all rest in their hands."[22] *The New York Times* acknowledged this fact when it reported in the midst of a slump in the economy in 2002: "Any chance that the United States economy will revive rests largely on the shoulders of corporate managers. It is their choices about fresh investment that will go a long way toward determining whether the nation limps along with modest growth or returns to robust economic health."[23]

This situation provides business with a unique advantage in the political arena. Elected officials are dependent on business to invest, create jobs, and increase the standard of living. In a capitalist system, where production is privately organized, these decisions are made by those who own and control the means of production. And capitalists will do the things society needs them to do only if they can make a profit. Elected officials, therefore, have an enormous stake in ensuring that the needs of business are satisfied. Consequently, government is under pressure to offer inducements to business. For example, in the 19th century, the federal government gave railroads

---

[19] For a powerful account that describes the struggle over work rules in two textile plants, see Daniel J. Clark, *Like Night and Day: Unionization in a Southern Mill Town* (Chapel Hill: University of North Carolina Press, 1996).

[20] The literature on this is fascinating and important. See, for example, the essays in David Montgomery, *Workers' Control in America* (New York: Cambridge University Press, 1979); Michael Buroway, *Manufacturing Consent: Change in the Labor Process Under Monopoly Capitalism* (Chicago: University of Chicago Press, 1979); and Donald Roy, "Quota Restriction and Goldbricking in a Machine Shop," *American Journal of Sociology* 57 (1952): 427–42.

[21] Richard B. Freeman and Joel Rogers, *What Workers Want* (Ithaca, NY: Cornell University Press, 1999), p. 1.

[22] Charles Lindblom, *Politics and Markets: The World's Political-Economic Systems* (New York: Basic Books, 1977), p. 172.

[23] *New York Times*, September 22, 2002.

more land than the entire area of France in order to encourage the construction of the transcontinental railroad. Today, the government offers business more prosaic inducements, such as patent protection, tariffs, tax breaks, research and development subsidies, vocational training, and military protection. Politicians offer incentives in order to inspire business confidence. If business does not invest and a recession or depression occurs, politicians risk being held responsible and voted out of office. Elected officials' political careers are, therefore, dependent on continued prosperity, which is heavily influenced by business decisions. Moreover, prosperity means more tax money flowing into government coffers to pay for programs that earn politicians credit with voters. Consequently, it is in politicians' self-interest to offer inducements to business in order "to motivate them to provide jobs and perform their other functions," according to Lindblom.[24]

The special political advantage business enjoys by virtue of its economic power can be described by the term "the mobilization of bias," coined by political scientist E. E. Schattschneider. Political scientists Peter Bachrach and Morton S. Baratz have argued that a mobilization of bias occurs when "the rules of the game" tend to favor one group over another. Their point is not that the resources groups have in the struggle over policy may be unequal—that may be true, too!—but that the playing field may unfairly favor one group over others. How the game is set up may have as much to do with the outcome as the relative strengths of the players on the field.[25]

The U.S. economic and political system contains a mobilization of bias in favor of business that is built into the political framework and limits the extent of American democracy. That is, even before the first vote is cast, the first campaign contribution is made or the first lobbyist contacts a member of Congress, business starts with an advantage in the political arena based on its control over the means of production. Take an important illustration of how the mobilization of bias operates: Presidents constantly look over their shoulder to see how their proposals register with the stock and bond markets. They worry that, if investors oppose their policies, these investors will pull their money out of the market, causing stock and bond prices to fall. Business confidence will sink and companies will not invest, with consequences that are all too reminiscent of what happened to Flint, Michigan.

An example of the mobilization of bias at work occurred when the House of Representatives considered a bill designed to stimulate a faltering economy in 2001. The $100 billion package included over $70 billion in corporate tax breaks but provided very little direct financial assistance to the growing number of unemployed and low-income workers. House Ways and Means Chair Bill Thomas defended the bill against criticism as nothing more than a

---

[24] Charles Lindblom, "The Market as Prison," *Journal of Politics* 44 (1982): 327.

[25] Peter Bachrach and Morton S. Baratz, *Power and Poverty: Theory and Practice* (New York: Oxford University Press, 1970). For a brilliant discussion of the different dimensions of power, see John Gaventa, *Power and Powerlessness: Quiescence and Rebellion in an Appalachian Valley* (Urbana: University of Illinois Press, 1980), pp. 1–33.

AP/Wide World Photos

President George W. Bush emerging from a meeting with business leaders following his election.

form of corporate welfare by reminding his colleagues of the structural power of business: "Something very important has gotten lost in the furious slinging of accusations over who benefits from the business components of this bill. And that is the plain fact that businesses are America's employers. . . . You can't restore a dysfunctional economy without helping business stabilize and recover."[26] Two years later, in the midst of an economy that continued to deteriorate, President Bush offered a similar defense of his proposal to eliminate the tax on stock dividends, creating a windfall for the rich, who are the largest stockholders. Bush explained, "It will encourage investment and that's what we want. Investment means jobs."[27]

The fact that business begins with a special political advantage does not guarantee that government policy will always reflect capitalist interests. Just because business begins the race with a head start does not mean it will reach the finish line first. Political opposition forced both the corporate tax breaks in the bill passed by the House in 2001 and President Bush's proposal to eliminate the tax on stock dividends to be scaled back. As Neil J. Mitchell explains, business must engage in policy struggles characterized by unreliable politicians, "a shifting set of adversaries, and volatile public preferences."[28]

---

[26] Thomas is quoted in *The New York Times*, October 25, 2001.

[27] *New York Times*, January 7, 2003.

[28] Neil J. Mitchell, *The Conspicuous Corporation: Business, Public Policy and Representative Democracy* (Ann Arbor: University of Michigan Press, 1997), p. 167.

Despite its advantages, business's success in the policy struggle is highly contingent and no sure thing. The mobilization of bias in favor of business is not constant across the entire agenda of issues or equally powerful at all times.

Public officials enjoy considerable latitude despite the presence of a mobilization of bias for two reasons.[29] First, capitalists have different political interests and compete with each other. Capital or business is rarely united and cohesive. On many issues, business firms have different interests depending on the region in which they are located, whether they produce for local or international markets, whether they are capital or labor intensive, and so on. Political struggles among different business groupings have occurred in American history from the time slaveholders and manufacturers fought over the tariff in the 1800s to more contemporary struggles over trade policy between domestic producers and export-oriented firms. These conflicts enable elected officials to play one business interest against another and respond to other groups.

Second, democratic procedures require policymakers to respond to the larger public. Movements from below have achieved significant political victories over business, despite capital's threat that reform would undermine business confidence. For example, the Family Medical Leave Act, which permits employees to take unpaid family or medical leave, was passed in 1993 over business's objections. Public support for the measure offset business warnings that the bill would reduce profits, cost jobs, and erode management autonomy. Several years later, another popular measure, an increase in the minimum wage, sailed through Congress despite threats from business that passage of the bill would be inflationary. With the 1996 election just three months away and polls indicating that four out of five Americans supported an increase in the minimum wage, the bill passed easily. Raising the minimum wage even received a majority of votes from Republicans in Congress who normally oppose such measures, despite the opposition of every GOP congressional leader.[30]

A similar victory over business opposition occurred during President George W. Bush's presidential tenure, following corporate scandals that included the issuance of fraudulent financial statements, stock analysts recommending stocks that they knew to be losers, and insider trading. Two large companies, Enron and WorldCom ended up in bankruptcy after their fraudulent accounting caught up with them, while one of the Big Five accounting firms, Arthur Andersen, went out of business after it was the object of criminal prosecution. Public outrage forced Congress to pass legislation providing for tougher penalties for accounting and securities fraud and tougher regulation of accounting and securities laws. The momentum

---

[29] This issue is treated meticulously in Hal Draper, *Karl Marx's Theory of Revolution,* vol. 1, bk. 1, *State and Bureaucracy* (New York: Monthly Review Press, 1977), pp. 311–39.

[30] *New York Times,* August 3, 1996. See also Sherrod Brown, *Congress From the Inside: Observations from the Majority and the Minority* (Kent, OH: Kent State University Press, 2004), pp. 192–94.

for reform was so great that it overcame lobbying by business against the bill, went further than President Bush's own proposals, and marked a reversal of policy for Congress, which just six years earlier had weakened measures designed to prevent corporate crime.

In these cases, democratic pressure from below overcame the mobilization of bias that operates in favor of business. Elected officials cannot simply ignore popular challenges. Sometimes challenges are sufficiently powerful that policymakers must recalculate the risks of conceding to business and instead support alternative interests and values. When the public is mobilized and organized, politicians may redefine their self-interest and oppose business.[31] While the political burden of proof is much greater for movements from below than it is for business interests, the power of democratic pressure to influence public policy cannot be dismissed.

Politics matters. If, as the political scientist Neil J. Mitchell argues, the "house" always won, then citizens would think the game is fixed and lose interest. Instead, citizens play with gusto because business does not always win. The "house" sometimes loses.[32] The state stretches and bends in response to the political pressures exerted on it. Even though business derives an enormous advantage from the mobilization of bias, political struggles matter. The power that business derives from the mobilization of bias depends on whether politicians regard business's threat to disinvest or withhold investment as credible, whether groups opposed to business are mobilized and united, and whether business is organized enough to translate the mobilization of bias it enjoys into specific policies. None of these can be taken for granted or are automatic.

Business sectors the world over enjoy a mobilization of bias in their favor. But American business derives especially great political benefits from it because the opposition it faces here is weaker. The result has been a different mix of government policies, such as a less extensive and less generous welfare state (see Chapter 10), which helps to produce more inequality in the United States than in other industrialized democracies. Just because American business has faced weaker political challenges in the past, permitting it to exploit the mobilization of bias more effectively, does not mean these challenges will remain weak. Political struggle is highly variable. Contingency rules. The future is always open.

This book examines the sometimes tense, sometimes smooth relationship between democratic politics and the undemocratic private government of capitalism. The politics of power is affected by the capitalist organization of the economy, and the capitalist organization of the economy is affected, in turn, by the fact that the political system is democratic. We believe that, in order to understand American politics, one must appreciate both that the mobilization of bias constitutes a powerful pressure in favor of business and

---

[31] Mitchell, *Conspicuous Corporation*, pp. 167–89.

[32] Ibid., p. 11.

that democratic pressure is capable of mitigating, if not counteracting, it. *The Politics of Power* describes both sides of this complicated coin. In the next section, we review the overall characteristics of the private government exercised by corporate capitalism in the United States.

CORPORATE CAPITALISM

Suppose it was learned that a small group had gained control over vast concentrations of economic resources and political power in the United States. Imagine that, in a country with a population of 270 million people, several thousand Americans—unrepresentative, not democratically chosen, not even known to most people—controlled key aspects of American economic life. This small group determined what the level of investment would be, where investment would occur, what would be produced, and how production would be organized.

It owned and controlled the offices and factories in which production occurred, as well as the media that influenced the values and attitudes of many Americans. It hired, fired, and promoted a large proportion of Americans and produced the goods and services that they depended on. Because members of this group controlled much of the country's productive capacity, their decisions affected every American. Yet they based their decisions not on what the country needed but on what would be most profitable for them. This small group used its vast wealth to buy private islands in the Caribbean, drive luxury cars, and live in stately homes in various cities and fashionable vacation spots. At the same time, tens of millions of other Americans could not afford to obtain medical care, pay the rent, care for their kids, or put food on the table.

Further, the small group at the top of the wealth pyramid had enormous political influence. Candidates and political parties shaped their agendas around its concerns in exchange for campaign contributions. Members of Congress responded to lobbyists representing the group's interests, and many policymakers were members of the group themselves.

One can imagine the outcry that would greet the announcement that such a group existed. Its existence and power would be a betrayal of American democracy. And yet such a group does exist. All that has been described is fact, not fiction. A convenient shorthand label for the group that controls the process of production and derives immense political power from its control of the economy is corporate capitalism.

Corporate capitalism includes the largest mining and manufacturing companies, investment banks, financial services firms, retail chains, utilities, high-technology companies, media companies, and corporate law firms. The giant companies listed in the Fortune 500 are the core of corporate capitalism. The corporate sector is characterized by large firms that tend to be capital-intensive, highly productive, diversified, and global in their reach.

The corporate sector of the economy can be distinguished from the competitive sector, which includes the 22 million other businesses that exist in the United States. These firms range from convenience stores to car repair shops to locally owned restaurants. Firms in the competitive sector of the economy not only are smaller in terms of profits, sales, assets, and number of employees but also sell in smaller markets and are more labor-intensive than firms in the corporate sector.[33]

Firms in the competitive sector are not independent of the corporate sector. Small businesses act as suppliers to the corporate sector, are dependent on it for orders, provide retail sales outlets for its products, and repair what large firms produce. They also act as shock absorbers for the corporate sector: They are the first firms to fail when recessions occur because they lack the resources of the larger firms. In the cosmos of capitalism, the small, competitive-sector firms are planets that revolve around and rely on the heat and light of the corporate sun, which sustains them.

The corporate sector, on the other hand, is best characterized by the Fortune 500. The total corporate revenues of this group of giant corporations were $6.3 trillion in 1999, accounting for over half the gross domestic product (GDP) of the entire American economy and employing about one-seventh of the American workforce.[34] The 20 largest U.S. firms, listed in (Figure 2-1) have higher corporate revenues than the Gross Domestic Product of all but a few of the world's wealthiest countries.

According to the economist Eric Schultz, small may be beautiful, but power and profits go to those with size. Size has many advantages. Big corporate firms buy in volume so they pay less for goods; they are better credit risks, permitting them to receive lower interest rates when borrowing money; they can purchase advertising in order to better market their products; they can use their market power to charge more for goods they produce; and, finally, their size gives them political influence with which to obtain favorable policies.[35]

The trend in recent years has been toward greater concentration. That is, fewer firms account for a larger proportion of production and sales within an industry. A wave of corporate mergers and acquisitions over the course of the 1990s accelerated these developments. Oil giants like Mobil and Exxon merged to become the world's largest industrial corporation, and telephone companies merged to produce nationwide empires. Especially disquieting for the quality of American democracy were mergers in the news media. Disney purchased Capital Cities/ABC, resulting in a $16 billion communications empire; Time Warner merged with CNN, which resulted in a $20 billion

[33] Robert Averitt, *The Dual Economy: The Dynamic of American Industrial Structure* (New York: Norton, 1968).

[34] *Fortune*, April 17, 2000, F-19.

[35] Eric Schultz, *Markets and Power: The 21st Century Command Economy* (Armonk, NY: Sharpe, 2001).

■ FIGURE 2–1

FORTUNE 500 COMPANIES

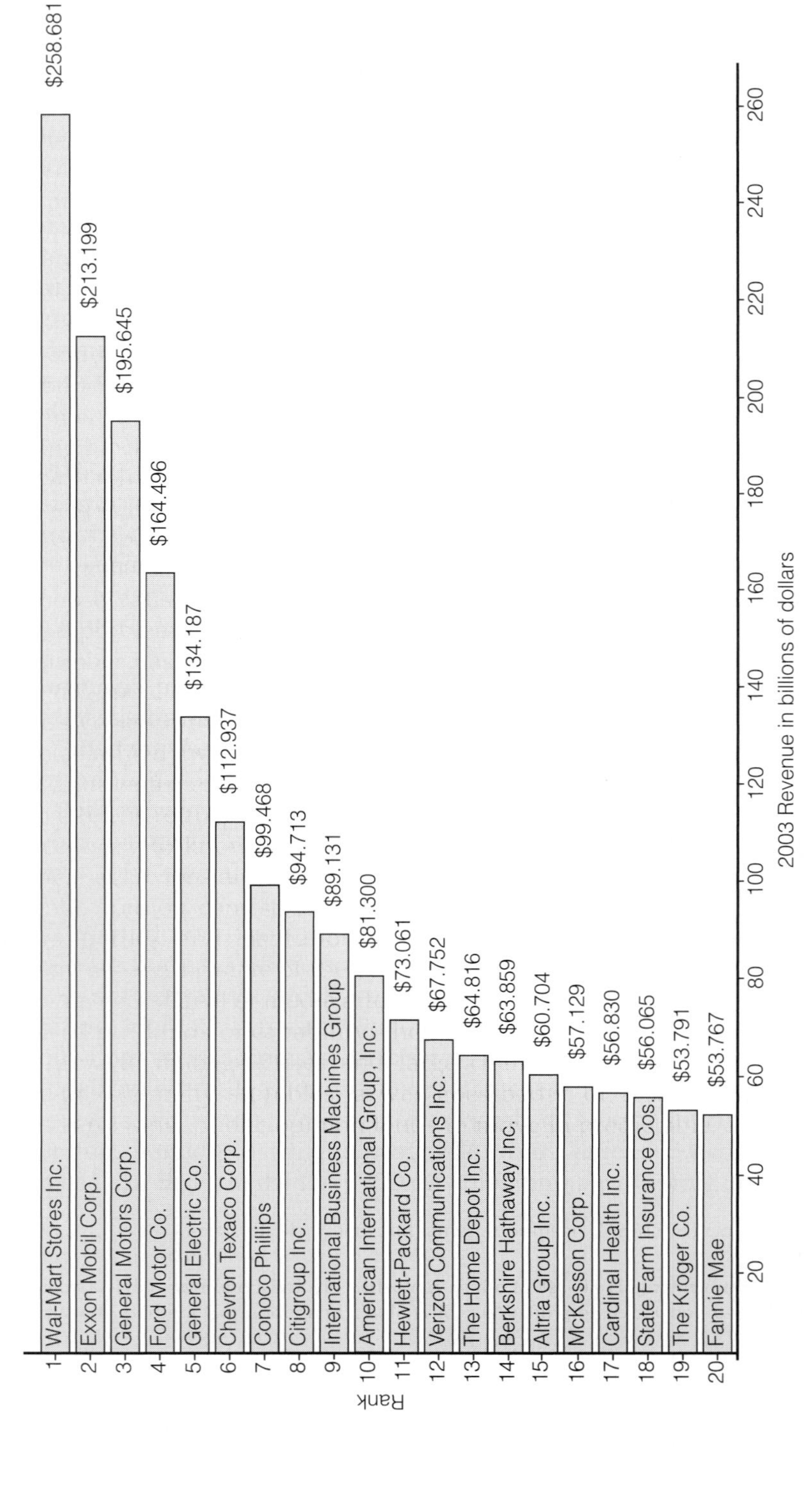
Rank
1 Wal-Mart Stores Inc. $258.681
2 Exxon Mobil Corp. $213.199
3 General Motors Corp. $195.645
4 Ford Motor Co. $164.496
5 General Electric Co. $134.187
6 Chevron Texaco Corp. $112.937
7 Conoco Phillips $99.468
8 Citigroup Inc. $94.713
9 International Business Machines Group $89.131
10 American International Group, Inc. $81.300
11 Hewlett-Packard Co. $73.061
12 Verizon Communications Inc. $67.752
13 The Home Depot Inc. $64.816
14 Berkshire Hathaway Inc. $63.859
15 Altria Group Inc. $60.704
16 McKesson Corp. $57.129
17 Cardinal Health Inc. $56.830
18 State Farm Insurance Cos. $56.065
19 The Kroger Co. $53.791
20 Fannie Mae $53.767
20 40 60 80 100 120 140 160 180 200 220 240 260
2003 Revenue in billions of dollars

SOURCE: *USA Today*, March 22, 2004.

conglomerate; and Westinghouse Electric Corporation bought CBS for $5.4 billion.[36] But these deals were dwarfed in 2000 when America Online, the Internet company, purchased Time Warner, the media empire, for $165 billion. Big companies used to eat small companies. Now they eat each other.

When production becomes concentrated, control becomes centralized in fewer hands. A cluster of privately owned companies that can squeeze their suppliers as well as their customers wields economic power. Even more dangerous, democracy is threatened because such a concentration of economic power tends to promote the concentration of political power. Business professor Jeffrey E. Garton warned that the big problem with concentration "is the growing imbalance between public and private power in our society." Corporate giants are so big that they have the resources to ward off prosecution by the government indefinitely or pay fines for environmental and labor law violations that amount to petty change to them.[37]

WHO OWNS AMERICA'S PRIVATE GOVERNMENT?

The answer to this question begins with identifying who owns stock in giant corporations. People who invest money in corporations receive shares in the assets—called stocks—of that corporation. Stockholders are entitled to a share of the corporation's profits in proportion to the amount of stock they own. Stockholders are also entitled to vote for the board of directors of the corporation, which chooses the corporation's top management and reviews its performance and decisions. The number of votes that investors cast depends on the amount of stock they own in the corporation.

Some argue that this creates a shareholder democracy in the United States. As one Wall Street executive explained, "In our system of free enterprise, the capitalist system, industry is owned by the American public."[38] But the idea of the economy being governed by a shareholder democracy is as implausible as it being ruled by a consumer democracy, which we reviewed earlier. A shareholder democracy is a perverse notion when one-half of all American households cannot vote because, as Table 2-1 makes clear, they do not own stock in any form, either directly or indirectly through a mutual or pension fund. Moreover, shareholding is unequally distributed among the remaining half who do own stock. In 1998, the wealthiest 1 percent of households held 42 percent of the value of all the stock in the United States; the

---

[36] Eric Alterman, *Who Speaks for America: Why Democracy Matters in Foreign Policy* (Ithaca, NY: Cornell University Press, 1998), p. 156.

[37] Jeffrey E. Garton, "Megamergers are a Clear and Present Danger," *Business Week* (January 25, 1999): 28.

[38] William Lynch, an executive of the stockbrokerage house Dean Witter Reynolds, interviewed by the *Voice of America*, February 3, 1985. Note that this statement was broadcast around the world as a description of the American system.

■ TABLE 2–1

CONCENTRATION OF STOCK OWNERSHIP BY
U.S. WEALTH CLASS, 1998

Wealth Class	Value of Stock Holdings			National Share of All Stock Owned	
	Any Amount	$5,000 or More	$10,000 or More	Total	Cumulative Total
Top 1 percent	93.2%	92.9%	91.2%	42.1%	42.1%
Next 4 percent	89.0	87.0	86.1	25.0	67.1
Next 5 percent	83.9	80.4	78.9	10.6	77.7
Next 10 percent	78.7	74.0	71.6	11.1	88.8
Second quintile	58.9	49.8	45.4	7.7	96.5
Third quintile	45.8	32.7	25.9	2.6	99.1
Fourth quintile	35.1	15.1	8.6	0.7	98.8
Bottom quintile	18.6	4.6	1.8	0.2	100.0
All U.S. households	48.2	36.3	31.8	100.0	

NOTE: Stock holdings include directly owned stock and shares owned indirectly through mutual funds, trusts, and retirement accounts. Data from the U.S. Bureau of the Census. Found in Edward N. Wolff, "The Rich Get Richer . . . and Why the Poor Don't," *American Prospect* (February 12, 2001), p. 15.

wealthiest 5 percent owned about two-thirds; the top 10 percent, more than three-quarters; and the top 20 percent (or "quintile," meaning one-fifth), about nine-tenths.[39] Finally, elections for corporate boards of directors often are not contested. Shareholders often have the option of voting for only one slate of directors. Companies have defended their right to offer just one slate of candidates on the odd claim that if there were competing candidates, "it would be difficult to predict which candidates would be elected."[40]

THE MODERN CORPORATION

In the 1800s, the ownership and control of a business were united in the same person. Robber barons, such as John D. Rockefeller, Jay Gould, and J. P. Morgan, managed their own businesses, from which they derived their reputations for ruthlessness and their great wealth. But as firms became

---

[39] Edward N. Wolff, "The Rich Get Richer . . . and Why the Poor Don't," *American Prospect*, (February 12, 2001): 15.

[40] This argument was offered by Verizon in response to a shareholder proposal requiring directors to nominate more candidates than there were seats on the company's board of directors. *New York Times*, April 13, 2003.

larger and multidivisional, operated in a range of industries, and needed more capital to expand, many firms sold shares and became public corporations.[41] Ownership and control of the corporation increasingly split apart. Owners, now transformed into large stockholders, no longer performed day-to-day operations but oversaw the work of corporate managers who carried out these tasks. Today's corporate executives tend to be faceless and unknown to the general public, unlike yesterday's titans of industry. In fact, in *Roger & Me*, Michael Moore never does complete his quest to talk to Roger Smith, the head of GM, who is protected from the public by an army of receptionists, security guards, and publicists.[42]

Many corporate executives come from upper-class families, attended the most selective colleges, are graduates of either business or law school or both, and are generally white and male, although there has been a small increase in minority members and women within the top ranks of the business elite.

Corporate executives are rewarded lavishly for their efforts. The average salary and bonus of corporate chief executive officers (CEOs) in 2000 amounted to $10.9 million, an increase of 16 percent from the previous year.[43] Although top management in the United States has always earned much more than the workers they employ, there has been a dramatic increase in inequality between the top and bottom of the corporate pyramid. In 1980, the CEO of the typical major U.S. corporation received 42 times the compensation of an average factory worker; by 1990, the ratio had doubled. By the time the decade ended, the average CEO made a whopping 475 times more than the typical factory worker.[44]

Corporate executives are paid more in one day than many of their workers earn in one year. Moreover, the gap between executive compensation and that received by the average manufacturing worker is higher in the United States than almost anywhere else, as Figure 2-2 demonstrates. Some argue that corporate executives deserve their high salaries because of the wealth they create. But in 2001, corporate profits declined by 35 percent, yet median executive salaries still rose by 7 percent. Corporate executive pay does not reflect performance as much as it reflects their power to direct the firm's assets to themselves.

Data on executive compensation suggests that "managers" are not merely salaried employees but also substantial owners of the companies they manage. Corporate executives often own large blocs of stock in the firms they direct. For example, Bill Gates, the chief executive of Microsoft, owns $35 billion worth of Microsoft stock; Philip Knight, the head of Nike, owns stock in his company

---

[41] The most significant work on this process is Alfred D. Chandler, *The Visible Hand: The Managerial Revolution in American Business* (Cambridge, MA: Harvard University Press, 1977).

[42] Ronald Edsforth, "Review of Roger & Me," *American Historical Review* 96 (October 1991): 1145.

[43] *New York Times,* February 26, 2001.

[44] The data in this paragraph, reported by the AFL-CIO Executive Paywatch Organization, are available at *www.paywatch.org.*

■ FIGURE 2–2

THE PAY GAP

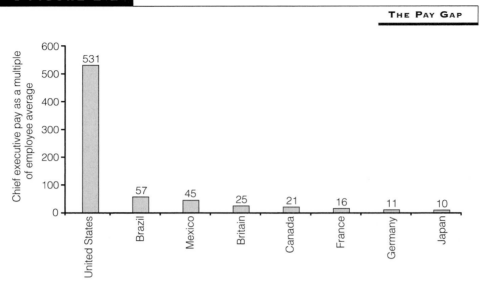

SOURCE: From "Explaining (or Not) Why the Boss Is Paid so Much" by Gretchen Morgenson, *New York Times*, January 25, 2004. Copyright © 2004 by the New York Times Co. Reprinted by permission.

worth $3.68 billion; and Michael Eisner, who runs Walt Disney, owns stock in his company worth $1.2 billion. Average managerial and director ownership has increased from 13 to 21 percent in the last 60 years.[45] One study of the 200 largest publicly traded companies found that chief executive officers owned an average of $57.8 million worth of their company's equity in 1997. Indeed, the separation of ownership and control within American corporations is diminishing. Grants of large blocs of stock to executives help align the interests of management with those of other large stockholders. This alliance is then sealed by the fact that many corporate executives not only actively manage the company but also sit on the firm's board of directors. Rather than the board serving as a check on corporate management, it becomes a social club of insiders.

THE CAPITALIST CLASS

Capitalist economies are dynamic and in constant motion. The engine of change is competition among firms for markets and profits. But corporate capitalism is characterized by cooperation and coordination among firms as well as rivalry and competition. In 1935, political scientist E. E. Schattschneider

---

[45] Donald Palmer and Brad M. Barber, "Challengers, Elites, and Owning Families: A Social Class Theory of Corporate Acquisitions in the 1960s," *Administrative Science Quarterly* 46, no. 1 (March 2001): 115.

noted, "Businessmen collectively constitute the most class-conscious group in American society. As a class they are the most highly organized, more easily mobilized, have more facilities for communication, are more like-minded, and are more accustomed to stand together in defense of their privileges than any other group."[46]

Capital is linked through a dense organizational network. Managers are united in their desire to protect their firm's autonomy and to pursue its economic and political interests with minimal interference from the state or popular movements. One mechanism through which capitalist class cohesion occurs is exclusive social clubs, such as the Links and Century clubs in New York, the California Club in Los Angeles, and the Pacific Union Club in San Francisco. Social clubs promote capitalist class cohesion by creating information and friendship networks among the elite. The exclusive social club is the last step in a long process of elite socialization that begins in prep school, is reinforced at prestigious private colleges, is strengthened at the best law and business schools, and is polished at corporate headquarters.[47] Along with the elite social club, informal exchanges of information and views are now conducted by organizations such as the World Economic Forum. This group hosts forums and panels at such posh Alpine resorts as Davos, Switzerland, where not only American but world business and political leaders exchange opinions and socialize.

Peak business associations are another source of capitalist class cohesion. At the very top of the industrial pyramid is the Business Roundtable, which tries to develop consensus on public issues among the managers of the largest corporate firms in the United States. Membership in the Business Roundtable is limited to the chief executives of the largest corporations. Currently the Roundtable has 140 members, whose companies employ 10 million people and have combined revenues of over $3.5 trillion. The Roundtable employs no support staff or lobbyists. Instead, the chief executives themselves convey the Roundtable's position on public issues to legislators and policymakers directly in one-to-one exchanges. Their positions and donations give them access and influence with decision makers.

At a broader, less elite level, thousands of large and small firms are members of the U.S. Chamber of Commerce and the National Association of Manufacturers. These peak associations seek to represent the collective interests of business across industries. At the level of specific industries, one finds countless trade associations, from the relatively inconsequential Fresh Garlic Association to the powerful American Banking Association, which represents the interests of firms in a particular sector. Table 2-2 presents some facts about contemporary business associations.

---

[46] E. E. Schattschneider, *Politics, Pressures and the Tariff* (New York: Prentice-Hall, 1935), p. 287.

[47] For a list of exclusive social clubs, see G. William Domhoff, *The Higher Circles: The Governing Class in America* (New York: Random House, 1970).

■ TABLE 2-2

AMERICAN BUSINESS ASSOCIATIONS

Organization	Year Founded	Budget in $Millions
Leadership Associations		
National Association of Manufacturers	1895	5
Chamber of Commerce of the United States	1912	70
Business Roundtable	1972	23
National Federation of Independent Business	1943	65
The Business Council	1933	1
Committee for Economic Development	1942	4
Trade Associations		
Chemical Manufacturers Associations	1872	41
American Bankers Association	1875	54
National Association of Broadcasters	1922	27
American Trucking Associations	1933	30
Air Transport Association of America	1936	45

SOURCE: Richard Levine, *Government and Business* (New York: Chatham House Publishers, 2001), p. 120.

A third source of capitalist class cohesion is corporate interlocks, in which the member of one corporate board of directors also serves on the board of another corporation. Interlocks facilitate communication between firms. According to sociologist Michael Useem, interlocks promote "the flow of information throughout the [corporate] network about the practices and concerns of most large companies, companies that are operating in virtually all major sectors of the economy and facing the full range of economic and political problems confronting business generally."[48] Directors who sit on multiple corporate boards comprise what Useem identifies as the "inner circle" of capital. Those in the inner circle form the leading edge of the capitalist class because their perspective goes beyond the interests of any particular firm or industry to encompass the interests of corporate capitalism as a whole. Capitalist class cohesion results from the activities and transcendent corporate perspective of the inner circle.

No single organization enforces discipline and unity among the firms that comprise corporate capitalism. Yet social clubs, peak business associations, and corporate interlocks form the infrastructure that promotes classwide understandings, if not specific positions, on policy. Unified political

[48] Michael Useem, *The Inner Circle: Large Corporations and the Rise of Business Political Activity in the U.S. and U.K.* (New York: Oxford University Press, 1984), p. 56.

action by capital is rare. But it is more likely to occur when managerial authority is threatened than at any other time. Threats to managerial authority come from two sources: the labor movement in the form of collective bargaining and the government in the form of business regulation. Indeed, the threat from unions was the impetus that spurred capitalists to organize in the first place. In 1906, one leader of the newly formed National Association of Manufacturers (NAM) admitted, "It is surprising how many of our members take issue with us on everything except the labor question. . . . On that the manufacturers are a unit. The minute you get away from it there is no unity."[49]

Relations within corporate capitalism are characterized by both conflict and cooperation. Some issues provoke conflict within the business community. Other issues might politically mobilize firms in one industry while other firms remain indifferent. And on still other issues, such as challenges posed to managerial autonomy by unions and government regulation, the business community stands armed and united. Overall, according to political scientists Kay Lehman Schlozman and John T. Tierney, "[C]ooperation within the business community is far more commonplace than conflict." Members of the business community are more likely to identify other business interests as political allies than as antagonists.[50]

THE STRUCTURE OF EMPLOYMENT

Below the top level of corporate executives that comprise the capitalist class is a workforce that is changing shape in response to the needs of capital. An industrial occupational order based on manual, blue-collar factory workers is being replaced by a new post-industrial order in which service and white-collar office workers predominate.

Industry first began to overtake agriculture as the basis of employment after the Civil War. Workers employed in manufacturing increased from just 2.5 million in 1870 to over 11 million by 1920. Labor historian Melvin Dubofsky writes, "Both in its growth and its distribution, then, the American labor force from 1865 to 1920 became concentrated in the primary (extractive) and secondary (manufacturing) sectors of the economy."[51] Hand tools were

---

[49] Quoted in Julie Greene, *Pure and Simple Politics: The American Federation of Labor and Political Activism, 1881–1917* (New York: Cambridge University Press, 1998), p. 92.

[50] Kay Lehman Schlozman and John T. Tierney, *Organized Interests and American Democracy* (New York: Harper & Row, 1986), p. 401. These impressions were confirmed statistically by Jeffrey M. Berry, who found twice as many cases of no conflict within and across industries on bills pending in Congress as examples of inter- or intra-industry disagreement. See Jeffrey M. Berry, *The New Liberalism: The Rising Power of Citizen Groups* (Washington, DC: Brookings, 1999), p. 79.

[51] Melvin Dubofsky, *Industrialism and the American Worker, 1865–1920,* 2nd ed. (Arlington Heights, IL: Harlan Davidson, 1985), p. 3.

replaced by machines, workshops were replaced by factories, artisans were replaced by unskilled manual workers, and crafted items were replaced by standardized products. Foreign immigrants and native farmers took jobs as industrial workers in factories, transforming villages into towns and towns into cities. Pittsburgh grew up around steel, Akron around rubber, and Detroit around cars. But nowhere was the industrial transformation as rapid as it was in Flint, Michigan. Flint was transformed from a sleepy town of 13,000 in 1900 into a bustling city of 150,000, where over 60,000 industrial workers were employed—many of them in GM factories—by 1929.[52]

As the industrial workforce grew and defined its era, it created the need for a new post-industrial occupational order based on the growth of white-collar occupations that would eventually overtake it. As productivity in industry increased, firms hired salespeople and market researchers to find and create new outlets for their prodigious output. As capitalists discovered the benefits of applying science to production, firms hired technical experts to develop new products and improve existing methods. As companies took the skill out of jobs, firms hired engineers to design the labor process and supervisors to manage it. As companies increased in size and became more bureaucratic, the number of office workers and levels of management increased to coordinate the flow of work within the firm. As the advance of industry broke down traditional social relations, the demand for service workers increased as people turned to the market to purchase what they previously provided themselves. The number of fast-food workers, cleaning-service workers, child-care workers, and nursing home workers grew. Finally, as industrial capitalism developed, so did the white-collar, public-sector workforce in order to provide essential services and cope with the escalating costs of industrial development. That is, the growth of a post-industrial workforce did not occur separately or independently from the grimy world of material production but emerged in response to the demands of industry and the social changes it provoked.

The shift from an industrial to a post-industrial workforce is reflected in Figure 2-3 from the U.S. Department of Labor's *Report on the Workforce.* In 1970, the number of manufacturing and service workers were just about equal. By 2000, the traditional industrial working class, consisting of craft workers and operatives, comprised just over 25 percent of the total workforce. These occupations have declined in the face of the enormous growth of white-collar occupations.

As the post-industrial occupational order emerged, so have disturbing signs that the occupational structure is bifurcating. That is, both good and bad jobs are growing at the expense of the middle. According to Figure 2-3, such good jobs as manager or professional—jobs that are well compensated and require education—have increased in number. Indeed, the increase in

---

[52] Ronald Edsforth, *Class Conflict and Cultural Consensus: The Making of a Mass Consumer Society in Flint, Michigan* (New Brunswick, NJ: Rutgers University Press, 1987), pp. 39–71.

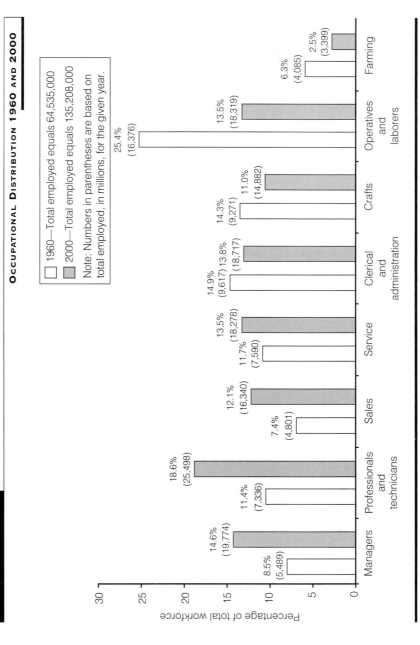

■ FIGURE 2-3

OCCUPATIONAL DISTRIBUTION 1960 AND 2000

☐ 1960—Total employed equals 64,535,000
▨ 2000—Total employed equals 135,208,000

Note: Numbers in parentheses are based on total employed, in millions, for the given year.

Percentage of total workforce

SOURCE: Table 593, *Report on the American Workforce* (Department of Labor, 2001) pp. 380–82. For 1960 figures, see *Historical Statistics of the United States: Colonial Times to 1970* (Part 1) (Washington DC: US Government Printing Office, 1971), p. 139.

managers led economist David M. Gordon to argue that American corporations are top-heavy with managers compared to their foreign counterparts. Managers comprise 14.6 percent of total employment in the United States compared to 3.9 percent in Germany, 4.2 percent in Japan, and 2.6 percent in Sweden.[53]

While good jobs have increased, so have bad jobs right alongside of them. Concentrated in the service and sales occupational categories, bad jobs tend to be poorly paid, offer few fringe benefits, and require menial and routine labor. According to the U.S. Bureau of Labor Statistics, seven of the ten occupations with the greatest job growth through 2012 will be low-wage jobs requiring little education, such as janitors, cashiers, nurse's aides, and salespeople. The increase in the number of bad jobs is highlighted by the fact that GM, which has traditionally provided its workers with solid wages and benefits, has been replaced as the country's largest private employer by Walmart, which offers part-time, low-wage work without benefits. In effect, the middle, represented by General Motors' full-time jobs at union wages, is giving ground steadily to both good jobs at the top and, in larger measure, to bad jobs at the bottom. A group of leading labor economists reported at the end of the 1990s boom: "The labor market has become increasingly bifurcated. Worsening inequality in wages is a reflection of this underlying characteristic of the job market. Despite the prosperity of recent years, the low-wage labor market not only has persisted but shows some signs of growth. A substantial portion of the work force seems trapped in bad jobs and able to experience the 'new economy' only through media reports."[54] Furthermore, this same study found that workers mired in bad jobs could not expect much mobility out of them. It reported that "for a substantial fraction of adults the low-wage, low-skill labor market is not a staging area but a final destination."[55]

The bifurcation of the occupational order into good and bad jobs helps explain why wage disparities are higher in the United States than elsewhere. Economist Richard B. Freeman found that the distribution of wages (and income) is more unequal in the United States than in any other advanced country.[56] A comparison of the wages that the top 10 percent receives with those received by the lowest 10 percent shows that the United States has the highest degree of wage dispersion among industrialized democracies.[57] Wage inequality is double what it is in Sweden, which has the most egalitarian wage structure. The fact that inequality varies so much among comparably

---

[53] David M. Gordon, *Fat and Mean: The Corporate Squeeze of Working Americans and the Myth of Managerial "Downsizing"* (New York: Free Press, 1996), pp. 33–61.

[54] Paul Osterman, Thomas A. Kochan, Richard Locke, and Michael J. Piore, *Working in America: A Blueprint for a New Labor Market* (Cambridge, MA: MIT Press, 2001), p. 55.

[55] Ibid., p. 52.

[56] Richard B. Freeman, "How Labor Fares in Advanced Economies," in *Working Under Different Rules,* ed. Richard B. Freeman (New York: Russell Sage Foundation, 1995), p. 12.

[57] OECD, Employment Outlook (Paris: OECD, July 1996).

affluent countries suggests that the reasons are political, not economic. For example, what are considered junk jobs here are compensated better elsewhere due to the greater power of unions and government regulations that raise wages at the bottom to above-market rates. Inequality intensifies in the absence of a political force to check the tendency of the market to generate winners and losers.

EXTREME MARKET CAPITALISM

Capitalism comes in many flavors; the American variant, which we refer to as extreme market capitalism, is just one of them. Extreme market capitalism has three distinctive features. First, as we have already noted, American corporate managers enjoy more autonomy, less interference from unions or government regarding the management of their firms, than their counterparts elsewhere. Unions, for example, are smaller and weaker here than in virtually any other rich democracy. As Table 2-3 reveals, a smaller proportion of workers are unionized in the United States than in any West European country, with the exception of France. Union membership among workers that peaked at 37 percent of the workforce in 1960 has fallen almost continuously to less than 13 percent today. In the absence of unions, employers can unilaterally set wages and working conditions; they do not have to bargain with workers' representatives over the conditions of employment.

The decline of American unions is due to many factors. First was the failure of unions to organize in the South. The South was a refuge for nonunion firms that would later become the vanguard, setting the nonunion standard for the rest of their industry.[58] The South also harbored conservative, anti-union politicians who contributed to the second reason why unions have declined: restrictive labor legislation. Laws, such as the Taft-Hartley Act of 1947, placed obstacles in the way of union-organizing campaigns and restricted strike activity.[59] Third, employer strategy toward unions changed from one of reluctant acceptance to uncompromising opposition.[60] Management began to illegally discharge union activists and actively oppose union-organizing drives. Demands for concessions in bargaining were often used as a pretext by employers to instigate strikes, permanently replace workers, and rid themselves of unions entirely. Finally, unions share some of the blame for their decline. They did not inspire their members, invest in organizing, or respond effectively to the new offensive by employers.

---

[58] See, for example, Bruce E. Kaufman, "The Emergence and Growth of a Nonunion Sector in the Southern Paper Industry," in *Southern Labor in Transition, 1940–1995,* ed. Robert H. Zieger (Knoxville: University of Tennessee Press, 1997), pp. 295–330.

[59] Paul Wieler, "Promises to Keep: Securing Workers' Rights to Self-Organization Under the NLRA," *Harvard Law Review* 96 (1983): 1769–1827.

[60] Thomas A. Kochan, Harry C. Katz, and Robert B. McKersie, *The Transformation of American Industrial Relations* (New York: Basic Books, 1986).

■ TABLE 2–3

COMPARATIVE UNIONIZATION RATES

	Year	Union Membership as a Percentage of Non-agricultural Labor Force
Australia	1995	28.6
Austria	1995	36.6
Belgium	1995	38.1
Canada	1993	31.0
Denmark	1994	68.2
Finland	1995	59.7
France	1995	6.1
Germany	1995	29.6
Ireland	1993	36.0
Italy	1994	30.6
Japan	1995	18.6
Netherlands	1995	21.8
Norway	1995	51.7
Spain	1994	11.4
Sweden	1994	77.2
Switzerland	1994	20.0
United Kingdom	1995	26.2
United States	1995	12.7

SOURCE: *http://www.ilo.org/public/english/dialogue/ifpdial/publ/wlr97/annex/tab12.htm.*

Uninhibited by collective bargaining agreements with unions, management is also relatively free from government regulation. For example, laws in many European countries that require managers to negotiate with workers' councils in their shops, stipulate that workers are entitled to representation on the company's board of directors, or restrict employers' right to lay off workers are all absent in the United States. Beyond anti-discrimination laws and some safety and health standards, the regulatory hand of the U.S. government within the workplace is quite light. "By most international standards," one study commissioned by the Ford and Rockefeller Foundations concluded, "American employers are . . . confronted with fewer direct regulations of employment conditions than employers in other countries."[61]

---

[61] Osterman et al., *Working in America*, p. 47.

Second, the American model of extreme market capitalism is distinctive in how little the government is relative to the size of the economy. Compared to contemporary Western governments, the public sector in the United States is quite small. State, local, and federal employment account for just 15 percent of the nation's workforce, far less than the one-quarter to one-third of total employment that the public sector typically comprises in most other rich democracies. In addition, no advanced industrialized country collects a lower proportion of its GDP in the form of taxes than the United States, and the United States is also near the bottom when it comes to the proportion of its GDP allocated to government spending. The smaller public sector in the United States is reflected in fewer public services that citizens receive from the government. Other countries have public programs to finance or directly provide such benefits as health care. In the United States, this and other services are considered commodities and must be purchased in the marketplace—if citizens can afford them.

Finally, the American model of capitalism is unusual in the extent to which it lets markets rule.[62] When government plays such a small role in the economy, who gets what, where, and how is left to the market to determine. This permits those with power in the market, those who own and control the means of production, to influence critical decisions that affect the general welfare.

The result of letting markets rule is greater instability and greater inequality. Without shock absorbers to curb the market's excesses, the effects of booms and busts are more exaggerated here than elsewhere. Incomes and jobs increase more during prosperity, while employment and standards of living decrease more during recessions. Instability creates anxiety among people because they cannot plan their future with any confidence, and they feel powerless because their fate is in the hands of hidden, potent market forces they cannot control.

Letting markets rule also contributes to greater social inequality, as indicated in Table 2-4. According to a study released in 1999 by the Center on Budget and Policy Priorities, the share of income going to families in the wealthiest fifth of the income pyramid increased from 44.2 to 50.4 percent between 1977 and 1999, while the share going to the remaining four-fifths of the population declined. The income of the poorest fifth declined (in constant dollars) by over 10 percent, while the share of the wealthiest fifth increased by 38 percent.[63] The richest 1 percent of Americans had as much annual income as the bottom 49 million of their fellow citizens in 1977. In 1999, the income of the richest 1 percent, that is, 2.7 million Americans, was equal to the combined income of the bottom 100 million.

---

[62] The Fraser Institute, a conservative think tank in Canada, ranks countries according to their degree of "economic freedom." This approximates the degree to which markets guide their economies. The United States consistently ranks in the top five of the Fraser Institute's standings of more than 120 countries.

[63] *New York Times*, September 5, 1999.

■ TABLE 2-4

SHARE OF NATIONAL INCOME BY INCOME GROUPS,
1977–1999

Household Groups	Share of All Income*		Average After-Tax Income (Estimated)		
	1977	1999	1977	1999	Change
One-fifth with lowest income	5.7%	4.2%	$ 10,000	$ 8,800	▼ 12.0%
Next lowest one-fifth	11.5	9.7	22,100	20,000	▼ 9.5%
Middle one-fifth	16.4	14.7	32,400	31,400	▼ 3.1%
Next highest one-fifth	22.8	21.3	42,600	45,100	▲ 5.9%
One-fifth with highest income	44.2	50.4	74,000	102,300	▲ 38.2%
1 percent with highest income	7.3	12.9	234,700	515,600	▲ 119.7%

*Figures do not add to 100 due to rounding.

SOURCE: Isaac Shapiro and Robert Greenstein, "The Widening Income Gulf," *Center on Budget and Policy Priorities* (September 5, 1999).

The American model of extreme market capitalism is unique in the autonomy it gives corporate management, the weakness of organized labor to check managerial authority, the relatively light regulatory touch and small size of the government, and the degree to which market power determines who gets what in society. Extreme market capitalism has been held up as a model for the rest of the world to emulate. Its alleged virtue is that it creates prosperity, whatever other byproducts it may produce. But this threatens to give the American model more credit than it deserves. While economic growth has been higher in the United States than in Western Europe, the United States is only in the middle of the pack when it comes to productivity increases. Nor can we attribute the United States' enviable employment record over the course of the 1990s to extreme market capitalism either. Denmark, the Netherlands, and Austria all practice a very different model than extreme market capitalism, and all enjoyed low unemployment— without greater inequality—in the 1990s. Whatever better employment record the United States might have had than its competitors was due more to lower interest rates and looser fiscal policies than it was to greater market freedom.

The model of extreme market capitalism can also boast that the American economy is the largest and most dynamic in the world. In 1999, the Swiss-based

International Institute for Management Development examined 287 different criteria and ranked the United States the most competitive economy in the world. But powerful as it is, the American economy has not repealed the business cycle that governs the rise and fall of capitalist economies. Record stock market gains and job creation in the 1990s were replaced with three years of stock market declines and job losses from 2000 to 2003. The response of the Bush administration has been to make the model of extreme market capitalism more extreme than it already is! It has tried to shrink the size of government through tax cuts. It has redirected resources to the wealthy. It has not enforced regulations that govern corporate behavior and has placed more obstacles in the way of organized labor. It has practiced extreme market capitalism with an exclamation point!

CONCLUSION

Capitalism does not simply distribute money and wealth unequally. It also distributes economic power unequally. People who own and control the means of production have power over the working lives of their employees and have the power to make decisions that have consequences for the entire society. Capitalists decide whether to invest, where to invest, and what to invest in, based on what will yield the greatest profit, not the greatest good. Moreover, their economic wealth and power enable capitalists to wield great political influence. Their wealth provides them with the money to contribute to political campaigns, while their economic power creates a mobilization of bias in their favor. If the former gives them more powerful weapons with which to wage political combat, the latter tilts the rules of combat in their favor.

Yet the results of political struggle remain open, depending on a host of factors. Chief among them is how unified capitalists are, which cannot be taken for granted, and the extent of popular opposition they encounter. Mobilization from below can mitigate and counteract the power of business.

This chapter has described the economy as based around a few hundred large, diversified, global corporations upon which innumerable small businesses depend. A small elite class of corporate executives and large shareholders make policy for these corporate behemoths. Below this group is a workforce that is increasingly divided between professional, technical, and educated workers who are well compensated and workers who do menial and routine labor that is poorly paid. Finally, the chapter argues that the American model of capitalism is best described as extreme market capitalism, which is characterized by managerial autonomy, weak unions, small government, and relatively unregulated markets. In the next chapter, we focus on how extreme market capitalism became the form of the political economy in the United States.

3

THE AMERICAN STATE
AND CORPORATE CAPITALISM

In Chapter 2 we described how capitalism creates a mobilization of bias that gives the corporate elite a decisive advantage. Ownership and control of the means of production give it the power to manage the workforce, organize production, make investment decisions, and retain profits. These decisions, made in corporate boardrooms and not by elected public officials, are beyond the reach of democratic decision making. Yet politicians have a stake in such decisions; their reelection depends on them because corporate control over investment, employment, production, and plant location affect whether incomes grow, jobs are available, and standards of living increase. If voters' economic conditions deteriorate, politicians risk being repudiated at the polls. Consequently, politicians try to promote their own career goals by encouraging investment through offering inducements and incentives to corporations.

This chapter examines the relationship between the American state and corporate capitalism. By state, we mean the totality of public institutions that form the government of a country. The core of the state is the executive—in the United States, the president, the office of the president, and the executive branch or bureaucracy along with the military. But the state also includes Congress, the courts, and, in a federal system such as ours, state and local governments.[1]

Capitalism is often described as a system in which production for private profit is organized and coordinated through markets that are free of political direction. But the free market has always been a fiction. Markets cannot exist without a government to maintain order, enforce contracts, create currency, and provide a host of other public goods. Markets require a protective, facilitating political order in order to function.

Even in the United States, where the state's role within the economy has been less extensive than elsewhere, the state was deeply implicated in the economy from the very start. Soon after the founding of the United States,

---

[1] The use of the term *state* for both state governments and the more inclusive state as defined here complicates descriptions of American politics. However, the text should be clear as to which of the two referents is intended.

following ratification of the Constitution in the late 18th century, state and local governments developed a commercial code and legal framework to bring order and stability to economic activity, created a common currency to facilitate trade and exchange, employed a military and police to secure property and markets, financed the building of roads and bridges to facilitate production and trade, and provided rudimentary social services. As capitalism matured, the different forms of state assistance increased. The invisible hand of the market has always been supplemented and supported by the visible hand of the state.

The relationship between the state and market-based production for private profit (or capitalism) is especially complicated in those countries, such as the United States, in which capitalist production exists alongside democratic political institutions. A tension may exist between capitalism, an economic system based on profits for the few; and democracy, a political system based on democratic rights for the many.[2]

This tension is resolved through political struggle, the outcome of which is nearly always open and contingent. But this is not to say there are not clear and regular winners. Throughout American history, employers, workers, men, women, racial minorities, and farmers have often been in conflict, as each group tried to impose its own vision of the proper balance between free markets and state regulation. Business has been the most frequent winner, unusually successful in these struggles. It has limited the government's ability to influence the behavior of private firms, shaped the institutions through which intervention would occur, and influenced the policies those institutions would implement. As a result, the steering capacity of the government regarding production and investment decisions has been weak by intention.

But under popular pressure, state policy has sometimes diverged from business interests. The relative weakness of the American state's steering capacity has been a durable aspect of American history, and business interests have constantly tried to prevent insurgent groups from fashioning a different role for the state in the economy.

One can discern periodic swings throughout American history in which the government has supported and limited the play of free markets. Since World War II, as we shall describe in more detail, there have been two long swings of the pendulum. In the postwar period, building on the expansion of government during the Great Depression of the 1930s and the government's enormous success in steering the economy during World War II, the state played a more expansive role than in the past. From the 1930s through the 1970s, the government's size and scope increased enormously.

Beginning in the late 1970s, especially following the election of Ronald Reagan to the presidency in 1980, the pendulum shifted in the opposite direction. Now the principal aim was to free markets from the "shackles"

---

[2] For classic analyses of these dilemmas, see Charles Lindblom, *Politics and Markets: The World's Political-Economic Systems* (New York: Basic Books, 1977); and Claus Offe, *Contradictions of the Welfare State* (Cambridge, MA: MIT Press, 1984).

imposed during decades of government regulation. As a result of the "Reagan Revolution," groups seeking to restrict market forces in order to defend the environment, help the less affluent, protect consumers, and safeguard the interests of workers have been thrown on the defensive. This trend received further impetus under George W. Bush's presidency, with more rollbacks of state regulation and greater consideration given to the needs of business. But Stephen Roach, chief economist of Morgan Stanley, the Wall Street investment company, believes the pendulum may be shifting once again. Roach warned his colleagues in the investment community that a backlash to the triumph of markets is gathering momentum. Investors, Roach warned, have deceived themselves into believing that they have discovered the equivalent of the capitalist fountain of youth in unregulated markets. The pendulum is beginning to swing away from markets, according to Roach, and "trapped in their comfort zones, few will ever see it coming."[3] While the future direction of state involvement in the economy is unclear at this point, it will depend heavily on the course of political struggles.

In this chapter, we study the state's changing relationship to the economy, focusing on the change ushered in by President Franklin Delano Roosevelt's New Deal in the 1930s, the reversal of the New Deal policy paradigm by President Ronald Reagan in the 1980s, and its aftermath in the Clinton and George W. Bush administrations.

THE FIRST WAVE OF EXPANSION

The first expansionary phase in American history, starting in the 1840s, was based on a revolution in transportation.[4] New roadways, canals, and railroads allowed farmers in the Ohio and Mississippi valleys to ship their products more quickly to seaboard cities like New York, Baltimore, and Philadelphia. Shipping midwestern grain to New York by wagon took almost two months; by canal, it took three weeks; by rail, it took just seven days.[5] Regional and even national markets in labor and commodities soon developed as a result of these efficiencies in transportation. Railroads especially were a dynamic force propelling the entire economy forward. Their demand for massive inputs of labor and material created new markets, encouraged new technologies, and produced new corporate forms.

---

[3] Stephen Roach, "Angst in the Global Village," *Challenge* (September-October 1997): 95–108.

[4] We focus here on the development of what became the industrial base of the American economy in the North and Midwest. The story of southern economic development, based on a semifeudal plantation economy dependent on slave labor, highlights one of the most shameful aspects of American history. But since the southern economy was increasingly marginal to national economic development, our focus in this chapter will be on the development of the industrial base.

[5] Bruce Laurie, *Artisans into Workers: Labor in Nineteenth Century America* (New York: Noonday Press, 1989), pp. 15–47.

But the revolution in transportation would not have had nearly the impact attributed to it had it not been for the role of government. Almost a century ago one historian wrote that, despite popular images of the United States as "the land of private enterprise *par excellence;* the place where 'State interference' has played the smallest part, and individual enterprise has been given the largest scope, it is a fact that this country was one of the first to exhibit the modern tendency to extend the activity of the State into industry."[6] The mistaken impression of minimal state interference in the economy persists because people often look for the state in the wrong place. *State governments,* far more than the federal government, were involved in shaping the contours of the pre–Civil War political economy.[7] State governments had the authority to regulate labor relations, including slavery; determine public policy regarding corporations; collect their own taxes; plan and build their own public works; and expropriate private property under laws of eminent domain.

Nowhere was the influence of state governments more apparent than in their contribution to railroad development. For example, a number of state governments built and operated railroads themselves, or invested heavily in privately owned railroads. State and local governments financed almost 30 percent of the more than $1 billion invested in railroads before the Civil War. In addition, state governments regulated railroads through charters they issued to private railroad companies, through appointments to railroad commissions, and through the railroad rates they set.[8]

During this classic era of competitive capitalism, prior to the rise of giant corporations, the federal government's role was quite limited. Political scientist Stephen Skowronek found that "[t]he national government throughout the nineteenth century routinely provided promotional and support services for the state governments and left the substantive tasks of governing to these regional units."[9] The national government's jurisdiction in economic matters was limited basically to establishing tariff policy and banking and monetary policy, managing public lands, collecting taxes, and maintaining order.

The activities pursued by state and national government in the early 19th century were essential to creating a framework within which business could grow. They challenge the common belief that, prior to the 20th century, government did little to influence the economy. But the economic role governments played in the early 19th century paled in comparison to the range and

---

[6] Guy S. Callender, "The Early Transportation and Banking Enterprises of the States in Relation to the Growth of Corporations," *Quarterly Journal of Economics* 77 (November 1902): 111–62. Quoted in Colleen A. Dunlavy, *Politics and Industrialization: Early Railroads in the United States and Prussia* (Princeton, NJ: Princeton University Press, 1994), p. 97.

[7] See the important article by Harry N. Scheiber, "Federalism and the American Economic Order, 1789–1910," *Law & Society Review* (Fall 1975): 57–119.

[8] See Dunlavy, *Politics and Industrialization*, pp. 45–98.

[9] Stephen Skowronek, *Building a New American State: The Expansion of National Administrative Capacities, 1877–1920* (Cambridge, England: Cambridge University Press, 1982), p. 23.

level of activity that governments pursued later in that century, as they tried to respond to the challenges posed by industrialization, the rise of corporate capitalism, and economic instability.

The first wave of economic expansion, which was initiated by the transportation revolution, ended in 1873. Prices fell 25 percent throughout the last quarter of the 19th century as fierce competition drove entrepreneurs to introduce new, efficient production methods in an attempt to cut costs and prices. The downturn initiated a wave of business consolidations and acquisitions, creating large corporations that could dominate their markets. Citizens were at their mercy, forced to accept the wages corporations offered and the prices they charged. Labor historian Melvin Dubofsky quotes a Pennsylvania coal miner who lamented: "The working people of this country . . . find monopolies as strong as government itself. They find capital as rigid as absolute monarchy. They find their so-called independence a myth."[10]

These grievances soon found expression in organized political movements. In the 1870s, farmers mobilized through the Farmers Alliance and the Grange to put pressure on state legislatures and on Congress to demand fairer rates from the railroads. The historian Russell Nye captured the kinds of grievances Midwestern farmers organized against "[t]he 'plutocrat' [who] planted no corn or wheat, built no towns, and battened on the labor of those who did; he foreclosed mortgages, raised freight rates, charged high interest, stole public lands, and bought legislatures."[11]

Workers also mobilized in what became known as the Great Uprising of 1877. Railway workers from Baltimore to San Francisco struck to protest wage cuts. Local governments were either sympathetic to the workers' demands or so overwhelmed by their protests that the federal government had to dispatch troops to crush the first national strike in U.S. history. The Great Uprising was followed in 1886 by the Great Upheaval, when another labor organization, the Knights of Labor, emerged from obscurity to lead a series of strikes by workers for the eight-hour day. At the same time that workers manned picket lines, farmers in the South and the West joined the Populist Party. The Populists challenged both major political parties and criticized their ties to banks and large corporations.

All of these disparate movements opposed the growth of large corporations able to dominate their markets at the expense of farmers, workers, and consumers. They shared a belief in equality; a sense that labor, not capital, created wealth; a fear that big business and their Wall Street financiers had captured political power; and an optimism that the majority could tame the corrupting influence of capital. This general critique was embodied in specific proposals for change, for example, cooperatives owned and managed by farmers and

---

[10] Quoted in Melvin Dubofsky, *Industrialism and the American Worker, 1865–1920* (Arlington Heights, IL: Harlan Davidson, 1985), p. 53.

[11] Nye is quoted in Kevin Phillips, *Wealth and Democracy: A Political History of the American Rich* (New York: Random House, 2002), p. 308.

workers as an alternative to the traditional privately managed firm. They also demanded changes in government policy to reflect the power of the "producing classes," of workers and farmers, as opposed to the selfish influence of merchants, bankers, and capitalists.

While these broad-based social movements failed to capture government from the capitalists they believed had usurped it, they did leave a legacy. First, these movements left a local heritage of radicalism, which later generations could draw on. For example, in the 1900s, the Socialist Party garnered remarkable support from farmers in the Southwest because it could draw on an earlier tradition of Populism in the region.[12] Second, the political program of these groups became the basis for later reforms of the Progressive period, which sought to restrain corporate capitalism.[13] Finally, these movements created an alternative to the dominant culture of competitive individualism— one based on the dignity of labor, the benefits of a rough equality, the value of solidarity, and the virtues of self-sufficiency.[14]

THE SECOND WAVE OF EXPANSION

A second wave of expansion began at the turn of the century, sparked by the development of new power sources. The electric motor and the internal combustion engine now powered industry and increased productivity. By 1890, American industrial output had surpassed that of Britain, France, and Germany as more workers were engaged in applying more efficient techniques to industry. Pig iron production increased by 1700 percent from 1865 to 1900; crude oil production increased by 9000 percent; and soft coal by 2000 percent. Technological innovation not only increased productivity but contributed to the concentration and centralization of production. Historian David Noble points out that, in such varied industries as petroleum, steel, rubber, and transportation, "the systematic introduction of science as a means of production presupposed, and in turn reinforced, industrial monopoly."[15] Small firms that existed in competitive markets were steadily being driven out of business or were capitulating by combining with larger firms. "American industry is not free," Woodrow Wilson wrote, because "the man with only a little capital is finding it harder to get into the field, more and more impossible to compete with the big fellow. Why? Because the laws of this country do not

---

[12] James R. Green, *Grass Roots Socialism: Radical Movements in the Southwest, 1895–1943* (Baton Rouge: Louisiana State University Press, 1978), pp. 228–70.

[13] Elizabeth Sanders, *Roots of Reform: Farmers, Workers and the American State, 1896–1917* (Chicago: University of Chicago Press, 1999).

[14] This point is made forcefully in Lawrence Goodwyn, *The Populist Moment* (New York: Oxford University Press, 1979).

[15] David F. Noble, *America by Design: Science, Technology, and the Rise of Corporate Capitalism* (New York: Oxford University Press, 1977), p. 6.

prevent the strong from crushing the weak."[16] The result was a wave of corporate mergers and greater industrial concentration. By 1904, 318 trusts held
40 percent of all U.S. manufacturing assets. The House of Morgan alone held
341 directorships in 112 corporations with a net worth totaling $22 billion,
more than twice the assessed value of all property in the states of the Old
Confederacy and more than the assessed value of all the property in the
22 states west of the Mississippi River.

What is called the Progressive era, from 1900 to 1916, marked a profound
change in the American political economy. The rise of trusts—large corporations that had the raw power to dominate their markets and exploit consumers,
farmers, and employees—generated popular demands for government action.
In the past, state governments had intervened in the economy to *promote* business. Now citizens demanded that the federal government intervene to *regulate*
it. President Theodore Roosevelt articulated the view of many citizens when he
argued that if the trusts, "this irresponsible outside power is to be controlled in
the interest of the general public, it can be controlled in only one way—by giving adequate power of control . . . to the National Government."[17] Under popular pressure, the federal government assumed increased responsibility for
regulating business activity but in a distinctively American way. Corporate
behavior would be regulated in a manner that not only avoided big government but retained a great deal of freedom for corporations.[18] Rather than
closely scrutinizing corporate behavior as many demanded, the federal government would simply prohibit corporations from engaging in what was
described as "unreasonable restraint of trade," such as price fixing. Hence,
firms would continue to enjoy a free hand, and government's role would be
limited to preventing unfair business practices.[19]

Government intervention in the economy substantially increased during
World War I (1917–1919) because of the pressing need to mobilize all available resources. The federal government formed tripartite committees, composed of representatives from business, labor, and the government, to
develop policy that would coordinate production for the war effort. Although
highly successful, the tripartite committees were disbanded at business's
insistence when the war ended. Except during a wartime emergency, business interests opposed this kind of cooperative arrangement, which provided
labor and government with a role in what business saw as its own private
domain. In the ensuing prosperity of the 1920s, national income rose throughout the decade. But it rose faster for those at the top of the income scale than

[16] Woodrow Wilson, *The New Freedom: A Call for the Emancipation of the Generous Energies of
a People* (New York: Doubleday, 1918), p. 15.

[17] Roosevelt is quoted in Arthur Schlesinger, Jr., "A Question of Power," *The American Prospect*
(April 23, 2001): 27.

[18] Frank Drobbin, *Forging Industrial Policy: The United States, Britain and France in the Railway
Age* (Cambridge, England: Cambridge University Press, 1994), pp. 28–91.

[19] Ibid., pp. 324–33.

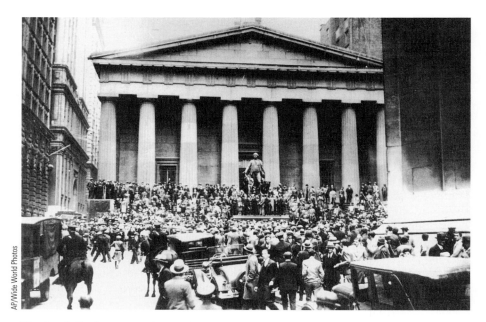

AP/Wide World Photos

The Stock Exchange in New York City on the day the market crashed in 1929.

it did for those at the bottom. Despite the boom, a majority of families did not have sufficient income to reach "the American standard," a modestly defined measure of minimum comfort, and almost one-quarter of all families lived in severe poverty.[20]

The Roaring Twenties ended on October 21, 1929, when the stock market crashed and the bubble burst that had been created by investors' irrational calculation that the rise in stock prices could perpetually outstrip economic growth. The Dow Jones Industrial Average, a barometer of the entire market, lost half its value in just two weeks. The "era of good feelings" was replaced first by gloom and then by despair. Unemployment rose steadily, from 4 million in January 1930, to 6 million by November, and then to 8 million by the following January. Employers increased the distress by cutting wages. Each line of defense against poverty—first, family savings; next, private charities; and then state and local government relief programs—was overwhelmed by the demands for help placed upon it. Meanwhile, Republican President Herbert Hoover stubbornly remained faithful to the prevailing economic orthodoxy, which claimed that the government should not engage in spending and active policies to lift the economy out of depression.

---

[20] Irving Bernstein, *A History of the American Worker, 1920–1933: The Lean Years* (Boston: Houghton Mifflin, 1960), pp. 47–83.

The depth and persistence of the Depression undermined people's faith in capitalism, in capitalists, and in a government that did nothing to help. Bread lines, soup kitchens, and millions of unemployed led people to demand large-scale change. Farmers struck, refusing to bring their crops to market because prices had dropped below production costs. Workers in the great manufacturing centers began to organize into unions. General strikes closed down San Francisco and Minneapolis. Rubber workers in Akron, Ohio, and autoworkers in Flint, Michigan, held sit-down strikes and occupied factories until their demands for union recognition were met. A group of unions broke away from the conservative American Federation of Labor (AFL) in order to organize unskilled workers in mass production into a new, more militant labor federation called the Congress of Industrial Organizations (CIO). By the end of the thirties, unions affiliated with the CIO boasted over 3.6 million members.

A NEW DEAL

From one end of the country to the other, from farms to factories, people demanded change. In 1932, a new electoral coalition of working people, Catholics, Jews, and southerners elected Democratic candidate Franklin Delano Roosevelt as president. In dramatic contrast to President Hoover's dithering, FDR boldly promised a New Deal. He proposed that the government devise measures to end the Depression, provide relief, and manage the economy. The contrast between Democratic and Republican approaches to the Depression was portrayed by one union newspaper as "a titanic struggle between the old and the new, between reaction and progressivism, between abuses of capitalism on the one hand and the masses of workers and common people on the other, between the strong who would grab everything within reach and the 'weak' who became tired of exploitation—yes, a conflict between $ interests and human welfare, nothing more. It's basically simple as that."[21]

Roosevelt believed that a fundamental restructuring of the economy and a new relationship of the state to the economy were necessary to restore economic growth, reduce unemployment, and satisfy voters. FDR was not hostile to capitalism but believed that greater management by the federal government was required to save it. But as the Depression was superseded by a new emergency—World War II—a subtle but significant shift in prevailing economic ideas occurred. The Roosevelt administration's priorities shifted from promoting growth through greater state intervention to promoting growth through increasing consumption. The government would increase the level of demand in the economy—put money in people's pockets

---

[21] Quoted in James D. Rose, *Duquesne and the Rise of Steel Unionism* (Urbana: University of Illinois Press, 2002), p. 146.

to buy things—by running budget deficits. Deficit spending represented a less sweeping form of government intervention than the other measures New Dealers had first proposed in response to the Depression. According to historian Alan Brinkley, New Dealers now spoke less about redistributing economic power and more about increasing mass purchasing power.[22]

This new economic paradigm, in which consumption drove the economy, was based on ideas first developed by British economist John Maynard Keynes. Keynes claimed that the major cause of the Depression (which afflicted not only the United States but European economies as well) was inadequate consumer demand. Private industry was caught in a vicious circle in which mass unemployment reduced the demand for goods. As inventories piled up for lack of consumers to purchase them, firms laid off even more workers. Private industry, by itself, was incapable of escaping from this downward spiral of unemployment, since private business firms were accurately reacting to signals indicating a lack of demand in the market. To break the vicious circle, government would have to step into the breach. By running a deficit in the federal budget—spending more money than it collected in tax revenue—the government would increase the total amount of money in circulation and thereby increase demand. Once people had money to spend again, business would react to the new consumer demand by rehiring workers and stepping up production. With workers back on the job earning and spending wages, demand would grow, and the economic recovery would become self-sustaining. Thus, Keynes argued that deficit spending by the government in times of slack demand was the key to transforming vicious circles of economic stagnation into virtuous ones of economic growth.

Corporations frightened by the potential radicalism of the New Deal found Roosevelt's new emphasis on increasing consumption preferable to earlier, more ambitious New Deal proposals. Budget deficits required no change in the distribution of economic power between government and business, whereas the initial proposals had involved more sweeping structural reforms.[23] In the new approach, business remained in control. Although government was more active than in the pre–New Deal era, its role now consisted of providing those in need with resources to purchase privately produced goods. Thus, the American form of Keynesianism, as the new demand-side theory came to be called, represented the least threatening way to use government to counter tendencies toward recession and depression. (It should be noted that Keynesianism took a very different form in West Europe at this time, where it helped inspire various forms of government planning and state-provided social services.) For the next four decades, from

---

[22] Alan Brinkley, *The End of Reform: New Deal Liberalism in Recession and War* (New York: Knopf, 1995), pp. 230–31.

[23] Ibid., p. 268. This interpretation of the transformation of New Deal economic reform is based on Brinkley's work. A similar view is offered by John W. Jeffries, "The 'New' New Deal: FDR and American Liberalism, 1937–1945," *Political Science Quarterly* 105, no. 3 (1990): 397–418.

the 1930s to the 1970s, both Democratic and Republican administrations followed Keynesian prescriptions of economic management.

As it was developed in the United States, Keynesianism came to command such wide support in part because it was a safe alternative to more audacious proposals for state economic intervention. In many ways, the Depression and World War II emergencies represented a missed opportunity to regulate private economic power.[24] Certainly, the changes that occurred were substantial. For example, the outlines of the welfare state were forged during the New Deal, offering citizens some protection against the swings of the business cycle. Unemployment insurance and Social Security created at least a minimal safety net where none existed previously. The labor market also came in for a degree of regulation, as child labor was outlawed and a minimum wage law was passed. Labor unions grew from 3 million members in 1929 to 14 million by 1945, offering workers some protection against the unilateral power of management. The federal government also grew. Federal expenditures that were just 3 percent of GDP in 1929 were 10 percent of GDP a decade later. The number of federal employees almost doubled in the same ten-year period. The growth of the welfare state, unions, and the federal government were consolidated after World War II and were accepted as legitimate by most Democrats and Republicans until the 1970s.

But set against comparable developments that occurred in Europe, the results were quite meager. In Europe, following World War II, Keynesianism inspired a more expansive form of government intervention. Governments developed a range of social programs to cushion citizens from economic instability, including public health programs, public housing, and publicly organized or financed child-care facilities. European governments also developed more powerful levers with which to steer the economy, regulate the market, and influence the behavior of private firms. European governments did not rely predominantly on deficit spending to promote economic growth but instead nationalized such basic industries as telecommunications, airlines, utilities, railways, and steel. Interestingly, the United States had an opportunity to travel a similar path of public ownership after the war but chose not to follow it. In order to meet wartime production requirements, the federal government built manufacturing plants and leased them to private industry, which operated the facilities. By the end of the war, the government owned 40 percent of all capital assets in the United States, including all the nation's synthetic rubber and magnesium production facilities, in addition to

---

[24] Andrew Shonfeld writes, "The New Dealers . . . perceived the future as a new mixture of public and private initiatives, with the public side very much reinforced but still operating in the framework of a predominantly capitalist system. Considering the opportunities for radical experiment offered by twenty years of uninterrupted Democratic administration from 1933 to 1952, it is surprising how little follow-through there was from this original impulse into the postwar world." See Andrew Shonfeld, *Modern Capitalism* (London: Oxford University Press, 1970), p. 308.

significant stakes in aircraft manufacturing and aluminum production. Continued ownership of the plants would have provided government with the potential to exert a powerful influence on the postwar economy. But under pressure from conservative groups, wartime reconversion plans required the government to sell the plants in order to prevent the government from competing with private industry.[25]

Not only did American economic reform reject public ownership but the Keynesian approach it adopted was applied in a conservative form. For example, Keynes believed that full employment was essential to increasing aggregate—total—demand. Consistent with this belief, President Truman (who replaced President Roosevelt when the latter died in office) submitted the Full Employment Act to Congress in 1945, just two weeks after the end of World War II. However, conservatives in Congress proceeded to dilute the bill beyond recognition.[26]

Keynes also believed that some kind of redistribution of income from the top to the bottom was required. He identified as one of the "outstanding faults of the [capitalist] economic society in which we live . . . its arbitrary and inequitable distribution of wealth."[27] But Keynes's prescription to redistribute wealth was rejected in America. Welfare state spending was lower and less redistributive in the United States than in Europe. Finally, the conservative form Keynesianism took in the United States was evident in the way it ran deficits. Both Democratic and Republican administrations chose to pursue deficit spending through cutting taxes rather than increasing public spending.[28] A consequence was that while many people were well off in the United States, public facilities, such as schools and parks, were starved for funds. Economist John Kenneth Galbraith described the result as "private affluence amidst public squalor."[29] And even within the category of government expenditures, American Keynesianism was given a conservative twist. A large proportion of government expenditures were for the military as opposed to the welfare state. Defense spending accounted for three-quarters of all discretionary spending by the federal government in the 1950s, generating military orders, jobs, and new technologies for the economy. As

---

[25] Brinkley, *End of Reform*, pp. 240–45.

[26] Alan Wolfe, *America's Impasse: The Rise and Fall of the Politics of Growth* (Boston: South End Press, 1981), pp. 52–53.

[27] Quoted in Ibid., p. 51.

[28] In 1964, President Lyndon Johnson defended his administration's tax cut in the very same terms that Republicans 20 years later used to defend their tax cuts. Johnson told an audience of business people, "We put some of the money back for the people to spend instead of letting the government spend it for them. We put some of the money back for business to invest in new enterprise instead of the government investing it for them." Quoted in Judith Stein, *Running Steel, Running America: Race, Economic Policy and the Decline of Liberalism* (Chapel Hill: University of North Carolina Press, 1998), p. 75.

[29] John Kenneth Galbraith, *The Affluent Society* (Boston: Houghton Mifflin, 1963).

Business Week, a management publication, pointed out, "There's a tremendous social and economic difference between welfare pump priming and military pump priming. . . . Military spending doesn't really alter the structure of the economy. It goes through regular channels. As far as a business man is concerned, a munitions order from the government is much like an order from a private customer."[30]

In brief, a conservative form of Keynesianism became the new economic orthodoxy following the war, accepted not only by Democrats but eventually by Republicans as well. The American version of Keynesianism included only a symbolic commitment to full employment; economic stimulation through military spending, not redistribution; and deficit spending through tax cuts, not public investment. When recast in this form, even business, which was initially hostile to Keynesianism, came to appreciate its benefits. Although the Democratic Party was the first to embrace Keynesianism, by the 1970s even Republican President Richard Nixon could declare, "We are all Keynesians now."[31]

THE GOLDEN AGE OF CAPITALISM

Many feared that the economy would slide back into recession once the artificial stimulus of World War II was removed. Instead, the United States experienced the most prosperous 25 years in its history, often dubbed the golden age of capitalism. Median family income almost doubled between 1950 and 1970. As historian Jack Metzgar recalls in his memoir of the period, the affluence of the postwar years was "new, and surprising—like a first kiss."[32] Urban working families moved out of tenements and acquired new homes in the suburbs. Televisions, cars, washing machines, and telephones— beyond the reach of most families in 1940—were now owned by a majority of families just 20 years later.

The success of the U.S. economy can be attributed to an unusual coincidence of national and international factors that distinguish this period from what came before—and after. First, pent-up consumer demand fueled the postwar economy. Production for the war effort restricted the supply of consumer goods at the same time that it put people to work and money in their pockets. The combination of disposable income and pent-up demand led Americans to spend freely once wartime controls were lifted.

---

[30] Quoted in Robert M. Collins, *The Business Response to Keynes, 1929–1964* (New York: Columbia University Press, 1981), p. 199.

[31] Herbert Stein, *Presidential Economies: The Making of Economic Policy from Roosevelt to Clinton* (Washington, DC: American Enterprise Institute, 1994), p. 135.

[32] Jack Metzgar, *Striking Steel: Solidarity Remembered* (Philadelphia: Temple University Press, 2000), p. 210.

© H. Armstrong Roberts/Corbis

Family buying a car in the 1950s.

Second, the huge demand for consumer goods led businesses to expand capacity and invest in new plants and equipment. Capital investment not only created jobs as a result of new plant construction but also increased labor productivity as firms invested in new technology. Third, labor relations simmered down following the 1946 strike wave, the largest in American history. Employers did not fully accept the legitimacy of unions but now resentfully acknowledged them as a fact of life they could not avoid. Fourth, big government contributed to the new affluence. Government spending climbed steadily from $47.1 billion in 1950, or 21 percent of gross domestic product (GDP), to $236.1 billion by 1970, or almost 27 percent of GDP. (A substantial percentage of this increase was military spending that ballooned during the Cold War.) Big government was not a drag on economic growth during the golden age of capitalism but, rather, was essential to it.

Finally, the postwar economy profited from the emergence of U.S. global dominance. American firms not only were busy satisfying the voracious appetite of American consumers but also were supplying war-torn Europe with food and clothes, as well as equipment and other supplies with which to rebuild its devastated economies. Moreover, American firms had the world market to themselves. The only potential competitors, in Europe and Japan, were heavily damaged from World War II and needed to devote their resources to wartime recovery.

By mid-century, the terms of the informal national bargain that had been struck between business and government were clear. Strategic decisions governing the American economy—how much to invest, where to invest, what to invest in, how to organize the work—would be made by corporate capital. Government would not intrude on corporate decision making or engage in economic planning that might interfere with business's right to manage. Instead, by smoothing out the business cycle, educating workers, stimulating consumption, funding research, and protecting corporate markets and investments abroad, government would create a political and economic environment that would encourage corporate investment and job creation.[33]

Over the course of the 1970s, however, the Golden Age waned as the economy began to experience stagflation, an unprecedented situation in which unemployment and inflation occurred simultaneously. In the past, unemployment and inflation moved in opposite directions. Now they both rose together. The average rate of unemployment was 6.2 percent in the 1970s, compared to just 4.8 percent in the 1960s. The inflation record was even worse. The exceptional conditions that so clearly favored American firms in the Golden Age crumbled. For example, European and Japanese industry, which were in ruins following World War II, had been rebuilt and could now compete with American manufacturers in world markets.

Symptomatic of America's economic decline was slower productivity growth, which squeezed profits. Firms at first raised prices in order to stay ahead. But this threatened to price U.S. products out of their markets. Then employers tried to maintain earnings by engaging in corporate takeovers and mergers. Economic resources were frittered away in rearranging assets rather than being invested in new plants and equipment that could maintain the competitiveness of American industry.[34] Finally, managers tried to restore productivity growth and relieve the profit squeeze by coercing employees to work harder for less money. Business threatened to close plants if unions did not agree to wage and work rule concessions in collective bargaining. Meanwhile, business engaged in old-fashioned union busting in order to reassert managerial control and intensify labor. In 1978, Auto Workers President Douglas Fraser bitterly charged, "I believe leaders of the business community, with few exceptions, have chosen to wage a one-sided class war in this country—a war against working people, the unemployed, the poor, the minorities, the very young and the very old, even many in the middle class of our society. The leaders of industry, commerce, and finance in the U.S. have broken and discarded the fragile, unwritten contract previously existing during a period of growth and progress."[35]

---

[33] Robert B. Reich, *The Wealth of Nations: Preparing Ourselves for 21st Century Capitalism* (New York: Knopf, 1991), p. 67.

[34] Ira C. Magaziner and Robert B. Reich, *Minding America's Business: The Decline and Rise of the American Economy* (New York: Vintage Books, 1982).

[35] Quoted in Taylor E. Dark, *The Unions and the Democrats: An Enduring Alliance* (Ithaca, NY: Cornell University Press, 1999), p. 113.

Conservative Keynesianism, which had provided the logic behind the golden age of capitalism, collapsed in the 1970s. Unemployment, inflation, lower productivity growth, and rising trade deficits defeated it. A new economic paradigm, articulated by a resurgent Republican Party, soon replaced discredited conservative Keynesianism.

REAGANOMICS

In 1980, American voters, battered by stagflation and polarized by race, turned to the Republican Party and elected Ronald Reagan president. Reagan was at the forefront of a new majority coalition that articulated a new economic philosophy, which departed from the Democrats' exhausted Keynesian formula. Prosperity would no longer depend on the welfare of workers whose wages propelled aggregate demand. Now, according to the new theory of supply side economics, prosperity would depend on the welfare of the affluent, whose savings supplied the capital for investment.

Supply side economics argued that the economy suffered from insufficient investment capital, not insufficient demand. In order to boost the supply of investment capital, Reagan proposed to cut taxes—most of all for the rich. Supply side economists forecast that the powerful growth resulting from the tax cuts produced by economic expansion would increase tax revenue despite the cut in tax rates. But the opposite occurred. The Reagan tax cuts, combined with an enormous increase in military expenditures, produced what were the largest budget deficits in American history at the time. Interest payments to cover this immense debt consumed 12.4 percent of all federal outlays in 1984, nearly twice their proportion of a decade earlier.

At the same time that Reagan directed tax cuts to the rich, he directed spending cuts to the poor. Until an outraged public forced the decision to be reversed, the Reagan administration even tried to define ketchup as a vegetable so that the government could reduce subsidies for the school lunch program! He also proposed to roll back regulations, such as environmental standards and consumer protections, that restricted corporate behavior. Deregulation, Republicans argued, was necessary to restore business's right to manage without expensive, burdensome rules. Finally, the Reagan administration tried to weaken unions in order to give management more power on the shop floor to increase production and corporate profits. At the beginning of his presidency in 1981, President Reagan fired 14,000 air traffic controllers who were on strike. The government proceeded to hire permanent replacements for the striking workers. Employers took the signal from the federal government to impose their own hard line on their organized workforce.

But deregulation, deunionization, and supply side economics failed to spur economic growth. Instead, the economy contracted by 1.2 percent in 1982 and experienced its deepest recession since the 1930s. Ironically, when there was eventually a recovery, it was motored more by unfashionable Keynesian fiscal stimulation than by new supply side investment. *Business Week* commented, "In the short run at least, the combination of budget deficits and tax cuts has produced a recovery that looks less like a supply side miracle than an old fashioned super-Keynesian expansion."[36]

The Reagan administration, as well as the administration of George H. W. Bush that followed, failed to restore economic growth to postwar levels, deliver balanced budgets, prevent government outlays from growing, or improve productivity.[37] Real wages stagnated amidst growing inequality. But Republican administrations were successful in shifting the terms of debate by placing government on the intellectual defensive and promoting the virtues of free markets. Unlike in the Keynesian era—when government intervention was regarded as useful in helping to reduce the inequality that markets produce, in policing corporate behavior so that the public interest was protected, and in moderating the business cycle in order to prevent another depression—the burden of proof had shifted. Now markets and corporations were regarded as beneficent, and government was regarded as guilty until proven innocent.

CLINTONOMICS

The large sign in the "War Room," where the Clinton team plotted their strategy before the 1992 presidential election, was a reminder of the issue they wanted to drive home to voters, one they believed would catapult their candidate into the White House. The sign was simple and direct: "It's the economy, stupid."

Clinton was able to ride this message to two election victories. Whether by default or design—the fortuitous accident of being president during an upturn in the business cycle or the result of deft policy making—Clinton's presidency coincided with the longest economic expansion in American history. During his administration, the Gross Domestic Product grew by 37 percent after adjusting for inflation, unemployment reached a 40-year low, median household income reached an all-time high, and a federal budget that ran a $290 billion deficit when Clinton took office ran a $9.5 billion surplus when he left.[38]

In some ways, Clinton tacked within the new economic orthodoxy of Reaganomics. Clinton ran as an alternative to traditional spend-and-tax Democrats. He was as critical of big government as any Republican. Clinton's

---

[36] *Business Week,* September 3, 1984, p. 75.

[37] George H. W. Bush, the 41st president of the United States, is the father of George W. Bush, the 43rd president.

[38] The following paragraphs draw heavily from Thomas B. Edsall, "Review of Dead Center," *The American Prospect* 11, no. 8 (February 28, 2000): 48–52.

trade policy also differed little from previous Republican administrations. He worked with Republicans and against members of his own party to push through Congress a free trade agreement that his predecessor had negotiated with Mexico. Finally, he was willing to sacrifice his campaign promise of new public investments on the altar of deficit reduction in order to appease the business and financial communities.[39]

In other ways, Clinton diverged from and reversed some of the policies associated with Reaganomics. He sponsored tax increases that helped reduce enormous budget deficits, and he strengthened regulatory agencies that had been neutralized in the Reagan and Bush years. He appointed members to the National Labor Relations Board who were sympathetic to unions and issued executive orders penalizing firms that engaged in union busting. Finally, despite his disavowal of government in principle, he embraced it in practice. In his first term he proposed an ambitious plan to provide health insurance to all Americans. In his second administration, he sponsored bills that expanded federal programs in virtually every field, including education, housing, criminal justice, health care, and research and development. No one would accuse Clinton of scaling back government, despite his rhetoric critical of it.

The prosperity of the 1990s under Clinton differed from the Golden Age of prolonged growth from 1947 to 1973 in how the returns were distributed between labor and capital. In the boom following World War II, wages kept pace with productivity growth. In the 1990s, however, the wealth created by increasing productivity was captured by corporations in the form of rising profits, not rising wages. A 1997 study by the investment company Goldman Sachs concluded that "[t]he share of gross value added going to wages and salaries has declined on trend in the U.S. since the 1980s. . . . We believe that the pressures of competition . . . have forced the U.S. industry to produce higher returns on equity capital and that their response to this has been to reserve an increasingly large share of output for the owners of capital."[40]

In 1995, President Clinton sadly acknowledged the paradoxical economic record his administration had compiled: "I came to this job committed to restoring the middle class and I did everything I knew how to do. We lowered the deficit. We increased investment in education, in technology, in research and development. We expanded trade frontiers. We have seven million more

---

[39] Bob Woodward, *The Agenda: Inside the Clinton White House* (New York: Simon & Schuster, 1994), pp. 64–147. Woodward states that a critical turn occurred early in Clinton's first term. Clinton met with his advisers, who informed him that prosperity depended on low interest rates and that interest rates would come down only if the financial markets were convinced the president was serious about deficit reduction. Woodward reported, "At the president-elect's end of the table, Clinton's face turned red with anger and disbelief. 'You mean to tell me that the success of the program and my reelection hinges on the Federal Reserve and a bunch of [expletive deleted] bond traders?'" p. 84.

[40] Quoted in Ronald Dore, *Stock Market Capitalism: Welfare Capitalism* (New York: Oxford University Press, 2000), p. 4.

jobs. We have a record number of millionaires. We have an all-time high stock market. We have more new businesses than ever before. . . . And most people are still working harder for lower pay than they were making the day I was sworn in as president."[41]

His practice of using government to solve social problems spoke louder than his words criticizing it. After Clinton, Republicans could not simply present themselves as market fundamentalists, decrying government at every turn. Now they would have to present themselves to voters as what Clinton's successor George W. Bush called compassionate conservatives, not simply old-fashioned conservatives. They would have to acknowledge that the market cannot do everything and that government is sometimes necessary to assist those whom markets have left behind.

GEORGE W. BUSH: REAGANOMICS ON STEROIDS

George H. W. Bush ran against Ronald Reagan in the 1980 Republican presidential primary. On the campaign trail, he condemned Reagan's proposal to cut taxes, raise military spending, and balance the budget all at the same time as "voodoo economics." Twenty years later, President George W. Bush would follow the same prescriptions his father had condemned so dismissively a generation ago.

President George W. Bush took office promising American citizens that he would cut taxes, expand Medicare to include an expensive prescription drug program for the elderly, and still avoid pushing the federal budget into deficit. The budget surplus generated under Clinton not only made all three possible, argued Bush, but he would avoid dipping into revenue earmarked for Social Security. Previous administrations had used this revenue to pay for current expenses. But with the budget running a surplus, Bush promised to set this money aside so as to meet looming social security obligations in the future, when the baby boom generation retired.

The Bush program began auspiciously. The 2001 tax cut was the largest in a generation, going back to Ronald Reagan. The bill cut taxes by $1.4 trillion through 2010 by lowering income tax rates, eliminating the estate tax, and giving rebates to taxpayers. Although working-class people received some immediate tax relief through the rebate checks they received, the lion's share went to the rich as lower tax rates on high incomes and elimination of the estate tax were phased in.

Initially, the Bush administration argued the tax cut was affordable given the budget surplus that had accumulated under Clinton. But the economy turned sour. The stock market declined in 2000 and unemployment rose.

---

[41] Quoted in William Greider, *One World, Ready or Not: The Manic Logic of Global Capitalism* (New York: Simon & Schuster, 1997), p. 197.

Slow growth reduced tax revenue in addition to tax cuts pushed through by the Bush administration and turned a projected ten-year budget surplus of $5.6 trillion when Bush took office into a projected ten-year budget deficit of $2.3 trillion by 2003—a stunning $8 trillion reversal in just two years. Not only did the tax cuts push the federal budget deeper into deficit, but they forced the government to dip into the social security surplus, which Bush had promised not to spend, in order to meet expenses. Despite the stimulus provided by the tax cuts, rising deficits, and record-low interest rates, the economy remained stagnant. Two days before the September 11, 2001 terrorist attacks on the World Trade Center and the Pentagon, a dozen prominent and worried Republicans met with Bush and warned him that if he did not do more to revive the economy, he would be a one-term president like his father.

Although the economy proceeded to grow modestly over the course of Bush's first term, it didn't seem that way to many Americans. The economy lost 2.5 million jobs in the first three years of his presidency, the longest sustained period without job growth in 60 years. The stock market declined more steeply than at any point since the deep recession of the 1970s, and pretax corporate profits fell more than at any point since the 1980s. The answer, as always, was more tax cuts: in 2002 a tax cut of $30 billion and then a much larger $330 billion tax cut the following year. The 2003 tax bill cut the rates on capital gains and dividends, accelerated income tax rate reductions, and increased the child-care credit. Like its predecessors, the distributive effect of the tax bill was regressive, giving the biggest tax breaks to those who needed them least. Most tax relief was directed to the wealthy—millionaires received 44 percent of the law's benefits in 2005—while 6.5 million taxpayers earning less than $20,000 received no tax breaks at all.

Tax policy under Bush became a form of Robin Hood in reverse, giving to the rich and taking from the poor. It provided little medicine to an ailing economy because Bush's tax cuts provided only modest relief to working- and middle-class people, those most likely to spend what they received in tax relief. In any event, the economy did not suffer from too little consumer spending but too little business investment. Tax cuts cannot induce new investment when business already suffers from excess capacity as a result of the investments it made in the heady days of the 1990s, before the stock market bubble burst. In March 2003, the Congressional Budget Office, which offers expert economic analysis to Congress, concluded that the effect of Bush's tax cuts and spending plans on the American economy would be negligible. The congressional report was especially noteworthy because it was supervised by Douglas J. Holtz-Eakin, an advocate of tax cuts and supply side economic theory—one of the faithful—and the former chief economist at President Bush's Council of Economic Advisors.[42]

Politically, however, the tax cuts made a lot of sense. First, they directed benefits to the wealthy, President Bush and the Republican Party's staunchest

---

[42] *New York Times*, April 17, 2003.

supporters. But the political consequences of the tax cuts go beyond a crass payoff to loyalists. Second, their intent was to raise the profile of private power at the expense of public power, to starve the government of the funds it needs to pursue policies that offer an alternative to the marketplace. Budget deficits limit the growth of public investment and social programs. They create fiscal constraints that discourage spending on programs like medical care for the aged, even as the need and demand for them increases. When such programs are deprived of adequate financing, people look to the private sector to provide them. They go to the market to purchase health care—if they can afford to buy it. Not only do budget deficits restrain spending on existing programs but they prevent the government from adequately funding additional programs to meet new challenges, such as homeland security. Despite the President's "pay any price" rhetoric to protect Americans from further terrorist attacks, President Bush was unwilling to spend the money to do it. In 2002, he vetoed as too expensive a spending bill passed by Congress that included homeland security funding, provided money to first responders only by shifting money from existing grants to police and firefighters, and denied budget requests from his own Cabinet officials to upgrade security in their areas.[43] The same was true with regards to Bush's education policy. The No Child Left Behind Act imposed new mandates on states—raising educational standards and increasing accountability—but did not provide the states with enough money to meet them. Bush's budget paid for his tax cuts by cutting crucial educational programs, such as money for teacher training, better facilities, and after-school programs.

As a result of tax cuts, government revenue declined for three years in a row—the first time that had happened since the 1920s. Federal government revenue fell from 20.9 percent of GDP in 2000 to just 15.7 percent in 2004, the lowest it has been since 1955. Actual government receipts declined from $2.03 trillion in 2000 to $1.8 trillion four years later, the result of an ailing economy and tax cuts. Government spending, however, increased by 29 percent from 2000 to 2003. The gap between lower revenues and increased spending was reflected in President Bush's 2004 budget proposal that projected a deficit of $450 billion, which threatened to beat the record deficit of $374 billion recorded just the year before in 2003.

Historically, the Republican Party has stood for fiscal responsibility, such as balanced budgets. They criticized deficit spending by the Democrats as reckless, creating liabilities that future generations would have to pay. Under President Bush, however, the Republican Party became the greatest offender of what it previously had condemned. Republicans in control of the House, Senate, and Presidency created deficits that would have shamed even the Democrats! Tax cuts have created deficits into the future as far as the eye can see and reduced federal revenues as a percentage of GDP to their lowest level since 1959—before such expensive government programs as Medicare

---

[43] Jonathon Chait, "The 9/10 President," *The New Republic* 228, no. 9 (March 10, 2003): 18–23.

and Medicaid existed, before terrorists posed a threat to American security, and before social security faced looming claims from pensioners. More than hypocrisy is going on in this apparent change of heart regarding deficits. Condemning deficits in the past was a ploy to oppose government spending just as creating deficits today is a gambit to prevent government spending. The purpose was the same in either case: to shrink government and alter the distribution of public and private power in the American political economy.

After his reelection in 2004, burgeoning deficits did not prevent President Bush from proposing to partially privatize social security, another move to reduce public spending. The controversial plan would authorize employees to divert a portion of their payroll taxes to individual retirement accounts. The result would both reduce by a corresponding amount the funds available to pay benefits to current retirees and leave workers vulnerable to instability in the stock market, the type of instability that occurred at the beginning of the decade.

CONCLUSION

The American political economy, the balance struck between state and markets, between public and private power, has been the result of unremitting conflict. Initially, conflict over the degree and purpose of state intervention in the economy was fought out between farmers and industrialists. With the eclipse of agriculture, struggle over the scope and direction of state power occurred between employers and their workers. Currently, employers have the upper hand as unions are in decline and the frontiers of the state have been rolled back. The American model of extreme market capitalism is triumphant. But political economies must succeed politically as well as economically. The model of extreme market capitalism has been brilliantly successful in this domain as well. With the partial exception of Bill Clinton's presidency, the model has commanded electoral victories for Congress and the presidency ever since the election of Ronald Reagan in 1980. One reason has been the Democrats' failure to pose an appealing alternative. Another has been the presence of social issues like abortion and gay marriage that have contributed to Republican victories. But the economic inequalities and difficulties created by the model of extreme market capitalism are generating heavy costs for current and future generations of Americans.

Public Opinion and Political Participation

Part II examines whether public opinion is contrived or genuine and whether political participation is substantial or feeble. It is hard to imagine a thriving democracy where public opinion is manipulated or disregarded, or where citizens are apathetic and do not engage in political activity.

Chapter 4 examines public opinion. It reviews the level of knowledge that citizens have about politics, how political attitudes are formed, and what the preferences of the American public are. What people know about politics and how they interpret what they know, the meaning they give to it, are important because ideas form the basis of political activity. The political participation of citizens is based upon a set of values, beliefs, and orientations that citizens hope to realize through their activity. How these ideas are generated, what they assert or imply, and the amount of conflict or consensus around them are all significant issues in American politics. Chapter 4 also discusses the preferences or views that Americans hold.

Chapter 5 examines political participation, what Americans do when they act on their beliefs. Citizens participate by voting, writing letters to newspapers, engaging in social movements, contributing money to candidates, lobbying policymakers, and joining interest groups. The various forms of political participation are not sealed off from one another. In fact. the opposite is true; citizens who engage in one form of political activity are more likely to engage in another.

The politics of power is evident in both the realm of ideas and the realm of action. The most privileged are the most well-informed. And when it comes to influencing public opinion, business has more resources to shape public preferences in such a way that they reflect its interests. But this advantage does not imply that it can simply gull the public into adopting its values. People receive cues from many different sources, and they test ideas against their experience to see how well they work. When received ideas don't work, citizens modify them to suit their needs.

Similar circumstances apply when considering political participation. The most privileged are the most active. And business again has an advantage over other political actors when it comes to political participation, just as it does in the realm of ideas. It has more money to contribute to campaigns, is more active lobbying policymakers, is more organized to deploy resources efficiently, and is more adept at influencing public opinion—to say nothing of the mobilization of bias business enjoys as a result of the special position it has in the economy. But as is true with regard to public opinion, these advantages do not necessarily translate into political victory. A contested politics of power exists despite these sources of inequality when it comes to political participation. Unlike dictatorial regimes where political participation is actively repressed, in the United States citizens can develop their political voice to influence policymakers. This is especially true when large numbers of people are mobilized in organizations, at the polls, or in social movements. Political participation, which so often reinforces privilege, can also counteract advantages of wealth, color, ethnicity, and gender.

4

THE POWER OF OPINION

On a daily basis, we are inundated by reports about what the public thinks or wants. Open any daily newspaper or listen to any major newscast, and you are likely to be told about the distribution of this or that opinion. How is the President doing? Does the public support abortion, gun control, or tax cuts? Who is in the lead in an upcoming election? How secure does the public feel despite the threat of terrorism? A great deal of money is invested in technologies, especially opinion polling, that try to replace hunches with facts about what the public is thinking about such questions. But the meaning and status of all this opinion is not quite as clear as this persistent attention implies.

Writing in 1940 to defend the development of the public opinion poll, the country's leading pollster, George Gallup, identified the development of such surveys, then still an "infant science," with democratic values. "For the first time in democratic history . . . public opinion research," he observed, "provides an objective week to week description of the values to which the people hold, and the prejudices and attitudes which they have formed out of their own experiences." Further, he wrote, "[T]heir judgments on hundreds of recent social, political, and economic issues are on file for all to examine and to evaluate." In this way, polls provide "a continuous chart of the opinions of the man in the street." Rule by public opinion, Gallup maintained, is the core principle of democracy. The alternative is rule by what he called the self-chosen. "The life history of democracy," he concluded, "can be traced as an unceasing search for an answer to this vital question . . . What is the common man thinking?"[1] Democratic government, on this view, listens to and carries out the policy wishes of the people.

Gallup was not only explaining the significance of survey instruments. In arguing that public opinion is the driving force behind what American government does, he was advancing a view that the public is both capable and in the driver's seat. "It is important to realize," he insisted, "that ignorance, stupidity, and apathy are the exception, not the rule." To the contrary, he expressed

---

[1] George Gallup and Saul Forbes Rae, *The Pulse of Democracy: The Public Opinion Poll and How It Works* (New York: Simon and Schuster, 1940), pp. v, 286, 285.

"enormous admiration for the honesty and common sense with which an enormous number of ordinary people in all walks of life and at all levels of the economic scale have continued to meet their responsibilities as citizens." In the country's system of majority rule, their opinions guide what political leaders do. This, he argued, is the central hallmark of a democracy as opposed to a dictatorship.[2]

Gallup sought to contradict the "gloomy picture of the disenchanted man living in a world 'which he cannot see, does not understand, and is unable to direct'" that the country's leading journalist, Walter Lippmann, had described 15 years earlier in a bestseller called *The Phantom Public*.[3] It is a myth that the public governs, Lippmann had argued, because the public does not exist as a population with an informed body of opinion. Most Americans, he showed, are not well-informed about politics and policy. Busy with their private lives and often uninterested in public affairs, they lack the basic information that they would need to reach rational conclusions about public affairs. Most citizens do not follow key debates, possess basic information about who governs and which choices exist, or even care that much about American government in action. Public opinion cannot govern, Lippmann maintained, because it hardly exists.

Both views—the one claiming the people govern because political leaders follow their informed opinions, the other maintaining that the people are incompetent and thus cannot govern—contain elements of truth. Each, we will discover, however, is an exaggerated cartoon. Each underscores only some elements of a more complex truth. To better understand the character and influence of public opinion, we will need to grasp four sets of issues.

In what sense is the public well or poorly informed about key issues? As scores of researchers have confirmed since Lippmann expressed his skepticism about the knowledge and interest of the public, people vary enormously in the degree of attention they pay to and in the information they command regarding public policy. Many, often most, know only a little. Yet, looked at over long periods and across a range of issues, the views of the American public in fact are quite stable and rational. Taken as a whole, public opinion seems smart. What explains this combination? Is it possible for there to exist what two leading students of public opinion, Benjamin Page and Robert Shapiro, have called the paradox of "individual ignorance" and "collective wisdom"?[4] This is our first question.

Second, what do Americans believe? Thanks to Gallup and tens of other pollsters, we now have a massive amount of information about what members of the public think and prefer. What does the substance of public opinion look like? How do citizens assess the big issues, including the status of

---

[2] Ibid., p. 287.

[3] Ibid., p. 13; Walter Lippmann, *The Phantom Public* (New York: Harcourt Brace, 1925).

[4] Benjamin I. Page and Robert Y. Shapiro, *The Rational Public: Fifty Years of Trends in Americans' Policy Preferences* (Chicago: University of Chicago Press, 1992), p. 15.

democracy and capitalism, which shape the politics of power? Do they condemn or accept the substantial inequalities of wealth and power that characterize American society? How do they orient themselves to debates about social welfare and the role of government? Are these views and preferences distributed evenly across groups and parts of the country?

Third, how are these views fashioned? Where do they come from? Which people and institutions affect public opinion? Broadly, there are two main possibilities. From one perspective, what people prefer is the result of who they are. People from similar backgrounds and educated in similar ways, who read similar newspapers and watch similar television, and who live in similar neighborhoods are very likely to express similar opinions. Alternatively, what matters is how individuals are influenced to develop and change their views by activists in different kinds of organizations. Much effort is devoted by political leaders, interest groups, political parties, think tanks, advertising, and the mass media not just to discover but to persuade and change mass opinion. What matters from this second view is less who people are than how they are influenced by these individuals and organizations.

Finally, what role does public opinion play within the democratic system? To what degree does public opinion actually drive what government does? To what extent do the people rule? Do all opinions count equally? Of course, no government anywhere on the globe can simply ignore the views held by the population it governs. Even dictatorships, however brutal and oppressive, must take these preferences into account when conducting the affairs of government. Otherwise, they risk resistance and rebellion. But, at least in theory, the importance of public opinion is greatest in democracies like the United States. Such governments formally rest on the consent of the governed. To what extent does American government respond to the ideas, attitudes, values, and beliefs of its citizens? In what ways, both direct and indirect, do the public's attitudes and beliefs affect what our government does or might do?

After all, unless these preferences influence to a considerable degree the decisions political leaders take, the political scientist V. O. Key observed, "all talk about democracy is nonsense." For that reason, he defined public opinion as "those opinions held by private persons which governments find it prudent to heed."[5] Does public opinion of this kind exist? Always? Sometimes? When and how does it shape the activity of political leaders? To answer these questions, we will need to consider both how citizens make evaluations, identify with ideologies and parties, and develop preferences about what government should and should not do. In turn, we will need to be concerned with how political leaders both shape and respond to the range of views held by the American people.

We will discover that, within the range of issues that appear on the public agenda, Americans are sufficiently well-informed to make judgments about

---

[5] V. O. Key, Jr., *Public Opinion and American Democracy* (New York: Alfred A. Knopf, 1963), p. 14.

political life. Their opinions present a paradox. Overall, public opinion is ideologically more conservative than liberal but more liberal than conservative on most specific issues. Most Americans champion democracy ardently and support capitalism as the best available economic system. Although they are ambivalent about big government, they strongly prefer that public policy help ensure equal opportunity for all. Their views are influenced by many sources, especially their own experiences, the media, and cues offered by experts and political leaders. Increasingly, over the past three decades, the political education offered by politicians, think tanks, the press, radio, and television have tilted in a conservative direction. Symptomatic of this movement has been the quite successful assault on the word *liberal*. Today, many politicians are proud to be conservatives, but few announce that they are liberal. More generally, politicians work hard to shape public opinion because, ultimately, in a democracy they are required to heed what the people want if they wish to stay in office.

IGNORANCE AND KNOWLEDGE

At first blush, the mass public lacks political knowledge to a shocking degree. During the height of the Cold War, in 1964, just under four in ten Americans thought the Soviet Union was a member of NATO, the military alliance organized to counter Soviet military might. In 1987, when press attention focused on how the Reagan administration had organized a covert effort to channel arms to the Contras seeking to overthrow the Sandinista government in Nicaragua, nearly half the public did not know which side the United States was on or even that Nicaragua was in Central or Latin America. Polls show that under 10 percent of Americans can identify the Chief Justice of the Supreme Court (many more have heard of television figures like Judge Judy or Judge Wapner). Even fewer can name the head of the Federal Reserve or either of their United States Senators.[6] Survey after survey, a major study found, reveals that "most Americans are, at best, fuzzy about the details of government structure and policy. They do not know with any precision how much money is being spent on the military, foreign aid, education, or food stamps. They have only a dim idea of what is going on in foreign countries or (in many cases) even where those countries are. They do not know much about monetary policy or economic regulation or labor relations or civil rights."[7] Perhaps even more unsettling, some students of public opinion have found that the same individuals often answer the same question about a given public policy differently from

---

[6] Page and Shapiro, *Rational Public*, pp.9–13; Michael X. Delli Carpini and Scott Keeter, *What Americans Know About Politics and Why It Matters* (New Haven, CT: Yale University Press, 1996), p. 101.

[7] Page and Shapiro, *Rational Public*, pp. 13–14.

© Jeff Greenberg/The Image Works

Pollsters at work.

one moment to another, indicating that many citizens lack "meaningful beliefs, even on issues that have formed the basis for intense controversy."[8]

Given this high level of unawareness and lack of knowledge, was Lippmann right? Is public opinion a phantom? Such a conclusion would be misleading. Many kinds of evidence persuasively indicate that it is not. In the first instance, exercises aimed at finding out what Americans are informed about and understand often overstate their unawareness. Even if the public does not have a keen sense of many details, many indications show that most Americans are politically literate at a basic level and thus competent as citizens.

During presidential campaigns, when a great deal of attention is focused on political choices, the public, in fact, is quite well-informed. The candidates are known by almost every American. Significant majorities can place the candidates' positions accurately on key issues like defense, taxes, and abortion. The majority also know which party controls the Senate and the House. More broadly, poll data indicates that most Americans, in addition to knowing where candidates, parties, and officeholders stand with regard to key issues, understand the key institutions and concepts of political life: party platforms, presidential vetoes, civil liberties. They also are informed about such key terms in political economy like *deficit, recession,* and *foreign trade.*[9]

---

[8] Philip Converse, "The Nature of Belief Systems in Mass Publics," in *Ideology and Discontent,* ed. David Apter (New York: Free Press, 1964), p. 245.

[9] Delli Carpini and Keeter, *What Americans Know,* pp. 102–103.

The situation in terms of individual political information thus is mixed but not nearly as dire as Walter Lippmann and other doomsayers have thought. Despite often stark levels of individual ignorance about particular issues at specific times, Americans on the whole do have a level of political knowledge adequate to make judgments, based on experience and information, about political questions. George Gallup's admiration for the political sense of the public is largely borne out, but not quite as strongly as he insisted or democratic theory would like. Lippmann assumed that only a tiny number of Americans are well-informed, and thus only their opinions really should count. If he were right, an elite model of democracy would make sense because the people would not be competent to govern. Gallup, by contrast, implied that the great majority of citizens have lots of information and thus can play a strong role as knowledgeable participants in political life. In fact, the distribution of political information is not like either model. It is more like that which Michael Delli Carpini and Scott Keeter call "pragmatic democracy," a situation in which "the distribution of knowledge is diamond-shaped." The population is "divided into a few very informed people, a few totally uninformed people, and most people who cluster in the middle ranges of knowledge" who possess "at least a moderate amount of political knowledge" sufficient to evaluate and act effectively.[10]

Viewed as a whole, then, public opinion is based on a decent level of knowledge. Further, as Page and Shapiro famously have argued, the collective rationality of the public has been demonstrated over time by the way its opinions have proved durable and consistent about most issues. When we observe what Americans collectively think about particular policy questions over long periods, we discover a great deal of stability and continuity. The major long-term study of public opinion, covering all available poll results from 1935 into the 1990s, discovered that for both domestic and foreign policy issues, poll results have been quite consistent from one moment to the next. During the course of these decades, for example, quite steady proportions of Americans, ranging from 55 to 70 percent, reported thinking the country was spending too little on improving education, protecting the environment, or improving the nation's health. "Opinion changes of substantial magnitude," the authors concluded, "are uncommon."[11]

Where there have been large changes, these usually have gone hand in hand with big social developments, or they have reflected major historical events. Two of the largest long-term shifts in public opinion have concerned the role of women and the legitimacy of racism. Public approval of married women working outside the home has jumped dramatically. In the late 1930s, only 18 percent of respondents told the Gallup Poll they favored women entering the labor market when their husbands earned enough to support a family. By the mid-1970s, such support had grown to more than 70 percent.

---

[10] Delli Carpini and Keeter, *What Americans Know*, p. 153

[11] Page and Shapiro, *Rational Public*, p. 52.

Today, nearly nine out of ten Americans support the employment of women. With the development of a significant women's movement in the 1960s and early 1970s, other attitudes about gender also began to change. In 1970, just over 40 percent of Americans indicated their support for the women's movement and for gender equality; today, those numbers hover around 80 percent.[12] Likewise, there have been dramatic shifts concerning race. In the early 1940s, only 31 percent thought blacks and whites should attend the same schools, while 72 percent favored separate restaurants and 86 percent thought it important that blacks and whites live in separate parts of cities. These preferences have radically reversed. By the 1980s, well over 90 percent of Americans favored integrated schools and opposed any forms of racial segregation.[13] These results both reflect and were causes of some of the most massive social changes in the United States in the 20th century.

There is an important distinction between political knowledge measured by knowing the name of a United States Senator or recalling a member of the Cabinet, and information concerned with big historical issues. There also is a big difference between the kind of close factual knowledge most Americans don't have and their assessment of needs and desires for better schools or clean air based on personal experience and values, or their support for fundamental shifts in relationships between men and women or between whites and blacks. On most issues, the public has consistently preferred particular kinds of governmental action, while on a small number of key subjects they have responded to social movements and social change by steadily shifting their opinions in the direction of tolerance and equality. These are hardly the hallmarks of ignorance or irrationality.

Further, a great deal of evidence shows that the views Americans hold about particular sets of issues come in coherent bundles. Issues about which individuals have preferences—taxes, social welfare, fiscal policy, and the environment—tend to line up together as choices about whether the federal government should do more, or less. Americans may know a little or a lot about any particular area, but they tend to have clear and coherent thoughts about the scope of what the national government should be doing. This, of course, is the question that most divides Republicans and conservatives, who tend to favor less activity, from Democrats and liberals, who tend to favor more. Here, something of a complex pattern emerges. When asked directly to choose ideological labels or the general question of whether government should do more or less, more Americans describe themselves as conservatives than as liberals, and a majority consistently say that government is too large, too intrusive, or spends too much. Yet when Americans are asked specific questions about spending to achieve particular policy goals— environmental beauty, better nutrition for poor children, improved schooling,

---

[12] Leonie Huddy, Francis K. Neely, and Marilyn R. Lafay, "The Polls—Trends: Support for the Women's Movement," *Public Opinion Quarterly* 64 (Fall 2000): 311, 318–321.

[13] Page and Shapiro, *Rational Public*, Chapter 3.

and the like—some six out of ten consistently favor liberal positions.[14] In light of this distribution of opinion, as we have seen in Chapter 2, American public opinion, as the political scientists Kathleen Knight and Robert Erikson have put it, "may be philosophically conservative but operationally liberal."[15]

Other issues, like those that concern abortion or the death penalty, cluster differently. Here, in dealing with moral and cultural questions, Americans don't judge what they want in ways that map neatly onto their usual policy liberalism and conservatism. During the past half-century, Catholics and Jews, for example, have tended to be more liberal in their preferences about the role of government than Protestants; but Catholics and evangelical Protestants are a good deal more likely to oppose abortion than other Protestants and Jews. There is more than one dimension to public opinion.

Robert Erikson, Michael MacKuen, and James Stimson treat these distinctive dimensions as policy moods about government and culture. These basic building blocks of mass opinion, they find, do change over time but not radically or haphazardly. Since 1960, the liberal policy mood, measured by support for specific governmental programs, hit a high of 70 percent in 1961 and a low of 52 percent in 1980. Most of the time, it has hovered around 60 percent.[16] At the same time, a growing number of Americans have identified with conservatism and markets, rather than government-oriented solutions to social problems. In 1971, 43 percent described themselves as liberals; today, that number has declined to 33 percent.[17] The biggest shifts occurred in the late 1960s and 1970s, when the term *liberal* came, for many, to mean cultural permissiveness rather than generous government. In turn, even progressive politicians shied away from the label, fearing electoral retribution.

Yet another aspect of "rational" and informed public opinion is the way in which citizens retrospectively evaluate the performance of government. It is not necessary to know every detail of tax or labor market policy to judge whether secure jobs are being produced or inflation is in check. A good part of public opinion consists of judgments about the competence of political leaders, parties, and institutions. The two most important bases for these assessments are the state of the economy and how particular current events receiving a good deal of media attention have been handled. Political leaders promise both kinds of capability: the ability to produce prosperity and the know-how to manage crises and large challenges, at home and abroad. When the economy stumbles, a war goes badly, or a sense of control of events is missing, public opinion tends to move in predictable, and rational,

---

[14] Robert S. Erikson, Michael B. MacKuen, and James A. Stimson, *The Macro Polity* (New York: Cambridge University Press, 2002), pp. 193–205.

[15] Kathleen Knight and Robert Erikson, "Ideology in the 1990s," in *Understanding Public Opinion*, eds. Barbara Narrander and Clyde Wilcox (Washington, DC: Congressional Quarterly Press, 1997), p. 102.

[16] Erikson, MacKuen, and Stimson, *Macro Polity*, pp. 203–210.

[17] Ibid., pp. 222–228.

directions. Not just the beliefs of the public but the amount of attention they pay to particular issues varies a lot by event. Almost no American took much notice of Iraq before the country invaded Kuwait in 1990 or before discussions of a new war began in earnest in late 2002 and early 2003. But once the United States government had decided on war, and especially after a quick military victory was followed by a difficult aftermath that cost many lives, the public focused quite intensively on Iraq, so much so that it became a dominant issue in the presidential campaign of 2004.

In sum, most Americans know rather little about the details of political life or about the contours of the fine grain of public policy most of the time. But taken as a whole, the population has reasonably consistent views, ideological positions, and the ability to make judgments about how well their leaders are doing. They also focus intensively on particular issues when warranted by events. Individual ignorance and collective wisdom can indeed go hand in hand.

MANY PUBLICS, NOT JUST ONE

It is a mistake, moreover, to simply think about "the public" as a single entity. The United States is a huge country with a diverse population divided by class and race, gender and geography. Its citizens also pay different levels of attention to politics and perform different roles in public life. Furthermore, the intensity of their concern for specific issues can vary quite a lot. So to speak of an undifferentiated or singular set of mass opinions cannot possibly capture the variety and distribution of views in the population.

Opinions do not only exist; they have a location. That is, they are anchored in particular experiences that come from how, and where, individuals and families live, work, and worship. Sectionalism, for example, long has exerted a powerful influence on opinion. Not surprisingly, in light of the country's history of Civil War, Reconstruction, segregation, and struggles about civil rights, the most important regional distinction has divided the view of Americans who live in the South from those who live elsewhere in the country. Two years after the Supreme Court ruled in *Brown v. Board of Education of Topeka, Kansas* that racial segregation in public schools is unconstitutional, the Survey Research Center at the University of Michigan asked members of the public whether they agreed or disagreed with the statement "The government in Washington should stay out of the question of whether white and colored children go to the same school." Within the South, 60 percent strongly agreed, and 20 percent strongly disagreed (the others hovered in a more moderate middle range); outside the South, just 30 percent strongly agreed, while 40 percent strongly disagreed.[18]

---

[18] Survey Research Center, University of Michigan, cited in Key, *Public Opinion*, p. 102.

The most dramatic differences in opinion distinguish the views of white and black Americans. When asked in a recent survey about the main causes of racial inequality in the United States, 64 percent of blacks ascribed this situation to past discrimination, but only 35 percent of whites agreed. By contrast, when asked if conditions of African Americans had improved in recent years, 36 percent of blacks said yes compared to 65 percent of whites. Just 12 percent of black respondents say that police in most cities treat blacks as fairly as whites, while a majority of whites, 54 percent, think they do.[19] Not surprisingly, black and white Americans also disagree about what should be, or needs to be, done at present, especially with regard to remedies based on race, like affirmative action, school busing, and the enforcement of open housing laws.[20] These differences are particularly important today because there has been a major change in the place race occupies in the spectrum of public opinion. When V. O. Key published his classic study in 1960, he found that attitudes about race, especially segregation in the South, were quite independent of those about other issues that divided Americans along a left to right continuum of liberals and conservatives. More recently, racial matters have become central to this left-right divide. Mass beliefs about many political questions have come to be shaped in good measure by how people think about racial issues.[21]

Though class does not influence public opinion to the same extent, these divisions in the population also matter a good deal for the formation of public opinion. Over and over again, those less well-off report greater support for social welfare programs and an enlarged role for government in reducing economic differentials. Interestingly, the more people know about politics, the more polarized they are by class. That is, the better informed poor and working class Americans are, the more likely they are to adopt strong views favoring a strong welfare state and redistributive tax policies; the more substandard their political knowledge, the more conservative they tend to be. A similar pattern prevails for the wealthiest Americans. The higher their political knowledge, the more likely they are to resist such policies.[22]

There also is a significant gender gap in American public opinion on some issues. Women comprise a category less united in views than African Americans or even the working class. Support for some issues that especially concern women, including abortion and whether the constitution should contain an Equal Rights Amendment, show no significant differences between men and

---

[19] Robert C. Smith and Richard Seltzer, *Contemporary Controversies and the American Racial Divide* (Lanham, MD: Rowman & Littlefield, 2000), pp. 34, 121.

[20] Paul M. Sniderman and Thomas Piazza, *The Scar of Race* (Cambridge, MA: Harvard University Press, 1993); Delli Carpini and Keeter, *What Americans Know*, pp. 247–248.

[21] Key, *Public Opinion*, pp.100–109; Edward G. Carmines and James A. Stimson, *Issue Evolution: Race and the Transformation of American Politics* (Princeton, NJ: Princeton University Press, 1989), Chapter 5, especially pp. 125–137.

[22] Delli Carpini and Keeter, *What Americans Know*, pp. 242–243.

women.[23] Women, though, are somewhat more likely to support liberal and Democratic candidates than men. They also are more likely to favor social welfare policies and oppose assertive foreign policies. Where men and women differ most is in the priorities they set. On most matters, their views are not different. But the order in which they rank issues is dissimilar. Women give a higher position to family issues like parental leave, to support for feminist policies, and to the election of female candidates.[24]

Americans within and across all groups differ in the amount of attention they pay to political life and the degree of knowledge they possess. Some people have strong or weak opinions; others have none. Some shape opinion; others defer. Some know quite a lot about a given issue; others, little or nothing. Broadly speaking, the population falls into three categories. At one end of the distribution are individuals who rarely engage with politics and who get little or no information about public affairs. Their views tend to be the least systematic, least consistent, and most likely to be based on thin political knowledge. Most of the "don't know" answers to questions posed by pollsters tend to come from this relatively uninformed part of the population. At the other end is an upper knowledge class, including political activists and committed partisans who know and care a lot about issues, candidates, and policy. In the middle lie the majority, who are moderately attentive, reasonably informed, and episodically concerned. Most of the time, they are occupied with other matters, but at particular moments, mobilized by political leaders, the media, or intrusive events, they give quite a lot of notice to public affairs. Because the ill-informed, often with random views, tend to cancel each other out and because the best informed tend to have fixed commitments, changes to collective public opinion are mainly produced by this middle group characteristic of most Americans, influenced by the best informed, most active set of leaders.[25] From the perspective of the debate that divided Gallup and Lippmann, this is largely good news because it means that a significant majority of Americans fall within the two best informed groups.

But not all the news is positive. Political information and ignorance are not distributed evenly. The least informed tend to be Americans who are poor or young or black. Women also tend to have less political knowledge than men. These groups that, arguably, most need and have the most to gain by effective participation in political life tend to be less well-informed than Americans who are older, white, and male.

---

[23] Carl Everett Ladd and Karlyn H. Bowman, *Public Opinion about Abortion* (Washington, DC: American Enterprise Institute, 1997); Nancy Burns, "Gender: Public Opinion and Political Action," in *Political Science: State of the Discipline*, eds. Ira Katznelson and Helen Milner (New York: W.W. Norton & Company, 2002), p. 477.

[24] Nancy Burns, Kay Lehman Schlozman, and Sidney Verba, *The Private Roots of Public Action: Gender, Equality, and Political Participation* (Cambridge, MA: Harvard University Press, 2001).

[25] John R. Zaller, *The Nature and Origins of Mass Opinion* (New York: Cambridge University Press, 1992), pp. 18–21; Erikson, MacKuen, and Stimson, *Macro Polity*, pp. 431–432.

Delli Carpini and Keeter, in their research to determine how political knowledge is distributed, surveyed Americans about their acquaintance with the institutions, rules, key figures, and policy choices in political life. They discovered, perhaps predictably, that awareness tends to be consistent across areas of information. People who are poorly informed about a particular area are unlikely to know much about others. In turn, people who know quite a bit about a given facet of political life usually know a good deal about many others. Bearing this bunching in mind, Della Carpini and Keeter proceeded to identify Americans who fell into an "upper class" of knowledge (with an average score of 71 percent in correctly identifying the information about which they were polled), a "middle class" (averaging 49 percent) and a "lower class" (just 26 percent).[26] Although most citizens possess at least a moderate level of knowledge that makes them functional as citizens, there are big differences across these groups, with the top tier scoring at a rate nearly three times higher than the lowest. Political information on which public opinion is based thus is unevenly distributed in American society.

More disturbing is the lack of randomness in the placement of people in each of these three categories. "The overall pattern is compelling: men are more informed than women; whites are more informed than blacks; those with higher incomes are more informed than those with lower incomes; and older citizens are more informed than younger ones." These gaps are large. Men were about one and a half times more likely than women to give correct responses to the battery of questions Delli Carpini and Keeter tested. The same ratio characterized the disparity between members of families earning, in 1989, more than $50,000 a year from those earning under $20,000, and individuals from the pre–baby boom generation of the post–World War II years from those born after the baby boom. Whites, they found, were twice as likely to respond correctly than blacks. The best-informed Americans, they found, were older white men whose family income exceeded $50,000. They possessed political knowledge at a rate two and a half times higher than the least-informed group: black women with a family income below or just above the poverty line.[27]

This pattern of distribution is worrying not because, as Lippmann thought, the great majority of Americans lack the means to create thoughtful public opinion but because those who have the least political knowledge need it most. The more people know, the more likely they are to form consistent opinions, develop a structure of attitudes that can guide their political efforts, understand how the political world affects them, accurately identify their interests and link them to such political attitudes, and effectively participate in politics. In matters of substance, moreover, the more people who are less well-off or minorities know, the more they support the active government

[26] Delli Carpini and Keeter, *What Americans Know*, p. 154.

[27] Ibid., pp. 156–161.

policies they need. Without sufficient information or attention to politics, those closer to the bottom of the social structure thus tend not to make the kinds of demands about politics and policy that would help them most. All in all, it does not make much sense to ask how much the public, in general, knows about policy and politics without also taking into account the striking disparities in political knowledge and their largely conservative effects.

POLITICAL CULTURE: CAPITALISM AND DEMOCRACY

Public opinion does not simply consist of views about particular candidates, policies, and events. Nor is it simply based on the degree of knowledge and information citizens possess. At the heart of the formation of American public opinion lies an array of visions and values that enjoy broad popular support. These features of the political culture are grounded in the country's most important sets of institutions—liberal democracy and capitalism—as well as in the country's unusually high degree of religious commitment and its history of race relations.

Most Americans subscribe both to democracy and capitalism. They overwhelmingly support a political system based on consent, elections, free speech, the rule of law, fair procedures, protection against arbitrary action by government, and moral and religious freedom. Despite many disagreements about particular issues, the status of liberal democracy as the way in which Americans wish to govern themselves is strong and secure. So, too, is the powerful emphasis on freedom in the country's political culture. Furthermore, the great majority of Americans have a high degree of tolerance for the expression of minority opinions and unconventional ideas.[28] Indeed, over the course of American history, the scope of liberty in religion, the press, and in matters that concern morals and sexuality have all grown as public support for tolerance has increased.[29]

Further, set against the country's history of slavery and segregation, and long-standing patterns of discrimination against women, ethnic minorities, and homosexuals, the country today, as a matter of values, seems deeply committed to political equality and to the dignity and human worth of each person. The great majority think it goes against the American idea of equality to teach that some kinds of people are better than others or undeserving of equal treatment. Some 95 percent subscribe to the view that "every citizen should have an equal chance to influence government policy." More than 90 percent

---

[28] An important confirmation of the growing tolerance among Americans is the study by Alan Wolfe, *Moral Freedom* (New York: W.W. Norton, 2001).

[29] Herbert McClosky and John Zaller, *The American Ethos: Public Attitudes Toward Capitalism and Democracy* (Cambridge, MA: Harvard University Press, 1984), pp. 18–61.

think "everyone should have a right to hold public office,"[30] a preference in some tension with the current pattern of office-holding drawn mainly from a small pool mostly of white, affluent men.

Americans also tend to strongly support the existence of a capitalist economic system. Survey after survey has shown strong backing for the view that people should be free to earn as much as they can and the view that values achievement, ambition, and a strong work ethic. When asked to respond to such statements as "there is nothing wrong with a man trying to make as much money as he honestly can" and "the profits a company or a business can earn should be as large as they can fairly earn," huge majorities of Americans—of all political persuasions—say yes. To the proposition that "government should limit the amount of money any individual is allowed to earn in a year," nine out of ten say no. Furthermore, well over 80 percent believe that the "private ownership of property is necessary for economic progress" and that a system of free enterprise is "necessary for free government to survive."[31]

As a result of these strong commitments both to democracy and capitalism, the country's political culture contains a deep and permanent tension between its priorities and values. When two leading students of public opinion, Herbert McCloskey and John Zaller, introduced their powerful study of these two traditions of belief, they observed that they are not mutually consistent or harmonious. Rather, democracy and capitalism represent two traditions—one maximizing freedom and participation, the other maximizing earnings and profit—that offer discordant, often clashing priorities. "Capitalism tends to value each individual according the scarcity of his talents and his contributions to production," they write, whereas "democracy attributes unique but roughly equivalent value to *all* people." Further, "capitalism stresses the need for a reward system that encourages the most talented and industrious individuals to earn and amass as much wealth as possible; democracy tries to ensure that all people, even those who lack outstanding talents and initiative, can at least gain a decent livelihood." Finally, they observe, "capitalism holds that the free market is not only the most efficient but also the fairest mechanism for distributing goods and services." By contrast, "democracy upholds the rights of popular majorities to override market mechanisms when necessary to alleviate social and economic distress."[32]

One way in which Americans deal with these tensions is to compartmentalize them; that is, to hold fast to both sets of commitments without directly confronting how they might be incompatible. Another is to debate the relative priority democratic and capitalist values should have. How free should the market be? When should government act to ensure that political equality is backed by a sufficient degree of economic equality to make it meaningful?

---

[30] Ibid., p. 74.

[31] Ibid., pp. 120, 123.

[32] Ibid., p. 7.

Such choices provide much of the content in public opinion and define the choices our politics offer.

The dominant way in which most Americans manage these tensions is by subscribing to a cluster of values often gathered under the heading of "the American dream" that stresses the importance of equality of opportunity, the chance for all Americans to freely and actively pursue their ambitions in the public and private realms. Of course, there are mythical qualities to this dream. Not everyone can participate in the quest for success equally. People tend to blame themselves, rather than more impersonal and distant forces, for their failures. But given the depth of commitment Americans have to both democracy and capitalism, no other ideological position exists that successfully competes with this vision of equal opportunity.[33] This is a perspective that permits more than one kind of policy. At times, as in the New Deal of the 1930s, the quest for equal opportunity strongly supported the push for a more effective government that could limit and tame the inequalities generated by the economic system. Over the past quarter-century, since the start of the Reagan presidency in 1980, equal opportunity has underpinned an assault on big government with the argument that the people, not the national state, should keep as much as possible of the money they earn and that this orientation will best help make the economy grow and spread opportunity.

Over time, the implications of equal opportunity for public opinion about the role of the federal government has changed quite a lot. We can see this kind of transformation over the long haul of American history. In the early years of the Republic, most Americans thought that a strong central state would become the tool of the privileged. Equal opportunity thus required a relatively small national state that would undertake only basic responsibilities for defense, trade, and internal communications. But with industrial development in the late 19th and 20th centuries and the growth of new patterns of inequality as capitalism expanded, more and more Americans looked to the federal government to pass laws and institute regulations that could level the playing field to create conditions within which the notion of equal opportunity could be realized. Today, large majorities of Americans—more than two out of three—support the idea of increased spending for education and to provide child care, assist the elderly, improve health care, and fight poverty.[34] They often differ about how this should be done, but government now has achieved a durable role in making the norm of equal opportunity at least something of a reality for most citizens. What government does thus has reduced the tensions between democracy and capitalism, but those tensions haven't disappeared nor can they be entirely eliminated. In recent decades,

---

[33] For a particularly thoughtful discussion, see Jennifer L. Hochschild, *Facing Up to the American Dream: Race, Class, and the Soul of the Nation* (Princeton, NJ: Princeton University Press, 1995), esp. Chapters 1–4.

[34] Martin Gilens, *Why Americans Hate Welfare: Race, Media, and the Politics of Antipoverty Policy* (Chicago: University of Chicago Press, 1999), p. 28.

moreover, when public policy has stressed market values and inequalities of income and wealth actually have been increasing, the place of government in making real equal opportunity possible has become more charged.

Much of the time, such friction is managed by a distinction between issues thought to be political, and thus subject to democratic life and popular control, and those considered to be economic, which are largely placed in private hands. But more and more, such a distinction is difficult to sustain. Government policy plays a huge role in economic life. Moreover, the big enterprises and jumbo corporations, like General Electric, Microsoft, General Motors, and Walmart, that dominate our economic life possess enormous political clout. As the political scientist Robert Dahl observes, "A large firm is . . . inherently a *political* system because the government of the firm exercises great power, including coercive power. The government of a firm can have more impact on the lives of more people than the government of many a town, city, province, state."[35] Further, big corporations can participate as partisans in political life because, legally, as we have seen, they have the standing of a person.[36]

So the tensions remain. Much public opinion is formed in the crucible of tough-to-resolve differences between capitalism and democracy. Whereas both sets of institutions command high regard by the public, surveys reveal that Americans are often divided—sometimes divided against themselves— about how to find the proper balance between the two. For example, although significant majorities, about two-thirds, believe the private enterprise system to be "generally fair and efficient" and that "workers and management share the same interests in the long run," a slightly larger majority thinks both that corporations and the wealthy don't pay their fair share of taxes and that "corporations and people with money really run the country."[37]

In all, the range of conflict about these matters, when situated in a comparative framework, is relatively modest. Most Americans have views that range from weakly to strongly procapitalist, and virtually all support democracy. Much public opinion, and a good deal of our politics, consists of efforts to reconcile these allegiances.

POLITICAL CULTURE: RELIGION AND RACE

Infusing public life—its rhetoric, precepts, and motivations—is a profound paradox. More than almost any other country, the United States insists on an institutional separation of church and state. There is no state church. There are no religious tests for holding office. Though the great majority of Americans

---

[35] Robert A. Dahl, *Dilemmas of Pluralist Democracy* (New Haven, CT: Yale University Press, 1982), p. 184.

[36] See Charles Lindblom, *Politics and Markets* (New York: Basic Books, 1977), p. 356.

[37] McClosky and Zaller, *American Ethos*, pp. 176, 177, 179.

are Christian, fewer than one in five think the country was meant to be a Christian nation; more than four in five believe firmly in a country made up of many religions. Over 90 percent think religious toleration is either somewhat or extremely important. A much larger proportion of Protestant Americans than in the past are now willing to support Catholic and Jewish candidates for office, including the presidency. "By 1999," a thorough review of the poll data reported, "the numbers suggest a practically identical disposition toward a Baptist, Catholic, or Jewish presidential candidate in American elections," with well over 90 percent saying yes with regard to all three religions.[38] At the same time, Americans overall are a deeply religious people. Ever since the Gallup Poll started asking the question in the 1940s, 95 percent or more of the respondents have said they believe in God. Over time, there has been a slight decline in absolute certainty (declining from 87 percent in 1952 to 72 percent in 1996), but the persistence of faith in a secular age is an overwhelming feature of American life and politics. Three in four citizens report they would not vote for a candidate for president who does not believe in God.[39]

During the past quarter-century, conservative religious movements based in Protestant evangelical churches, including the Moral Majority and the Christian Coalition, have played a growing role in mobilizing public opinion. These organizations have sought to tap into the country's religiosity, with a considerable degree of success. A key result has been the growing importance of moral issues—including abortion, family life and values, and sexual preference—often at the expense of issues concerning economic policy and patterns of inequality. But just as support for democracy does not necessarily imply backing for social welfare policies or just as support for capitalism does not necessarily lead to an espousal of policies restricting regulation, religious feeling does not necessarily produce opinion that follows the lead of the conservative Christian movement. Indeed, most Americans think it to be a divisive force. When asked in 1995 when the movement was at its peak whether it strengthened or divided the Republican party, 27 percent said "strengthened" and 56 percent responded "divided," while the rest did not know.[40]

Like democracy and capitalism, religion is what the political scientist J. David Greenstone called a boundary condition in American life.[41] Political conflict and choice largely play out inside the limits each establishes. Public opinion is shaped within the borders that these institutions and values set.

Race provides the final key component of American political culture. The long history of racial injustice in the United States has made it virtually

[38] Ibid., pp. 24, 32; Mariana Servin-Gonzalez and Oscar Torres-Reyna, "The Polls—Trends: Religion and Politics," *Public Opinion Quarterly* 63 (Winter 1999): 596.

[39] George Bishop, "The Polls—Trends: Americans' Belief in God," *Public Opinion Quarterly* 63 (Fall 1999): 428–31; Servin-Gonzalez and Torres-Reyna, "Religion and Politics," p. 614.

[40] Servin-Gonzalez and Torres-Reyna, "Religion and Politics," p. 600.

[41] J. David Greenstone, *The Lincoln Persuasion: Remaking American Liberalism* (Princeton, NJ: Princeton University Press, 1993).

impossible for African Americans to understand their experiences and identities, or shape their political views, other than by looking at the country through a racial lens. Further, as the political scientist Michael Dawson has shown, "black ideologies"—distinctive positions that include black nationalism and black feminism—"dramatically shape black political opinion."[42] Blacks share many common understandings and beliefs about politics with white Americans. At the same time, African Americans draw on distinctive traditions of thought, language, and belief in forming their views and preferences. Above all, what distinguishes these perspectives is the high degree to which blacks believe their fate is linked to each other and that their chances in life are connected to the fate of their group.

It is this feature of black opinion that leads Dawson to argue that a "black counterpublic" exists. Overall, Americans self-identify more as conservatives than liberals. Most African Americans are liberals. In the black community, critics of liberalism tend not to be conservatives. There are black conservatives, of course, but only a very small proportion of the group. Most critics of liberalism within black America, by contrast, including black nationalists, feminists, and some Marxists, are on the left of the political spectrum rather than on the right. Like other liberals, black liberals support government when it intervenes in the marketplace, favor social welfare programs, and would like tax policy to be far less generous to the rich. But their liberalism tends to be much more skeptical in the face of what they perceive as a continuing pattern of racism. It also is less willing to celebrate the American experience. As a result, Dawson argues, black liberalism has more variety, with more diverse shades of view, than the liberalism of white America. It tends to be more egalitarian, more ambitious for government, and, as we have seen, more disillusioned with what has been accomplished thus far.[43]

MAKING AND USING OPINION

Public opinion is the product of two main factors: who we are and how we are influenced. The development of political attitudes begins in childhood. Children raised in conservative and Republican families, especially when both parents share ideological and political views, are likely to be conservative and Republican; those reared in liberal and Democratic families are disposed to be liberal and Democratic. The more political knowledge her

---

[42] Michael C. Dawson, *Black Visions: The Roots of Contemporary African-American Political Ideologies* (Chicago: University of Chicago Press, 2001), p. xiii.

[43] Ibid., pp. 238–313. Also see Michael C. Dawson, *Behind the Mule: Race, Class, and African American Politics* (Princeton, NJ: Princeton University Press, 1994); Donald R. Kinder and Lynn Sanders, *Divided by Color: Racial Politics and Democratic Ideas* (Chicago: University of Chicago Press, 1996); and Katherine Tate, *From Protest to Politics: The New Black Voters in American Politics* (Cambridge, MA: Harvard University Press, 1993).

parents have, the more likely a person will hold informed opinions about politics and policy. The place of parents in the class structure helps determine the opinions of children, with working class families more likely to produce liberal offspring. On balance, then, the family is a source of continuity in public opinion.[44]

More generally, the influence of families is part of a constellation of factors that help determine the political identities of citizens. Particular neighborhoods, regions, and states have collective political orientations that make it more likely that a person will conform to prevailing and common opinions than dissent. People choose to belong to interest groups and social movements that both conform with and reinforce their political views. Belonging to some categories in the population, most notably the fact of being black, makes it highly likely that individuals will hold opinions that correspond with other group members.

Public opinion, in short, is shaped in part by how we experience daily life where we live and where we work. We tend to be influenced by those like us and close to us. Most people, even before they are the targets of public appeals of different kinds, are strongly disposed to one or another position or opinion. But public opinion is not fixed or strictly determined by the identities and happenings in people's lives. Public opinion is made by politicians, activists, and institutions who seek to shape it by providing information, by appealing to emotions, and by contradicting opposing views.

One way in which politicians deal with public opinion is to gather information, often through polls, about what the public is thinking and caring about. Then they try to create policies that respond to what public opinion wants. When observers like what they do, they call this democratic responsiveness. When they don't, they call it pandering to the public, a sign of cowardly or missing leadership.[45]

A second manner in which politicians handle opinion is to try actively to craft it. They use survey instruments to find out less what the public wants than how to convince the public to support the policies they would like to enact. In this way, Lawrence Jacobs and Robert Shapiro detect, "politicians use polls and focus groups not to move their positions closer to the public's but just the opposite: to find the most effective means *to move public opinion closer to their own desired policies.*"[46] They call this effort "crafted talk" because it is directed in subtle ways by the cues polls offer about which words, constructs, and arguments are likely to win public support for their own policy goals.

This type of effort to tap into and redirect public opinion, they argue, has been increasing at the expense of more genuine responsiveness. Likewise,

---

[44] Key, *Public Opinion*, Chapter 12.

[45] Lawrence R. Jacobs and Robert Y. Shapiro, *Politicians Don't Pander: Political Manipulation and the Loss of Democratic Responsiveness* (Chicago: University of Chicago Press, 2000), pp. xiv–xv.

[46] Ibid., p. xv (italics in original).

political scientist Alan Monroe's research has found that the policies the government has adopted since 1980 were less receptive to the signals given by majority public opinion than policies enacted between 1960 and 1979.[47] The key term here is "majority." Political leaders are still being responsive but less and less to majorities, some of whom are paying only modest attention to political life, but more to minorities with intense interests in specific issues. For many years, one of the main truisms in political analysis has been that politicians move to the political center to find moderate voters. But in recent years, as politics has become more polarized, many candidates and office holders have pitched their campaigns instead to the most partisan and most active part of the population. These are the people more likely to select candidates in primaries or donate funds to political campaigns. They also track and respond to the views of interest groups with an intense interest in a given subject because they know that these organized interests have the capacity to mobilize voters within their constituency.

Political leaders also have views of their own about what good policy consists of. With the erosion in number of liberal or moderate Republicans and conservative Democrats, politicians increasingly tend to be individuals with strong policy preferences that put quite a distance between the two political parties. As a result of these factors, rather than seeking votes in the middle by adopting restrained policy positions, they increasingly use crafted talk to move people in the middle of the political spectrum to their own policy positions. In this way, rather than assume public opinion is fixed, they work to change it. In so doing, they can "pursue policy goals independent of centrist opinion without unduly sacrificing their chances for reelection."[48]

The growing ideological distance between Republicans and Democrats in the past quarter-century has been accompanied by a dramatic increase in the number of interest groups, most of which belong to the business community, that have specialized and intensely focused concerns. With growth of the religious right and especially the number of registered lobbyists and the presence of corporations with offices in Washington (see Chapter 3), as well as the decline in influence of organized labor as a political force (see Chapter 2), and the growing importance of money in politics that these groups can mobilize (see Chapter 5), politicians are now strongly pressured to pay less attention to the broad sweep of the public's views than to the concentrated concerns of activists. Especially when they share the groups' policy positions, they are likely to turn to crafted talk to bring the mass public along.

In such efforts, the media—newspapers, radio, television, and, increasingly, the Internet—play a crucial role because it is from the media, rather than from political leaders directly, that citizens obtain the information they use in

---

[47] Alan D. Monroe, "Consistency Between Public Preferences and National Policy Decisions," *American Politics Quarterly* 7 (January 1978); Alan D. Monroe, "Public Opinion and Public Policy, 1980–1993," *Public Opinion Quarterly* 62 (Spring 1998).

[48] Jacobs and Shapiro, *Politicians Don't Pander*, p. 20.

developing their view about public issues. Politicians thus have a keen interest in shaping what the media report and how they say it. Accordingly, they invest a great deal of effort to develop a message and supply it to the media.

One effect is to "dumb down" public discourse. Rather than try to explain to citizens the content and complexities of policies and their merits by reasoned arguments, they tend instead to use mass communications to shift public opinion by doing what social psychologists call priming. This is an effort to "raise the priority and the weight that individuals assign to particular attitudes already stored in their memories."[49] Staying on message with simple themes and repeated language is used to control the terms and content of debate by shaping how the issue gets reported. In circumstances where most Americans support spending for many government programs for social welfare but are against big government, opponents of these programs prime the public to think that the issue at hand is the size of the federal establishment, not the particular goal of the program.

The environment in the press has changed, making such priming more likely to be successful. With technological change, the world of the mass media has become more fragmented and increasingly competitive in journalistic and economic terms. Once, newspapers and news magazines were the major source of political information, but no longer. These suppliers of news are still important, but most Americans now get their information from television, radio, and the Internet. Rather than a main hometown newspaper, now hundreds of competing sources of information have to attract audiences. Even television, once concentrated in three main networks, has been fragmented by the revolution in cable and satellite means of delivery. Like politicians, the new media have an incentive to dumb down as they search for more viewers, listeners, and readers and to treat the news as a source of entertainment more than information. Further, as individual institutions, they tend to have fewer resources than the big papers or the major TV networks. So they depend more on the cues and language offered to them by politicians. As a result, less distance and independence separate what political leaders want to get reported and what does.

The amount of press coverage tends to vary with the strategic campaigns of politicians, and the content of what gets reported is shaped by the language and cues they offer. Press objectivity in these circumstances has come to mean covering as factual both sides of political controversies in the terms each side offers to the public. These usually are designed to fit the desire of the media to offer up news in an entertaining and enticing way.[50] Because the cost of collecting the news is great, higher than most outlets can afford, they

---

[49] Ibid., p. 50.

[50] For an important history of the media, see Paul Starr, *The Creation of the Media: Political Origins of Modern Communications* (New York: Basic Books, 2004). There is an excellent discussion of priming and the political use of the media in Jacobs and Shapiro, *Politicians Don't Pander*, pp. 49–61.

rely heavily on such joint services as the Associated Press that disseminate the same basic stories to the media at large, which then reshape them to the level and perceived preferences of their particular audiences. They also depend on information provided by the massive public relations efforts of political leaders and activists to mold how they, and their views, are presented to the media and the public.

The relationship between the media, politicians, public opinion, and democracy is not one-dimensional. Individuals are not easy to manipulate. People live within dense networks of personal influence and social relationships that shape their experience and their views. The media and their use by politicians and interest groups cannot easily change public opinion because the public itself is fragmented and not open to mass suggestion of a simple kind. Most people have reasonably stable views and ideological commitments that are not radically affected by public relations efforts. The fragmentation of the media also means that there is at least some representation of minority and unpopular ideas.

OPINION, POLICY, AND THE CONSERVATIVE DRIFT

It does not take massive collective shifts to change public opinion and its impact on public policy. Consider the role public opinion played in the rise and fall of the far-reaching plan to reform American health care President Bill Clinton launched in September 1993. In the following months, culminating in his State of the Union address four months later, he primed the public with a "Security for All" message that "publicly highlighted the benefits of health reform as a substitute for a detailed discussion of how to pay for the plan and implement it."[51] In this period, public opinion polls reported that support for this initiative never fell below 50 percent. At some points, it rose to 60 percent. Only a third of the country opposed this reform. Most pundits, observing the positive trend of public opinion, predicted that the President's suggestions would become law. Soon, however, the tables turned. By July 1994, pollsters reported that only 40 percent still backed the Clinton health care program; opposition had grown to 56 percent of the population. The legislation soon failed, and health care reform was shelved.

Both preceding and just after President Clinton's election in 1992, the country's two leading polling organizations regularly asked Americans about health care. "In your opinion, is there a crisis in health care in this country today, or not?," the Gallup Poll inquired. "Which of the following statements comes closest to expressing your overall view of the health care system in this country?" the Harris Poll asked. "On the whole, the health care system works pretty well, only minor changes are necessary to make it work better; there

---

[51] Jacobs and Shapiro, *Politicians Don't Pander*, p. 51.

are some good things in our health care system, but fundamental changes are needed to make it work better; the American health care system has so much wrong with it that we need to completely rebuild it."[52]

The poll results had been so striking that they surely had emboldened the President to seek major reforms. In 1992 and in early 1993, nine out of ten Americans thought the health system was in crisis. Even more striking was growing support for fundamental change—"completely rebuild it." Between 1990 and September 1993, backing for a restructuring even greater than "fundamental change" grew from 24 percent to 42 percent of the population. Only 6 percent thought that just minor changes would suffice. All in all, then, 94 percent of respondents preferred substantial alterations to the health care system. Paralleling the decline in support for Clinton's measures, however, these numbers, the polls reported, started to drop quite quickly in the fall of 1993. Within a short period, responses identifying a crisis in health care had dropped by 18 points and support for rebuilding the system fell to 31 percent.

Alongside these poll results were others that consistently displayed more skepticism by the public about the role Washington should play in health care. When asked to choose between paying higher taxes and placing government "in charge of the organization and delivery of health care services," or paying "more money out of your own pocket directly to private doctors and hospitals, with government involvement only for people who cannot pay their own care," support for governmental responsibility peaked at 46 percent, never getting over the 50 percent mark. By the end of 1993, this degree of support had fallen to just 39 percent. It was this sentiment that opponents of the Clinton reforms used to build opposition. By utilizing a series of television advertisements featuring a married couple, Harry and Louise, and by stressing the complexity and costs of the scheme, and in mobilizing press attention, "opponents of the president's health reform proposal consistently stuck to the simple message that 'big government' would reduce quality."[53]

In this case, as in most other battles to shape public opinion in order to achieve, or stop, new public policies, it was not necessary to change everybody's views. Indeed, relatively small shifts can have large consequences. The targets of priming and public relations campaigns tend not to be the best informed and most committed citizens. Nor is it the group that is least informed and least committed. Rather, the objective is to influence the majority of citizens in the middle knowledge class, those who have broad and quite general information about American politics and who pay attention from time to time. It does not take many converts to change the contours of public opinion in aggregate. The dramatic fall of 18 points about whether the health care system was in crisis required only that 9 of every 100 people change their views.

---

[52] Cited in Ibid., p. 345.

[53] Ibid., p. 52.

Tracing the history of debate and press coverage of the Clinton reform initiative, two leading journalists, David Broder and Haynes Johnson, argued that those with the most to lose if Clinton's plan had passed—the insurance industry—played a key role in funding negative advertisements and leading a negative campaign in the press.[54] What these firms understood is that business rarely can get its way directly in American politics but must find the means to influence the public by helping to shape their views and preferences.

In the recent past, the capacity of business to persuade the public has been enhanced by the rise of think tanks—private not-for-profit organizations that investigate issues concerning public policy—that politically lean to the right. In evaluating and promoting policy proposals, these institutions often directly seek to influence politicians and policy experts. But they also have an important, if more indirect, impact on public opinion. They help shape public preferences by developing arguments and producing evidence that makes a particular course of action more attractive. Behind public opinion, in short, lies a battleground of ideas in which think tanks—left, right, and center—dispute and compete. Most Americans do not have direct access to the materials they produce. Rather, they are geared to find their way to the media, where they are disseminated and shape the views held by the public.

As not-for-profit organizations, think tanks need financial support to hire staff, publish papers, hold conferences, and advocate in the mass media. Seeking to counter what they believed had been a liberal bias in think tanks and the media from the New Deal of the 1930s to the Carter administration in the 1970s, business leaders made a concerted effort to provide funding for an intellectual infrastructure for conservatives. In the 1970s, funding for the previously unimportant American Enterprise Institute grew tenfold, based mainly on corporate funding. Financial support from Joseph Coors was critical to the creation in 1973 of the Heritage Foundation; soon it had funds from 87 companies in the Fortune 500. During the 1970s and 1980s, other key think tanks on the right were created or greatly expanded, including the Cato Institute, the Hudson Institute, and the Manhattan Institute.[55]

Soon, there was a significant shift in the way the media covered policy issues. A study of think tanks and the media by the political scientist Mark Smith found that liberal think tanks had a small advantage over conservative ones in reports in the media in the 1970s. Since 1980, however, conservative institutes have gained the upper hand, often in dramatic fashion. All in all, the conservative organizations "have been more effective over time than their

[54] Haynes Johnson and David Broder, *The System: The American Way of Politics at the Breaking Point* (Boston: Little Brown, 1996). Jacobs and Shapiro argue this is something of an exaggeration, since such business sources accounted for far less media coverage than experts, other advocates, and politicians. But this, in turn, underestimates who the experts were and how they were funded.

[55] Mark A. Smith, *American Business and Political Power: Public Opinion, Elections, and Democracy* (Chicago: University of Chicago Press, 2000), p. 173.

liberal counterparts in generating publicity for their views." Business, he concluded after a careful investigation both of the impact of think tanks on the media and of the media on the public, had gained power by its growing ability to shape public opinion. "As think tanks grew in prominence and corporations directed their contributions toward overtly conservative ones, . . . business added a new weapon to its arsenal."[56] Alongside the rise of the Christian right and the erosion of influence in the labor movement, this development has been the most significant means by which public opinion has been nudged in a more conservative direction.

CONCLUSION

For more than a generation, leading scholars writing about public opinion have focused on two main issues: Does the public know enough to be competent in political life? Do political leaders and institutions promote public understanding of issues and choices, or do they manipulate public opinion by providing biased and false information? We have seen that Americans, in the main, do possess adequate, if in many respects limited, information about politics and have a sufficient level of interest to be thoughtful and rational citizens. In the main, they acquire and hold coherent policy preferences that remain stable over time. When these change, they usually do so in response to important events and historical trends. Citizens tend to form political views sensibly based on their experiences, underlying values and core beliefs, and a decent level of information. Public opinion is not a phantom.

But there are no grounds for complacency, particularly regarding the quality and, sometimes, the truthfulness of information available to the public when citizens fashion their views. Unfortunately, the record is uneven. Much of the time, the clash of opinion, the range of information, and the thoughtfulness of debate about public policy help produce an informed public and guide knowledgeable choices. Yet, the country's history over the past half-century has been punctuated by efforts to shape public opinion that contradict this standard. As a candidate for President in 1960, John Kennedy declared a missile gap with the Soviet Union that was not true; and even after his administration knew that this worst-case scenario was false, it repressed the information in order to justify a rapid build-up in weapons. In 1964, President Lyndon Johnson wrongly claimed North Vietnamese attacks on two U.S. destroyers in the Gulf of Tonkin in order to persuade Congress to authorize war making in Vietnam. In 1985 and 1986, President Ronald Reagan disguised covert efforts to trade arms and hostages with Iran in a complicated scheme to help Contra rebels in Nicaragua fight a guerilla war against the elected leftist Sandinista government. In the months before the

---

[56] Ibid., pp. 185, 192, 194.

United States went to war against Iraq in 2003, President George W. Bush exaggerated the military threat from that country in his State of the Union address, even to the point of citing forged documents about an Iraqi attempt to obtain nuclear fuel in the African country of Niger.

The judgment announced in the classic work on public opinion by V. O. Key still holds. "Politicians," he wrote, "often make of the public a scapegoat for their own shortcomings; their actions, they say, are a necessity for survival given the state of public opinion. Yet that opinion itself results from the preachings of the influentials, of this generation and of several past genera- tions." He further noted that political "leaders who act as if they thought the people to be fools responsive only to the meanest appeals deserve only scorn."[57] Critical responsibility for the depth and quality of public opinion, in short, lies with the character of education provided by our schools, the range and rigor of reporting by the mass media, the standards used by experts who care about public policy, and the thoughtfulness and responsibility exhibited by politicians.

---

[57] Key, *Public Opinion*, pp. 557, 555.

5

POLITICAL PARTICIPATION: PARTIES, ELECTIONS, AND MOVEMENTS

INTRODUCTION

Like fraternal twins, the 2000 and 2004 elections had the same genetic code but different personalities. They resembled each other in that George W. Bush won the presidency due to the overwhelming support he received from the South, the Great Plains, and the Rocky Mountain West in each election. But the two elections differed in their meaning and significance.

The 2000 election could not have been more dramatic. Election night extended over 36 days before citizens knew who the new president would be. Although Democratic candidate Al Gore received 550,000 more votes nationwide than his Republican opponent George W. Bush, presidential elections are decided by who wins a majority in the Electoral College and not in the popular vote. (The Electoral College is discussed in more detail in Chapter 6.) The race was so tight that Florida's 25 electoral college votes would provide either candidate with the majority he needed to become president. At first, the television networks called Florida for Gore. A few hours later they reversed themselves and declared the state for Bush, and then they corrected themselves once again and acknowledged the state was simply too close to call. Bush enjoyed a slim margin of a few hundred votes in Florida out of more than five million that were cast statewide. As attention was riveted upon the state, charges of massive voting irregularities and disputed ballots in Florida emerged, casting suspicion upon the results. Gore sued to have Florida's disputed ballots counted manually. Bush tried to prevent the recount. The legal case eventually landed in the Supreme Court, which, in a controversial decision, ruled 5–4 to stop a recount of ballots that was already underway. This decision put Florida's 25 electoral college votes in Bush's column, giving him a majority in the Electoral College. When Al Gore conceded the next day, it was not clear whether he had lost by the official total of 537 votes in Florida or by just one vote on the Supreme Court. George W. Bush proceeded to become the fourth president in American history to be elected with fewer votes than his opponent.

The 2004 election lacked the drama of a disputed outcome that made the 2000 election so tense and gripping. And just like the results of four years before, Bush owed his victory to his strength in the South, the Plains states, and the Rocky Mountain West. But as much as the 2004 presidential election lacked the tumult of the previous one and the results resembled it, the 2004 elections still have a significance of their own. First, Bush was able to win not only a majority in the Electoral College in 2004 but he also won the popular vote, which had eluded him in 2000. He won by a margin of over 3,500,000 votes nationwide. He became the first presidential candidate to win a majority of the popular vote, with 51 percent of the vote to 49 percent for his Democratic opponent John Kerry, since his father George H. W. Bush managed to do so in 1988. Second, the election was marked by large voter turnout. While traditional Democratic voters, such as blacks, turned out in record numbers, this was even more true of traditional Republican voters, such as Christian evangelicals.

Finally, in 2004 the party system crossed a Rubicon toward which it had been moving since the 1960s. With Republicans winning the presidency—winning a majority in the Electoral College and the popular vote—as well as increasing their majorities in the House of Representatives and the Senate and controlling a majority of state houses in the form of governorships, the GOP firmly established itself as the new majority party in the nation. If the 2000 election had been a perfect tie, reflecting an exquisite balance between the parties, that was no longer true four years later. The Republican Party is the new dominant party in American politics, with the Democrats now cast as the minority party. After four decades of catching up to and finally drawing even with the Democrats, the Republicans now stand alone at the summit of American politics. Their conduct in power and the outcome of future elections will determine how long they can stay at the mountaintop.

This chapter analyzes the emergence of the Republican Party as the new dominant party in American politics and the corresponding decline of the Democrats. It also examines the history of the American party system, the impact of money on elections and campaigns, and the different forms of political participation.

TURNOUT AND AMERICAN VOTERS

According to political scientist E. E. Schattschneider, "The political parties created modern democracy and modern democracy is unthinkable save in terms of the parties."[1] Political parties are the agency that organizes and transmits the will of the majority to the government. They are the heart of any democracy because they pump the blood of electoral consent that informs and flows through political institutions. Political parties are not only organizations committed to winning elections, but they also educate and mobilize voters, and recruit and nominate candidates for office. In addition, they advocate policies that link voters to candidates and connect elected officials from the same party to each other.

---

[1] E. E. Schattschneider, *Party Government* (New York: Holt, Rinehart & Winston, 1942), p. 1.

If, as Schattschneider claims, political parties are the measure of democracy's health, then American democracy is in urgent need of medical care. American political parties are suffering from a case of severe political anemia, reflected in alarmingly low voter turnout. While the patient certainly showed signs of recovery in 2004—with turnout at 59 percent, the highest recorded since 1960—it still cannot be given a clean bill of health. Political parties may have performed better at bringing voters to the polls in 2004 than they have done in the past, but compared to other countries the American party system still lacks vitality. The United States continues to bring up the rear in comparisons of turnout with other industrialized democracies. In one study, the United States ranked second to last in turnout, finishing ahead only of Switzerland![2]

Many factors contribute to low turnout in U.S. elections. First, low turnout is a symptom of widespread popular cynicism directed at politicians from both parties. "Us" versus "them" no longer refers to the partisan division of the electorate between Democrats and Republicans. It now describes skeptical citizens on one side and the governing class on the other side. Citizens are sullen and suspicious of political elites from both parties, who are perceived as simply out for themselves. Citizens express their disgust by withdrawing from a process that they regard as corrupt and unresponsive to their interests.

Second, the political scientist Robert Putnam argues that low turnout is due to generational replacement. The elderly, who vote regularly, are dying off and being replaced by a new generations of citizens who are not in the habit of casting a ballot. Or to put the point in very personal terms: The students who read this book (and their parents) are much less likely to vote than their grandparents. Putnam argues that the older generation developed the habit of voting and confidence in the electoral process because parties responded effectively to the Depression and World War II, which shaped this generation's consciousness. The habits and values of succeeding generations were similarly shaped by their history. But instead of confirming the value of parties and elections, the lessons that these generations drew from events made them skeptical and cynical.[3]

Third, citizens have expressed their disappointment with the choices offered them by not going to the polls. The limited options provided by the two-party system were humorously portrayed in the Halloween episode of the *The Simpsons* that aired just before the November 1996 elections. Homer Simpson discovers that aliens have abducted incumbent Democrat Bill Clinton and Republican challenger Bob Dole and are posing in disguise as

---

[2] Russell J. Dalton, *Citizen Politics: Public Opinion and Political Parties in Advanced Industrial Democracies*, 3rd ed. (New York: Chatham House, 2002), p. 36. For comparative turnout levels, see Table "International Voter Turnout, 1991–2000," which can be found at *www.fairvote.org/turnout/intunout.html*.

[3] Robert D. Putnam, *Bowling Alone* (New York: Simon & Schuster, 2000) pp. 33–34. See also Warren E. Miller and J. Merrill Shanks, *The New American Voter* (Cambridge, England: Cambridge University Press, 1996).

these presidential candidates. Homer thwarts the aliens' plans by attending a presidential debate, where he leaps on stage and tears off their masks. The audience at the debate is horrified and disgusted when the true identities of the choices offered are revealed to them. One of the aliens turns to the audience and says, "It's true, we are aliens. But what are you going to do about it? It's a two-party system. You have to vote for one of us."

Since parties are in the business of electing their candidates to office, one would expect them to try and increase turnout. But party competition does not ensure that they have an incentive to attract nonvoters to the polls. Parties are reluctant to raise issues that appeal to nonvoters because they may not interest the party's core supporters. To promote such issues would upset the power that elites currently exercise within the party. Similarly, candidates are more responsive to wealthy donors and current voters than they are to nonvoters. They receive a better return on their scarce resources by investing in voters who tend to have strong partisan feelings and are likely to vote than those who are not. Candidates and parties, therefore, are often content with the low level of turnout and have little interest in changing it. Party competition, in short, does not ensure responsiveness to citizens' demands.[4]

Nonvoting is not distributed randomly but tends to be concentrated among the lower class. The greatest difference between the rich and the poor is not whom they vote for but whether they vote at all. According to political scientist Walter Dean Burnham, there is a hole in the American electorate where the working class should be.[5] Lower-class citizens in the United States vote at roughly 60 percent of the rate of upper-class citizens, a much greater difference in voting participation between classes than one finds in other Western nations.[6]

The failure of parties and candidates to articulate the demands of lower-class voters confirms Schattschneider's profound insight: *"The definition of the alternatives is the supreme instrument of power."*[7] Parties, which set the agenda of government, have done so in a way that effectively disfranchises the lower classes by failing to articulate their demands. The result has been massive nonvoting by the underprivileged and a bias of the electoral process—and of the benefits that can be derived from government through elections—toward

---

[4] Richard F. Hamilton, *Class and Politics in the United States* (New York: Wiley, 1972), pp. 1–22. See also Paul Frymer and John David Skrentny, "Coalition Building and the Politics of Electoral Capture During the Nixon Administration: African Americans, Labor and Latinos," *Studies in American Political Development* (Spring 1998): 131–61. Frymer and Skrentny write, "Instead of competitive parties being uniquely suited to aid the incorporation of group interests into the political system, we argue that party competition can at times hinder such efforts" (p. 161).

[5] Walter Dean Burnham, "The 1980 Earthquake: Realignment, Reaction or What," in *The Hidden Election: Politics and Economics in the 1980 Presidential Campaign*, eds.Thomas Ferguson and Joel Rogers (New York: Pantheon, 1981), pp. 126–27.

[6] Jan E. Leighley and Jonathon Nagler, "Socioeconomic Class Bias in Turnout, 1964–1988," *American Political Science Review* 86 (1992): 725–36.

[7] E. E. Schattschneider, *The Semisovereign People: A Realist's View of American Democracy* (Hinsdale, IL: Dryden Press, 1975), p. xxvi (emphasis in original).

those who are more fortunate. Party competition does not correct this bias by giving the losing party an incentive to mobilize nonvoters. Instead, it serves to legitimize the results as fair and democratic even though the alternatives offered are unrepresentative and truncated. Elections obscure citizens' lack of representation with the fig leaf of party competition.

But the 2004 elections indicate there are circumstances when party competition does in fact contribute to high voter turnout. When candidates and parties compete for the allegiance of an electorate that is polarized, evenly split, and absorbed in politics, then all bets are off. In 2004, both presidential candidates offered voters more of a choice than in previous elections as they appealed to their partisan base instead of to moderate swing voters. They did not try to soften their message by playing to undecided voters, of whom there were quite few, but instead sought to emphasize their differences by appealing to their core supporters. In addition, with the country at war, the issues in the election were too important for voters to dismiss cynically. Finally, with the memory of how close the 2000 election was, both parties and interest groups devoted more resources and effort to increasing turnout in the expectation that mobilizing new voters could be decisive for the outcome.

THE ORIGINS OF THE TWO-PARTY SYSTEM

The Constitution made no provision for political parties; they have no official status in our political system. Indeed, the authors of the Constitution viewed political parties with contempt and believed they were a threat to liberty. The Founders, according to historian Richard Hofstadter, "hoped to create not a system of party government under a constitution, but rather a constitutional government that would check and control parties."[8] Both Thomas Jefferson and James Madison, who founded the Republican Party (the forerunner of today's Democratic Party), and Alexander Hamilton and John Adams, who led the Federalist Party, viewed political parties, at best, as necessary evils.

Yet, even as the framers of the Constitution condemned parties in theory, they helped create them in practice. It is ironic, Hofstadter notes, that "the creators of the first American party system on both sides, Federalists and Republicans, were men who looked upon parties as sores on the body politic."[9] Parties emerged quickly in Congress as legislators formed opposing stable alliances in response to pressing issues. Legislators then appealed to the people to settle party divisions brewing in Congress. A partisan press emerged, officials began to campaign for office, and July 4th celebrations turned into partisan rallies. Party in government gave birth to party in the electorate.[10]

---

[8] Richard Hofstadter, *The Idea of a Party System: The Rise of Legitimate Opposition in the United States, 1780–1840* (Berkeley: University of California Press, 1969), p. 53.

[9] Ibid., p. 2.

[10] John H. Aldrich, *Why Parties?: The Origin and Transformation of Political Parties in America* (Chicago: University of Chicago Press, 1995).

From the start, parties proved to be a democratizing force in the United States. They expanded political participation, mobilized eligible voters, and broke down a deferential system of politics in which only the socially privileged and wealthy could participate.[11] By the time of Andrew Jackson's presidency (1828–1836), the historian Michael Schudson writes, "the rule of gentlemen was replaced by the rule of majorities."[12] In 1824, turnout of eligible voters for president was under 30 percent; by the time parties were fully established in 1840, turnout had increased to 78 percent.

As the 19th century proceeded, parties got stronger. They developed solid organizational bases and a mass following.[13] With voters mobilized through parties, the United States was in an important respect the first popular government in the world. This point, however, must be qualified because women and blacks at the time were excluded from the electorate. The United States did not become a fully realized democracy with universal suffrage until the 1960s, when southern blacks were finally as free to vote as other Americans.

The existence of a two-party system is taken for granted by many Americans. In fact, two-party systems are unusual; most democracies throughout the world have multiparty, not two-party, systems. One reason why our party system took such a distinctive form has to do with the electoral rules that stipulate whoever gets the most votes wins. Under such rules, there are no rewards for parties and candidates that lose. Consequently, voters fear wasting their votes on candidates from small third parties that cannot win and tend to choose among the candidates from the two major parties. Under different electoral rules, such as proportional representation, where legislative seats are allotted to parties based on their percentages of the vote, multiparty systems flourish. Parties receiving less than a plurality receive some representation in the legislature. Voters can vote their conscience without fear that they are throwing their vote away, as would be the case under our winner-take-all rules. This avoids the situation depicted in the cartoon shown here in which the limited choices of a two-party system often force Americans to choose between the lesser of two evils.

The two-party system is further strengthened by our presidential system. Strong presidencies create an incentive for groups to form broad coalitions in order to create majorities that can win the ultimate prize, the most powerful office in the entire government. Finally, third parties must contend with a strong media bias. The media devote most of their coverage to the two major parties and ignore third-party candidates. Consequently voters do not perceive

---

[11] Richard P. McCormick, "Political Development and the Second Party System," in *The American Party Systems: Stages of Political Development*, eds. William Nesbitt Chambers and Walter Dean Burnham (New York: Oxford University Press, 1977), p. 102.

[12] Michael Schudson, *The Good Citizen* (Cambridge, MA: Harvard University Press, 1998), p. 112.

[13] Walter Dean Burnham, *Critical Elections and the Mainsprings of American Politics* (New York: Norton, 1970), p. 21.

GABLE
THE GLOBE AND MAIL
Toronto
CANADA

third-party candidates as viable alternatives. The result is a self-confirming prophecy: Since only candidates from the two major parties are considered as serious contenders, voters view them as such, polls reflect this sentiment, and the media follow the polls by confining coverage to the two parties' candidates.

Although the factors reviewed here have made it difficult for third parties to break the two-party mold, it has been done. The Republican Party emerged in the 1850s as a third party and successfully replaced the Whigs. In addition, third parties can take advantage of American federalism and establish themselves at state and local levels. There are many examples of third parties electing mayors and other local officials. Although there are countless "third parties"—actually, then, third, fourth, and fifth parties—on the ballot in virtually every election, the two major parties tend to monopolize voter choice.

CRITICAL ELECTIONS AND PARTY DECAY

The two-party system limits the choices available to voters and creates parties that consist of broad coalitions composed of diverse and sometimes conflicting groups. For example, at one time, the Democratic Party included both blacks who supported integration and southerners who opposed it.

American political parties try to contain such conflicts by being evasive on issues. They do not offer the kind of clear, ideologically distinctive programs that voters are offered in multiparty systems. American political parties believe that to stake out clear positions on issues might antagonize groups they want to attract and thus jeopardize their chance of winning elections. Consequently, parties are unresponsive to emerging groups and their demands. The parties blur issues, ignore new demands, and fail to adapt to new conditions. The result is that demands build up, pressure in the system increases, and dissatisfaction with the lack of alternatives offered by the parties grows. The party system fails to reflect changes that are occurring in the broader society.

At first, citizens seek answers outside the existing party system, in the form of protests and social movements. But dissent eventually is expressed through the electoral system in what political scientists refer to as a *critical* or *realigning election*. Such elections are characterized by unusually high turnout and more intense ideological conflict between the parties. The issues that divide the parties change, and party conflict is organized around a new set of issues. Voters are realigned and party coalitions shift. Some groups defect, shifting their loyalty from one party to another. Or groups that were unattached now may identify with and give their support to one of the political parties. The result of these changes in voting patterns may give rise to a new party to replace one of the established parties, as occurred when the Republicans replaced the Whigs in the 1850s. Or the minority party prior to the critical election may become the new majority party, as happened to the Democrats in the 1930s. Or the majority party may capitalize on the dramatic changes to maintain its position on the basis of a new coalition and a new set of issues, as happened to the Republican Party in 1896.

Party systems have life cycles. A new party system is inaugurated by a critical election in which party coalitions are formed and party conflict is organized around a particular set of issues. But as new groups with new demands emerge, the parties do not respond or address their concerns. Demands build until another critical election occurs, ushering in a new party system—new party coalitions organized around a new set of issues—at which point the process begins again.[14]

American political parties were not always weak and unable to mobilize voters. In the late 19th century, parties were powerful organizations that, according to Stephen Skowronek, lent "order, predictability and continuity to governmental activity."[15] They were complex, well-staffed organizational structures that reached down into the grass roots, communicated to voters through a partisan popular press, and controlled the nomination of candidates

---

[14] The classic account of the theory of critical elections is Walter Dean Burnham, *Critical Elections*.

[15] Stephen Skowronek, *Building a New American State: The Expansion of National Administrative Capacities, 1877–1920* (New York: Cambridge University Press, 1982), pp. 24, 25.

and the platform on which they ran.[16] Turnout was high, and there was little of the class bias so evident in turnout patterns today. Still, one should avoid idealizing the political parties of this period, often considered the high point of American political party development. While parties were able to turn out the vote, they mostly depended on patronage and spoils to motivate activists and voters. Urban political machines integrated workers as voters, but in a way that insulated business from democratic challenge.[17] High voter turnout, especially among the working class, does not guarantee that party competition will be organized around class issues or that economic elites will be challenged. But it is hard to imagine class issues emerging or business being challenged politically in the absence of high levels of working-class turnout.[18]

Party decline set in following the critical election of 1896. Turnout in presidential elections declined from 79 percent in 1896 to 49 percent in 1924, with nonvoters concentrated among the working class and minorities. This demobilization was due to many factors. First, party competition declined dramatically following the 1896 election. Both the South and the North became one-party regions. The Democrats enjoyed a political monopoly in the South, where the party became the vehicle for the defense of white racism, while the Republicans dominated elsewhere. Both Republicans and Democrats were content with their monopolies of voters in different regions of the country and were under little pressure to compete on each other's turf. Without meaningful competition, voters lost interest and turnout fell.

Second, following the 1896 critical election, business groups and middle-class reformers made a vigorous and effective effort to weaken parties. They became impatient with the expense and corruption of urban political machines and feared that working-class politics might take an even more ominous, radical turn. As a result, business progressives tried to weaken political parties as organizations by cutting off the flow of incentives parties could offer voters. Civil service positions would now be awarded according to merit based on competitive exams and not by party control of patronage. In addition, the spread of the direct primary, in which the party's nominee is elected by party members, not selected by a caucus of party activists and officials, hastened the decline of party organization. The party organization no longer controlled who received the party's nomination to run for office; instead, rank-and-file party members had the decisive say.

Finally, turnout was depressed by new legal barriers to voting. Nowhere was the effort to put obstacles in the way of voting pursued with more vigor and ingenuity than in the South. Southern states, which traditionally relied

---

[16] See Burnham, *Critical Elections,* pp. 71–73.

[17] Ira Katznelson, "The Crisis of the Capitalist City: Urban Politics and Social Control," in *Theoretical Perspectives on Urban Politics,* eds. Willis D. Hawley and Michael Lipsky (Englewood Cliffs, NJ: Prentice-Hall, 1976), pp. 224–25. Also see Ira Katznelson, *City Trenches: Urban Politics and the Patterning of Class in the United States* (New York: Pantheon, 1981).

[18] Francis Fox Piven and Richard Cloward, *Why Americans Don't Vote* (New York: Pantheon, 1988), pp. 28–41.

on fraud and violence to keep blacks from the polls, now institutionalized racial—as well as class—repression through such devices as poll taxes (which required paying a hefty fee to vote), literacy tests, and tests of "good character." Three-quarters of all citizens in the South, especially blacks and poor, uneducated whites, lost the right to vote through these stratagems. Turnout in the South in presidential elections declined from 57 percent in 1896 to a mere 19 percent of eligible voters by 1924.[19]

Northern elites pursued the same goal as their southern counterparts, but with less spectacular results. Complicated voter registration systems discouraged voting by imposing residency requirements, setting early closing deadlines to register to vote, and opening the voter registration office only for short and inconvenient periods. While the formal right to vote remained, helping to legitimize the United States as a democracy, the introduction of these procedural obstacles prevented millions of citizens from actually exercising that right.[20]

The 1896 critical election set in motion a process of party decay that has continued, with twists and turns, through the present. For example, in an exhaustive survey of party organizations in all 50 states, political scientist David R. Mayhew found that the strength of "local [party] organizations . . . sloped downward between 1950 and the late 1960s and have fallen precipitously since."[21] Party organizations decayed as the resources they depended on slipped from their grasp. More ominously, from the party's standpoint, the functions they previously provided candidates lost their value. Today, campaigns depend on money and technology that candidates provide themselves and not on labor and organization that parties once supplied. Candidates raise their own money through computer-generated direct mail and fundraisers with affluent supporters. They hire polling organizations and political consultants to conduct focus groups and do market research to advise them how to fine-tune their message. Candidates reach voters through television advertising and no longer need campaign workers the party would recruit to promote them. An era of candidate-centered politics has replaced a period of party-centered politics.

Some political scientists suggest that American parties are experiencing a revival in the past few years. While local party organizations may be hollow, state party organizations now have full-time staffs, ample budgets, and services they can offer to candidates and supporters.[22] Party organization is even

---

[19] J. Morgan Kousser, *The Shaping of Southern Politics: Suffrage Restrictions and the Establishment of the One-Party South* (New Haven, CT: Yale University Press, 1974).

[20] Piven and Cloward, *Why Americans Don't Vote.*

[21] David R. Mayhew, *Placing Parties in American Politics* (Princeton, NJ: Princeton University Press, 1986), pp. 220, 225.

[22] Cornelius P. Cotter, James L. Gibson, John F. Bibby, and Robert J. Huckshorn, *Party Organizations in America* (New York: Praeger, 1984), pp. 13–41. See also John F. Bibby, "State Party Organizations: Coping and Adapting," in *The Parties Respond,* 2nd ed., ed. L. Sandy Maisel (Boulder, CO: Westview Press, 1994), pp. 21–45.

more robust at the level of each party's national committee. The Republican National Committee (RNC) was the first to modernize its operations in the 1980s by raising money and hiring pollsters and political consultants. The RNC's success compelled the Democratic National Committee (DNC) to follow suit. According to political scientist Paul S. Herrnson, "[N]ational parties are now stronger, more stable and more influential in their relations with state and local party committees and candidates than ever before."[23]

However, one should not confuse increased levels of activity by party organizations with increased party strength. Party organizations have, in essence, become large political consulting firms at the service of candidates. Parties still control one unique and indispensable feature—nominating candidates for office—but they are mere shadows compared to the past. According to British political scientist Alan Ware: "A strong party organization is one, which, at the very least, can determine who will be the party's candidate, can decide (broadly) the issues on which campaigns will be fought by its candidates, contributes the 'lion's share' of resources to the candidate's election campaign, and has influence over appointments made by public officials."[24]

Judged by these reasonable and traditional standards, party organization in the United States remains feeble. Primaries have undermined party control of nominations, candidates raise their own money, and personal ties count more than party loyalty when elected officials make appointments to key administrative positions. The parties may be more active, provide more services, and raise more money than in the past, but *they do so in a context in which they play a more subordinate* role to candidates.[25] Parties, in John H. Aldrich's phrase, are in service to candidates but no longer in control of them.[26] Nor can the party renewal thesis hide a fundamental paradox: At the same time parties are institutionally stronger at state and national levels, they are weaker as agents of representation, at transmitting the demands of citizens to government.

American political parties have not always been weak. But they have always been decentralized. Party organization reflects the federal structure of government, with Democratic and Republican organizations located at the national, state, and local levels. Relationships among the different levels of the party are not hierarchical. The DNC or RNC do not have formal authority or informal power to issue instructions to the party's lower levels. To the contrary, the different levels of the party are relatively independent of each other, with state and local parties deciding on their own slate of

[23] Paul S. Herrnson, "The Revitalization of National Party Organizations," in *The Parties Respond,* p. 67.

[24] Quoted in John J. Coleman, "Resurgent or Just Busy? Party Organizations in Contemporary America," in *The State of the Parties: The Changing Role of Contemporary American Parties,* 2nd ed., eds. John C. Green and Daniel M. Shea (Lanham, MD: Rowman & Littlefield, 1996), p. 377.

[25] Ibid., p. 382.

[26] Aldrich, *Why Parties?*, p. 273.

candidates and programs without direction from above. Candidates and state and local parties are free to define for themselves what it means to be a Democrat or Republican. For example, the RNC (but not the Louisiana Republican Party) censured neo-Nazi David Duke but could not prevent the Louisiana Republican Party from nominating Duke for Senator and then for governor, or from running and winning a seat in the Louisiana state legislature as a Republican. The loose, disorderly party structure that characterizes both the Democratic and Republican parties once led Will Rogers to quip, "I don't belong to an organized political party. I'm a Democrat."[27]

The Republican and Democratic national party conventions possess formal authority over the parties. The parties hold conventions every four years to nominate the party's presidential and vice presidential candidates, adopt a party platform, select party officers, and review party rules. Party conventions were once significant because competition among contending candidates for the party's presidential nomination meant that convention delegates had a real choice over their party's nominee. An extreme example of this occurred when delegates to the 1924 Democratic Party convention cast 103 ballots before finally settling on John W. Davis as their presidential candidate. Today, however, the parties' nominating conventions have declined in significance because the parties' presidential nominees are now effectively chosen in statewide primaries, by party members who vote to select the party's candidate. National party conventions simply crown the candidate who has amassed the requisite number of convention delegates during primary season. Indeed, the last time either the Democratic or the Republican Party convention needed more than one ballot to select a presidential nominee was in 1952. Presidential primaries have so reduced the drama and spectacle of the party conventions that the television networks devote little coverage to them anymore.[28]

Primaries appear as a more democratic way for parties to nominate candidates than by selection at party conventions controlled by party leaders. But the matter is not so simple. Turnout in primaries is very low. When the primary electorate is so small, differences in resources among candidates loom larger. Candidates with money or close ties to interest groups that can mobilize on their behalf have an advantage over other candidates. In addition, the primary electorate is even more unrepresentative of the country than the general electorate. It is more ideological, more educated, and more upper-class than voters who turn out in regular elections.

---

[27] Quoted in Frank J. Sorauf and Paul Allen Beck, *Party Politics in America* (Glenview, IL: Scott Foresman, 1988), p. 101.

[28] After the 1984 Democratic convention, Daniel Patrick Moynihan, senator from New York, observed, "The convention does not decide and it does not debate. . . . [T]he nomination is settled before the convention begins. . . . We have to make up our arguments to have on the floor so that television has something to cover." Quoted in Theodore J. Lowi, *The Personal President: Power Invested, Promise Unfulfilled* (Ithaca, NY: Cornell University Press, 1985), p. 111.

MONEY AND ELECTIONS

Candidates need more than votes to succeed; they also need money—and lots of it. The comment by Mark Hanna, a key Republican strategist in the early 1900s, remains as relevant today as it did a century ago: "There are two things that are important in politics. The first is money, and I can't remember the second."[29] Money pays for political ads and media time, pollsters and political consultants, and research and advance work, as well as travel costs and overhead expenses. In 2000, more than $2.9 billion was spent on federal elections. The 2004 election year passed that mark with a total of $3.9 billion—about one-third more than just four years ago—being spent by interest groups, parties, and candidates on congressional and presidential races. President Bush set a fund-raising record of $365 million, while John Kerry raised $334 million—$82 million of that from online sources—to become the best-financed challenger in history.

Business firms and wealthy individuals provide the bulk of political contributions to candidates and political parties. Candidates appeal to these groups for contributions for the same reason that Willie Sutton said he robbed banks: because that's where the money is. One study found that families with incomes over $75,000 were ten times more likely to contribute money to political campaigns than poor families that earned less than $15,000, and that they were overrepresented in comparison to middle-income citizens as well.[30] Contributors to both major parties were given special privileges depending upon how much money they raised, just like the airlines give special rewards to their most loyal and lucrative passengers. Within the Republican Party, for example, the most productive fund-raisers were members of the Rangers, who raised $200,000 for President Bush's campaign, followed by the Pioneers, who each raised $100,000, and then the Mavericks for those under 40 years old who had raised $50,000.

In order to understand why wealthy donors and corporations contribute to political campaigns, it is useful to regard contributions as investments rather than donations. Jerome Kohlberg, a founding partner of the Kohlberg, Kravis Roberts & Co. investment firm, commented, "Even what we think of as large soft-money contributions are a small price for big corporations to pay to gain political influence. . . . [C]orporations give for one reason: self interest. They can easily justify their expenditures because they get an outstanding return on their investment."[31] The Enron Corporation, for example, which committed the largest corporate fraud in American history, had given money to no fewer than 71 senators and 188 members of Congress. Once Enron's fraud was exposed and $60 billion of investors' money was gone,

---

[29] Quoted in the *New York Times,* April 1, 2001.

[30] Sidney Verba, Kay Lehman Schlozman, and Henry E. Brady, *Voice and Equality: Civic Voluntarism in American Politics* (Cambridge, MA: Harvard University Press, 1995), p. 189.

[31] *New York Times,* July 8, 1998.

those same legislators were charged with investigating the company from which they had previously received campaign checks.[32]

Donors receive access and influence over government appointments and policies in return for their campaign contributions. Representative Michael G. Oxley of Ohio acknowledged, "It would be unrealistic to ask people to contribute and not let them have a voice, not let us know their opinion."[33] While it is illegal to exchange cash for a specific presidential decision or favorable vote in Congress, the typical contribution process is more indirect than that and therefore perfectly legal. Campaign contributions can motivate legislators to support a bill more energetically, intervene with federal bureaucrats on behalf of a contributor, recommend certain amendments to a bill, or reduce the intensity of a policymaker's opposition. Justin Dart, founder of Dart Industries and a large contributor to and fund-raiser for the Republican Party, expressed it well when he observed that dialogue with politicians "is a fine thing, but with a little money they hear you better."[34]

American political campaigns last longer, cost more, are less regulated, and are financed by a higher proportion of private (as opposed to public) funds than in any other Western democracy. Scandals and public outcry over large contributors buying political influence periodically result in the passage of reform legislation. But the power of money has time after time proven stronger than efforts to control it. In 1971, Congress passed the Federal Election Campaign Act (FECA) and amended it in 1974 to limit political contributions, control spending, and require public disclosure of all receipts and disbursements. But this effort at reform led donors to exploit loopholes that were even more abusive than the activities the law was intended to restrict. For example, FECA prohibited businesses, unions, and other groups from contributing money directly to federal election campaigns. Interest groups evaded this restriction by forming Political Action Committees (PACs) that solicit money from individuals and then funnel it to candidates. In 1974, 608 PACs registered with the Federal Election Commission (FEC), and they contributed a total of $34.1 million to political campaigns. Since then, the number of PACs and their resources has skyrocketed. In 2004, there were over 4040 PACs registered with the FEC, and their spending increased tenfold to over $384 million.

Business PACs account for much of the growth in PAC activity. The number of corporate PACs has grown from 433 in 1976 to 2,480 only 20 years later—more than half of all registered PACs in 1996—and they spent twice as

[32] There were 212 of the 248 House and Senate members on the 11 Congressional committees investigating Enron who had received contributions from either the company itself or from Arthur Andersen, its accounting firm.

[33] *Washington Post National Weekly Edition*, April 17, 2000, p. 13.

[34] Quoted in Elizabeth Drew, *Politics and Money: The New Road to Corruption* (New York: Macmillan, 1983), p. 78.

much as unions, the second largest group of contributors.[35] PAC money follows power. Congressional incumbents received two-thirds of all PAC money in 1996 and a whopping 84 percent of all PAC money in 1998. But the party that produces incumbents has changed. Prior to the 1994 congressional elections, when the Republicans took control of both houses of Congress, House Democrats enjoyed a two-to-one advantage in PAC money, while Senate Democrats ran even with their Republican counterparts. As the majority party in Congress at the time, Democrats shaped legislation, and it was therefore pragmatic for corporate PACs to contribute to their campaigns. But after 1994, Republicans became the majority party in Congress—business interests could now be both pragmatic and principled by contributing to Republican candidates. In 2004, corporate PACs gave two-thirds of their money to Republicans. The fact that corporations now account for a larger proportion of all PAC money and that most of this corporate money now goes to Republican congressional candidates has given them a large financial advantage in elections.

A decade of reform efforts failed to restrict PAC spending. But even as the issue of PAC money remained unresolved, it was superseded by a new and even more urgent problem. The swelling waves of PAC contributions looked positively innocent compared to the deluge of soft money that followed. Soft money refers to money that may be used for so-called educational and party-building purposes. This might include meeting a party's overhead and administrative costs, funding voter registration and get-out-the-vote drives, or paying for issue advocacy ads that suggest voters should support a candidate without saying so explicitly. Soft money, which is unregulated and unlimited, is distinguished from hard money, which is contributed directly to a candidate's campaign. There are ceilings on how much hard money donors can give directly to candidates, and such contributions must be reported. Soft money has the advantage of evading these inconveniences. Donors can give unlimited and unregulated amounts of soft money to parties who then spend it on issue advocacy ads that are hard to distinguish from those produced by the candidates themselves. Compared to the soft money loophole through which hundreds of millions of dollars flow into federal elections, PACs look positively benign.[36]

---

[35] These figures are drawn from document 5.3, Number of PACs Registered with the FEC, 1974–96, and document 5.4, Total PAC Contributions to Congressional Candidates, 1978–96, in Anthony Corrado et al., *Campaign Finance Reform: A Sourcebook* (Washington, DC: Brookings Institution Publications, 1997), pp. 140–41. We combined corporate and trade-membership-health PACs, composed mostly of business interests, to calculate the totals for business PACs and business PAC spending. See Thomas Byrne Edsall, *The New Politics of Inequality* (New York: Norton, 1984), p. 131. References to corporate or business PACs in the text combine the categories of corporate and trade-membership-health PACs, which the FEC uses.

[36] Diane Dwyer and Victoria A. Farrer-Myers, *Congress and Campaign Finance Reform* (Washington, DC: Congressional Quarterly Press, 2001), pp. 1–63.

What PACs and soft money have in common is that business is the primary source of funds for both forms of contributions. Three-quarters of the soft money donated to the parties in 2002 came from corporations or individual business executives. And as with PACs, most of the soft money that business donates goes to the Republican Party. Many firms, however, hedge their bets and give money to both political parties so that no matter which party wins, firms are assured access and influence. In 2004, for example, Citicorp divided $2.1 million in contributions between the Democratic and Republican parties; the Boeing Corporation contributed more than $1.2 million to both parties; and Comcast, the cable television company, distributed $442,000 to the Democrats and $371,000 to the Republicans.[37]

By 1996, the political scientist Anthony Corrado writes, the system created to regulate campaign spending "finally collapsed. Candidates and party organizations spent more money than ever before, including hundreds of millions of dollars from sources supposed to be banned from contributing in federal elections."[38] Public disgust with the sheer amount of money being spent to influence elections and the taint of corruption it carried fueled demands for reform. In 2002, Congress passed the Bipartisan Campaign Reform Act (BCRA), after four previous efforts at reform going back to 1995 had failed. BCRA's purpose was to restore contribution limits by closing the soft money loophole in FECA. The price for closing the soft money loophole was increasing the "hard money" limit that donors could give. Individuals who previously could give only $1,000 to a candidate could now donate $2,000, and the limit of what donors could contribute to a political party was also raised from $20,000 to $25,000.

Even as hard money limits have been raised, unlimited and unregulated contributions continue to flow into elections despite BCRA's efforts to stop them. No sooner is one loophole closed than another one opens up. Soft money that previously would have been channeled through political parties is now raised and spent by "527" groups, which are named after the section of the tax code authorizing them. The Federal Elections Commission (FEC) interpreted BCRA in such a way as to permit unlimited independent expenditures by 527s for registration, get-out-the-vote drives, and issue ads so long as their activity is not coordinated with a candidate's campaign. As a result, such 527 groups as Swift Vets and the Progress for America Voter Fund ran television commercials and organized register-and-vote drives on behalf of President Bush, while other 527s, such as the MoveOn.org Voter Fund and the Media Fund, did so on behalf of John Kerry. The taint of soft money that was previously collected and spent by political parties is now

---

[37] These numbers are from *www.opensecrets.org/industries/contrib.asp?Bkdn=DemRep&Cycle=2005, 2006, 2007.*

[38] Anthony Corrado, "Financing the 1996 Elections," in *The Election of 1996*, ed. Gerald M. Pomper (Chatham, NJ: Chatham House, 1997), p. 164.

reproduced by money collected and spent by 527s. These advocacy groups disbursed over $452 million during the course of the 2004 election.

Money has had corrosive effects on the electoral process. In 2004, 96 percent of the House races and 91 percent of the Senate races were won by candidates who outspent their opponents.[39] While it is true that money does not guarantee victory in politics or happiness in life, winning in politics or being happy in life is much harder without it. Another baneful effect of money is that it feeds public cynicism about politics. Because politicians are forced to hold out the begging bowl, this conveys the impression that politicians are for sale to the highest bidder. Of course, this impression is not entirely without foundation. But politicians are probably no less ethical than corporate executives, salespeople, carpenters, or college professors. Yet the system of private campaign finance—above all, politicians' need to raise ever larger campaign chests—taints the entire political sphere. During the 1997 Senate hearings into campaign finance reform, Senator Richard Durbin of Illinois acknowledged that legislators vote on issues with an eye on how it might affect their fund-raising. He observed that the flow of money has increased the voters' skepticism and that "if the system isn't corrupt, it's corrupting. It forces you into compromising yourself."[40] The Supreme Court even acknowledged the corrupting influence of money in politics when it upheld BCRA. The Court's majority opinion cited "substantial evidence to support Congress's determination that large soft money contributions to national political parties give rise to corruption and the appearance of corruption" as its pragmatic reason for upholding the constitutionality of campaign finance reform.[41]

Finally, the arena of political parties and elections is supposed to provide the most important means by which citizens can participate, convey demands to their representatives, and hold these representatives accountable. But this comforting view ignores the substantial difference in class location and political values between the general population and those citizens who provide the resources on which parties and candidates depend. Rather than the party system acting as an engine of democracy, the unquenchable thirst for money skews the political system toward the interests and preferences of affluent Americans. The system by which the United States finances political campaigns simply reproduces the inequalities of the private economic system within the public electoral sphere and corrupts genuine democratic government.

We have focused until now in this chapter on the institutional mechanisms that organize citizens' electoral choices. We now turn to describing and analyzing the changing social base of the Democratic and Republican

[39] These numbers are from *www.opensecrets.org/pressreleases/04results.asp.*

[40] Elizabeth Drew, *The Corruption of American Politics: What Went Wrong and Why* (Woodstock, NY: Overlook Press, 2000), p. 24.

[41] The Court's majority opinion upholding BCRA is excerpted in the *New York Times,* December 11, 2003.

parties. The social bases of each party provide important clues to the kinds of policies that governments will enact.

THE RISE AND FALL OF THE NEW DEAL COALITION

The critical election of 1932 voted Franklin Delano Roosevelt into office, ushering in a long period of Democratic Party dominance. The New Deal coalition that Roosevelt forged over four consecutive presidential terms (1933–1945) included blacks, who received some benefits from New Deal programs targeted for the poor and unemployed; southerners, whose Democratic sympathies dated back to the Civil War; immigrant Jewish and Catholic workers from southern and eastern Europe who appreciated Roosevelt's efforts to end the Depression; Irish supporters of big city machines; and some renegade financiers and corporate executives, who believed the New Deal would be good for business. Each group was attached to the Democratic Party for the benefits it could derive from the federal government, whose growth the party supported. But that was where the consensus that bound these diverse groups together ended. The New Deal coalition was a marriage of convenience, in which the partners were content to lead separate lives and use their union to enlarge the federal government in order to extract benefits from it.

The Democratic Party leadership was relatively successful in maintaining the support of the various elements in its coalition in the 1940s and 1950s. But this became increasingly difficult as the initial impetus of the Depression receded and conflict increased among the various coalition members. The most profound and destabilizing issue to upset the New Deal coalition was race.

Racial conflict deeply divided the southern and northern wings of the Democratic Party. Southern Democrats demanded that national party leaders not interfere with the region's laws enforcing racial segregation. But as the Civil Rights movement of the 1960s gained momentum, nonsouthern Democrats supported legislation that outlawed racial discrimination. Feeling betrayed, southerners began to abandon the Democratic Party. Native white southern identification with the Democratic Party dropped from 74 percent in 1956 to half that level by 1984.[42] At first, this change in party loyalty among white southerners was evident only in presidential voting. But it soon began to trickle down and influence southern elections for lower offices as well.[43] By 1994, for the first time in the 20th century, Republicans comprised a majority of the southern delegation to both the Senate and the House, and they occupied a majority of Dixie's gubernatorial

---

[42] Earl Black and Merle Black, *Politics and Society in the South* (Cambridge, MA: Harvard University Press, 1987), p. 241.

[43] See ibid.

offices. Southern realignment is the most important factor behind the success of the Republican Party and the reason why the number of people who identify themselves as Republican is now dead even with those who identify themselves as Democrat.[44]

Not only did the New Deal coalition lose its southern flank to racial conflict, but its base in the North was badly damaged by it as well. Beginning in the 1960s, race began to drive out class as the line that divided Democrats from Republicans in the minds of voters.[45] White working-class support for the Democratic Party began to erode. Some white workers defected from the Democratic Party because they were racists. But many defected because they were angry that the burden of racial change fell unfairly on them. Their children were more likely to attend schools subjected to court-ordered bussing orders to achieve racial integration, their jobs were more likely to be subject to affirmative action reviews, and their communities adjoining black neighborhoods were more likely to be integrated. White workers resented that the Democrats permitted upper-class whites to avoid the racial changes that they were experiencing.[46]

The New Deal coalition was also weakened by the emergence of new issues that created political and cultural conflict within the Democratic Party. The Vietnam War was fought within the Democratic Party, as students who thought of themselves as liberal Democrats challenged Democratic Party leaders who prosecuted the war. Feminism, gay rights, abortion, and crime also divided Democrat from Democrat and further fragmented the New Deal coalition. One faction was comprised of traditional working-class voters who were economically liberal but socially conservative. They supported federal regulation of markets and welfare state programs but opposed policies defending gay and abortion rights. The other wing was composed of wealthier, more educated, and more recent supporters. They were economically conservative but socially liberal. These Democrats saw the party as a vehicle for challenging gender hierarchies and sexual stereotypes but opposed programs that sought to redistribute wealth. Reconciling the two wings of the party was a difficult balancing act.

The New Deal coalition was further wounded by the decline of labor unions. Union membership as a proportion of the workforce has declined steadily from its peak of 33 percent in 1953 to just 13 percent today. The Democratic Party has suffered as a result of union decay because union

---

[44] John Petrocik, "Realignment: New Party Coalitions and the Nationalization of the South," *Journal of Politics* 49 (May 1987): 347–75.

[45] R. Robert Huckfeldt and Carol Weitzel Kohfeld, *Race and the Decline of Class in American Politics* (Urbana: University of Illinois Press, 1989).

[46] These points are made by Thomas Byrne Edsall and Mary D. Edsall, *Chain Reaction: The Impact of Race and Taxes on American Politics* (New York: Norton, 1991); see also Reg Theriault, *The Unmaking of the American Working Class* (New York: The New Press, 2003), pp. 175–79; and Anthony Lukas, *Common Ground* (New York: Knopf, 1985).

members are more reliable Democratic Party voters than their nonunion counterparts.

Finally, the New Deal coalition was a victim of policy failure. The New Deal policy of conservative Keynesianism offered economic growth without redistribution, and fiscal fine-tuning as a substitute for structural economic change. (See Chapter 3 for a fuller description of conservative Keynesianism.) The inadequacy of this formula first became apparent in the 1970s, when economic growth faltered and both inflation and unemployment accelerated. Conservative Keynesianism could no longer deliver the economic growth that the New Deal coalition needed to satisfy the demands of its various constituents. Nor could the Democrats develop a new economic formula around which to revive their faltering coalition. The decline of the New Deal coalition is apparent in Table 5-1, in which the percentage of Democratic identifiers has declined among all subgroups from the 1950s through 2000.

As the Democratic majority lost ground, the Republican Party gathered momentum and changed direction. The Republican Party's political and geographic transformation can be traced through the evolution of a political dynasty—the Bush family. The Bush family odyssey in politics began with Prescott Bush, father of the 41st president, George H. W. Bush (1989–1993), and grandfather of the 43rd president, George W. Bush (2001–2009). Prescott Bush was a Wall Street banker before being elected to the Senate from Connecticut in 1952. He was a moderate Eisenhower Republican who had a good civil rights record, voted for new federal programs, and accepted the legitimacy of the New Deal. He was a compassionate conservative.

His son, George H. W. Bush, was a transitional figure, connecting the Republican Party of the past, represented by Prescott Bush, to the Republican Party of today, represented by his son, George W. Bush. George H. W. Bush, like Prescott Bush, was a member of the Eastern Establishment and reflected its politics of moderate conservatism. When he ran in the 1980 Republican presidential primary, he disdainfully condemned Ronald Reagan's proposal to cut taxes and still balance the budget as "voodoo economics." When Reagan won the Republican nomination, he chose Bush as his running mate. For the next eight years, George H. W. Bush served as a loyal vice president within a Reagan administration that chipped away at the New Deal his father had accepted. When Bush himself was elected president in 1988, his administration accepted the new Republican orientation of smaller government. But at the same time he angered conservatives by breaking a campaign pledge not to raise taxes. As a traditional fiscal conservative, he feared increasing public deficits.

In 2000, Governor George W. Bush of Texas ran as the Republican candidate for president against the type of government his grandfather had helped to consolidate and that his father had once supported. While Prescott Bush made reluctant peace with the New Deal, his grandson hoped to repeal it. While his father criticized voodoo economics, his son practiced it, producing the largest

■ TABLE 5-1

DEMOCRATIC PERCENTAGE OF PARTY IDENTIFIERS
AMONG SUBGROUPS BY DECADE

	1952–1960	1962–1970	1972–1980	1982–1990	1992–2000	Change, 70s to 90s
Overall electorate	61%	63%	62%	57%	56%	−6%
Blacks	74	91	92	90	91	−1
Whites	59	60	58	51	50	−8
Northern males	56	58	55	46	47	−8
Northern females	52	57	56	51	56	0
Southern males	81	69	62	52	39	−23
Southern females	76	71	67	59	52	−15
Protestants	54	54	50	45	42	−8
Religious	NA	NA	44	40	34	−10
Less religious	NA	NA	54	48	49	−5
Catholics	74	74	71	59	56	−15
Religious	NA	NA	69	63	51	−18
Less religious	NA	NA	73	56	60	−13
Jews	83	90	83	74	87	+4
Other, no religion	64	70	68	58	63	−5
College	47	49	50	45	45	−5
No college	63	64	62	56	58	−4
Upper income	56	56	50	44	42	−8
Middle income	62	63	61	51	51	−10
Lower income	62	63	63	59	61	−2
Union household	71	73	70	62	62	−8
Married	60	60	56	48	46	−10
Unmarried	52	60	61	55	56	−5

SOURCE: From Alan Abramowitz, *The Voice of the People: Elections & Voting in the United States* (New York: McGraw Hill, 2004), p. 85. Data from American National Election Studies, 1952–2000.

NOTE: Percentages are based on Democratic identifiers, including independent Democrats, divided by combined total of Democratic and Republican identifiers. South includes the 11 states of the old Confederacy.

NA = Not available: question not asked.

budget deficits in American history. And while his grandfather and father were both members of the Eastern Establishment, their namesake made his home in the Southwest. George W. Bush started his business career in the Texas oil patch, assembled a group of partners to purchase the Texas Rangers baseball team, and was twice elected governor of Texas before his election as president.

The postwar history of the Republican Party is reflected in the history of the Bush family as it moved right politically and to the South and West geographically. But it is also a history of party revival. During Prescott Bush's time in the 1950s, the Republican Party was the minority party, trailing the Democrats electorally and politically. Two Bush generations later, the Republican Party is now the dominant, majority party in American politics. Its resurgence is due to four factors. First, white males became more Republican in their voting patterns, as Republican candidates successfully played to their fears about dismantling racial and gender hierarchies. Second, the party found an enthusiastic base among religious fundamentalists. The Christian Right mobilized through the Republican Party in order to challenge what they regarded as the moral decay around them. Third, the business community gave the party a boost by infusing it with money and funding think tanks to develop conservative policies. The party added to its traditional business base among northeastern financiers and midwestern industrialists with a new breed of maverick multimillionaire entrepreneurs from the Sunbelt, who were fiercely opposed to government regulation. Finally, the party has benefited from population growth in the suburbs and the Sun Belt, areas that are "sympathetic to Republican appeals of self-reliance and less government."[47]

The result of these forces was to re-center the Republican Party politically and geographically.[48] The key moment in this transformation was the party's nomination of Senator Barry Goldwater from Arizona for president in 1964. Goldwater's nomination signaled that power had shifted from the Eastern Establishment, which grudgingly accepted certain aspects of the New Deal, to hard conservatives from the South and the West, who were militantly anti-government, anti-taxes, anti-union, and anti-communist. The Sun Belt nourished conservative Republicanism because it was the home of many defense industries and military bases; the federal government owned large tracts of western land and was perceived as intrusive; and new, homogenous suburbs made it easier to find consensus and build institutions among a basically conservative group of middle-class migrants to the area.[49] Although Goldwater lost the 1964 election by the largest margin in American history, the conservative Sun Belt forces that engineered his nomination eventually triumphed. After years of patiently funding PACs, conservative think tanks, and grassroots groups, these forces were victorious in 1980, when their standard bearer, Ronald Reagan, was elected president. Acknowledging the similarities

---

[47] Jeffrey M. Stonecash, *Class and Party in American Politics* (Boulder, CO: Westview Press, 2000), p. 26.

[48] Nicol C. Rae, *The Decline and Fall of the Liberal Republicans from 1952 to the Present* (New York: Oxford University Press, 1989), p. 198.

[49] Lisa McGirr, *Suburban Warriors: The Origins of the New Right* (Princeton, NJ: Princeton University Press, 2001), p. 157.

between Goldwater and Reagan—each came from the West, each was militantly anti-communist, each wanted to downsize government and increase military spending—one historian wrote, "If there had been no Barry Goldwater, there would have been no Ronald Reagan."[50]

Today the Republican Party no longer orbits the Democratic Party, as it did in Prescott Bush's time. Today the party is electorally dominant, intellectually vibrant, and financially prosperous, and is based in the South and the West, the fastest-growing regions of the country. Although each election is distinctive, turning on specific events, personalities, and strategies that affect voters' decisions, voting patterns from one election to the next are relatively stable. Both the Democratic and Republican parties tend to attract different groups of voters, which helps to explain the parties' different policy orientations. Analyzing the 2004 presidential election results provides insight into contemporary party coalitions.

Even a casual inspection of Table 5-2, based on nationwide exit polls from voters who had just cast their ballots, reveals that the two major parties' presidential candidates in 2004 received different levels of support from different groups in the electorate. For example, no group is more united behind the Democratic Party than blacks. Support for the Democratic Party among blacks persists at extraordinarily high levels of 80 percent or more. Black voting is bloc voting. From Washington, DC to Washington State, from professors to postal clerks, blacks have voted as one to reward the Democratic Party for its support of welfare state programs and civil rights legislation.

Another reliable group of voters within the Democratic Party coalition is union members. On average, union member support for Democratic presidential, senate, and congressional candidates was 17 percent higher than for nonunion members from 1952–1998.[51] Other reliable Democratic coalition members include Jews, women, singles, urbanites, and low-income voters.

Some groups, such as Hispanics, have not clearly identified themselves with any party yet. Hispanics are a diverse group composed of Spanish-speaking citizens. Some emigrated from the Caribbean, some from Mexico, and still others from South and Central America. They came from various cultures and did not necessarily share a common experience once they arrived here, as blacks did. Turnout among Hispanics is notoriously low. For instance, although they are now the nation's largest minority group, Hispanics comprised almost one-third fewer voters than blacks in 2004. While Al Gore received almost two-thirds of the Hispanic vote in 2000,

[50] Mary C. Brennan, *Turning Right in the Sixties: The Conservative Capture of the GOP* (Chapel Hill: University of North Carolina Press, 1995), p. 141.

[51] Herbert B. Asher, Eric S. Heberlig, Randall B. Ripley, and Karen Snyder, *American Labor Unions in the Electoral Arena* (Lanham, MD: Rowman & Littlefield, 2001), p. 141.

Pct. of 2004 Total Vote	1984		1988		1992		
	Reagan	Mondale	Bush	Dukakis	Clinton	Bush	Perot
Total vote	59	40	53	45	43	38	19
77 White	64	35	59	40	39	40	20
11 Black	9	90	12	86	83	10	7
6 Hispanic	37	62	30	69	61	25	14
46 Men	62	37	57	41	41	38	21
54 Women	56	44	50	49	45	37	17
62 Married	62	38	57	42	40	41	20
37 Unmarried	52	47	46	53	51	30	19
Family Income Is:							
8 Under $15,000	45	55	37	62	58	23	19
15 $15,000–$29,999	57	42	49	50	45	35	20
22 $30,000–$49,999	59	40	56	43	41	38	21
23 $50,000–$74,999	—	—	—	—	40	41	18
14 $75,000–$99,999	—	—	—	—	—	—	—
18 Over $100,000	—	—	65	32	—	—	—
21 Liberals	28	70	18	81	68	14	18
45 Moderates	53	47	49	50	47	31	21
34 Conservatives	82	17	80	19	18	64	18
24 Union household	46	53	42	57	55	24	21
Size of Place:							
13 Population over 500,000	—	—	37	62	58	28	13
19 Population 50,000 to 500,000	—	—	47	52	50	33	16
45 Suburbs	61	38	57	42	41	39	21
8 Population 10,000 to 50,000	—	—	61	38	39	42	20
16 Rural areas	67	32	55	44	39	40	20
22 From the East	53	47	50	49	47	35	18
26 From the Midwest	58	41	52	47	42	37	21
32 From the South	64	38	58	41	41	43	16
20 From the West	61	38	52	46	43	34	23
41 White Protestant	72	27	66	33	33	47	21
27 Catholic	54	45	52	47	44	35	20
3 Jewish	31	67	35	64	80	11	9
17 18–29 years old	59	40	52	47	43	34	22
29 30–44 years old	57	42	54	45	41	38	21
30 45–59 years old	60	40	57	42	41	40	19
24 60 and older	60	39	50	49	50	38	12
36 White men	67	32	63	36	37	40	22
41 White women	62	38	56	43	41	41	19
5 Black men	12	85	15	81	78	13	9
7 Black women	7	93	9	90	87	8	5

SOURCE: *New York Times*, November 7, 2004. Based on Voters News Service and other exit polls.

1996			2000			2004	
Clinton	Dole	Perot	Bush	Gore	Nader	Bush	Kerry
49	41	8	48	48	2	51	48
43	46	9	54	42	3	58	41
84	12	4	8	90	1	11	88
72	21	6	31	67	2	43	56
43	44	10	53	42	3	55	44
54	38	7	43	54	2	48	51
44	46	9	53	44	2	57	42
57	31	9	38	57	4	40	58
59	28	11	37	57	4	36	63
53	36	9	41	54	3	42	57
48	40	10	48	49	2	49	50
47	45	7	51	46	2	56	43
44	48	7	52	45	2	55	45
38	54	6	54	43	2	58	41
78	11	7	13	80	6	13	85
57	33	9	44	52	2	45	54
20	71	8	81	17	1	84	15
59	30	9	37	59	3	40	59
68	25	6	26	71	3	39	60
50	39	8	40	57	2	49	49
47	42	8	49	47	3	52	47
48	41	9	59	38	2	50	48
44	46	10	59	37	2	59	40
55	34	9	39	56	3	43	56
48	41	10	49	48	2	51	48
46	46	7	55	43	1	58	42
48	40	8	46	48	4	49	50
36	53	10	63	34	2	67	32
53	37	9	47	49	2	52	47
78	16	3	19	79	1	25	74
53	34	10	46	48	5	45	54
48	41	9	49	48	2	53	46
48	41	9	49	48	2	51	48
48	44	7	47	51	2	54	46
38	49	11	60	36	3	61	38
48	43	8	49	48	2	55	44
78	15	5	12	85	1	13	86
89	8	2	6	94	0	10	90

George W. Bush cut into this margin decisively in 2004, winning 44 percent of their vote. Many Hispanics are new voters and, as is true of new voters generally, their partisan loyalty is still unsettled. As the largest and fastest growing minority in the United States, Hispanics will play an increasingly important role in American elections.

The Republican Party has a different clientele. It traditionally attracts wealthier voters. As one goes up the income ladder, the Republican vote increases.[52] White Protestants are also staunchly Republican, with Catholics who once identified with the Democratic Party now pretty evenly split between the two parties. But the most important religious division among voters is not what religion they belong to but how fervently they practice it. White Protestants, Jews, and Catholics who attend religious services regularly are more likely to vote Republican than their co-religionists who do not. The Republican Party also polls well among white men, married couples, and rural voters. While the Northeast and West Coast tend to be Democratic, the South, the Plains states, and the West tend to be Republican.

The electorate has always been split along social lines, such as those we just reviewed. But it is increasingly divided along ideological lines as well. Liberal voters are now more likely to ally themselves with the Democratic Party and conservatives to align themselves with the Republican Party. Voters' policy preferences now correspond more closely to their party identification. One effect of the increasing ideological division of the electorate has been to weaken ties that historically bound social groups to a particular party. Southern white males who are conservative, for example, have deserted their home in the Democratic Party, while well-educated men and women who are liberal no longer identify or vote with the Republican Party to the extent they once did.

One cleavage that post-election polls revealed may have cost Kerry the 2004 presidential election—and whose importance pre-election polls had not highlighted—was what was identified as a values cleavage. Voters who claimed that moral values had determined their vote were overwhelmingly likely to favor Bush. "Moral values" could range from support for a pro-life position on abortion to opposition to the rights of gays to marry, to a sense that President Bush appeared more authentic than his opponent.

Looking at the exit polls for 2004, it could be argued John Kerry ran remarkably well. He received 49 percent of the vote, despite having to run against a wartime incumbent and all the advantages this entails. George W. Bush could exploit a rally-round-the-flag effect by virtue of being commander in chief during wartime, and he could claim credit for benefits his administration provided by virtue of being the incumbent. Still, despite these disadvantages, Kerry received more votes than any presidential candidate in American history with the exception of the one who counted the

[52] Stonecash, *Class and Party in American Politics*, pp. 62–65.

most, his opponent George W. Bush. For a switch of just 140,000 votes in Ohio, Kerry would have won the election.

On the other hand, the exit polls reveal an erosion of Democratic support among virtually all groups compared to 2000. Kerry lost support among almost every category of core Democratic voters at the same time Bush increased his margin among almost every group of core Republican supporters. The Republican coalition in 2004 was both broader, taking in more voters outside its base, and deeper, harvesting its core voters more intensively, than it was four years ago. As we said at the outset of this chapter, the 2004 election marked the emergence of the Republicans as the new ruling party in American politics. The 2004 election was the first time since 1928 that the Republican Party won a majority in all three elective national institutions: the House of Representatives, the Senate, and the Presidency. Whether they will be able to maintain this position depends upon their performance in office over the next four years.

A POSTELECTORAL ERA?

Political scientists Benjamin Ginsberg and Martin Shefter argue that America has entered a postelectoral era, in which elections are no longer as decisive as they once were for resolving political conflicts and constituting governments.[53] Conflict and mobilization have shifted to arenas other than elections and to forms of political participation other than voting. Take the case of interest groups, formed by citizens who share common values and preferences to influence policymakers. Interest group formation surged in the 1960s and 1970s at the same time that parties and voter turnout declined.[54] New advocacy organizations, representing environmentalists, women, and minorities now took their place beside more established economic interest groups to scrutinize and pressure policymakers. The interest group explosion, which finally only leveled off in the 1990s, enlarged the policy agenda.[55] New groups raising new issues were now organized. But these were different types of organizations than those that had come before. They were more professional and less voluntary, more centralized and less participatory, more specialized and less inclusive. They catered more toward educated, middle-class citizens than toward working-class citizens. The shift from mass membership to professional organizations enhanced the variety of interest groups trying to influence public policy. But it also increased the influence of more

---

[53] Benjamin Ginsberg and Martin Shefter, *Politics by Other Means: The Declining Implications of Elections in American Politics* (New York: Basic Books, 1990).

[54] Jack L.Walker, Jr., "The Origins and Maintenance of Interest Groups in America," *American Political Science Review* 77 (June 1983): 390–406; Kay Lehman Schlozman and John T. Tierney, *Organized Interests and American Democracy* (New York: Harper & Row, 1986), pp. 75–76.

[55] Jeffrey Berry, *The Interest Group Society*, 3rd ed. (New York: Longman, 1997), p. 24.

wealthy and educated citizens who found the new type of professional organizations congenial, while the voice of workers was muted as the traditional mass membership organization they were accustomed to declined.[56]

Another form of political participation that has increased as parties and elections have declined are social movements. Social movements differ from more familiar and more common electoral and interest group activity in three ways. First, social movements are not as hierarchical or as well organized as political parties and interest groups. Second, social movements tend to be more contentious, more spontaneous, than conventional forms of political expression. Finally, social movements interrupt normal politics, often express strong ideological convictions, and move citizen participation to a more active and demanding level. Social movements often use extraordinary tactics, such as sit-downs and sit-ins, in order to bring groups that were previously excluded into the mainstream. Social movements, such as the labor, civil rights, or environmental movements, are often identified with liberal, progressive agendas. But social movements are not the exclusive property of the left. Conservative groups have also formed social movements in order to promote political change. The anti-abortion and evangelical movements of today demonstrate that ideological commitment and disruptive forms of activism can be found across the ideological spectrum.

Political participation has not only taken a more chaotic turn in the form of social movements but its opposite, a more formal turn, such as when citizens and groups resort to litigation. Political activists now try to win in the court of justice what they cannot win in the court of public opinion. For example, Senator Mitch McConnell of Kentucky, who opposed campaign finance reform, promised that "should the bill become law, I will be the lead plaintiff."[57] The day after the bill became law, the National Rifle Association and other opponents filed suit challenging its constitutionality.

In principle, anyone can vote, write his or her representative in Congress, join an interest group, file suit in court, participate in a social movement, or contribute to a political campaign. But some citizens are in a better position to take advantage of these opportunities than others. Political participation may be open, but it is not free. It is greatly facilitated by class-related factors, including adequate time, money, and civic skills; the ability to communicate well; a feeling of empowerment; and connections. Political scientists Sidney Verba, Kay Lehman Schlozman, and Henry E. Brady conclude from a massive survey of political participation that, "[o]ver and over, our data showed that participatory input is tilted in the direction of the more advantaged groups in society—especially in terms of economic and education position, but in terms of race and ethnicity as well."[58]

---

[56] Theda Skocpol, *Diminished Democracy: From Membership to Management in American Civic Life* (Norman: University of Oklahoma Press, 2003).

[57] *New York Times*, February 17, 2002.

[58] Sidney Verba, Kay Lehman Schlozman, and Henry E. Brady, *Voice and Equality* (Cambridge, MA: Harvard University Press, 1995), p. 512.

The postelectoral era is characterized by more political participation that flows outside electoral channels. Political participation takes different paths because political parties do not provide groups with what they consider to be adequate representation. Indeed, the postelectoral era has created a paradox. Given the different forms that political participation takes, government appears besieged. It is the target of more organized and unorganized pleading than ever before. At the same time, government appears more insulated and removed from democratic accountability than ever before. The paradox of the postelectoral era is that both appearances may be true, that government is simultaneously more besieged and more insulated.

CONCLUSION

The fundamental idea of democracy is that the preferences of citizens deserve equal consideration and that their ability to influence political outcomes should be equal. The mechanism by which these goals are accomplished is political participation. Citizens participate by voting, joining interest groups, expressing opinions, participating in social movements, contributing money to candidates, and filing lawsuits. Citizens use such strategies in order to influence public policy.

Unfortunately, political participation in the United States is slanted toward the rich, flouting democratic principles in which Americans believe. Every recent major study confirms that a pattern reported a half a century ago in a study of interest group membership remains true today. "The frequency of membership . . . increases from the lower to the upper reaches of the class structure."[59] Not only is participation slanted toward the wealthy in terms of interest group membership but also in terms of who votes, who contributes to political campaigns, who runs for office, and who engages in political activism. Uneven participation is a result of the uneven distribution of politically relevant resources, such as money, education, time, self-confidence, civic skills, and contacts with broader group networks. Despite these sources of inequality, all adult citizens potentially can develop their political voice. Unlike dictatorial regimes, where political participation is actively repressed, in democracies all adult citizens can participate and influence the laws that govern them. The majority is not voiceless, especially when large numbers of them are mobilized in organizations, at the polls, and in social movements. Political participation, which so often reinforces privilege, can also do the opposite: counteract advantages of class, race, and gender.

---

[59] David B. Truman, *The Governmental Process: Political Interests and Public Opinion* (New York: Knopf, 1951), p. 522.

POLITICAL INSTITUTIONS

A BRILLIANT AND MISCHIEVOUS DESIGN

The Constitution lays out the architecture of government. By architecture, we mean the design of political institutions—notably, the three branches of the federal government: the executive, legislative, and judicial. The Constitution also specifies how political authority is distributed among these different institutions, as well as between the federal and state governments. With over 88,000 governmental units of all types nationwide—from familiar state legislatures to obscure special district authorities—the design is complicated, with much overlap and jurisdictional conflict among different government bodies. The design of the American political system is quite distinctive because of the degree to which the Constitution disperses authority widely among a variety of political institutions. Authority is divided in two ways. First, the United States is a federal system, which means that authority is divided between national and state governments. The Tenth Amendment to the Constitution specifies that all power not expressly delegated to the national government by the Constitution is reserved to the states. For much of American history, state governments exercised the bulk of governmental power. In comparison, the national or federal government was lean and mean, primarily engaged in enforcing laws, arbitrating conflicts, issuing currency, and defending the country.

Today, political power is more concentrated at the federal than at the state level, although state governments continue to formulate, implement, and finance programs in vitally important domains like education, transportation, and property rights. Despite the fact that the Constitution created a federal system, with power distributed between national and state governments, one cannot neatly distinguish which level of government is responsible for which function. Sometimes there is a near-complete separation of functions: The national government alone decides whether to commit troops abroad; state governments are solely responsible for regulating marriage and divorce. But the typical situation is more complicated, with federal and state governments operating more or less cooperatively in the same policy areas. Political scientist Morton Grodzins suggested that American federalism resembles a marble cake, in which governmental functions are interwoven and shared among the different levels of government, as opposed to a layer cake, in which the national and state governments are neatly separated from each other and perform different tasks.[1]

The Constitution fragments governing authority in a second way. Political power is divided not only vertically between different levels of government but also horizontally between different branches of government. Rather than uniting power within a single powerful agency, as in the famed "Westminster model" of British parliamentary government, power is divided among the legislative, executive, and judicial branches of the federal government. The term *separation of powers* is often used to describe this dispersion of power among the different branches of government. But like the layer cake image of federalism, the concept of the separation of powers can be misleading if taken to mean that each branch of government has exclusive authority in certain domains. In fact, the opposite is the case. A better term to describe how power is distributed within the federal government would be *shared* or *overlapping powers*, as opposed to separation of powers. For example, both the Congress and the president share power in the realm of foreign policy. The president can make treaties with foreign governments, but these must be ratified by a two-thirds vote in the Senate. The president can command the military, but Congress appropriates the necessary funds for military operations. Similarly, all three branches share power when it comes to legislation. Congress can pass a law, but the president is authorized to approve or veto it. Congress can then override a presidential veto with a two-thirds vote in both the Senate and the House. Finally, the Supreme Court can nullify the law by finding it unconstitutional.

It is this architecture of shared or overlapping powers that creates a system of "checks and balances." Each branch of government has the power to check the actions of the other branches and must depend on their cooperation to achieve its goals. We do not mean to imply by checks and balances that the three branches have equal power, only that government is designed in such a way that many policies and activities require the tacit or explicit support of all three institutions. Unlike a parliamentary system, where the executive and legislative branches are fused, the system of divided, yet shared, powers ensures that each branch possesses autonomous power.

Legislation must run a difficult gauntlet in a political system where each branch of government can check the other and success depends on the cooperation of all of them. Chances of completing this obstacle course are made even smaller by having each elected branch of government represent different constituencies. The president is elected nationally, senators are elected from each state, and members of the House of Representatives are elected from districts within states. In effect, our constitutional design requires legislation to win three different types of majorities—nationally, by state, and by district. That is, shared powers require groups to build overlapping, simultaneous

[1] Morton Grodzins, *The American System: A New View of Government in the United States,* ed. Daniel J. Elazar (Chicago: Rand McNally, 1966).

majorities at the level of the presidency, the Senate, and the House. Legislation must run the equivalent of a triathlon (neglecting the courts for the moment), a series of three different athletic events requiring three different kinds of skills: running, cycling, and swimming—but with one important difference. In a triathlon, a contestant can lose one event but still be declared the winner so long as he or she has the highest combined score at the end of the contest. This would be insufficient under our system of government. The Constitution requires contestants to win all three events *outright*. Groups who desire political change must win at every step of the process, while those groups who want to defend the status quo have to win just once to block a bill. Legislation must pass the House, be approved by the Senate, and then be accepted by the president (excluding the difficult task of overriding a presidential veto), or it will fall short of passage.

The design of government in the Constitution, with its system of shared powers among independent institutions representing different constituencies, has conservative implications that were intended by the Founders who created it. On the one hand, the designers of the Constitution embarked on a remarkable political experiment in 1787. They proposed to create the first republic in which political authority would be located in the hands of the people instead of a king. The architects of the Constitution were intent on protecting the government against tyranny, which they had just fought a revolution to defeat. On the other hand, the Founders were frightened by the audacity of their own democratic inclinations. They believed that democracy, if left to its own devices, posed a threat to the natural hierarchy in society. Political scientist Robert Dahl observes that the Founders were "alarmed by the prospect that democracy, political equality, and even political liberty itself would endanger the rights of property owners to preserve their property and use it as they please."[2] They thus devised checks and balances as a way to protect the unequal social order without taking away any of the majority's democratic rights. Checks and balances, they believed, would protect the rich by requiring workers and farmers to build concurrent majorities at every level of government. Majorities would have to be built in the House of Representatives by districts based on population, in the Senate according to states, and in the presidency across the entire country. The Founders anticipated the result would be deadlock and government paralysis, as majorities would find it difficult to win at every level required of them.

The Founders sought to create a government powerful enough to promote market-based economic development but not so powerful that it could be used as an instrument of popular forces to restrict the rights of property. They succeeded brilliantly at this task of constitutional engineering. When public power is unable to rule because it is gripped by deadlock, private power rules in its place.

---

[2] Robert Dahl, *A Preface to Economic Democracy* (Berkeley: University of California Press, 1985), p. 2.

The next three chapters, covering the presidency, Congress, and the courts, respectively, examine the institutional structure of government and how power is distributed within and among the three branches. The structure of government, the relationships among the different institutions of government, and the formal and informal rules that govern how they work internally have important consequences for policy. In other words, institutions count. Policy is not simply a reflection of economic and social forces; rather, these social forces are refracted through institutions whose rules and relationships affect the outcome of their struggle. Some groups win and some groups lose, depending on the structure of government. But the structure of government, the relationship among institutions, and their formal and informal rules are not set in stone and are themselves subject to political conflict. The Constitution may have created the architecture of government more than 200 years ago, but the design is constantly being remodeled. The executive branch does not look like it did 50 years ago, nor is its relationship to Congress the same as it was 50 years ago. Groups struggle over not only who will occupy the government but also what it will look like. The result is that the institutional form of government changes as a result of political conflict. Political institutions—through their relationships to each other and their internal procedures—reflect the larger distribution of power in society at the same time they help to shape it. The focal point of the federal government, and therefore the place we begin our study of political institutions, is the presidency.

THE PRESIDENCY: IMPERIAL OR IMPERILED?

Delegates to the Constitutional Convention arrived in Philadelphia in 1787 with many complaints about their form of government. One of their objections to the Articles of Confederation, which established the first American government that emerged from the Revolutionary War in 1776, was that it did not provide for a single official responsible for directing the executive branch who would be independent of Congress. The Founders believed that a new government required an autonomous and energetic presidential office, as opposed to the weak executive that labored under the Articles. But the Founders disagreed over the powers that should be invested in this new presidential office and how it should be filled. Alexander Hamilton, a brilliant 30-year-old delegate from New York, shocked the gathering by praising the British monarchy—against whom the colonies had revolted a mere decade before—as a suitable model to emulate. Recognizing that hereditary monarchy would never be accepted in America, Hamilton suggested that the new federal government be directed by an elected monarch who would hold office for life.

Hamilton's view was an extreme one among the delegates in Philadelphia. But it made the arguments of those who supported a stronger executive appear moderate in comparison. A strong executive was needed, advocates argued, because elected assemblies succumbed to popular demands too easily. The constitutional architects specifically designed the office of the president as independent of Congress in order to check what they perceived as the latter's democratic excesses.

The creation of a single executive independent of Congress was one of the innovations that distinguished the new form of government under the Constitution from that under the Articles—and, indeed, from any other government in the world at that time. The creation of the presidential office is one of the key institutional innovations of the American Constitution. While the delegates to the Constitutional Convention could agree that a more powerful and independent executive was necessary, they could only settle the

AP/Wide World Photos

The White House.

question of specifying the president's powers by leaving them undefined, ambiguous, and incomplete.[1]

Aside from being unsure what powers to invest in the president's office, delegates to the Constitutional Convention also disagreed over how presidents should be chosen. James Wilson of Pennsylvania proposed that the executive be elected by the people. But the delegates rejected this proposal because it would make the president responsive to the very democratic spirit they were intent on taming. After creating an executive independent of Congress, delegates were not about to propose selecting the president through direct election, which would reflect the same popular opinion they saw lurking in legislatures. "Each solution" for selecting the president, Robert Dahl argues, was "worse than the rest."[2] James Wilson fretted that the question of how the president should be chosen was "in truth the most difficult of all which we have had to decide."[3] With more desperation than confidence, the convention delegates devised a plan by which a majority of members of the newly created electoral college would elect the president.

---

[1] Richard M. Pious, *The American Presidency* (New York: Basic Books, 1979).

[2] Robert Dahl, *How Democratic Is the American Constitution?* (New Haven, CT: Yale University Press, 2001), p. 74.

[3] Wilson is quoted in Dahl, *How Democratic Is the American Constitution?*, p. 74.

The Constitution specifies that states have as many votes in the electoral college as they have members of Congress. That is, each state is given a number of electoral votes equal to the total number of senators and representatives in Congress from that state. As a result, the electoral college tends to overrepresent small states. For example, Wyoming, with 3 electoral votes, has one electoral vote for every 166,000 citizens in the state, while California, with 55 electoral votes, has one electoral vote for every 600,000 citizens. If a citizen lived in California and then moved to Wyoming and voted in the next presidential election, his or her vote would have about four times the weight at the new address than it did previously, given the distribution of electoral votes per citizen in the two states.

Over time, a pattern developed in which the presidential candidate who receives the most votes in a state receives all of that state's votes in the electoral college.[4] This is known as the unit rule.[5] If no presidential candidate wins an absolute majority of votes in the electoral college (presently 270 votes), the House of Representatives selects the president by majority vote.

The unit rule permits presidential candidates who win the most votes in a particular state to get all of that state's votes in the electoral college even though the difference separating the two candidates in the actual election may be just a few votes out of millions that were cast. As a result, the electoral college vote for president may diverge from the popular vote. For example, in 2000, the presidential election hinged on several hundred votes separating Al Gore and George W. Bush in Florida. Bush was awarded all of Florida's 25 electoral votes even though he won the state by only 537 votes out of almost 6 million votes cast statewide. In other words, he won 100 percent of Florida's electoral votes even though he carried the state by .0001 percent of the vote. By the same token, Al Gore benefited from the unit rule when he won all of the electoral votes from Iowa (7), New Mexico (5), Oregon (7), and Wisconsin (11), even though he carried each of those states by less than 1 percent of the popular vote. In the 2004 elections, the unit rule delivered all of Iowa and New Mexico's electoral college votes to Bush even though he won each state by less than 1 percentage point, just as it delivered all of New Hampshire and Wisconsin's electoral votes to Kerry, who likewise carried those states by less than 1 percent of the vote.

The unit rule, by which all of a state's electoral votes go to the statewide winner regardless of how narrow the margin of victory, so distorts the popular vote that it is even possible for a presidential candidate to win the popular vote nationwide and to lose in the electoral college. This is precisely

---

[4] By 1836, every state but South Carolina had decided to cast all its votes as a unit for the candidate who received the most votes within the state, regardless of how narrow the margin.

[5] Although most states have enacted the unit rule, either by state law or custom, there are exceptions. For example, Nebraska allocates two electoral votes to the candidate who has received a plurality of votes at the state level but divides its remaining votes in the electoral college on the basis of who wins pluralities in each of Nebraska's congressional districts.

what happened in 2000. Al Gore received over 550,000 more votes than George W. Bush in the popular election but lost 271–267 in the electoral college. Most of the time, however, the effect of the unit rule within the electoral college is not to reverse the result of the popular vote but to exaggerate it. For example, in 1996, Bill Clinton received 49 percent of the popular vote but received 70 percent of the votes in the electoral college. In 1992, Ross Perot finished third in the presidential election with 19 million votes, but he received *no electoral votes* because he did not finish first in any state.

Presidential candidates campaign with the strategic goal of winning a majority in the electoral college—270 votes. Because most states follow the unit rule in the electoral college, presidential candidates tend to lavish particular attention on states where the outcome is uncertain, on the reasonable assumption that this is the most efficient way to allocate scarce resources of time and money. Thus, in the 2004 presidential campaign, George W. Bush ignored California, with the most electoral votes of any state, because polls showed him to be hopelessly behind there. John Kerry, on the other hand, made only a token effort to campaign in Texas, which has the second highest total of electoral votes, because Bush already had the state sewn up. Both presidential candidates instead concentrated on large battleground states like Pennsylvania, Ohio, Michigan, and Florida, which were up for grabs.

Some political scientists argue that Republican presidential candidates have an advantage in the electoral college in that they start out with more assured

Stewart Cairns for NYT

New York electors cast vote for the Electoral College in the 2004 presidential election, Albany, New York.

electoral college votes than Democrats can depend upon.[6] Republicans have won at least two-thirds of the South's electoral votes in every election since 1972, with the exception of 1976. In addition, they can count on winning votes from the Mountain and Plains states, which have also gone Republican in election after election.[7] This allows Republican presidential candidates to start the campaign with about 170 votes in their pocket from these regions—about 62 percent of the electoral votes needed to win.[8] Democrats, on the other hand, begin the campaign assured of only 13 electoral votes from the reliable Democratic enclaves of Minnesota and the District of Columbia. They must get at least 72 percent of the electoral votes from the other states

---

[6] Earl Black and Merle Black, *The Vital South: How Presidents Are Elected* (Cambridge, MA: Harvard University Press, 1992).

[7] By the South, we mean the 11 states that comprised the old Confederacy. The Mountain and Plains states include Arizona, Colorado, Idaho, Kansas, Montana, Nebraska, Nevada, New Mexico, North Dakota, Oklahoma, South Dakota, Utah, and Wyoming.

[8] We derive the figure of 170 electoral votes by taking two-thirds of the South's electoral votes and the electoral votes of every state that voted Republican in every presidential election but one from 1968 to 2004. This group of states includes the Plains states of North Dakota, South Dakota, Nebraska, Kansas, and Oklahoma and the Mountain states of Idaho, Montana, Wyoming, Colorado, Utah, and Arizona. The other consistently Republican states in presidential elections are Indiana and Alaska.

in order to win, whereas their Republican opponent needs to win only 28 percent of the remaining electoral votes.

However, in the 1992 and 1996 presidential elections, the Republican presidential candidates' base of strength in the South and the Mountain and Plains states turned into a ghetto when the party's candidates were unable to attract sufficient support outside these regions. These heavily Republican states tend to be more agricultural, more religious, more culturally conservative, and whiter than the rest of the country. These attributes, which gave Republicans a virtual lock in certain regions before the campaign began, prevented the party from extending its appeal to other regions during the campaign itself. What made the Republicans so attractive to their loyal following *in* the South and the Mountain and Plains states made the Republicans harder to sell *outside* of them.

In 2000, George W. Bush was able to escape the limits of the Republican ghetto that had contributed to the defeat of his two predecessors. But only barely. He won the Border states of Missouri, Kentucky, and West Virginia, which had gone Democratic in 1992 and 1996. Inasmuch as these states reflect their southern neighbors in many ways, this is really a case not of breaking out of the box but of extending it a bit. But Bush also won New Hampshire and Ohio, which is evidence that he was able to pick up electoral votes outside Republican strongholds.

But the real secret of George W. Bush's success in both 2000 and 2004 was not how well he performed outside of Republican citadels but how well he performed within them. Bush defended Republican states spectacularly well, preventing almost any defections from the party's base in the South, the Plains, and the West—only New Mexico voted for Gore in 2000—and there were no defections in 2004. Holding his base firm, Bush was able to win just enough electoral college votes outside of it to win in 2000 and 2004.

THE HISTORICAL PRESIDENCY

In the debates over the Constitution in Philadelphia, Alexander Hamilton defended the office of the president as one that would give "energy" to the government. He believed that a strong executive was necessary to provide leadership and decisiveness to a government that could otherwise drift and be stalemated in a system of checks and balances. According to political scientist Stephen Skowronek, the "energy" that Hamilton sought to invest in the office has made the president a powerful source of political change. Far from being defenders of the status quo, presidents regularly upset it. More than other government officials, presidents routinely "disrupt systems [and] reshape political landscapes."[9] Regardless of whether they are liberal or

---

[9] Stephen Skowronek, *The Politics Presidents Make: Leadership from John Adams to George Bush* (Cambridge, MA: Harvard University Press, 1993), p. 6.

conservative, Democrat or Republican, all presidents, according to Skowronek, are agents of change. They set the wheels of government in motion in order to remake it in their own image.

Today the president remains the energy center of the government, just as Hamilton envisioned it, in part by default. Congress is often too decentralized and fragmented to compete for leadership with the president. But there are no constitutional or political guarantees that the president will be successful in wielding power. Presidential power must be constructed; it cannot be taken for granted. The contingent nature of presidential power is evident in how long it took the office to play a commanding role within the government—a position it must struggle continually to defend. Prior to the Civil War, most presidents exercised relatively few powers because the responsibilities of the national government itself were quite limited. Chief executives in the 19th century were "chief of very little and executive of even less," according to one scholar.[10] The president was regarded a bit derisively as the nation's "chief clerk." Bold innovators like Andrew Jackson and Abraham Lincoln were isolated exceptions, not the rule.

As late as the end of the 19th century, the presidency was viewed as a relatively weak office. In 1885, a young Princeton professor published an influential study of American politics entitled *Congressional Government*, in which he asserted that Congress was the foremost policy-making institution of American government. The president, this scholar argued, was powerful in the legislative domain only to the extent that he exercised veto power over bills passed by Congress. Twenty-three years later the author changed his mind and, in *Constitutional Government in the United States*, developed a far more expansive view of the presidency. Soon after, by his actions as president, Woodrow Wilson, the former Princeton professor, contributed even more directly to the creation of a powerful presidency.

Through much of the 19th and 20th centuries, there were swings between strong and weak presidents, between presidential and congressional supremacy. But as corporate capitalism developed, the federal government grew in both size and power, and the presidency as an institution expanded along with it. First, the regulatory role of the federal government increased because corporations had outgrown the police power of mere states. Only federal law could regulate the behavior of firms that now operated nationally. Second, the federal government became responsible for economic management, as both business and workers looked to it to protect them from the boom-and-bust swings of the business cycle. Third, the federal government took on new social responsibilities, creating a welfare state that would distribute resources to the elderly, unemployed, and disabled who could no longer provide for themselves. Finally, the federal government grew in response to the global character of corporate capitalism and the rise of the

---

[10] Michael Schudson, *The Good Citizen: A History of Civic Life* (Cambridge, MA: Harvard University Press, 1998), p. 206.

United States as a global power. As the focal point of the federal government, the presidency was well positioned to take advantage of these developments. The growth of big government, the rise of corporate capitalism, the emergence of the United States as a world power, and the expansion of presidential power occurred together in a mutually supportive relationship.

Since Franklin D. Roosevelt, who served as president from 1933 to 1945, the balance of power among the three branches of government has tilted clearly toward the president, although this does not mean that presidents are able to achieve their goals easily. FDR gave birth to the modern presidency; as a result, the office is now looked upon as "the preeminent source of moral leadership, legislative guidance, and public policy."[11] Roosevelt led people to expect the federal government to respond to problems and led them to look to presidential leadership in resolving those problems.[12] Joseph Cooper writes, "The New Deal and World War II permanently established the president as the single most powerful figure in both the legislative and administrative processes of government, as well as the elected official charged, in the eyes of the public, with primary responsibility for initiating and securing policies in the public interest."[13] The executive branch expanded as a new array of regulatory and administrative agencies were created, providing the president with new tools to pursue his policies quite apart from Congress, the courts, and political parties. The New Deal and World War II supersized the presidency and executive branch to their current proportions.

THE IMPERIAL PRESIDENT

The symbolism and substance of presidential power are so vast that the president might best be seen as towering over the other parts of the government, a veritable Gulliver standing over the Lilliputians. The perquisites attached to the office are enormous. Presidents draw an annual salary of $400,000, and another $150,000 is available for expenses. A staff of more than 500 assistants as well as limousines, helicopters, and a small fleet of planes are available to assist them. The presidential family resides at the most exclusive address in the world—1600 Pennsylvania Avenue—in the 123-room White House.

---

[11] Sidney M. Milkis and Michael Nelson, *The American Presidency: Origins and Development, 1776–1990* (Washington, DC: Congressional Quarterly Press, 1990), p. 260.

[12] Theodore Roosevelt, not FDR, first used the media in a systematic way. He was the first president to have a press secretary, a press office, and frequent meetings with reporters. In his famous phrase, he used the presidency as "a bully pulpit." However, FDR's presidency coincided with the diffusion of radio, which enabled him to establish direct contact with vast audiences.

[13] Joseph Cooper, "The Twentieth-Century Congress," in *Congress Reconsidered,* 7th ed., eds. Lawrence C. Dodd and Bruce I. Oppenheimer (Washington, DC: Congressional Quarterly Press, 2001), p. 335.

A staff of about 100 attends to the First Family's personal needs at a cost of about $8 million per year. For privacy and relaxation, the president can go to Camp David, a 180-acre retreat in the mountains of Maryland. To ease the transition from office, ex-presidents receive a special grant of $1 million to cover expenses for the return to private life, as well as a generous lifetime pension.[14]

While presidents are well compensated, few get rich from the job. Indeed, presidents of medium-sized corporations earn more than presidents of the United States. The relatively modest remuneration of presidents—in comparison to their peers in the private sector—reflects a populist vigilance. But it also reflects the low evaluation of public affairs in the United States. That the private sector is more significant than the public sector in the United States is symbolized by the greater compensation given to corporate presidents, and even many college presidents, than to presidents of the United States.

The president has substantial power and authority, but the nature and extent of that power vary considerably and are based on quite diverse sources. The president's authority is based only in part on the powers enumerated in the Constitution. The Founders, as we argued previously, were reluctant to specify the president's powers and preferred to ascribe a general grant of powers to the office. Article II of the Constitution, which addresses the power of the presidency, has been referred to as "the most loosely drawn chapter of the Constitution."[15] The Constitution empowers the president to veto legislation passed by Congress, act as commander in chief of the armed forces, execute the laws, pardon criminals, make treaties, call Congress into special session, appoint government officials, and recognize foreign governments.

But presidential power lies not only in explicit constitutional grants of authority but also in the use presidents make of them. Presidential power is based on elements that are as real as the powers enumerated in the Constitution and as subtle as their reputation among members of Congress, their standing with the media, and their popularity among ordinary citizens. It is based on the inescapable authority attached to the office and on often fickle impressions of the president's professionalism and popularity. It is based on both legal and political grounds.

The president's greatest political resource is the unique authority derived from being the one official in the country (along with the vice president) to be voted upon in a nationwide election. No one else can make a legitimate claim that he or she represents the national interest, as no one else was elected on a national basis. The president, thus, embodies the nation, with all the emotional and patriotic symbols attached to it. Unlike parliamentary regimes, where prime ministers are head of the government and others perform

---

[14] A good but dated list of the fringe benefits presidents receive appears in Pious, *The American Presidency*, p. 4.

[15] E. S. Corwin, *The President: Office and Powers*, 3rd ed. (New York: New York University Press, 1957), p. 2.

ceremonial duties as head of state, the President of the United States is both head of state and head of the government. The office fuses real and symbolic power, making the presidency "the focus for the most intense and persistent emotions in the American polity," according to presidential scholar James David Barber.[16]

As chief executive, presidents command media attention through which to deliver their message. The office is a powerful bully pulpit, in President Theodore Roosevelt's words, that permits presidents to appeal directly to the people for support. By attracting the media, political scientist Bruce Miroff writes, "the president gains an unparalleled advantage in defining political reality for most Americans. . . . Press or partisan criticism may challenge a president . . . but the outline of reality that he has sketched is usually left intact."[17] For example, on the second anniversary of September 11, seven out of ten citizens believed that Iraq's dictator Saddam Hussein was linked to the terrorist attacks of 2001 as a result of repeated claims by President George W. Bush that linked the two—despite the absence of supporting evidence.

Realizing the usefulness of the media in molding public opinion, presidents have made increasing use of them. The number of presidential appearances and addresses has increased over time.[18] Sometimes presidents go to extraordinary dramatic lengths in order to deliver their message. One need only recall President Bush's "Top Gun" landing on board the aircraft carrier *U.S.S. Abraham Lincoln* in which he declared victory prematurely in the war on Iraq.[19] Such staged events add spice to the constant daily reporting about the president that tends to reinforce the image of the presidency as an essential institution at the center of political life. The extent of coverage devoted to the president is as helpful in promoting a favorable image of the office as the deferential reporting it generally receives.

Presidential power is further bolstered by their management of the federal bureaucracy, which includes over 2.7 million employees and a budget of over $2 trillion. Through management of the executive branch, presidents influence how federal policy is interpreted and implemented. They influence federal agencies by reviewing their policies and proposing changes to their budgets. But their most potent means of control over federal agencies is through staffing. Presidents make over 3,000 appointments to different federal agencies—more than chief executives of other countries get to make— permitting presidents to place political allies throughout the government.

---

[16] Barber is quoted in Gary L. Gregg II, "Dignified Authenticity," in *Considering the Bush Presidency*, eds. Gary L. Gregg II and Marc J. Rozell (New York: Oxford University Press, 2004), p. 89.

[17] Bruce Miroff, "Monopolizing the Public Space: The President as a Problem for Democratic Politics," in *Rethinking the Presidency*, ed. Thomas E. Cronin (Boston: Little, Brown, 1982), p. 220.

[18] Jeffrey K. Tulis, *The Rhetorical Presidency* (Princeton, NJ: Princeton University Press, 1987).

[19] President Bush co-piloted a fighter jet that landed on the aircraft carrier as a banner on deck waved "Mission Accomplished." American casualties in Iraq more than doubled in the year following President Bush's triumphant landing.

© Reuters/Corbis

President Bush lands on the *U.S.S. Abraham Lincoln*, May 2003, to announce the end of the war in Iraq.

For example, President George W. Bush and Vice President Dick Cheney are both from the energy industry and came into office intent on helping that industry by removing environmental restrictions and increasing oil and gas exploration. They pursued their objective by naming over 30 energy industry executives, lobbyists, and lawyers to influential positions within the federal bureaucracy. Frederick D. Palmer, executive vice president of external affairs for Peabody Energy acknowledged, "The people running the United States government are from the energy industry. They understand it and believe in energy supply."[20]

Presidents can also issue executive orders requiring or authorizing federal agencies to take some action. They are important tools that permit presidents

---

[20] *New York Times*, April 21, 2002. Bush political appointees from the energy industry include: Assistant Secretary of Land and Minerals Management Rebecca Watson, a lawyer who defended many timber and mining companies; Assistant Secretary of Water and Science Bennet W. Raley, who in 1994 lobbied against reauthorization of the Clean Water Act; J. Stephen Griles, who worked as a mining industry lobbyist before becoming Deputy Secretary of the Interior; and Associate Deputy Secretary of Interior James. E. Cason, who served in the Reagan administration where he tried to stop limits on drilling for oil and gas in national forests. Other influential appointees in the Bush administration from the energy industry include Secretary of Commerce Donald L. Evans, who worked for a Denver oil and gas company; and Philip Cooney, who was a lawyer for the American Petroleum Institute, a lobbying arm of the industry, before he was appointed chief of staff for the Council on Environmental Quality in the president's Executive Office.

to act unilaterally in implementing important domestic and foreign policies. For example, President Harry Truman ordered the racial integration of the armed forces by executive order. Through executive orders and other forms of executive lawmaking, presidents can "establish policy, reorganize executive branch agencies, alter administrative and regulatory processes, [and] affect how legislation is interpreted and implemented," according to political scientist Kenneth R. Mayer.[21] When George W. Bush came to office, he issued a number of executive orders reversing his predecessor's policies. For example, Bush issued an executive order banning aid to international organizations engaged in family planning that rescinded a previous executive order under President Clinton authorizing such assistance. Another flurry of executive orders occurred in response to September 11. The Bush administration issued executive orders that froze the assets of suspected terrorist groups and created the Office of Homeland Security within the Executive Office of the President. When presidents cannot obtain cooperation from federal agencies, when executive orders and their appointment powers are not enough, they can rely on the extensive bureaucracy in the Executive Office of the President (EOP), which is more subject to their direct control. Almost 1,600 people work in the specialized offices within the EOP, such as the Council of Economic Advisors, the Office of Management and Budget, and the National Security Council. These units provide presidents with expertise, perform management tasks on their behalf, and are a dependable resource to which they can turn for help.

Presidents also have rewards they can dispense in order to obtain compliance with their policies. For example, they have patronage, including judgeships and ambassadorships, and benefits, such as invitations to the White House, with which to repay loyal supporters and persuade holdouts who may need more convincing. They can strike bargains by offering inducements to members of Congress in return for votes. In 2001, the Bush administration was threatened with defeat on the floor of the House on a bill to give the president more authority to make trade agreements with other countries.[22] To secure victory, the Administration promised Representative Jim Demint from South Carolina that it would cancel trade preferences given some South American nations whose exports competed with textile mills in his district. Demint switched his vote in the final seconds, and the bill passed the House 215–214.

Presidents have sticks to punish opponents as well as carrots to obtain support. They can exclude opponents from White House social events, deny access to the president, and use their office to orchestrate pressure on reluctant members of Congress. Take a relatively "small" example—although not

---

[21] Kenneth R. Mayer, "Executive Orders and Presidential Power," *Journal of Politics* 61 (May 1999): 445.

[22] The bill was to give the president fast-track authority, which requires Congress to vote up or down, without amendment, trade agreements negotiated by the president.

so small to those involved! When Senator Richard Shelby from Alabama opposed Clinton's 1993 budget package, he was given only one ticket to the White House ceremony honoring the University of Alabama national championship football team. In contrast, Howell Heflin, Alabama's other senator, who supported the president's budget, received more than 25 tickets.[23]

Presidents are party leaders and can use this to appeal for loyalty from party members in Congress and elsewhere. In return, they can lend the aura of their office to party members by making appearances on their behalf, raising money for them, or supporting their pet projects.

Finally, presidents have benefited more than any other political institution from the rise of the United States as a global power. As the United States has become the dominant actor on the world stage, presidents are in a privileged position to write the script because they are uniquely situated to speak for the national interest. As the world becomes smaller, as foreign policy decisions touch people's lives in more intimate ways, from war and threats of terrorism to economic globalization and global warming, presidents become bigger. The more foreign policy matters, the more presidents matter. The power of the presidential office has grown with the economic and military power of the United States and its influence throughout the world.

The rapid growth in size and power of the presidency can be illustrated by a single statistic. When Herbert Hoover served as president from 1929 to 1933, a personal secretary and two assistants aided him. Today the president is assisted by a White House staff of more than 500 people. The bold innovations of one president to extend the powers of the office have come to be accepted as a normal feature of presidential power by the next. "In instance after instance," Richard E. Neustadt, the most influential scholar on the modern presidency, has observed, "the exceptional behavior of our earlier 'strong' Presidents has now been set by statute as a regular requirement."[24] Expressions of presidential powers that were once thought to be extraordinary have become routine.[25]

The modern presidency (which, as we will describe, extends far beyond the president) commands the most powerful military in the world, manages a vast bureaucracy, sets the agenda of government, defines the national interest, monopolizes the media, provides party leadership, and has a vast supply of benefits with which to reward supporters. If this were the whole story, the president would be a modern Leviathan. Why, then, do some scholars describe the presidency not as imperial but as imperiled?

---

[23] James P. Pfiffner, *The Modern Presidency*, 2nd ed. (New York: St. Martin's Press, 1998), p. 145.

[24] Richard E. Neustadt, *Presidential Power: The Politics of Leadership* (New York: Free Press, 1963), p. 5.

[25] Richard S. Gilmour, "The Institutionalized Presidency: A Conceptual Clarification," in *The Presidency in Contemporary Context*, ed. Norman C. Thomas (New York: Dodd, Mead, 1975), p. 155.

THE IMPERILED PRESIDENCY

In *Gulliver's Travels*, Jonathan Swift's satire on the modern condition, Gulliver not only found himself standing over the Lilliputians, towering above them, but also, at times, tethered by them. Presidential impotence is conveyed in the famous remark President Harry Truman made as he imagined what would happen when his newly elected successor, popular World War II hero General Dwight D. Eisenhower, took office. Truman predicted, "He'll sit here and he'll say, 'Do this! Do that!' *And nothing will happen.* Poor Ike—it won't be a bit like the Army. He'll find it very frustrating."[26] A sense of the president's weakness is reflected in the plea for help that the President's Committee on Administrative Management issued in 1937. The report's opening sentence, "The President needs help," has been reaffirmed many times by subsequent reports since then.[27]

Beginning in the 1970s, political scientists began to reassess the presidency and to characterize it as a weak and ineffective institution. The debacle in Vietnam under President Johnson and the criminality involved in Watergate under President Richard Nixon weakened the office of the president, temporarily removing the awe and veneration previously attached to it. With the aura surrounding the president tarnished, the media and Congress were now more ready and willing to resist presidential leadership.

The end of the golden age of capitalism in the 1970s also weakened the presidency. Since at least the New Deal, the president's fortunes have been closely tied to the fate of the economy. The power and prestige of the president (as well as that of the entire government) have prospered when corporate capitalism has prospered; and when the economy stagnates, the president's popular and professional standings fall. The decline in presidential favor corresponds to the heightened economic fears and insecurities people feel as inequality increases, globalization proceeds, and the economy gyrates between periods of boom and bust.

Recent presidents have also been confronted by a resurgent Congress, often led by the opposing party. In the 1950s and 1960s, Congress was willing to follow the president's lead because it agreed with the president's policies. For example, during the Cold War, Congress often deferred to the president because it shared the president's goal of containing Communism. But when Congress and the president began to disagree over substantive issues of domestic and foreign policy beginning in the 1970s, Congress acted to recover its lost prerogatives. For example, Congress tried to legislate limits on presidential powers in the War Powers Act of 1973. It also sought to create its own expertise to match that available to the president when it created the Congressional Budget Office in 1974.

---

[26] Quoted in Neustadt, *Presidential Power,* p. 9 (emphasis in original).

[27] This point is taken from Theodore J. Lowi, *The Personal President: Power Invested, Promise Unfulfilled* (Ithaca, NY: Cornell University Press, 1985), pp. 1–7.

The reassertion of Congress was, in part, driven by the almost routine appearance of divided government beginning in the 1970s, in which different parties controlled Congress and the presidency. Democrats held majorities in Congress throughout much of the Republican presidencies of Richard Nixon, Ronald Reagan, and George H. W. Bush, just as the Republicans held majorities in Congress through six of Bill Clinton's eight years in the White House. Divided government gives Congress an incentive to challenge, not cooperate with, the president.

Finally, presidents have been weakened by the proliferation of interest groups. The institutional universe of political action that presidents face today has, according to Skowronek, "gotten thicker all around." Skowronek argues that, for presidents, "there are more organizations and authorities to contend with, and they are all more firmly entrenched and independent."[28] Going over the heads of interest groups to build their own personal coalitions may free presidents of obligations to other political actors. But the flip side of this is that interest groups are similarly less obliged to remain loyal members of the president's team, making it difficult for presidents to govern once they are elected.

In conclusion, presidential power sometimes appears imperial and sometimes appears imperiled. A rough periodization of presidential power would indicate the emergence of an imperial presidency in the 1930s and 1940s, with the New Deal and the emergence of the United States as a world power following World War II. The presidency then became imperiled in the 1970s with the conflict surrounding the Vietnam War and President Nixon's abuse of presidential power in the Watergate scandal. However, Ronald Reagan reversed this trend in the 1980s as a result of his skillful actions and bold agenda. The imperial presidency was then tempered under Presidents George H. W. Bush and Bill Clinton, both of whom had to contend with divided governments in which the opposing party controlled Congress, only to have it reemerge even more vigorously under George W. Bush. Bush has pushed presidential powers to their limit, and in the view of some, even beyond it.

Whether presidencies are strong or weak, imperial or imperiled depends on particular circumstances and the ability of presidents to take advantage of them. Some presidents, as we shall argue, are more fortunate than others. They encounter a less resistant environment when they take office, one in which the opposition is in disarray and their party commands a working majority in Congress. Other presidents are not so lucky. And some presidents are simply more skillful than others at using the political resources available to them.

Presidential power is exercised most decisively and effectively when the president opposes some action. The Constitution authorizes the president to veto bills passed by Congress. Vetoing a bill does not require the cooperation of any other political actor—just a pen that works. The veto is very effective

---

[28] Skowronek, *Politics Presidents Make*, p. 55.

because the House and the Senate are often unable to assemble the two-thirds majority in each chamber required to override it.

But presidents get elected and make their mark not by preventing action but by promoting it. It is thus ironic that presidents find their power magnified and most effective when they thwart change and find their power diminished and most constrained when they try to promote it. The independence of Congress, the inflexibility of the federal bureaucracy, and the influence of special interest groups are daunting obstacles for presidents to overcome. And yet, as we argued at the beginning of this chapter, presidents are agents of change in our political system despite these obstacles, if only by default. No other office in our political system can muster comparable initiative and coherence to assemble its resources on behalf of a concerted course of action. That presidents may not succeed when they do so says less about their weakness and more about the power of the obstacles they must overcome.

PRESIDENTIAL STYLES

While all presidents reach office by promising to sponsor change, presidents construe their role in quite different ways. Presidential styles are, in part, a function of personality. John F. Kennedy was supremely confident to the point of arrogance, Lyndon Johnson was beset by profound insecurity, and Richard Nixon was suspicious by nature. In more recent times, Bill Clinton wanted to please so badly that he was called "slick Willie" because of his tendency to tell people what they wanted to hear, while George W. Bush was not as interested in intellectually mastering problems as he was in trusting his instincts in responding to them.

Presidential style is also a function of the unique skills and aptitudes presidents bring to office with them. Ronald Reagan had little patience for the details of policy but was brilliantly effective at communicating their broad themes to the public. Jimmy Carter was just the opposite. He brought his training as an engineer to the presidency and was intensely interested in the details of policy. (Some idea of the enormous range of issues with which Carter dealt—and his grueling schedule—can be gleaned from Figure 6-1.) Richard Nixon and George H. W. Bush each came to office with an interest in foreign policy, while Bill Clinton preferred domestic policy and, like Carter, participated in detailed policy discussions within his administration. George W. Bush, on the other hand, delegates authority to trusted subordinates and tends to view issues in stark, moral terms.

Presidents shape the office in their own image. This is reflected in how the White House is organized and run. Some presidents are hands-on managers, while others prefer to delegate authority. Some are comfortable with a rigid chain of command, while others prefer to improvise. Journalist Elizabeth Drew writes that the Clinton White House was so unstructured during his

■ .FIGURE 6-1

From	To	Activity
5:00		The President received a wake up call from the White House signal board operator
5:36		The President went to the Oval Office
7:15	7:20	The President met with his Assistant for National Security Affairs, Zbigniew Brzezinski
7:32	7:38	The President talked with Senator Russell B. Long (D–LA)
7:45	7:55	The President met with his Assistant for Congressional Liaison, Frank B. Moore
8:00	9:00	The President hosted a breakfast meeting for Democratic Congressional leaders
9:20	9:25	The President met with his assistant, Hamilton Jordan
9:30	9:48	The President telephoned the Chief of Government of the Republic of Panama, Brig. Gen. Omar Torrijos Herrera
9:33	9:46	The President met with: Warren M. Christopher, Deputy Secretary of State Stephanie R. van Reigersberg, Dept. of State interpreter Mr. Lordan
9:46	10:00	The President met with: Rex L. Granum, Deputy Press Secretary Jerrold L. Schecter, Associate Press Secretary, NSC
10:30	10:45	The President participated in an arrival ceremony in honor of the Prime Minister of Israel, Menachem Begin
10:48	1:00	The President participated in a meeting with U.S. and Israeli officials
1:00	1:04	The President met with Mr. Brzezinski
1:04	1:30	The President met with Vice President Walter F. Mondale
1:30	1:53	The President met to discuss urban policy with: Richard G. Hatcher, Mayor (D–Gary, IN) Lee A. Alexander, Mayor (D–Syracuse, NY) Henry W. Maier, Mayor (D–Milwaukee, WI) Stuart E. Eizenstat, Assistant for Domestic Affairs and Policy Jack H. Watson, Jr. Assistant for Intergovernmental Affairs Bruce Kirschenbaum, Associate for Intergovernmental Affairs
2:15	2:27	The President participated in a ceremony to present the National Teacher of the Year Award to Mrs. Henry (Elaine) Barbour of Montrose, Colorado

SOURCE: Michael W. Link, "The Presidential Kaleidoscope: Advisory Networks in Action," in *Presidential Power: Forging the Presidency for the Twenty-First Century*, eds. Robert Y. Shapiro, Martha Joynt Kumar, and Lawrence R. Jacobs (New York: Columbia University Press, 2000), p. 237.

first term that one White House aide described it as an "adhocracy."[29] The opposite is true of his successor George W. Bush, who runs a tight ship in which loyalty and teamwork are prized over brilliance and freelancing. If Clinton's White House team resembled a jazz ensemble where the musicians go off on their own riffs, Bush's resembles a military drill team in which the musicians play the music they are given and march together in lockstep. Each president puts a personal stamp on the office, but it is hard to draw a straight line from personality to policy. The institutional and political configuration that presidents face is far more important than their personality in explaining presidential decisions and determining their success. Presidential success depends far more on the circumstances they encounter than on their character.

According to Skowronek, presidents elected in the wake of an electoral realignment, with the opposition in disarray, are in a favorable position to impose their will on the nation. Effective presidents, Skowronek argues, come to office following electoral upheavals, when "government has been most thoroughly discredited, and when political resistance to the presidency is weakest."[30] More successful presidents simply take office under conditions that permit them more freedom to maneuver.

Crisis and war also permit presidents to overcome blockages that would normally compromise presidential power. The terrorist attacks of September 11, 2001, constituted such a crisis, and the Bush administration took full advantage of them to leverage the president's power. Prior to the attacks, the Bush administration was floundering. Poll numbers were low and the economy was in recession. But then came September 11. A presidency that had appeared small now loomed large. Approval ratings for President Bush soared and stayed that way longer than for any other president in the history of polling. Congress increasingly deferred to the president. The system of checks and balances became seriously unbalanced as President Bush used the threat of terrorism to increase presidential power. The Patriot Act, for example, gave the executive branch new, far-reaching surveillance and seizure powers. Bush also used his authority as commander in chief of the armed forces to create his own criminal justice system with its own rules removed from the ordinary oversight of Congress and the courts. He claimed the authority to classify terrorist suspects as "enemy combatants" and detain them indefinitely without access to a lawyer or even knowledge of the charges against them. Bush administration lawyers had even gone so far as to conclude that the president's authority as commander in chief meant that he was not even prevented by international treaties or federal laws from authorizing the use of torture against prisoners.

The sense of crisis over the terrorist attacks was then appropriated to justify war on Iraq, which consolidated power in the executive branch even further. The president's role as symbolic leader of the country was used to rally

---

[29] Elizabeth Drew, *On the Edge: The Clinton Presidency* (New York: Simon & Schuster, 1994), p. 231.

[30] Skowronek, *Politics Presidents Make*, p. 37.

public opinion. Congress, interest groups, administrative agencies, and the media offered little resistance. They did not want to appear at odds with the White House and be accused of undermining the war effort. Only the Supreme Court put up some belated resistance when it rejected President Bush's claims of power to deny suspects their rights. The Court reminded the Bush administration that "[a] state of war is not a blank check for the president when it comes to the rights of the nation's citizens."[31]

THE EXERCISE OF PRESIDENTIAL POWER

Given how central the president's position is within American government and how poorly that position is defined in the Constitution, scholars have tried to understand the bases of presidential power. For many years, the most influential treatment was offered by political scientist Clinton Rossiter, who identified the president's various "hats" or roles. Rossiter designated them as chief of state, chief executive, commander in chief of the armed forces, chief diplomat, chief legislator, chief of the party, voice of the people, protector of the peace, manager of prosperity, and world leader.[32] Political scientist Thomas E. Cronin reduced Rossiter's extensive list to just four spheres or subpresidencies: foreign policy, economic management, domestic policy, and symbolic or moral leadership.[33] Aaron Wildavsky, a specialist in public policy, suggested a still simpler classification by distinguishing two presidencies, one for foreign affairs and the other for domestic affairs.[34]

Using these classifications as a point of departure, we suggest three broad purposes on behalf of which contemporary presidents exercise power: to defend corporate capitalism and American power abroad, to foster economic growth and assist the system of corporate capitalism at home, and to maintain social control.

DEFENDING CORPORATE CAPITALISM ABROAD

The growth in the power of the presidency is inseparable from the rise of the United States as a superpower. As we alluded to previously, presidential power has thrived on foreign involvement, crisis, and war.

The Constitution gives the president authority to negotiate treaties, receive ambassadors from foreign countries (which implies the right to recognize or refuse to recognize the government of a particular country), and,

---

[31] From Sandra Day O'Connor's opinion for the Supreme Court majority quoted in *The New York Times*, June 28, 2004.

[32] Clinton Rossiter, *The American Presidency*, rev. ed. (New York: Harcourt, Brace, 1960), ch. 1.

[33] Thomas E. Cronin, "Presidents as Chief Executives," in *The Presidency Reappraised*, ed. Rexford G. Tugwell and Thomas E. Cronin (New York: Praeger, 1974), p. 235.

[34] Aaron Wildavsky, "The Two Presidencies," *Trans-action* (December 1966): 7–14.

above all, command the armed forces. The framers of the Constitution intended the president's power as commander in chief to be confined to the limited authority of a military leader once hostilities begin. The Constitution granted Congress, not the president, the power to declare war and appropriate funds for military expenditures. But as Representative Roy Blount confessed in regard to the war in Iraq, Congress was a mere passenger in a car driven by the president. Blount acknowledged: "The truth is that in time of war, beyond oversight and some extraordinary legislation, there is not a whole lot for members of Congress to do."[35]

Presidents have expanded the power of the presidency by interpreting broadly their authority as commander in chief. Supreme Court Justice Robert Jackson once warned that, as commander in chief, the president essentially has the power "to do anything, anywhere that can be done with an army or navy."[36] Presidents have used this open-ended authority invested in them to deploy American troops in pursuit of their foreign policy objectives. For example, President James K. Polk provoked war with Mexico in 1846 by sending American troops into disputed land between Texas and Mexico. When Mexican forces fired on the troops, Polk quickly extracted from Congress a declaration of war. Polk's actions brought forth an angry reaction from a young Illinois congressman: "Allow the president to invade a neighboring nation, whenever *he* shall deem it necessary to repel an invasion . . . and you allow him to make war at his pleasure. Study to see if you can fix *any limit* to his power in this respect."[37]

The words of the young congressman, Abraham Lincoln, proved prescient. Indeed, when Lincoln himself became president, he vigorously used presidential war powers during the Civil War to expand the power of his office. He refused to call Congress into special session in the first months of the war and sponsored numerous unauthorized measures in its absence: blockading southern ports, expanding the armed forces beyond their congressionally prescribed size, and spending money for purposes not approved by Congress.

Contemporary presidents, like their predecessors, have often deployed troops first and asked for congressional approval later, if they bothered to seek approval at all. President Carter informed Congress only after he had sent troops on an ill-fated mission to rescue American hostages held in Iran. In 1983, President Reagan ordered U.S. troops to invade the tiny Caribbean nation of Granada and overthrow its government without seeking authorization from Congress. After Saddam Hussein of Iraq invaded Kuwait in 1991, President George H. W. Bush sent 200,000 troops to neighboring Saudi Arabia

---

[35] Quoted in *New York Times*, March 23, 2002.

[36] Quoted in Byron W. Daynes, Raymond Tatalovich, and Dennis L. Sodin, *To Govern a Nation* (New York: St. Martin's Press, 1997), p. 265.

[37] Quoted in Arthur M. Schlesinger, Jr., *The Imperial Presidency* (Boston: Houghton Mifflin, 1973), p. 42 (emphasis in original).

to protect its oil fields and only asked Congress to approve of his actions when the number of American troops in the area had doubled. Two political scientists contend that when Congress considered what to do it "had little choice except to grant the president the authority he requested" because a number of military and diplomatic actions had already been taken by the Bush administration. They comment, "As most legislators were doubtless aware, withholding such approval would mean that the United States stood in real danger of incurring a serious diplomatic and military defeat in the Middle East. This was an outcome for which few legislators were willing to take responsibility."[38]

Following the terrorist bombings of the World Trade Center and Pentagon in 2001, Congress passed a resolution permitting the president to do what was necessary to fight terrorism, provided him with money with which to do it, and granted him new law enforcement powers. Only later did Congress complain that it was being bypassed and try to recover its constitutional authority.[39] When the Bush administration refused to consult with Congress or share information with it, Representative Dan Burton, a Republican and Chair of the Government Reform Committee, complained, "This is not a monarchy. His title is President George Bush, not King George."[40]

Presidents frequently defend their actions on the basis of their unique access to secret information. "If you knew what I know," President Lyndon Johnson once asserted, "then you would be acting in the same way."[41] But such arguments have a suspiciously self-serving ring to them. Presidents do their utmost to withhold information in order to prevent citizens from knowing what presidents know. Presidents frequently invoke "executive privilege" to prevent sharing their information with Congress and the wider public.

No administration has been more intent on limiting and controlling the flow of information than that of George W. Bush. His administration initially refused to release documents to and cooperate with the congressional committee investigating the September 11 attacks; it refused to turn over to an arm of Congress the names of business executives who advised Vice President Cheney's Energy Task Force; it ordered federal agencies to resist Freedom of Information requests; and it issued an executive order delaying the release of presidential papers from previous administrations.

Presidents try to monopolize the flow of information by classifying it for security purposes and thereby restricting access to it. More and more information is restricted to classified use for reasons that have less and less to do

---

[38] Cecil V. Crabb and Kevin V. Mulcahy, "George Bush's Management Style and Desert Storm," *Presidential Studies Quarterly* 25 (Spring 1995): 262.

[39] *New York Times*, March 13, 2002.

[40] *New York Times*, March 16, 2002.

[41] Robert T. Nakamura, "Congress Confronts the Presidency," in *1984 Revisited: Prospects for American Politics*, ed. Robert Paul Wolff (New York: Knopf, 1973), p. 82.

with national security. As one reporter observed, "Most of what is concealed through classification is anything whose revelation might be politically embarrassing to the Administration in power, or to individual officials, in terms of the enemy at home, the opposition party, the Congress, the press, and thereby the wider voting public."[42] National security is invoked to protect presidential interests as much as the security of the United States. President Nixon mentioned national security 31 times during a speech he gave while trying to escape responsibility during the Watergate affair.[43] James Oliver, a student of presidential foreign policymaking, observes, "Authoritarian and totalitarian governments are often accused of trying to divert the attention of their populations from domestic difficulties by means of wars or fabricated international crisis. It seems, however, that American presidents faced with their own domestic pressures are no less susceptible to [this temptation]."[44]

Presidents also use national security as a smokescreen with which to pursue their broader political agenda, to achieve policy goals under the cover of national security that have little to do with defense. For example, the Bush Administration had argued that oil drilling in the Arctic National Wildlife Refuge in Alaska was necessary to meet the energy crisis. When the energy crisis failed to materialize, the administration switched its argument to national security in the wake of 9/11, arguing that drilling for oil was a matter of natural security, as it would reduce our dependence on foreign oil. Similar arguments were offered as to why Congress should give the president more authority to make trade agreements with other nations. U.S. Trade Representative Robert B. Zoelleck argued that such authority was part of the "economic counteroffensive against terrorism." He explained, "Sometimes, tragedy presents opportunities for those who are alert."[45]

Following World War II, presidents had a relatively free hand in foreign policy. According to Aaron Wildavsky, presidents have enjoyed more success in foreign policy than they have in domestic policy because checks and balances are simply not as effective in foreign policy as they are in domestic policy, as we saw with regard to the critical issue of committing American troops abroad. Wildavsky claimed that presidents enjoy more success in the foreign policy arena because they have more expertise available to them and encounter less interest group opposition, and because Congress is more reluctant to challenge them.

But according to political scientists George C. Edwards III and Stephen J. Wayne, at the very moment when Wildavsky presented his thesis in 1964,

[42] Quoted in Daynes, Tatalovich, and Soden, *To Govern a Nation*, p. 283.

[43] Charles M. Hardin, *Presidential Power and Accountability: Toward a New Constitution* (Chicago: University of Chicago Press, 1974), p. 24.

[44] James K. Oliver, "Presidents as National Security Policymakers," in *Rethinking the Presidency*, ed. Thomas E. Cronin (Boston: Little, Brown, 1982), p. 397.

[45] Zoellick is quoted in Jeff Faux, "Trading on Terrorism," *The American Prospect* (December 3, 2001), p. 16.

the two presidencies were collapsing into one. The distinction between foreign and domestic policy that Wildavsky highlighted became harder to justify. American workers, firms, and consumers were more susceptible to economic forces beyond their borders due to the globalization of trade. The environmental movement made people aware of the global effects of pollution, and the media now brought visceral images from around the world into people's living rooms. As the world got smaller, and impinged on citizens' lives more directly, the latitude presidents enjoyed in foreign policy began to contract.[46]

In the 1970s, Congress began to reclaim the prerogatives it had ceded to the president during the Cold War. Given impetus by the Vietnam War protests, Congress tried to restore its constitutional authority when it passed the War Powers Act in 1973 over President Nixon's veto. The law required that the president gain congressional approval after deploying American troops abroad.

Congress was also spurred to play a more independent role in foreign policy by the changing interest-group environment around these issues. Organized interest-group pressure in foreign affairs used to be dominated by groups representing business, such as business associations interested in trade policy and the corporate-dominated Council on Foreign Relations. Today these groups compete in a more crowded and diverse interest-group environment that includes ethnic groups interested in policies affecting their countries of origin, human rights groups, and environmentalists. Presidents find they must satisfy, or at least neutralize, more groups to build support for their foreign policies than they did in the past. Finally, divided government has led Congress to become more assertive and less likely to follow the presidents' lead in foreign policy.

Congressional and popular resistance to presidential direction of foreign policy has had an impact. Yet the presidency retains immense power and initiative in foreign affairs. First, presidents still enjoy the authority granted them by the Constitution, such as their position as commander in chief of the armed forces, which presidents have successfully exploited. Second, presidents can use crises, even manufacture them, to focus attention on their office and put Congress in a position where it would not dare challenge it. Third, presidents retain the initiative in foreign affairs and control the flow of information regarding them. Fourth, presidents have the staff resources of the entire defense establishment at their disposal and enjoy unique access to the media to defend their actions. Fifth, while Congress is more assertive than it has been in the past, there is still substantial agreement between the two branches over the goals of foreign policy: to protect and promote the interests of American corporate capitalism.

---

[46] These paragraphs on the "two presidencies" draw on the analysis in George C. Edwards III and Stephen J. Wayne, *Presidential Leadership: Politics and Policy Making,* 4th ed. (New York: St. Martin's Press, 1997), pp. 460–64.

DEFENDING CORPORATE CAPITALISM AT HOME

The presidency operates as the central planning agency for an American political economy that is highly concentrated and interdependent. There is no institution comparable to the presidency that can present a coherent program, mobilize public support for it, and implement policies to stabilize and strengthen capitalist democracy. Presidential planning is an essential feature of modern capitalism, no less under a laissez-faire ideologue like Ronald Reagan than under a "New Democrat" like Bill Clinton or a "compassionate conservative" like George W. Bush. It is the nerve center of corporate capitalism.

But presidents have a hard time getting the different parts of the executive branch that they manage to cooperate. Getting the federal bureaucracy to implement presidents' wishes does not occur automatically. In fact, presidents find this difficult to achieve. The enormous size, diversity, and fragmentation of the federal bureaucracy means that it is a lumbering giant. Commands issuing from the top have a curious way of being distorted or ignored at the bottom. (Recall President Truman's rueful observation that his successor, Dwight Eisenhower, would say "do this, do that" and nothing would happen.) For example, one study of the Carter presidency (and the findings are doubtless valid for earlier and later periods as well) found that two years after Carter issued an order on a topic that required 75 administrative agencies to issue their own implementing regulations, only 15 had done so.[47] Presidents may be located at the top of the bureaucratic chart, but they are a world away from where the real administrative action takes place. They must compete with other actors for influence over federal agencies. Presidential direction of the bureaucracy is an aspiration, not a guarantee.

Presidents seek to impose their will on the bureaucracy through the specialized agencies located within the Executive Office of the President (EOP). The EOP has grown in size over the years, befitting the growing demands on presidents to manage corporate capitalism. About 1,600 people are employed in the different units within the EOP. Most are political appointees who were likely to have had a close association with the president prior to their appointment. For example, different FOBs, or "Friends of Bill," were distributed throughout the Executive Office under the Clinton administration. According to one estimate, 80 percent of the White House staff under President George W. Bush were either volunteer or paid workers in his presidential campaign.[48] Members of the EOP, especially the White House staff, are personally loyal to the president, owe their position to the president, and share the president's goals.

---

[47] Ron Duhl, "Carter Issues an Order, But Is Anybody Listening?," *National Journal* (July 14, 1979): 1156–58.

[48] John P. Burke, "The Bush Transition," in *Considering the Bush Presidency*, eds. Gary L. Gregg and John L. Rozell (New York: Oxford University Press, 2004) p. 29.

The EOP includes the National Security Council, the Council of Economic Advisors, the Office of the Vice President, and the White House Office (which includes the president's personal staff and advisers). But the largest office within the EOP is the Office of Management and Budget (OMB), which prepares the president's budget.[49] Agencies that reflect an administration's agenda are likely to be rewarded with fatter budgets, while those that engage in activities to which the president is opposed have to rely on Congress to restore proposed cuts in the president's budget.

The EOP is the first in a series of concentric circles surrounding the presidential center (see Figure 6-2). It is the part of the executive branch most responsive to the president, orbiting closest to the president, absorbing and reflecting its heat most intensely. The next ring out from the president is the "permanent government," comprised of the 15 departments in the executive branch, including the Department of Defense, the Department of Commerce, and the Treasury Department. Departments are umbrella organizations into which most of the agencies and bureaus that comprise the federal bureaucracy are placed. For example, the Department of Commerce includes over 25 different offices and agencies, with responsibilities as diverse as those of the Bureau of the Census, the Patent and Trademark Office, and the National Oceanic and Atmospheric Administration within it. When President George W. Bush created the Department of Homeland Security, he simply filled it with agencies, such as the Immigration and Naturalization Service (Justice), the Customs Service (Treasury), and the Lawrence Livermore National Laboratory (Defense), that were pulled from other departments. About three-quarters of all federal workers work in the executive branch departments and they spend two-thirds of all federal money.

The president appoints a secretary to lead each department, and the 15 department secretaries compose the president's cabinet. The cabinet does not play an important role in presidential decision making. Presidents come to office promising to consult frequently with their cabinet, but none ever do so. For example, President Clinton met with his cabinet only 18 times over the course of his first term and had even fewer cabinet meetings in his second. The classic story about presidents' relations with their cabinet involves Lincoln's announcement when he disagreed with his entire cabinet: "Eight votes for and one against; the nays have it."

Presidents also try to exert influence over the federal bureaucracy through their power of appointment. Presidents appoint those who share their political values to direct the departments and to staff other key government positions. President Bush, for example, has the power to appoint 15 department secretaries, 24 deputy secretaries, and 275 assistant secretaries, as well as another 2,500 people to lesser positions within the federal government.

---

[49] A complete description of the different agencies within the EOP is available in Bradley H. Patterson, Jr., *The Ring of Power: The White House Staff and Its Expanding Role in Government* (New York: Basic Books, 1988).

■ **FIGURE 6–2**

EXECUTIVE BRANCH

Executive Office of the President (EOP)
includes
Council of Economic Advisors
National Economic Council
National Security Council
Office of Management and Budget

Cabinet Departments
Agriculture
Commerce
Defense
Education
Energy
Health and Human Services
Homeland Security
Housing and Urban Development
Interior
Justice
Labor
State
Transportation
Treasury
Veterans Affairs

Independent Regulatory Commissions
includes
Federal Reserve Board
National Labor Relations Board

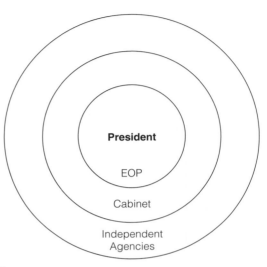

Regardless of whether the president is a Republican or a Democrat, political appointees are drawn overwhelmingly from the ranks of Washington insiders and the corporate elite, with financiers and corporate lawyers predominating. Each administration comes to Washington promising to bring new people with it, but they somehow all arrive from the same revolving corporate door. President Clinton came to office promising to appoint a cabinet that "looked like America." While he appointed more minorities and women to his cabinet than any previous president, many Clinton appointees—including the minorities and women—had the same corporate connections as their predecessors.

The same was true of President George W. Bush's Cabinet. It too was diverse in terms of race and gender, with the same corporate thread running through its members. When Bush's Cabinet was first announced, *USA Today* gushed, "No president, administration and Cabinet has been as marinated in capitalism." Secretary of Commerce Donald Evans ran an oil and gas company; Vice President Dick Cheney was chief executive of Halliburton, an oil field service company; Paul O'Neill was previously CEO of Alcoa, the largest aluminum company in the world; and Donald Rumsfeld headed G.D. Searle and General Instrument before becoming defense secretary. According to journalist James Surowiecki, "Bush had more former CEOs in his Cabinet than any previous president."[50]

The third ring out from the president, enjoying more autonomy from the president than the departments, is the independent regulatory commissions, such as the National Labor Relations Board (NLRB) and the Federal Reserve Board. While presidents appoint members to the independent regulatory commissions, subject to confirmation by Congress, these appointees—unlike secretaries of departments—serve for a fixed term and cannot be fired by the president. The terms of independent regulatory commission appointees often straddle administrations, and new presidents must wait for members to resign or for their terms to expire before appointing new members.

As this description of the federal bureaucracy makes clear, the federal government is not organized hierarchically but rather in concentric circles that surround the president, as depicted in Figure 6-2. The federal bureaucracy is like a solar system in which some planets orbit closer to the presidential sun, reflecting its heat and light, more than others do. But federal agencies are under the magnetic pull of another sun in the galaxy that threatens to draw them away from presidents' directions. The system of shared powers also endows Congress with influence over federal agencies, exerting a gravitational pull on them that competes with the force of the president. Federal agencies depend on Congress for appropriations, and they get their legislative mandate—their job description—from Congress, which performs oversight to ensure they comply with it.

Not only do presidents have to worry about Congress imposing its will on federal agencies, but bureaucrats also have their own sources of power to defy presidential direction. They have knowledge of the files and expertise that they can make available to or withhold from presidents' appointees. Presidential appointees often find themselves dependent on the knowledge bureaucrats possess and have to become advocates of the agency in order to obtain it. Consequently, presidents often complain that their appointees abandon them, "go native" on them. Rather than acting as the president's agent, ensuring that the agency complies with the president's program, the appointee is "turned" and becomes a double agent, representing the agency's interests to the president.[51]

Finally, presidential command of the bureaucracy is challenged by private groups that develop mutually supportive, friendly—sometimes called clientelistic—relationships with federal agencies. In exchange for tax breaks, subsidies, and favorable rulings, special interests give the agencies political support in bureaucratic struggles over "turf" (jurisdiction), OMB budgeting,

---

[50] James Surowiecki, "Bush's Buddy Economy," *The New Yorker* (September 2, 2002), p. 38.

[51] Hugh Heclo, *A Government of Strangers: Executive Politics in Washington* (Washington, DC: Brookings, 1977).

and congressional appropriations. Presidential management of the bureau-cracy is thwarted when private groups are powerful enough to capture a government agency. The agency has legal authority in a policy area that spe-cial interests "rent" for their benefit. Clientelism works best when these rental agreements are exclusive—that is, when other rival agencies and private groups can be excluded from participating in the agency's domain.

When presidential powers are not sufficient to defeat congressional, bureaucratic, and special interest challenges to their management of the executive branch, presidents circumvent the bureaucracy altogether. As one White House staff person explained, "Everybody believes in democracy until he gets to the White House and then you begin to believe in dictator-ship because it's so hard to get things done."[52] Presidents increasingly draw inward and bring policymaking inside the EOP, concentrated among people whom they know and trust, and who are personally loyal to them. This was particularly true during the Reagan administration. According to presidency scholars Sidney M. Milkis and Michael Nelson, policymaking in the Reagan administration "was concentrated in the White House Office and the Executive Office of the President." The Reagan administration, they con-tinue, "resumed the long term trend toward concentrating power in the White House that had been briefly suspended in the aftermath of Vietnam and Watergate."[53]

The Clinton presidency was no different. James F. Pfiffner, a scholar of the presidency, reports that "the main policy initiatives of the Clinton Administration were run out of the White House, not in the departments or in the cabinet policy groups set up by the president."[54] Pfiffner cites the example of Clinton utilizing special task forces organized by the White House to draft his economic plan and health care proposals as evidence of how White House–centered the policy process had become.

The policy-making process within the Bush Administration was as insu-lated as it had been under his predecessor. His patient bill of rights and energy, tax, education, environmental, and homeland security policies were all devel-oped within the confines of the White House, without much participation by Cabinet members responsible for those areas. Secretary of Education Rod Paige played so little a role in developing Bush's "No Child Left Behind" edu-cation bill that one education policy specialist gave him a grade of "I—for Irrelevant."[55] Sometimes, the extent to which Bush Cabinet members were out of the loop was embarrassing. A week after EPA Director Christine Whitman announced that the administration supported a mandatory reduction of car-bon dioxide emissions as stipulated in the Kyoto global-warming treaty, the White House announced it was abandoning such controls.

---

[52] Quoted in Thomas E. Cronin, *The State of the Presidency* (Boston: Little, Brown, 1980), p. 223.

[53] Milkis and Nelson, *American Presidency,* pp. 342–43.

[54] Pfiffner, *Modern Presidency,* p. 110.

[55] *New York Times*, August 5, 2001.

In Bush's second term, he tried to gain greater control of the bureaucracy by replacing some Cabinet members with trusted advisors who had formerly served within the Executive Office. Secretary of State Colin Powell was replaced by Bush's former National Security Advisor, Condoleeza Rice. Attorney General John Ashcroft was replaced by Bush's former General Council, Alberto O. Gonzales, and Secretary of Education Rod Paige was replaced by Bush's former domestic policy advisor, Margaret Spellings. By moving some key Executive Office personnel from his first administration into the field in his second term, Bush hoped to extend his influence throughout the bureaucracy.

SOCIAL CONTROL

Capitalist production systematically generates dislocations, inequalities, and discontent. This provides the structural context for the third arena of presidential activity, containing the conflicts generated by the collision of democratic politics and capitalist production. Thomas E. Cronin suggests that "calibration and management of conflict is the core of presidential leadership."[56] Presidents are concerned with keeping conflict from threatening the stability of the capitalist system, most often among wage earners and racial and ethnic minorities.

The legitimacy of American corporate capitalism depends on the periodic ratification of existing arrangements by electoral majorities and on popular acceptance of presidential policies. When discontented groups express grievances, presidents often take to the media to mollify them. Sympathetic symbolic gestures are made on behalf of the aggrieved group. For example, President Clinton was known for his ability to empathize. To illustrate, during the 1992 campaign, he assured an AIDS activist, "I feel your pain."[57] Sometimes presidents try to defuse an issue by forming commissions to study it. "These commissions," according to one skeptic, "study the situation and, in due course, issue a report, which after a flurry of publicity, is filed away, its recommendations unimplemented and forgotten."[58] For example, in 1997, President Clinton formed the Commission on Race, directed by John Hope Franklin, a distinguished African American historian, to advise the president on the topic and stimulate a national conversation. After one year and many public meetings, the commission's report was ignored and quickly forgotten, like countless presidential commissions preceding it.

---

[56] Thomas E. Cronin, "'Everybody Believes in Democracy Until He Gets to the White House. . . .': An Examination of White House–Department Relations," *Law and Contemporary Problems* 35 (Summer 1970): 575.

[57] Quoted in James L. Nolan, Jr., *The Therapeutic State* (New York: New York University Press, 1998), p. 236.

[58] Derrick Bell, quoted in *New York Times*, June 14, 1997.

Presidents can also wrap themselves in the flag and appeal to patriotic sentiments as a tool of social control. Presidents try to project themselves as indistinguishable from the nation and the American people. Presidents may draw on the salience and pomp of the presidential office to characterize those who disagree with them as unpatriotic and beyond the pale. For example, President Bush's appearance at Ground Zero of the World Trade Center following its collapse helped identify the president with this national calamity and efforts to heal. Patriotism operates as a functional substitute for a state religion in the United States, with the president acting as the high priest.[59]

Social control also occurs through presidential manipulation of the media. No other person in the world enjoys as much access to the media, and presidents spare no effort in managing how they are presented through it. Almost one-third of the president's White House staff is devoted to packaging the president for media consumption. Speechwriters, press secretaries, pollsters, and media consultants strive to present the presidents and their policies in a favorable light. The Clinton Administration used the media aggressively to package his presidency. When the Starr report provided details of Clinton's affair with a White House intern, Clinton took pains to appear presidential, appearing in public at the United Nations and beside world leaders who enjoyed moral standing, such as South African leader Nelson Mandela and Czech President Vaclav Havel.

The Bush White House has been no less concerned with appearances than its predecessor. Bush's "Top Gun" landing on the aircraft carrier to announce victory in the war against Iraq was delayed three hours until the lighting was right so that the president could touch down on the carrier against a setting sun. When Bush made a speech at Mount Rushmore, the platform was positioned so that "television cameras would catch the president in profile with his face aligned perfectly against the four presidents carved in stone."[60]

Another aspect of the selling of the presidency is the degree to which governing and campaigning have blended together. During the Clinton presidency, political consultants participated more in policy discussions within his administration than under any previous president. George C. Edwards described the Clinton administration as "the ultimate example of the public presidency—a presidency based on a perpetual campaign to obtain the public's support and fed by public opinion polls, focus groups, and public relations memos."[61] Clinton traveled throughout the country giving more speeches that promoted his administration's work than any previous president.

President George W. Bush picked up where Clinton left off, making speeches in 26 states in his administration's first 100 days, a record for the

---

[59] Henry Fairlie develops this point in *The Kennedy Promise: The Politics of Expectation* (Garden City, NY: Doubleday, 1973).

[60] *New York Times*, May 16, 2003.

[61] George C. Edwards, "Bill Clinton and His Crisis of Governance," *Presidential Studies Quarterly* 28 (Fall 1998): 755.

start of a presidency. Similar complaints surfaced about the degree to which politics determined policy under Bush as under Clinton. When Bush's Director of the Office of Faith-Based and Community Initiatives John DiIulio, Jr. resigned, he complained about the influence of the president's political advisors on policymaking and how policy was being sacrificed to image and political calculation.[62] *New York Times* columnist Thomas Friedman, a supporter of the war in Iraq, complained that the Bush administration's policy toward Iraq was driven more by domestic political concerns in the United States than by its stated aim of bringing democracy to Iraq. Freidman writes, "That is why, I bet, Karl Rove [President Bush's political advisor] had more sway over this war than Assistant Secretary of State for Near Eastern Affairs Bill Burns. Mr. Burns knew only what would play in the Middle East. Mr. Rove knew what would play in the Middle West."[63]

Today the public face of the presidency is highly managed and contrived. Reporters covering presidents work in a controlled environment. The news is managed with regard to what the administration chooses to reveal and when it chooses to reveal it. Asked why President Bush waited until September to begin beating the drums of war against Iraq, his chief of staff Andrew Card explained, " From a marketing point of view you don't introduce new products in August."[64] Presidential addresses and public appearances that can be scripted and managed for maximum impact have increased in number, while the number of presidential press conferences, in which reporters raise questions without advance notice, has declined. Complaints about spin and lack of press access reached new levels—always high—with the Bush administration. President Bush's team has been intent on preventing leaks and staying on message. But its success at these endeavors has been at the cost of less information being reported and a less transparent government.

Of course, sometimes presidents wish that some things they have done would escape the media's spotlight, and they cannot control the spin the media give to a story, such as the Monica Lewinsky scandal or the pictures of American soldiers torturing Iraqi prisoners. While the media can turn ugly, exposing presidents and their policies in a less than flattering light, it is really the presidents' game to win or lose.

Sometimes presidents find that symbolism and style are not enough to achieve social control. Presidential expressions of concern, blue ribbon commissions, and other symbolic gestures may not suffice. At these times, if the challenge to the existing order is sufficiently great, presidents may propose new policies or expand existing programs to satisfy aggrieved groups. Francis Fox Piven and Richard Cloward found that welfare funding

---

[62] Ron Suskind, "Why Are These Men Laughing?," *Esquire* (January 2003): 96–105.

[63] *New York Times*, May 13, 2001.

[64] Quoted in James P. Pfiffner, "Introduction: Assessing the Bush Presidency," in *Considering the Bush Presidency*, eds. Gary L. Gregg II and Mark J. Rozell (New York: Oxford University Press, 2004), p. 13.

expanded "during the occasional outbreaks of civil disorder produced by mass unemployment" and then contracted when political stability was restored. For example, labor unrest in the 1930s and black militancy in the 1960s provoked concessions by the government in the form of new welfare programs. Such programs were designed to pacify the protesters and were then cut back when the political challenge subsided.[65]

Presidents may also use force along with concessions in an attempt to restore order in times of crisis. They have called out the National Guard, mobilized the armed forces, engaged federal marshals, and used the FBI to maintain political order. The police power under the presidents' command is the iron fist cloaked by the velvet glove of presidential symbolism, media glorification, and policy concessions. Following 9/11, federal agents arrested approximately 1,200 foreign nationals, refused to release their names, detained them in secret locations, and began deportation hearings for many without offering access to an attorney or permitting family members or the press to attend the hearings. The most frequent use of domestic repression by presidents has been to break strikes by workers and to quell urban protests by minorities.

CONCLUSION

Political power is centralized in the executive branch, and within the executive branch, political power is concentrated in the Executive Office of the President. The presidency is at the apex of the government in a privileged position to coordinate the different parts of the government behind a coherent program. It is a key institutional site where conflicting demands in society are sifted to promote the general interests of capitalism. The presidency enjoys this exalted position by virtue of the constitutional power vested in it and as a result of its unique position as the only office elected on a national basis. The fact that only presidents are elected by a national constituency is a powerful political asset, permitting presidents—and only presidents—to claim that they speak for the nation as a whole and represent the national interest. But presidential power is highly contingent. Presidents must contend with countervailing pressures from citizens organized into interest groups and mobilized by social movements. In addition, powers shared among the legislative, executive, and judicial branches create a system of checks and balances that can thwart presidents. Presidential success requires obtaining the cooperation of Congress and the Courts, which are independent and may not be acquiescent. Even federal agencies in the executive branch, which are supposed to be under the president's management, are subject to

---

[65] Francis Fox Piven and Richard Cloward, *Regulating the Poor: The Functions of Public Welfare* (New York: Vintage, 1971), p. xiii.

various influences that pull them away from presidential direction. In such circumstances, presidents tend to move policymaking inside the EOP, where staff are more loyal and subject to their direct control. They tend to depend more on executive orders, recess appointments, and executive agreements; make more claims of executive privilege; and exert more political control over appointments, the budget, and rule making in order to avoid congressional impasses and minimize bureaucratic obstructions.[66]

But presidents are elected to make change, not prevent it. Presidents themselves encourage the impression that they are supposed to provide leadership and initiative to the government. Ironically, presidents find their power is most compromised by the system of checks and balances when they attempt to do just that! Presidential power is most effective when it is least important (when preventing change) and least effective when it is most important (when creating change). Even with all the political resources at their disposal, presidents find it very difficult to overcome interest group opposition, congressional resistance, adverse court rulings, and bureaucratic obstruction.[67] In these circumstances, presidential power looks more imperiled than imperial. Yet, for all the obstacles presidents might encounter from other political institutions, they are in a better position than any other part of the federal government to provide energy and direction to it. Presidents are at the center of government and attempt—not always successfully—to motor and direct it as well. Presidents attempt to provide initiative and coherence to the federal government as it pursues and protects the interests of corporate capitalism abroad, defines and promotes capital's interests at home, and engages in social control to cope with the dislocations that its policies in the first two arenas produce.

---

[66] Joseph Cooper, "The Twentieth Century Congress," in *Congress Reconsidered*, 7th ed., eds. Lawrence C. Dodd and Bruce I. Oppenheimer (Washington, DC: Congressional Quarterly Press, 2001), p. 356.

[67] Ibid.

7

CONGRESS

Writing in 1885, 28 years before he became the president of the United States, Woodrow Wilson analyzed "the essential machinery of power" in America. He believed "that, unquestionably, the predominant and controlling force, the center and source of all motive and regulative power, is Congress."[1] Rather than applaud this situation, Wilson was suspicious of congressional power. Congress, he concluded, was too unwieldy, too unpredictable, and too interested in patronage and spending to produce good government.

Wilson's argument that Congress is central to American government, but unfocused and irresponsible, reflects the misgivings that many Americans have had regarding this institution. Americans consistently express less confidence in Congress than in either the presidency or the Supreme Court. While confidence in all political institutions has declined, none is as low in public esteem as Congress.

Political scientists John Hibbing and Elizabeth Theiss-Morse argue that the public's contempt for Congress is not a reaction to the policies it adopts but to the procedures Congress uses to arrive at them. Congress is perceived as inefficient, "loaded with staffers, committees and perquisites" that suit the selfish needs of members of Congress but do little to meet the needs of the country.

But people also perceive procedures that are unfair, not simply inefficient, at work in Congress. Hibbing and Theiss-Morse write, "[T]he people believe they see processes that are not just, processes that are not equitable. A minority—the extremists, the special interests—are seen as having more access and influence than 'the people.' Lobbyists are in and ordinary people are out, so there is a clear injustice present."[2] The public lacks respect for Congress because it is perceived as captured by special interests who contribute

---

[1] Woodrow Wilson, *Congressional Government: A Study in American Politics* (New York: Meridian Books, 1958), p. 25.

[2] John R. Hibbing and Elizabeth Theiss-Morse, "What the Public Dislikes About Congress," in *Congress Reconsidered*, 6th ed., eds. Lawrence C. Dodd and Bruce I. Oppenheimer (Washington, DC: Congressional Quarterly Press, 1997), p. 77.

Courtesy of the Washington Conventions & Visitors Bureau

The U.S. Capitol.

to congressional campaigns, employ lobbyists to influence legislation, and enjoy special access to its members.

A paradox is at work. On the one hand, Congress is the most open and accessible of the three branches of the federal government. As a result, it reflects and represents public opinion well. Members of Congress have to be alert to shifts in the public mood because their jobs depend on it.[3] This means that Congress is often responsive to pressures from less privileged groups because, according to Elizabeth Sanders, its members are "bound to local constituencies," making them "exquisitely sensitive to the economic pain and moral outrage of their electorates."[4] On the other hand, Congress's openness also makes it easier for the most privileged to exert influence within it. They are best positioned to take advantage of Congress's accessibility. The wealthy are more likely to vote, contact their senator or representative, donate money, and belong to interest groups. "The flaw in the

---

[3] Robert S. Erikson, Michael B. MacKuen, and James A. Stimson, *The Macro Polity* (New York: Cambridge University Press, 2002).

[4] Elizabeth Sanders, *Roots of Reform: Farmers, Workers, and the Administrative State, 1877–1917* (Chicago: University of Chicago Press, 1984), p. 396.

pluralist heaven," political scientist E. E. Schattschneider once wrote, "is that the heavenly chorus sings with an upper-class accent."[5] Congress tends to hear the upper-class members of the chorus better because their money, their votes, and their organization amplify their accented voices.

While both the presidency and Congress are more responsive to groups that have wealth and power, a division of labor exists between them. Congress, according to the Founders, was supposed to represent local constituencies, while the president, in Thomas Jefferson's words, was "the only national officer who commanded a view of the whole ground."[6] Congress's perspective is parochial in the type of demands and issues it addresses. The particularistic local and regional demands Congress responds to reflect the local and statewide constituencies its members represent. The president, on the other hand, as we argued in Chapter 6, tries to condense these specific demands, examine them in relation to each other, and modify them into a coherent program.[7] In contrast to Congress, the purview of the president tends to be national and international, reflecting the constituency from which the president is elected and the foreign policy leadership the president is expected to provide. For example, while members of Congress may represent powerful local business interests that reflect their limited constituency, presidents tilt toward the interest of "advanced internationally competitive enterprises and finance capital" which share that office's national and global perspective.[8]

What happens inside Congress is not simply a function of outside forces brought to bear on it in the form of lobbying, campaign contributions, and election results. Senators and representatives come to office with their own preferences and ideological orientations. They are not blank pads on which outside interests simply inscribe their views. Moreover, policy is a product of Congress's own structure, rules, and procedures. The most important aspect of Congress's structure is its division into two parts, the Senate and the House of Representatives. Each chamber of Congress represents different kinds of constituencies. The Senate represents states, with each state electing two members to the Senate, while the House of Representatives represents districts within states based on population. Senators and representatives serve for different terms: six years for senators and two years for representatives. Each chamber is governed by its own formal and informal rules, which

---

[5] E. E. Schattschneider, *The Semisovereign People* (New York: Holt, Rinehart & Winston, 1960), p. 35.

[6] Quoted in Jeffrey Tulis, "The Two Constitutional Presidencies," in *The Presidency and the Political System*, ed. Michael Nelson (Washington, DC: Congressional Quarterly Press, 1984), p. 68.

[7] Or, as Jon Stewart of *Comedy Central* accurately described it, "If the president is the head of the American body politics, Congress is its gastrointestinal tract." The former may enjoy more dignity and prestige, but the grimy, malodorous excretions of the latter are just as crucial to the health of the American political system. Jon Stewart, Ben Karlin, and David Javerbaum, *America (The Book): A Citizen's Guide to Democracy Inaction* (New York: Warner Books, 2004), p. 57.

[8] Sanders, *Roots of Reform*, p. 395.

affect how they consider laws, certify appointments, conduct investigations, and remove officials from office.

This chapter will review the origins of Congress, the changing fortunes of congressional power, the legislative process, the different cultures and procedures of both the Senate and the House, and their relationship to the wider society.

THE ORIGINS OF TWO LEGISLATIVE CHAMBERS

James Madison put the matter bluntly to the delegates at the Constitutional Convention in Philadelphia in 1787. The problem confronting them was to devise a political formula that would guard against the "inconveniences of democracy" in a manner that was still "consistent with the democratic form of government."[9] The Founders, who believed in sovereignty by the people, also were concerned that democracy would threaten the social order. They perceived their task as one of "preserving the spirit and form of popular government," while avoiding what experience under the Articles of Confederation had taught them was its consequence: that the majority would use their democratic rights to pursue their economic interests through the government— what many Founders condemned as "the leveling spirit."

In order to protect the government against what the Founders perceived as the excesses of democracy, they created the presidency, as we saw in Chapter 6. But they did not stop there. The Founders also sought to check too strong a popular voice in the government by creating a legislature with two separate chambers: a House of Representatives, whose members would be elected by popular vote; and a Senate, whose members would be chosen by the various state legislatures.[10]

It was widely assumed at the convention, political scientist Robert Dahl has written, that a popularly elected House of Representatives with small districts and frequent elections "would be the driving force in the system; that the people's representatives would be turbulent and insistent; that they would represent majorities and would be indifferent to the rights of [elite] minorities; that the people would be the winds driving the ship of state and their representatives would be the sails, swelling with every gust."[11] The Founders also believed that the will of the majority expressed in the House of Representatives needed to be modified and checked by a

---

[9] Quoted in Merrill Jensen, *The Making of the American Constitution* (Malibar, FL: Krieger, 1979), p. 47.

[10] Senators were not popularly elected until the passage of the Seventeenth Amendment to the Constitution in 1912.

[11] Robert Dahl, *Democracy in the United States: Promise and Performance*, 2nd ed. (Chicago: Rand McNally, 1973), p. 151.

Senate.[12] While the House might be filled by commoners, the Senate was to be composed of society's natural aristocracy, its wealthy, educated, cultivated elites.[13] Senators were not to be elected directly but were to be appointed by state legislatures, presumed to be more favorable to mercantile, financial, and business interests than the electorate as a whole. The Founders sought to further ensure the autonomy of senators by permitting them to serve for a term three times longer than that of members of the directly elected House of Representatives. The independence, character, and virtue of senators, the Founders believed, would stand as a bulwark against what they feared would be the irresponsible democratic tendencies of representatives. The Senate, in the words of George Washington, would be "[t]he cooling saucer into which the hot coffee from the cup of the House should be poured."[14]

The most enduring protection against democratic excess that the Founders designed into the Senate was the way seats in that chamber were to be apportioned. Each state, regardless of whether it was large and populous or small and barely inhabited, was entitled to the same two members in the Senate. This deliberate malapportionment, in which voters in small states are more represented within the Senate than voters in large states, violates democratic principles of political equality. The 480,000 people in Wyoming, our least populous state, receive the same two votes in the Senate as the 32 million people who live in California, our most populous state. When the Senate is measured by the one person, one vote standard, political scientist Arend Lijphart found it was the most malapportioned legislative body in the world. Forty percent of all U.S. senators come from the smallest states in terms of population, together comprising just 10 percent of the population; more than 80 percent of all senators come from states that together account for just one-half of all Americans.[15] Not only is unequal representation greater in the Senate, but its effects are more meaningful. In other countries with two separate legislative houses, the chamber not based on population, such as the House of Lords in Britain and the Senate in France and Canada, is always the weaker of the two. By contrast, the U.S. Senate is never less than equal in power to the House of Representatives, and even possesses powers not granted to the House, such as approving presidential appointments and foreign treaties.[16]

---

[12] Jensen, *Making of the American Constitution*, p. 58.

[13] Elaine K. Swift, *The Making of an American Senate: Reconstitutive Change in Congress, 1787–1841* (Ann Arbor: University of Michigan Press, 1996).

[14] Quoted by Newt Gingrich in William F. Connelly, Jr., and John J. Pitney, Jr., "The House Republicans: Lessons for Political Science," in *New Majority or Old Minority: The Impact of Republicans on Congress,* eds. Nicol C. Rae and Colton C. Campbell (Lanham, MD: Rowman & Littlefield, 1999), p. 186.

[15] Arend Lijphart, *Patterns of Democracy: Government Forms and Performance in Thirty-Six Countries* (New Haven, CT: Yale University Press, 1999), p. 208.

[16] Malapportionment and its consequences are examined thoroughly in Frances E. Lee and Bruce I. Oppenheimer, *Sizing Up the Senate: The Unequal Consequences of Equal Representation* (Chicago: University of Chicago Press, 1999), p. 2.

The inequalities between large and small states reflected in the Senate are not innocent.[17] For example, large urban states are disadvantaged compared to smaller rural states. In addition, the fact that minorities are concentrated in the most populous states, such as California and New York, means that they are most disfranchised by the equal number of votes given to both large and small states in the Senate. On the other hand, whites, who comprise the overwhelming majority in racially homogenous small states like Wyoming and North Dakota, are given more weighted votes.[18]

THE HISTORICAL CONGRESS

The Constitution gives the House and the Senate substantial responsibilities. Article I, section 8 enumerates Congress's powers to levy taxes, borrow and spend money, regulate interstate and foreign commerce, declare war, support the armed forces, create courts inferior to the Supreme Court, and, more generally, "make all laws which shall be necessary and proper for carrying into execution the foregoing powers, and all other powers vested by this Constitution in the government of the United States, or any department or officer thereof." In addition, the House of Representatives was given the power to impeach—that is, bring charges against—members of the executive and judiciary branches. The Senate then acts as a trial court for all impeachments, requiring a two-thirds majority of those voting in order to convict.

The House of Representatives reached the height of its powers in the early years of the 20th century, appearing to confirm the Constitutional Convention's conception of the House as the driving force of the government. The House's power lay in its structure, which was highly centralized, with power concentrated in the Speaker, who led the majority party in the House. Joe Cannon, the Speaker of the House from 1903 to 1911, was considered by many to be even more powerful than the president. The Speaker led his party's caucus, which adopted a formal legislative agenda, which was then passed by disciplined party majorities.

The House of Representatives thrived during this period of party government. But the centralization of power in the Speaker and his ability to provide effective leadership to the majority party in the House came at the expense of individual representatives, who were reduced to near impotence. The House of Representatives as an institution may have been powerful, but individual members outside the majority party leadership enjoyed little of it. By 1910,

---

[17] Gary C. Jacobson, *The Politics of Congressional Elections*, 4th ed. (Washington, DC: Congressional Quarterly Press, 1997), p. 11.

[18] On the advantages of small states in the Senate and the benefits whites derive from this at the expense of minorities, see Francis E. Lee and Bruce I. Oppenheimer, *Sizing Up the Senate*, pp. 21–23.

the rank and file of the House rebelled and stripped Cannon of much of his power. Ironically, the big winner from this revolution inside the House of Representatives was the presidency. Party unity imposed by the Speaker, which once brought representatives together, now gave way to the tug of diverse local interests, which pulled them apart. With power now decentralized and the majority party unable to act in a disciplined fashion in support of a common program, it was easier for the president to seize the initiative and exercise legislative authority. Once the era of party government came to an end in the House of Representatives, the presidency assumed legislative leadership.

This shift in the congressional-presidential balance of power first began to unfold during Woodrow Wilson's administration (1913–1921) and accelerated under Franklin Delano Roosevelt's presidency. Elected in 1932 during the Depression, Roosevelt presented a presidential program to address the crisis in his first 100 days. Congress was content to follow the president's lead in responding to the Depression. And when Congress balked at presidential direction, Roosevelt went over its head and appealed directly to the public through press conferences and radio "fireside chats" for support of his New Deal. While Roosevelt had to continue to bargain with Congress to get his legislation passed, it was now clearly the president who initiated policy and set the agenda of government.

During the golden age of capitalism, from 1945 to 1973, Congress played a subordinate role to the presidency. Congress was content to let the president provide leadership and even encroach on congressional powers because it largely agreed with the president's policies. Once Congress left the broad design of policy to the president, its role, according to Samuel Huntington, was "largely . . . reduced to delay and amendment."[19]

But the uneasy consensus on foreign and domestic policy that had existed in the 1950s began to collapse in the 1960s. Racial issues, which had been kept off the domestic agenda, permitting the appearance of a satisfied consensus, exploded in the streets of Birmingham, on the roads of Mississippi, and in the slums of Detroit, Newark, and Los Angeles. At the same time racial turmoil emerged to upset the consensus on domestic policy, college campuses erupted in protest to the war in Vietnam, shattering the consensus on foreign policy. Policy disagreements between the presidency and Congress soon were reflected in institutional combat between the two branches. Congress appropriated funds for domestic programs that President Richard Nixon refused to spend, and Nixon pursued a covert war in Cambodia despite congressional action proscribing it. Moreover, divided government, in which different parties are in control of the presidency and

---

[19] Samuel Huntington, "Congressional Responses to the Twentieth Century," in *The Congress and America's Future*, ed. David B. Truman (Englewood Cliffs, NJ: Prentice-Hall, 1965), p. 23.

one or both houses of Congress, became the norm. When government is divided between the parties congressional leaders have more incentive to pursue agendas independent of the president.

Congress began to reassert itself in the 1970s and reclaim the authority it had ceded to the president. Congress tried to restrict the president's encroachment on Congress's war-making powers through the War Powers Resolution of 1973, match the president's budgetary powers by revamping its own budgetary procedures, challenge claims of presidential prerogatives, increase Congress's resources to equal those available to the president, scrutinize presidential appointments more carefully, and alter the president's legislative proposals. As the policy differences separating the legislative and executive branches of government increased, so did their battles over "turf" and conflict over institutional prerogatives.

The resurgence of Congress reached its peak in 1994, when a majority of Republicans were elected to both the Senate and the House. Republicans had drafted a "Contract with America", a ten-point legislative program that they pledge to enact if elected. The new Republican Speaker of the House, Newt Gingrich, claimed the election was a mandate to enact the Republican agenda, even though polls revealed that a majority of voters had never even heard of it. After a hiatus of 85 years going back to Speaker Joe Cannon, party government had returned to the House of Representatives.

But this moment of party government was brief. President Clinton successfully portrayed the House Republicans and their leadership as extremists willing to hold the government hostage if he did not capitulate to their radical demands. The 1995 government shutdowns in November, and again in December, turned the public against the Republican House leadership and broke the momentum of the Republicans' 1994 election victory. With House Republicans on the defensive, the legislative initiative passed to the president once again.

It would be inaccurate to view conflicts between the president and Congress as a zero-sum game, in which one institution grows in power at the expense of the other. Congress retains formidable power rooted in the Constitution, which requires presidents to obtain the approval of an independent Congress for their programs to succeed. The authority Congress derives from the Constitution makes it more powerful and more capable of independent action than any other legislature in the world. Moreover, as government has grown, so has Congress's power. As more and more legislation is proposed by the president, more and more legislation must be disposed of by Congress. Its ability to say "no," to oppose presidential measures, to amend legislation, to deny presidential appointments, to ignore the president's budget requests, and to challenge the president's management of federal agencies has become more consequential as the agenda and work of government have grown. The decline of Congress is thus not absolute but rather a decline relative to the powers of the presidency, which have grown even more.

CONGRESSIONAL CAREERS

Senators and representatives have desirable jobs. They are treated with respect, they have a chance to influence policy, they meet interesting people, and their work is varied and stimulating. Their salary in 2004 was $158,100. Members of the House and Senate also receive generous pensions (if they last at least five years in office), inexpensive life insurance, tax breaks (if they own two homes), allowances for their offices, almost unlimited mailing privileges, nearly free medical care, free parking, frequent trips abroad at government expense, and a large staff. Congress also provides many services as amenities for its members. The Senate alone has swimming pools, a health club, a barbershop, and a variety of restaurants for use by its members.

But such benefits are available also to high-priced lawyers and corporate managers in the private sector. What being a member of Congress provides that cannot be found in the private sector is the deference accorded to members of this exclusive club. "The most seductive part of it," a congressman from the Midwest acknowledged, "is the deference. My God, its amazing how many people can never seem to be able to do enough for you, here or when you go home. . . . Maybe I could and maybe I couldn't make more money in private business, but I do know this: I'd never have my ego fed half so grandly."[20] Or as former Senator Larry Pressler from South Dakota commented in 1998 regarding his return to private life after 22 years in Congress: "I feel like Cinderella after the ball. Poof! . . . Overnight my staff dropped from more than 100 down to one. My personal assistants disappeared into thin air. . . . Christmas season is an eye opener. The traditional flood of holiday cards has dwindled to about one-fourth of the senatorial level. And speaking of cards, I now hand out business cards. United States Senators don't do business cards. Everyone knows who they are."[21]

While some members of Congress have retired recently, complaining that the job is not as rewarding as it used to be, there is no lack of applicants to replace them. Congress continues to be filled with professional politicians who view their job in Congress as their career. Even those members elected to Congress promising to leave after serving for a certain number of terms find the rewards of office so enticing they want to extend their stay beyond what they said would be their limit. Indeed, political scientist David R. Mayhew argues that most of the behavior of representatives and senators follows from their principal goal of getting reelected. In pursuit of this goal, members of Congress will try to generate favorable publicity that will impress voters back home, respond to interest groups that can supply them with money for their campaigns, avoid controversial issues that might offend voters, and claim

---

[20] *New York Times*, May 30, 1978.

[21] *New York Times*, August 17, 1998.

credit for benefits that they bring back to their district.[22] For example, no member of Congress matches Senator Robert C. Byrd of West Virginia in the amount of federal projects he has diverted to his state and that bear his name in testimony for his efforts. There is the Robert C. Byrd Courthouse in Charleston, the Robert C. Byrd National Aerospace Education Center in Bridgeport, the Robert C. Byrd Locks and Dam at Gallipos Ferry, as well as health clinics, highways, bridges, and academic buildings that also bear the Byrd name and were paid for in part with federal money. Citizens in West Virginia reward Senator Byrd with their votes in return for the federal benefits he brings back to the state.

Political scientist Morris Fiorina found that the electoral connection between voters and Congress is based more on solving problems that constituents have with federal agencies, such as replacing a lost Social Security check, than on taking coherent and consistent positions on political issues. More and more members of Congress, according to Fiorina, prefer "to be reelected as an errand boy than not be reelected at all."[23] One House member told Richard F. Fenno, Jr., who studied what representatives did back in their local districts, "This is a business, and like any other business you have to make time and motion studies" as to what activities are most electorally rewarding.[24] Since the first order of business is to stay in business by getting elected, representatives develop what Fenno called a "home style," calculated to make members identify with voters in their district.

MONEY AND CONGRESSIONAL ELECTIONS

But all of this—developing a home style, getting and keeping your name before the voters, satisfying various constituencies back in your district— costs money . . . lots of money. Congressional candidates have to raise their own money and organize their own campaigns. Their success depends in no small part on how effective they are at these tasks. In order to be a credible candidate, a candidate for the House needs about $600,000, while a candidate for a Senate seat needs $2 million to be taken seriously. As Will Rogers once quipped, "It takes a lot of money to even get beat nowadays."[25] In comparison, when Abraham Lincoln ran for Congress in 1846, he had only one campaign expense—a barrel of cider. Candidates need to raise so much

---

[22] David R. Mayhew, *Congress: The Electoral Connection* (New Haven, CT: Yale University Press, 1979).

[23] Morris Fiorina, *Congress: Keystone of the Washington Establishment* (New Haven, CT: Yale University Press, 1977), pp. 36–37.

[24] Richard F. Fenno, Jr., *Home Style: House Members in Their Districts* (Boston: Little, Brown, 1978).

[25] Rogers is quoted in Sherrod Brown, *Congress from the Inside: Observations from the Majority and the Minority*, 3rd ed. (Kent, OH: Kent State University Press, 2004), p. 199.

money not because they want to, but because they are afraid not to. Campaign fundraising follows the same logic as an arms race: Incumbents and challengers alike try to build up their arsenals and raise more money in order to prevent their opponent from gaining a financial advantage. Fear ratchets up the cost of campaigns to higher and higher levels. Most of these funds are spent for television advertisements in order to enhance name recognition and image rather than discuss substantive issues. "Half the money you spend in a campaign is wasted," admitted one old-time politician. The only problem is "you just don't know which half."[26]

The sheer cost of running for office has many consequences. Congressional candidates are on the circuit continuously asking for money, attending fundraisers, and appealing to lobbyists. It does not matter whether a member of Congress has a safe seat and faces only token opposition, or won by a narrow margin in the last election and can expect another close contest. Either way the member will be out raising money relentlessly. While members from competitive seats are out raising money to hold off capable rivals, members from safe seats are building up war chests in order to discourage opponents.

The need to raise money also gives donors privileged access to members of Congress. The list of congressional donors is very long, and it reflects local as well as national interests. Money often flows into a representative's or senator's campaign coffers from beyond the district or state he or she represents. Interest groups contribute money to Congress members who sit on committees with jurisdiction over issues that affect them. The committee system, in which committees have jurisdiction over specific policy areas, makes it easy for groups to target their contributions to legislators who sit on committees and subcommittees that have jurisdiction over issues of concern to them. Most of these sources of funds are invisible to the average voter; and most buy access to the Congress member on behalf of issues that are of narrow concern to a particular group.

The high cost of running for office affects not only how members spend their time and who they spend it with but who gets elected to Congress. Money follows power. Contributors want a return on their investment. Since incumbents win nine out of ten House races and three out of four Senate races, they receive most of the money contributed to congressional candidates. The gap in campaign contributions between incumbents and challengers is wide and getting wider with each new election. In 1998, the typical incumbent in a contested House election spent 8 times more than the challenger; in 2000 the incumbent spent almost 13 times more. Money is so critical to making a race competitive where an incumbent seeks reelection that political scientists have found a direct relationship between the amount of money challengers raise and their odds of winning. Money permits challengers to escape obscurity, to get known and be recognized by voters. The problem is

---

[26] Brown, *Congress from the Inside*, p. 199.

that so few challengers can raise enough money to become a serious threat.[27] The fund-raising advantage incumbents enjoy explains, in part, why such a large proportion of them win and why most congressional elections are not really competitive.[28]

SAFE SEATS AND TURNOVER

Elections are mechanisms designed to hold Congress accountable to the voters. In 1787, George Washington endorsed the two-year term for members of the House of Representatives, expecting the House would turn over rapidly in membership. Power, he wrote, "is entrusted for certain defined purposes, and for a certain limited period . . . and, whenever it is executed contrary to [the public] interest, or not agreeable to their wishes, their servants can and undoubtedly will be recalled." Washington's expectation has not been borne out. In the 19th century, congressional turnover was very high; in 1870, more than half of the representatives sent to the House were newly elected. By 1900, new members comprised less than one-third; by 1940, less than one-quarter; and by 1988, less than one-tenth. Congress has become a career in which representatives and senators expect to serve long tenures. In 2004, only six incumbents lost in the general election, three of whom were defeated by other incumbents when they were redistricted. Ninety-nine percent of all incumbents were reelected.

Not only do incumbents continue to win, but they continue to win big. The number of marginal seats, where the winner received less than 55 percent of the votes, has declined. Conversely, the number of safe seats, those that are not very competitive, remains high. In 2004, there were only 43 contests for House seats—one-tenth of all races—where the winner polled less than 55 percent of the vote. Fifteen percent of all House members in 2004 faced no major party opposition; almost one-quarter of all House members won with more than 70 percent of the vote, and the average margin of victory to the House was 35 percent. Such figures indicate that there is little meaningful competition for House seats. When elections become mere rituals, turnout declines, voters become cynical, and representatives become less accountable. Senate elections tend to be more competitive and the incumbency advantage less powerful than in the House. Senate incumbents face more experienced, better-financed opponents, and their statewide constituencies are large enough that one party does not dominate them so clearly, as is often true in smaller House districts.

New blood is more likely to arrive in Congress by winning open seats in which the incumbent is not running than they are by defeating a sitting

---

[27] Jacobson, *Politics of Congressional Elections*, pp. 39–42.

[28] Gary Jacobson, *Money in Congressional Elections* (New Haven, CT: Yale University Press, 1980).

member seeking reelection. Incumbency is a powerful electoral asset because incumbents enjoy an enormous financial advantage over their opponents. In addition, incumbents have access to perquisites such as mailing privileges and staff with which to contact and serve voters back home, and they come from districts that have been carefully drawn to include voters already disposed to vote for members of their party.

MEMBERS OF CONGRESS

The ideal representative body mirrors the population as a whole. John Adams, the second president of the United States, once said that the legislature should be "an exact portrait in miniature, of the people at large."[29] No legislature in the world, of course, has the exact demographic profile of the citizens they represent. Nor is perfect symmetry necessary for the interests of the population to be represented. But a disproportionately unrepresentative legislature is likely to leave many members of the population without representatives who even minimally comprehend their life situations and needs, while others who are overrepresented are likely to have their views taken into account as a matter of course.

It is emphatically *not* the case that, just because someone comes from a certain social background, he or she will necessarily promote the interests of that group: former car dealers in Congress will not necessarily promote the interests of car dealers and wealthy members of Congress will not necessarily defend the interests of the rich. For example, Senators Jay Rockefeller and Ted Kennedy come from very wealthy families and are among the leading advocates of social programs for the poor. Similarly, a white member of Congress can do a very good job representing a black-majority district, as Lindy Boggs of New Orleans did for a number of years (1972–1989), and a black member of Congress can do a very good job representing a district where whites significantly outnumber blacks, as Ronald Dellums of Berkeley, California, did for a number of years (1971–1998).

The effects of social background on congressional decision making are more subtle than that. The social background of members of Congress is important because they bring assumptions to their work based on their life experiences. Inasmuch as some life experiences are more likely to be found in Congress than others, members of Congress are more likely to be sensitive to, intuitively aware of, some issues more than others. Consequently, it matters whether the social backgrounds of members of Congress are roughly similar to those of the people they ostensibly represent. It is certainly true that members of Congress, like all of us, are able to appreciate and understand issues that go beyond their own limited experience. But social background

---

[29] Quoted in Robert B. Kuttner, *Everything for Sale* (New York: Knopf, 1996), p. 349.

makes a difference in whether Congress members will have to make an extra effort or will gravitate naturally to the responses and issues they are familiar with based on their life experiences.

It is ironic that Congress, our most democratic institution, is so demographically unrepresentative of the people its members are supposed to represent. Congress does not look like America. Congress contains a much higher proportion of white, male, educated, rich, professional, and business people than the population as a whole. While Congress is less male and less white than it used to be, the average social background of members of Congress still differs strikingly from that of the rest of the population. For example, blacks comprise 12 percent of the electorate. Following the 2004 elections, they occupied 7 percent of the seats in the House and only 1 percent of all Senate seats. Hispanics are 8 percent of the electorate, and they occupied 3 percent of the seats in the House and only 2 percent of all Senate seats. Women make up 52 percent of all eligible voters, and they made up about 14 percent of the seats in the House and held about 16 percent of the seats in the Senate. Such imbalances have policy consequences. Female and minority representatives bring unique perspectives to Congress. Their disproportionate absence means that the concerns of minorities and women are not always pursued as vigorously as they might have been had their numbers in Congress better reflected their numbers at large.[30]

Not only is Congress unrepresentative of the American people in terms of race, ethnicity, and gender, but a great gap exists in terms of class position as well. In 2000, Congress included 100 members with a net worth over $1 million. The vast majority of members of Congress are lawyers, bankers, or businesspeople. Very few people from working-class occupations are ever seated. Only when electoral realignments occur, when new groups break through the party system, has the virtual monopoly that upper-class people have on seats in Congress been disrupted. Only during such turbulent periods have legislators from the lower class replaced the wealthy in winning congressional seats.[31]

THE LEGISLATIVE PROCESS

While the social background of Congress members influences what they do, more critical in our view for the shaping of legislation are the ways in which Congress is organized and the formal and informal rules that govern its decision making. Seemingly archaic and technical procedural rules, such as the

---

[30] On the difference women make in Congress, see Michele L. Swers, *The Difference Women Make: The Policy Impact in Congress* (Chicago: University of Chicago Press, 2002).

[31] Lester G. Seligman and Michael R. King, "Political Realignments and Recruitment to the U.S. Congress, 1870–1970," in *Realignment in American Politics: Toward a Theory,* eds. Bruce A. Campbell and Richard J. Trilling (Austin: University of Texas Press, 1980), pp. 157–75.

UPI/Roger L. Wollenberg/Landov

Senate Majority Leader Bill Frist, House Speaker Dennis Hastert, and Vice President Richard Cheney.

terms under which the Senate and House consider a bill, can determine the fate of legislation. Representative John Dingell of Michigan reportedly said, "If you let me write the procedure and I let you write the substance, I'll [beat] you every time."[32]

Although each member of Congress has only one vote, some members are more powerful than others. Legislators have different amounts of power depending on which committee they sit on, whether they are a committee or subcommittee chair, whether they are a member of the majority party, and whether they are a party leader. The procedures and rules of the House and the Senate determine the powers invested in these positions and are never neutral. Some groups win and some groups lose depending on how the rules distribute power within Congress.

---

[32] Quoted in C. Lawrence Evans and Walter J. Oleszek, "Congressional Tsunami? The Politics of Congressional Reform," in *Congress Reconsidered*, 6th ed., ed. Lawrence C. Dodd and Bruce I. Oppenheimer (Washington, DC Congressional Quarterly Press, 1997), p. 193.

The procedures of Congress, or what we might call the rules of the game, are constantly in flux as groups seek to adjust them in order to advance their interests. For example, liberals eager to curb the power of conservative committee chairs who thwarted their policy goals precipitated a wave of internal reforms to Congress in the 1970s. Similarly, the first day of business when Republicans became the majority in the House in 1995 was devoted to changing the rules that had been set by the Democrats.[33] Political struggle over the rules occurs, introducing change into the way Congress is organized and operates, because this affects legislative outcomes. Congress is always reforming itself, as legislators seek to change the process by which legislation is made in order to change the results.

The legislative process begins with the submission of a bill to both the House and the Senate. Most bills are introduced without any expectation of success. More than 6,000 pieces of legislation are introduced into Congress each year, with fewer than 400 actually having a chance of passage. Only members of the Senate and the House may submit bills. When legislators introduce a bill in Congress, they often are acting on behalf of constituents, interest groups, a federal agency, the president, or even their own personal convictions.

The bills that have the greatest chance of success and that generally define the agenda of Congress are those submitted by legislators on behalf of the president. The Office of Management and Budget (OMB), together with the congressional liaison staff in the Executive Office, coordinates the executive's legislative efforts. OMB acts as a clearinghouse, reviewing legislative requests from federal agencies and departments to ensure they conform to the president's program, while the legislative affairs officers in the White House coordinate presidential lobbying of Congress.

Once a bill is introduced in the House and the Senate, it is referred to a committee for consideration. Committee referrals made by the House Speaker and Senate Majority Leader are generally routine. Farm bills go to the House Agriculture Committee and the Senate Agriculture Committee, tax bills go to the House Ways and Means Committee and the Senate Finance Committee, and so on.[34] But as more issues cut across existing committee lines, Senate and House leaders have more discretion in referring bills to committee. This could affect the bill's chances of success because a legislative proposal might receive a warmer reception in one committee than it does in another.

Congress at work, Woodrow Wilson once said, is Congress in committees. Committees are legislative gatekeepers, "little legislatures," that perform the

---

[33] Even interior decorating within the Capital changed. The painting *Lawrence 1912: The Great Strike* by Ralph Fasanella, a self-taught painter who was also a union organizer, which had been displayed in the hearing room of the House Subcommittee of Labor, Health and Human Services, was ordered removed by the new Republican majority in 1994.

[34] Congressional Quarterly, *How Congress Works*, 1st ed. (Washington, DC: Congressional Quarterly Press, 1998), p. 61.

bulk of the legislative work in Congress. They collect information through hearings and investigations, they draft legislation in what are called markup sessions, and they report legislation to the floor of their respective chambers.[35] More than 90 percent of all bills submitted to Congress do not make it out of committee. While it is uncommon for the House or the Senate to review legislation that has not been reported to them from one of their committees, it is less unusual than in the past.

Once a bill leaves the committee, it is placed on the House and Senate calendars. In the House, the Rules Committee determines which bills will come to the House floor, when they will be scheduled, and under what conditions they will be debated. Such rules can put obstacles or ease a bill's path to passage. Consequently, in order to permit the majority party to control the flow of legislation on the floor of the House, the ratio of members from the majority party to those from the minority is much greater on the Rules committee than on any other.

The rules under which the House considered legislation began to change in the 1970s. Previously, legislation often came to the House floor under open rules from the Rules Committee, with no restrictions on germane amendments. But as the House became more partisan and divided in the 1980s and 1990s, the Democrats in the majority on the Rules Committee attached more restrictive rules to more legislation. Restrictive rules limited the time for debate and the amendments that could be offered on the floor of the House. House Republicans in the minority complained that such restrictive rules stifled debate and prevented them from amending legislation that came out of Democratic-controlled committees. But when Republicans became the majority in 1994, they used the Rules Committee in the same partisan manner the Democrats had previously to prevent the opposing party from delaying and amending the majority party's program on the House floor. In 2003, 76 percent of the bills coming out of the Rules Committee prohibited amendments. Under the Republicans, a higher proportion of bills now come out of the Rules Committee with the same restrictive rules they had complained about so vehemently when they were in the minority.

The Senate has no equivalent committee to schedule and set the terms of debate on the Senate floor. Scheduling is largely the work of the Senate majority leader, but he or she requires unanimous consent to bring a bill up for Senate consideration. Individual senators who want to prevent passage of a bill can filibuster—that is, hold the Senate floor and not give it up until the offending bill is removed from consideration. Nor does the Senate limit and set the terms of debate on the Senate floor, as the Rules Committee does for legislation considered by the House. The rules of the Senate are much more freewheeling than those for the House.

---

[35] Christopher J. Deering and Steven S. Smith, *Committees in Congress,* 3rd ed. (Washington, DC: Congressional Quarterly Press, 1997), pp. 11–20.

Even when the versions of a bill introduced in both the Senate and the House are the same, they may look very different after they come out of the committee process in both chambers. House and Senate committees mark up a bill without reference to each other, and amendments to it on the floor of the House and the Senate proceed independently. The result is that the version of the bill passed by the House may not look the same as the one passed by the Senate. The president can sign only bills that have been passed in identical form by both houses of Congress. Differences between the House and Senate versions of the bill are resolved in conference committees. Conference committees, composed of House and Senate members selected by the Speaker and the Senate Majority Leader, respectively, meet to reconcile differences in the versions of a bill passed by the House and the Senate. For example, following the September 11, 2001 terrorist attacks, the House passed a bill that would have the federal government regulate private security companies responsible for airport security, while the Senate passed a bill that would have the federal government, not private companies, perform airport security. The Senate was in a very strong position to prevail at conference because it had passed its bill unanimously and continued security violations at airports in the wake of the September 11 terrorist attacks put added pressure on House Republican negotiators. When the Conference report clearly reflected the Senate's preference for a complete federal takeover of airport security, Representative Dan Young, who led House members in negotiations, defended it to his colleagues, claiming, "I think I got the best deal I could."[36]

If conference can resolve the differences between the House and Senate versions of the bill, the new, reconciled version of the legislation is then sent back to the House and the Senate to be voted up or down, without amendment. If both houses vote to accept the conference report—that is, to accept identical versions of the bill—the final bill is then sent to the president for signature. The bill becomes law when the president signs it, or it becomes law without the president's signature ten days after the president receives it, provided Congress is still in session. The president may also veto the bill, but that veto can be overridden by two-thirds votes in both the House and the Senate.

The legislative process just discussed is noteworthy for the number of choke points, or opportunities to block legislation, it contains. "It is very easy to defeat a bill in Congress," President John F. Kennedy once observed. "It is much more difficult to pass one."[37] Following passage of a campaign finance reform bill in the Senate in 2001, Senator John McCain of Arizona, one of its sponsors, warned of the many dangers still ahead: "I think this is a victory, but I want to emphasize, I have no illusions about the House [of Representatives], about a conference, about the White House. We've just

---

[36] *New York Times*, November 16, 2001.

[37] Quoted in Congressional Quarterly, *How Congress Works*, p. 51.

taken the first step, and as we enjoy this moment, tomorrow we'd better fully understand that we've got a long way to go."[38] (McCain was prophetic as the campaign finance reform bill passed in the Senate later died in the House. Another, different campaign finance reform bill that successfully overcame procedural roadblocks was passed a year later in 2002.)

A bill can be waylaid at the subcommittee and committee levels; it may never be scheduled for consideration on the floor of the Senate or the House; it may fail to pass either the Senate or the House; conference may not be able to reconcile differences between Senate and House versions of the bill; the Senate or House may find the conference bill objectionable; the president may veto the legislation; and the Senate and House may be unable to marshal the two-thirds majority necessary to overturn a presidential veto. And all of these potential veto points must be successfully negotiated within the two-year life span of a single Congress or else the measure has to be reintroduced and the whole procedure repeated again when a new Congress is seated.

A legislative process loaded with so many points where new legislative proposals can be stopped is not politically neutral but serves to protect the status quo. The legislative process puts innumerable roadblocks in the way of those who seek to use the government to bring about change. Groups that are systematically disadvantaged and depend on political power and public policy to offset their lack of power in the marketplace often find themselves stymied by a legislative process that creates so many opportunities for blockage and defeat. They must build winning coalitions within both the House and the Senate at the subcommittee level, at the committee level, on the floor of each chamber, at conference, and then within the executive branch. Opponents, on the other hand, need to win only once at any level to defeat the bill. A legislative process that creates so many opportunities for obstruction, that promotes failure rather than success, makes it difficult for the disadvantaged to enlist public power against corporate private power.

The legislative process is so daunting that Congress deviates from it quite often to avoid its tendency toward gridlock. According to congressional scholar Barbara Sinclair, unorthodox lawmaking has become routine as Congress increasingly circumvents its own procedures. Committees are bypassed more frequently; bills are now more likely to be reworked after they emerge from committee; the content of legislation is more likely to be worked out in summits among executive and legislative leaders; and omnibus legislation, in which disparate bills are offered together in one legislative package, is now more common. Sinclair argues that it is no longer accurate to speak of one legislative process; rather, there are now many.[39] The legislative process has become a maze in which bills may now take

---

[38] McCain is quoted in Steven Weiss, "Campaign Finance Reform's Rocky Road," *Capital Eye*, Vol. VIII (Spring 2001), p. 1.

[39] Barbara Sinclair, *Unorthodox Lawmaking: New Legislative Processes in the U.S. Congress* (Washington, DC: Congressional Quarterly Press, 1997), p. 7.

many different paths through Congress on the way to enactment. The growth of unorthodox lawmaking has mitigated to some extent the tendency toward blockage and gridlock in Congress. But the legislative process as a whole still remains a challenging obstacle course for those who try to run it.

Next we examine the legislative process in more detail as it operates within the separate chambers of the Senate and the House of Representatives.

THE SENATE

In 1995, Republicans in the House of Representatives acted swiftly to pass the ten points in their "Contract with America." But the enthusiasm and kinetic energy of the House collided with the deliberative, obstructionist ways of the Senate. Even though Republicans took control of the Senate for the first time in eight years in 1994, the less centralized, more individualistic nature of the Senate prevented Republicans in that chamber from capitalizing on their new majority status as effectively as Republicans in the House. When one freshman Republican senator was asked what it was like to be part of the revolution in Washington associated with the 1994 class of new Republican legislators, he answered: "I don't know. I'm in the Senate!"[40]

The Republican victory in 1994 did not mean the same thing in the Senate as it did in the House because dramatic electoral shifts are moderated in the Senate by the fact that only one-third of its seats are contested each election. While the entire House must stand for election every two years and is thus exposed as a body to electoral swings, two-thirds of the Senate is not up for reelection and is insulated from hostile voters. The six-year terms for senators are staggered so that only one-third of all senators face election every two years. Electoral forces thus wind their way through the Senate more slowly than they do the House. In addition, the fact that senators represent large, diverse constituencies moderates their politics. Senators have to reach out and satisfy broader electorates, which tend to push them more to the political center than House members. The unique political and institutional characteristics of the Senate contributed to the irony that it was the Republican-controlled Senate, not a Democratic president, that stopped the "Contract with America" dead in its tracks.[41]

The sense of frustration the Republican majority in the House had with the Republican majority in the Senate was aggravated when President Bush took office in 2001 because now the possibilities were so tantalizing. For example, the House insisted on a bill to allow drilling for oil in Alaska,

---

[40] Nicol C. Rae, *Conservative Reformers: The Republican Freshmen and the Lessons of the 104th Congress* (New York: Sharpe, 1998), p. 131.

[41] Norman J. Ornstein, Robert L. Peabody, and David W. Rohde, "The U.S. Senate: Toward the Twenty-First Century," in *Congress Reconsidered*, 6th ed., eds. Lawrence C. Dodd and Bruce I. Oppenheimer (Washington, DC: Congressional Quarterly Press, 1997), pp. 1–2.

which the Senate blocked. The House had to settle for a lower tax cut than it preferred in order to get Senate approval in 2002. And in 2003, the House passed an energy bill that never cleared the Senate. "We expedite, they obstruct," a top House Republican aide complained.[42]

With only 100 members—compared to the House, which has 435—the Senate is a more intimate chamber, providing more latitude for action by individual members. In the past, the Senate's intimacy caused it to resemble a private, exclusive men's club where an elaborate set of formal and informal rules regulated the behavior of club members. In December 1956, newly elected Joseph Clark of Pennsylvania had lunch with an old friend, Senator Hubert Humphrey. Clark reports that he said to Humphrey, "Tell me how to behave when I get to the Senate." "He did—for an hour and a half. I left the luncheon I hope a wiser man, as well briefed as a neophyte seeking admission to a new order can be. In essence he said, 'Keep your mouth shut and your eyes open. It's a friendly, courteous place. You will have no trouble getting along. . . . You will clash on the filibuster rule with Dick Russell and the Southerners as soon as you take the oath of office. Don't let your ideology embitter your personal relationships. It won't if you behave with maturity . . . And above all keep your mouth shut for awhile.' "[43]

Humphrey advised Clark to abide by the Senate's unwritten rules: Members should work at their legislative tasks, becoming workhorses, not show horses; they should specialize in matters connected to their committee assignment and of direct interest to their state; they should be courteous to other senators and avoid personal conflicts; they should help colleagues when possible and keep bargains; and they should expect to serve a period of apprenticeship, during which they learn the Senate's customs.[44] Senators were expected to defer to senior members, be restrained in their use of power so as not to obstruct the work of the Senate, and be loyal to the institution. The Senate was "like a small town," according to accounts of those who served in it in the 1950s. Power in the town was distributed unequally, in that it was reserved for committee chairs with seniority. The committee chair set the committee's agenda, called committee meetings, appointed subcommittee chairs, and controlled the committee staff. Senators, who were all equal according to the Constitution, accepted this inequality because they expected to accumulate seniority and become a committee chair themselves someday. In the meantime, they were supposed to bide their time, concentrate on their own business, take pride in their institution, and be courteous to their colleagues.

Today senators are more rude and less familiar with each other, more equal in power and less restrained in using it, more individualistic and less willing to cooperate, more willing to poach on each other's business and less

---

[42] *New York Times*, May 12, 2003.

[43] Joseph Clark, *Congress: The Sapless Branch* (New York: Harper & Row, 1964), p. 2.

[44] Donald R. Mathews, *U.S. Senators and Their World* (New York: Random House, 1960).

willing to work hard at their own, and more interested in drawing attention to themselves than in the past. The customs and norms that governed behavior within the chamber have changed dramatically in the last 40 years.

The apprenticeship norm was one of the first Senate customs to go. According to three congressional scholars, "[N]ot only do junior members not want or feel the need for an apprenticeship, but also the senior members do not expect them to do so."[45] A mark of the decline of the apprenticeship norm is that freshmen are now more likely than in the past to sponsor amendments to legislation on the floor of the Senate.[46]

Another Senate norm that has disappeared is courtesy. As ideological differences among senators have increased, so has the level of incivility among them. Senator Joseph Biden of Delaware complained in 1982, "There's much less civility than when I got here 10 years ago. . . . Ten years ago you didn't have people calling each other [expletive deleted] and vowing to get each other."[47] Some senators have cited the decline of comity and civility as their reason for retiring from the Senate. The specialization norm is also a relic of the past. It is now standard behavior for senators to venture far from their committee's jurisdiction "to offer large numbers of amendments in a wide variety of issue areas." Senators are no longer reluctant to sponsor amendments to measures from committees on which they do not serve.[48] Even the norm of dedicating themselves to legislative work has receded. While senators in the past attended to tedious and politically unrewarding legislative tasks, today they leave that to their staff. Now senators are busy being show horses—running for president, attending fund-raisers, appearing on television—not workhorses concentrating on legislation.

Finally, the reciprocity norm is also in eclipse. The Senate permits unlimited debate, allowing members to hold the Senate floor and tie up the Senate's business with filibusters. It was previously understood that individual senators would restrain themselves and not obstruct the work of the Senate with filibusters except when important principles were at stake. But filibusters are now more common. More than one-third of all major legislation encounters some form of extended debate–related problem in the Senate today. And instead of filibustering only on issues involving matters of principle, senators now do it on relatively mundane concerns.[49] Filibusters are

---

[45] Norman J. Ornstein, Robert L. Peabody, and David Rohde, "The Changing Senate: From the 1950s to the 1970s," in *Congress Reconsidered*, eds. Lawrence C. Dodd and Bruce I. Oppenheimer (New York: Praeger, 1977), p. 8.

[46] Barbara Sinclair, *The Transformation of the U.S. Senate* (Baltimore: Johns Hopkins University Press, 1989), p. 83.

[47] Quoted in Alan Ehrenhalt, "The Senate of the '80s, Team Spirit Has Given Way to Rule by Individuals," *Congressional Quarterly Weekly Report* (September 4, 1982): 2176.

[48] Sinclair, *Transformation of the U.S. Senate*, p. 89.

[49] Barbara Sinclair, "The New World of U.S. Senators," in *Congress Reconsidered* 7th ed., eds. Lawrence C. Dodd and Bruce I. Oppenheimer (Washington, DC: Congressional Quarterly Press, 2001), pp.1–21.

now so common that the bar for passing legislation in the Senate has been raised in practice to 60 votes, the number needed to bring cloture, to end debate, as opposed to the simple majority the Constitution requires to pass a bill. This is not immaterial. Bills that could get a majority of votes and would have passed the Senate cannot get 60 votes to invoke cloture and are thus defeated. For example, campaign finance reform was defeated twice by filibusters in the Senate, first in 1998 and then again in 1999. Even though supporters had a majority of votes to pass these bills, they could not muster the supermajority of three-fifths required to stop a filibuster by the bill's opponents and bring campaign finance reform to the floor of the Senate for a vote.

More than Senate customs have changed. First, senators are spread thinner than in the past, serving on more committees and subcommittees. One result is that their staff, who are not elected and on whom they rely, have become increasingly important. It also forces senators to become generalists, not specialists.[50] Although senators are unable to meet the obligations involved in all their committee assignments, they are reluctant to reduce them. The more committees senators sit on, the more opportunities they have to pursue issues and get their fingers into more pies.

Finally, central leadership within the Senate remains weak. The vice president is the official president of the Senate, but its real head is the majority leader, selected by the majority party in the Senate. The majority leader's power is primarily procedural, such as scheduling the Senate's business. According to former Senator Alan Cranston of California, "A lot of leadership is just housekeeping now. Occasionally you have an opportunity to provide leadership but not that often. The weapons to keep people in line just aren't there."[51] With weak central leadership and the decline of committee chairs, the Senate is a more egalitarian institution than it used to be, with power distributed more evenly among senators than in the past. This has heightened the sense of individualism and independence among senators. They now pursue their own agendas, vote, propose amendments to bills on the floor of the Senate, and filibuster according to their own inclinations.

The result of these changes, Barbara Sinclair offers, is that the Senate has become more adept at promoting issues and articulating demands. The more even distribution of resources among senators, including committee assignments and staff, as well as the decline of Senate norms that once inhibited certain activities, has empowered 100 senators to promote their own agendas. More issues are pushed than in the past. But Sinclair argues that the Senate as an institution loses when each senator promotes a wide range of issues or threatens to filibuster over routine matters. The Senate becomes more undisciplined and inefficient.[52] According to journalist Alan Ehrenhalt, "The more individuals have to be personally satisfied for a bill to be enacted,

---

[50] Deering and Smith, *Committees in Congress*, pp. 80, 154.

[51] Ehrenhalt, "The Senate of the '80s," p. 2179.

[52] Sinclair, *Transformation of the U.S. Senate*, p. 214.

the more likely it is that there will be none."[53] Where it is every senator for himself or herself, it is difficult to legislate, to get things done. As one Republican senator lamented in frustration at the undisciplined, individualistic, inefficient ways of his own institution: "The Democrats are the opposition, but the Senate is the enemy."[54]

THE HOUSE OF REPRESENTATIVES

While the Senate has become less hierarchical, the House has become more so. A series of internal reforms initiated by House Democrats in the 1970s vested power in party leaders within the House of Representatives. The Speaker of the House; the House majority leader, who assists the Speaker in setting strategy; and the majority whip, who lines up votes among the party's rank and file, were empowered to promote goals supported by the Democratic House caucus.[55] The shift in power to the party leadership that began under the Democrats accelerated when Republicans became the majority in 1994 for the first time in 40 years. Both Democrats and Republicans in the House were comfortable with ceding power to their party leaders. Rank and file members believed this would help move legislation that the majority wanted through the House more efficiently.

Party leadership has replaced committee leadership as the locus of power within the House. Prior to the 1970 reforms, committee chairs held power in the House, just as they did in the Senate. Chairs were petty tyrants who ruled over their committees, independent of the party leadership and even the majority sentiment of their own party members. In 1953, George Galloway provided a neat summary of the powers committee chairs wielded:

> Just as the standing committees control legislative action, so the chairmen are masters of their committee. . . . They arrange the agenda of the committees, appoint the subcommittees, and refer bills to them. They decide what pending measures shall be considered and when, call committee meetings, and decide whether or not to hold hearings and when. They approve the lists of scheduled witnesses and authorize staff studies, and preside at committee meetings. They handle reported bills on the floor and participate as principal managers in conference committees. They are in a position to expedite measures they favor and to retard or pigeonhole those they dislike.[56]

Committee members were in thrall to committee chairs, who determined the fate of legislation within their committee's jurisdiction.

---

[53] Ehrenhalt, "The Senate of the '80s," p. 2175.

[54] Quoted in Evans and Oleszek, *Congress Under Fire*, p. 178.

[55] David W. Rohde, *Parties and Leaders in the Postreform House* (Chicago: University of Chicago Press, 1991).

[56] Quoted in Deering and Smith, *Committees in Congress*, p. 32.

Committee chairs were selected by the majority party in Congress on the basis of seniority. Seniority was perceived as a fair, apolitical way to distribute influence.[57] But all rules, even those like seniority, that are designed to be neutral create winners and losers. An unintended consequence of the seniority rule was to bestow power on southern Democrats within Congress. Southern Democrats were able to build up more seniority in Congress than other members of their party because they came from uncompetitive districts where they faced token Republican opposition, if any at all. Consequently, southern Democrats came to dominate the committee chairs and the most important committees in Congress.

As chairs, however, southern Democrats used their power to block liberal legislation that northern Democrats supported. In addition, these Dixiecrats often crossed party lines to vote with Republicans. Southern Democrats and conservative Republicans formed "the conservative coalition," which held the balance of power in Congress in the postwar period.[58] By the 1960s, the conservative coalition "had become a regular feature of congressional voting and a powerful obstacle to liberal and social legislation," according to political scientist Alan I. Abramowitz.[59] The conservative coalition appeared frequently in congressional voting and often enjoyed success when it did so, thwarting the policy goals of liberal Democrats in Congress.[60]

Liberal Democrats in Congress were irate over the apostasy of their own party's southern congressional delegation. Northern Democrats were increasingly resentful that their numbers were responsible for making their party the majority in the House—and thus able to select the committee chairs—but that southern Democrats dominated these posts through seniority. To add insult to injury, southern Democrats then used their positions to block civil rights, labor, and welfare state legislation that northern Democrats supported. Northern Democrats felt they had done all the hard work of planting the crops, only to see them harvested and consumed by southern Democrats.

---

[57] Although not as powerful as it once was, seniority is still a prevailing norm within Congress. A member's rank on committee is still largely determined by seniority, office selection for members of Congress is done by seniority, selection to serve on Conference Committees is often determined by seniority, and leadership of state delegations within each party is often based on seniority. Interestingly, no state legislature or, for that matter, any other legislative body in the world is as beholden to the seniority norm as the two houses of Congress.

[58] Initially, southern Democrats voted with Republicans only on civil rights and labor issues, but the range of issues on which the conservative coalition appeared expanded in the 1950s and 1960s to include tax, welfare state, and economic policy—bedrock issues for American liberalism. See Ira Katznelson, Kim Geiger, and Daniel Kryder, "Limiting Liberalism: The Southern Veto in Congress," *Political Science Quarterly* 108, no. 2 (Summer 1993): 283–305.

[59] Alan I. Abramowitz, "Is the Revolt Fading: A Note on Party Loyalty Among Southern Congressmen," *Journal of Politics* 42 (May 1980): 568–72.

[60] Alan Draper, "Be Careful What You Wish For . . . : American Liberals and the South," *Southern Studies* 4 (Winter 1993): 309–25.

Consequently, nonsouthern Democrats sponsored a series of internal reforms that changed the procedures and organization of the House. New rules and procedures, it was hoped, would bring different legislative results. Democratic reformers proceeded to reduce the power of committee chairs and make them more responsive to the Democratic House caucus at the same time they augmented the power of the party leadership.

While liberal Democratic reformers were trying to change policy results by tinkering with rules and procedures, removing the conservative veto that southern Democrats exercised as committee chairs, electoral forces were also making themselves felt. The Civil Rights movement precipitated an electoral realignment in the South, shifting its partisan sympathies from Democratic to Republican. In 1960, before the great civil rights struggles of that decade, the southern delegation in the House included only six Republicans from 106 congressional districts in the South. Since then, Republicans have become so competitive in southern congressional elections that they now comprise a majority of the southern House and Senate delegations. As southern Democrats lost seats to their Republican opponents, their proportion within the Democratic delegation in the House declined. In the 108th Congress (2003–2004), southerners comprised a little more than 25 percent of the Democratic delegation in the House compared to 46 percent in the 83rd Congress (1953–1954) (see Figure 7-1). Not only are there now fewer southern Democrats, but those that remain are more liberal and more likely to vote with their party than were their conservative Dixiecrat forebears.[61] Southern Democrats have become national Democrats.

The decline and nationalization of the southern Democratic congressional delegation spelled the end of the conservative coalition in Congress.[62] But the South continued to haunt American liberalism, even as the Dixiecrat influence in Congress faded away. Just as party realignment turned southern Democrats into national Democrats, it recreated the spirit of the old conservative Dixiecrats in a newly revived southern Republican Party. In 1975, southerners comprised 19 percent of the Republican delegation in the House. Thirty years later, southerners comprised about one-third of all House Republicans. This increase in the proportion of southerners within the Republican congressional party has moved it further to the right. Political scientist Charles S. Bullock III found that southern Republicans "form an almost monolithic bloc" across a wide range of issues in Congress and score higher on conservative tests of ideological purity than nonsouthern

---

[61] For party unity scores of southern Democrats, see Rohde, *Parties and Leaders in the Postreform House*, pp. 54–56. For the increasing liberalism of southern legislators, see Draper, "Be Careful What You Wish For . . . ," pp. 312–13.

[62] Norman J. Ornstein, Thomas E. Mann, and Michael J. Malbin, *Vital Statistics on Congress, 1993–1994* (Washington, DC: American Enterprise Institute, 1994), p. 203, Table 8.5. See also Alan Ehrenhalt, "The Changing South Perils Conservative Coalition," *Congressional Quarterly Weekly Report* (August 1, 1987): 1699.

■ **FIGURE 7-1**

DEMOCRATS' DECLINE IN SOUTH

Proportion of seats held by Democrats in 11 Southern states

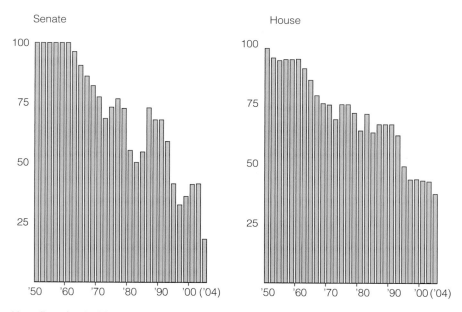

Note: Data for the House in 2004 do not reflect two seats to be decided by runoffs in December.

SOURCE: The *New York Times*, November 16, 2004. Data from Earl Black and Merle Black, *The Rise of Southern Republicans* (Harvard University Press, 2002), updated by Earl Black.

Republican legislators do.[63] Finally, the 1994 election thrust the southern wing of House Republicans into leadership, with the election of Newt Gingrich as Speaker.[64]

The least partisan and least ideological group of legislators, southern Democrats, are being replaced by the most partisan and most ideological

---

[63] Charles S. Bullock III, "Congressional Roll Call Voting in the Two-Party South," *Social Science Quarterly* 66 (December 1995): 803. For a similar analysis of the Senate, see Christopher J. Bailey, *The Republican Party in the Senate* (New York: Manchester University Press, 1988), p. 63.

[64] The Republican victory in the 1994 election thrust the South into leadership within Congress. Newt Gingrich (Georgia), the Speaker; Richard Armey (Texas), the Majority Leader; and Tom DeLay (Texas), the Majority Whip, were all southerners, as were the chairs of the most exclusive and important committees in the House of Representatives: Thomas Bliley (Virginia) of Commerce, William Archer (Texas) of Ways and Means, and Robert Livingston (Louisiana) of Appropriations.

group of legislators, southern Republicans. This has helped produce ideo-logically polarized parties in Congress. Members who could be considered moderates comprised 32 percent of the 92nd Congress (1971–1973), but their numbers declined to just 11 percent by the 105th Congress (1997–1999).[65] "The incredible shrinking middle," as one Senator referred to the decline of mod-erates in Congress,[66] has been due to the decline and nationalization of southern Democrats and the decline of northern Republicans within the GOP. The northern liberal wing of the Democratic Party has acted as a pole of attraction, pulling southern Democrats in the House to the left; at the same time, the southern conservative wing of the Republican Party has acted as a pole of attraction, pulling the rest of the GOP to the right. For example, Democratic House Minority Leader Nancy Pelosi has a 100 percent voting record according to the liberal Americans for Democratic Action (ADA), while her opponent across the aisle, House Majority Leader Tom DeLay, has a zero rating from the ADA. The political differences *within* the parties have declined, while the political differences *separating* the parties in Congress have grown. Parties within the House have become more cohesive and more polarized.

As these ideological differences became clearer, the impact of party on congressional voting increased. Partisan voting, in which a majority of Democrats vote against a majority of Republicans, is now more evident than in the past, as is the degree of party discipline.[67] The increasing parti-sanship in the House contributes to the public's lack of respect for Congress and its sense that Congress is out of touch. Citizens are frustrated with Congress because ideology and partisanship are not as intense among vot-ers as they are among members of Congress.

A byproduct of increasing partisan identification and conflict has been greater centralization of power in the House. When members of the major-ity party agree on policy, strengthening party leaders increases the chances that the majority's policy goals will prevail.[68] House party leaders are strong because party members want them to be strong. Centralizing power, especially increasing the power of the Speaker's office, helps prevent defec-tions from the party program and permits the majority to focus on its agenda, as opposed to seeing it dissipated by the parochial tug of commit-tees, interest groups, and constituents. Centralizing power also helps publi-cize the majority's agenda by giving the media a handful of party leaders to cover, as opposed to a larger group of committee and subcommittee chairs.

---

[65] Sarah A. Binder, *Stalemate: Causes and Consequences of Legislative Gridlock* (Washington, DC: Brookings Institution, 2003), p. 65.

[66] Senator John Breaux is quoted in Binder, *Stalemate*, p. 69.

[67] Rohde, *Parties and Leaders in the Postreform House.*

[68] Ibid., p. 172.

When the majority can speak through one voice, the Speaker's, it can better focus public attention and debate around its priorities.[69]

If substantial policy divisions reemerge *within* the parties, the willingness of members to cede power and defer to the party leadership will diminish. But with the decline of moderate northeastern Republicans as the left in their party and the decline of southern Democrats as the right in their party, both congressional parties are drifting further apart and becoming more ideologically cohesive internally. So long as electoral forces continue to increase the divide between the parties and reduce the conflict within them, the impact of parties and centralization will continue to be felt within the House.

CONGRESS, THE BUREAUCRACY, AND INTEREST GROUPS

When we considered the presidency, we observed that the president manages the federal bureaucracy but that Congress creates it. Each new federal agency originates with an act of Congress, which describes what the agency is supposed to do and provides the funding to do it. Congress is usually quite vague in its legislative instructions for agencies because it cannot anticipate all the contingencies an agency might encounter and because Congress hopes to avoid criticism and controversy by being too specific. As a result, agencies have a great deal of discretion in interpreting the mandate they receive from Congress. To ensure that federal agencies interpret and implement the law as Congress intended, Congress engages in *oversight* of the bureaucracy.

As government has grown, Congress has come to spend more time on oversight. In addition, oversight has grown as a result of the frequency of divided government. Congress monitors the bureaucracy more carefully to see that the laws are executed to reflect Congress's intent when Congress and the president come from different parties. Oversight is performed by congressional subcommittees and committees, which review the activities of agencies under their jurisdiction. They hold hearings at which members of Congress remind agency heads that Congress is the boss, that they get their appropriations from Congress, and that Congress expects deference from them.

Sometimes oversight becomes a form of subtle pressure to influence agency policy. For example, Republicans in Congress during the Clinton years were upset with what they considered the pro-union tilt of the National Labor Relations Board under its Chair, William B. Gould. Consequently, they held hearings at which members of Congress criticized and complained about the Board's practices and decisions. Employers critical of the Board were invited to testify much more frequently than union representatives who

---

[69] For the benefits of centralization, see Evans and Oleszek, *Congress Under Fire*, pp. 83–91.

defended it. As part of its oversight function, members of Congress also reviewed the Board's records. They were especially interested in Gould's activities, suspiciously examining his travel and correspondence, even going so far as to review his attendance at baseball games. Two Representatives wrote Gould: "In the documentation you provided regarding your travel to San Francisco, there is a copy of your August 9, 1996 letter to 'Dusty' in which you state, 'Many thanks for the seats. . . . ' Please identify Dusty by gender, position, and relationship to the San Francisco Giants, if any." Aware of Congress's power, Gould replied sarcastically: "Dusty Baker is a male. He is the manager of the San Francisco Giants, and in that connection, his relationship to the Giants is a prominent and important one."[70]

Just as Congress oversees federal agencies, its own activities are scrutinized carefully by a small army of lobbyists who seek to influence legislation. Lobbying has increased enormously as the reach of government has grown. In 1996, there were an estimated 80,000 people employed in the lobbying industry, working for 11,600 organizations whose combined annual operating costs were in the neighborhood of $12 billion.[71] In 1998, there were 18,590 lobbyists registered in Washington—38 lobbyists for each senator and representative.[72] When political scientists Kay Lehman Schlozman and John T. Tierney examined interest group presence in Washington, they found that 70 percent of all the organizations represented in their sample either were businesses and trade associations or were law and public relations firms hired by corporations to represent them in Washington.[73] The largest Fortune 500 companies were the best represented. They maintained their own lobbying arms in Washington, were members of their industrial trade group, and participated in peak organizations like the Business Roundtable. Moreover, the Washington corporate office was no longer a dumping ground where corporate executives placed their incompetent relatives to keep them out of harm's way. To the contrary, managers of corporate public affairs departments gained status within the corporate hierarchy. The *Wall Street Journal* found "the post of government-affairs executive has taken on added luster. A tour through the government-affairs department can be a quick route to the top."[74] Indeed, many corporate lobbyists are former government officials who bring their privileged access to former colleagues and knowledge of agency or congressional procedures to their new jobs. For example, by mid-May 2001, almost one-third of all retiring members who had served in the

---

[70] Mathew M. Bodah, "Congress and the National Labor Relations Board: A Review of the Recent Past," *Journal of Labor Research* 22, no. 4 (Fall 2001): 708.

[71] These figures on the lobbying industry are from John R. Wright, *Interest Groups and Congress: Lobbying Contributions and Influence* (Boston: Allyn & Bacon, 1996), pp. 9–11.

[72] *New York Times*, July 29, 1999.

[73] Kay Lehman Schlozman and John T. Tierney, *Organized Interests and American Democracy* (New York: Harper & Row, 1986), p. 67.

[74] Quoted in David Vogel, *Fluctuating Fortunes* (New York: Basic Books, 1989), pp. 196–98.

previous Congress and Cabinet-level officials from the departing Clinton administration had signed with lobbying or government relations firms.

Compared to other interest groups, business is the most organized, hires the most lobbyists, has the most contact, and devotes the most money to influencing policymakers. In fact, business spends a lot more on lobbying than it does on campaign contributions. For example, the energy industry spent more than any other industry on campaign contributions in the 2000 election cycle, distributing almost $30 million to candidates and parties. It spent 5 times that on lobbying in 2000, over $159 million; the pharmaceutical industry spent 7 times more on lobbying than on campaign contributions in 2000; and military contractors spent 15 times more than they spent on campaign contributions. It may be that industry devotes so much more money to lobbying than campaign contributions because lobbying delivers a higher return on the investment.[75]

Lobbying is a sophisticated, multifaceted operation today and requires an extraordinary amount of money to be effective. Take, for example, the case of Microsoft Corporation, which initially ignored politics. Prior to 1998 it employed one lobbyist working out of an office in a suburban Washington shopping mall and contributed less than $10,000 to candidates running for federal office. But Microsoft soon realized it needed friends on Capitol Hill when Congress began to consider legislation affecting the technology industry and the Justice Department sued the company for violating antitrust laws. Today, Microsoft invests a lot of money to influence policy. It contributes hundreds of thousands of dollars to parties and candidates, has hired a "Dream Team" of lobbyists, financed the writing of supportive op-ed pieces, and underwritten the work of academics and research groups who advocate Microsoft's positions.[76] Just in case legislators miss Microsoft's message in the media, the company gives money to local organizations that support Microsoft to make it appear that the company enjoys grassroots support. It also creates new trade groups that generate support for the company through websites and arranges meetings between Microsoft executives and congressional leaders.

Such lobbying efforts cost Microsoft tens of millions of dollars, much more than their public-interest lobbying opponents can afford to match. But this expense pales in comparison to what industry trade groups spend to influence policy. No group spends more on lobbying the government than the pharmaceutical industry. The drug lobby has more registered lobbyists than there are members of Congress. When they go to work, they are often

---

[75] *New York Times*, September 19, 2002.

[76] At one time, lobbyists on Microsoft's payroll included Ralph Reed, who was a senior advisor to George W. Bush's presidential campaign; Haley Barbour, former chair of the Republican National Committee; C. Boyden Gray, White House counsel to former President George H. W. Bush; and Lloyd N. Cutler, counsel to former Presidents Jimmy Carter and Bill Clinton.

lobbying their former colleagues, as more than one-half of all drug lobbyists are either former members of Congress or former staff members. Thomas A. Scully, who ran Medicare for President Bush, left government soon after Medicare reform passed to take a job with a law firm that represents companies in the health care industry. Representative Billy Tauzin did not wait until he left office to put his services up for bidding. After announcing that he would retire from Congress at the end of his term in 2004, he received a $2 million offer to direct the Pharmaceutical Research and Manufacturers of America (PRMA). The PRMA, which is the lobbying arm of the drug industry, had billions of dollars at stake in the 2003 Medicare prescription drug bill that Representative Tauzin helped guide through Congress.[77]

Table 7-1 shows the proposed $150 million budget that the PRMA planned to spend in 2004. (These expenditures do not include the millions of dollars the individual companies that are members of the PRMA plan to spend on lobbying.) PRMA warned that the industry needed to prepare itself to ride out "a perfect storm" that included the threat of price controls, bad press, demands for drug discounts, initiatives by states to make drugs more affordable, and access to cheaper drugs from abroad. As part of its $150 million budget to fight the approaching tempest, the PRMA planned to spend $1 million to produce an "intellectual echo chamber of economists" to speak against price controls, $1 million to "change the Canadian health care system," $2.5 million to research and policy organizations to generate "messages from credible sources" who were sympathetic to the industry, and $12.3 million to develop coalitions with doctors, minority groups, patients, and universities.[78]

Many Americans and some political scientists believe in a comforting picture of American politics. In their view, society is made up of relatively equal interests, with each one pursuing its own political goals and with government responding in an evenhanded way. But this is a partial picture, at best. Few groups can match Microsoft or the PRMA in the amount and variety of resources they can devote to lobbying public officials. In addition, capitalist countries depend on business to invest and produce, creating what we called in Chapter 2 a "mobilization of bias" in its favor. The result is a privileged position for business that has come to be seen as so natural that business is often not regarded as a special interest at all.[79] Finally, business's special position of privilege is augmented by a party system that is awash with corporate campaign contributions. That is, corporate capitalism enjoys a structural advantage (Chapter 2), an electoral advantage (Chapter 5), and an interest group advantage. These political advantages are cumulative, as they reinforce and augment each other.

[77] *New York Times*, February 7, 2004.

[78] *New York Times*, June 1, 2003.

[79] Mark Kesselman, "The Conflictual Evolution of American Political Science: From Apologetic Pluralism to Trilateralism and Marxism," in *Public Values of Private Power in American Democracy*, ed. J. David Greenstone (Chicago: University of Chicago Press, 1982), pp. 34–67.

PRMA PROPOSED BUDGET FOR FISCAL 2004

Division	In millions
Federal affairs	$ 14.4
Alliance Development *Pursues strategic alliances with economists, doctors, patients and influential members of minority groups to shape public opinion.*	12.3
State government affairs	11.7
Legal	9.7
Public affairs	9.4
Policy and research	9.4
International	6.3
Scientific and regulatory affairs	4.3
Finance and operations	4.3
Office of the president	1.5
SUBTOTAL	$ 83.3
OTHER EXPENSES	$ 66.7*
TOTAL	**$150.0**

*Includes an additional $6.3 million for a contingency fund and an addition to reserves.

SOURCE: *New York Times,* June 1, 2003, p. 33. Copyright © 2003 by the New York Times Co. Reprinted by permission.

CONCLUSION

Congress is decentralized and fragmented. It is separated into two chambers, a Senate and a House of Representatives. And within these chambers, power is dispersed widely, although this is much truer of the Senate than of the House. While Congress's decentralized structure makes it difficult for Congress to articulate a broad coherent program and to provide leadership to the government, except during unusual periods of party government, this structure is conducive to the expression of particularistic demands by organized groups. Congress is open to groups exerting influence because of the many points of contact and different power centers available within it. It is the country's most representative and accessible institution, which creates a certain irony. Congress's very openness to the social forces outside it means that the diversity and inequalities of the larger society are reflected within it. Those with the most political resources outside of Congress are in the best position to take advantage of Congress's accessibility, to cultivate relationships with its members, committee and subcommittee chairs, and party leaders. Inasmuch as business has more political resources than other groups, it can best take advantage of Congress's openness to influence the legislative process. The mobilization of bias, corporate lobbying, corporate campaign contributions, and the class background of members of Congress make Congress especially responsive to corporate concerns.

According to political scientist Nicol C. Rae, "Congress can delay and obstruct measures, and it can articulate the national mood, but except in highly unusual circumstances, it cannot lead."[80] Although Congress is usually unable to set the government's agenda, it remains a pivotal political institution. As Woodrow Wilson understood, Congress is central to policy making because of the powers conferred on it by the Constitution. It has the authority to delay, amend, or veto initiatives desired by the executive branch. As the world's most powerful legislature, its creative and disruptive capacities cannot be ignored.

---

[80] Rae, *Conservative Reformers*, p. 216.

8

THE JUDICIARY

Although Christmas was only two weeks away, there was little evidence of it on the taut, grim faces of the Supreme Court Justices as they left work on December 12, 2000. Their pained expressions registered the burden of the momentous and extraordinary decision they had just reached. They had good reason to feel anxious because their ruling was remarkable not only for what the Court had to say in this important case but for how the Court said it. For example, the Court normally announces its decisions in public session, summarizing its main points. But in this case, the Court released its decision at night when the Justices were not available to deliver their ruling. The Court's press room simply distributed a 65-page document that even omitted the usual synopsis that accompanies opinions and identifies how each justice voted.

Furthermore, the Court's opinion was labeled *per curiam*, meaning "by the court." This term is usually reserved for decisions so uncontroversial and on which such unanimity exists that the Court can dispense with a formal, written explanation. But there was nothing unanimous or uncontroversial about this case. It split the Court, elicited long written opinions by the Justices to explain their different rulings, and threatened to undermine the public's confidence in the Court itself.

Another unusual aspect of the decision was that it created a new Constitutional principle. But this was followed by an astonishing disclaimer indicating that this new principle would not apply to future cases. Supreme Court decisions normally try to articulate rules that apply generally, that can serve as precedents for future decisions. But in this instance, the Court went out of its way to indicate that its ruling applied only to this one case, this one time, to this one set of circumstances.

Moreover, members of the Court are pretty consistent in their views. But in this case, some Justices appeared to violate their own legal principles in order to reach the outcome they wanted. Justices normally concerned with states' rights and deference to lower courts set those views aside to rule the other way. They overruled state courts, state laws, and local canvassing boards in order to reach a verdict that was politically congenial.

AP/Wide World Photos

The entrance to the U.S. Supreme Court Building.

Lastly, the Court is reluctant generally to get dragged into unseemly election disputes and nasty partisan quarrels. But in this case, in *Bush v. Gore*, No. 00-949, a five-to-four majority of the Court decided to suspend a recount of disputed presidential votes in Florida, effectively electing George W. Bush as the 43rd president of the United States. Summarizing the extraordinary role a slim majority on the Supreme Court played in deciding the outcome of the 2000 presidential election, the comedian Mark Russell mused, "We have a new president. In this democracy of 200 million citizens, the people have spoken. All five of them."[1]

Federal courts interpret the Constitution, the supreme law of the land. They get to say what the law is, and their judgment is final. "We are under a Constitution," Chief Justice Charles Evans Hughes once remarked, and "the Constitution is what the judges say it is."[2] In addition, courts in the United States, unlike in many other countries, have the power of judicial review, permitting them to overrule the decisions of other political institutions. That

---

[1] See the excellent reporting by Linda Greenhouse in *The New York Times*, December 13, 2001. Russell is quoted in William Crotty, "Elections by Judicial Fiat: The Courts Decide," in *America's Choice 2000,* ed. William Crotty (Boulder, CO: Westview Press, 2001), p. 75.

[2] Bernard Schwartz, *A Basic History of the U.S. Supreme Court* (Princeton, NJ: D. Van Nostrand Co., 1968), p. 9.

is, the courts can nullify or overturn any federal, state, or public law that conflicts with the Constitution. Further, federal judges are appointed to life terms. They are free from pressures to raise funds and campaign for support that other political actors face. Judges thus enjoy extraordinary independence and autonomy.

Yet, for all its power and prestige, leading political observers have pointed to the judiciary's limitations since the founding of the Republic. Alexander Hamilton described the courts as the "least dangerous branch," having "no influence over either the sword or the purse; no direction either of the strength or of the wealth of the society; and can take no active resolution whatsoever." That is, the courts may rule on a case but must depend on other political institutions to implement their decision. For example, when President Andrew Jackson disagreed with a Supreme Court ruling, he reportedly snickered, "[Chief Justice] John Marshall has made his decision, now let him enforce it."[3] Likewise, Justice Tom C. Clark once complained of the Court's powerlessness to make its decisions effective: "We don't have money at the Court to hire an army and we can't take out ads in the newspapers, and we don't want to go out on a picket line in our robes. We have to convince the nation by the force of our opinions."[4] In addition, the courts depend on the other branches of government for their budget, staffing, jurisdiction, and the appointment and removal of judges.

The justice system is a system of written laws, legal procedures, and courts that resolve disputes and punish the guilty. Extending from the police walking their beat to judges hearing cases and jail guards locking down prisoners for the night, participants in the justice system often wear uniforms to signify that their actions are guided by the law, and not their private conscience or personal motives. The law thus presents itself as above politics and objective, with rules that apply to all citizens equally. This sentiment is captured in the words "Equal Justice Under the Law," which are engraved on the façade atop the columns of Italian marble at the entrance to the Supreme Court. Motivated by legal equality, the courts sometimes display independence and rule against the powers of the day.

But the Courts are also conservative institutions that often confirm the status quo. They defer to legal precedent in reaching decisions and thus bind the present to the past. The legal process, with its constant motions and appeals, is designed to work slowly and deliberately. Often the pace is torturous. Dependence and deference to other institutions usually make the courts handmaidens of convention and conformity, reinforcing the disparities that existing economic arrangements and social patterns produce. The law more often follows politics and power than the other way around.

---

[3] Quoted in ibid., p. 15.

[4] Quoted in Richard Kluger, *Simple Justice: The History of Brown v. Board of Education and Black America's Struggle for Equality* (New York: Knopf, 1976), p. 706.

In addition, the law can mask inequality by giving the impression that all citizens stand before the law as equals. For example, the individuals who sit on death row are poor, almost to a person—not because rich or middle-class individuals never commit murder but because the average number of hours of legal time assigned to defendants in capital cases who cannot afford a lawyer is just over 50 hours, hardly much time in trial preparation and the trial itself. Here the same basic procedures of trial by jury apply to all Americans, but the results are strongly shaped by the contrasting abilities of individuals to pay for defense lawyers. The illusion of justice, of formal equality under the law in a society marked with real, substantive inequalities, is captured best in Anatole France's famous remark: "The law in its majesty forbids the rich as well as the poor to sleep under bridges, to beg in the streets, and to steal bread."

Law and legal equality, nonetheless, are precious assets and should not be dismissed as mere pretense, an effort to beautify what is unseemly. Domination flourishes in the absence of equal rights. While the justice system may protect inequalities, a formal framework of rights and procedures also creates tangible resources that ordinary people can draw upon to make claims upon the rich and the powerful. It also sets limits on what the rich and the powerful may do.[5] They cannot simply assert their naked power but must abide by the limits of the law. The law may suit them, but they are its willing or unwilling prisoners as well. Even presidents can be penalized for violating the law, as when President Richard Nixon was induced to resign in the aftermath of Watergate. His resignation, of course, was mainly the result of a political process, but the courts made it far easier for Congress to proceed against him, ultimately forcing a resignation, by requiring that incriminating tapes he made in the White House be turned over to investigators. It is the law under the Constitution that grants and protects freedom of speech, freedom from unreasonable search and seizure, and freedom of religion. And ordinary citizens can appeal to the law in order to assert their rights, as civil rights activists did in the 1960s.

A DUAL COURT SYSTEM

If we are to understand this combination of judicial limits and power and how the courts both reinforce and counter inequality, we need first to understand how the courts are organized.

The United States has a dual court system; state and federal systems of justice exist side by side. Each of the 50 states and the federal government maintain their own systems of courts. Federal courts hear criminal matters

---

[5] For a nuanced appreciation of the role the law plays, see E. P. Thompson, *Whigs and Hunters: The Origin of the Black Act* (New York: Pantheon Books, 1975).

that concern federal law. They also hear noncriminal, or civil, cases that involve citizens of more than one state and complaints filed by the federal government. State courts hear all the rest. Sometimes there is conflict between federal and state courts over which has jurisdiction of a case. Although under the Constitution a defendant cannot be tried twice for the same crime, sometimes defendants can be tried in both federal and state courts for the same incident if charged for different crimes. In 1992, four Los Angeles police officers were acquitted in California state court of assaulting Rodney King, a black man, even though a videotape appeared to provide ample documentation for the charge. The federal district attorney in Los Angeles then brought federal charges against the police officers for violating King's civil rights. Two of the four policemen subsequently were convicted on these charges in federal court.

State courts are the workhorses of the justice system. Ninety-nine percent of all legal cases are tried in state courts—from divorce and child custody matters to criminal cases; from wills, trusts, and estate issues to small claims disputes. Their role and the incarceration system they oversee at the state and local levels have become increasingly visible at a time when the population in prisons has increased dramatically, nearly doubling to almost 2 million in 2003. Most of those behind bars are nonviolent offenders; about 70 percent are illiterate, 10 percent are afflicted with mental illness, and a disproportionate number are not white. Currently, 8 percent of African American men in their late twenties are or have been incarcerated (nearly 30 percent, at current rates, will spend some time in prison during their lives). The total population in American jails and prisons has grown at a rate exceeding 6 percent per year since 1970. Out of every 100,000 people in the country, 461 were behind bars in 2001. By way of comparison, from 1920 to 1970, the proportion behind bars was about 110 people per 100,000.[6]

By contrast, the federal courts have much less routine criminal business to conduct. Federal court rulings interpret the Constitution and apply federal laws that govern all Americans. In addition, federal courts have the power to review the decisions of state courts to ensure they comply with federal law.

The federal court system is divided into three levels (see Table 8–1). The lowest is comprised of 94 district courts. Most federal cases begin and end here. However, a litigant unhappy with a decision at the district court level may appeal it to the next level, the court of appeals. There is one U.S. court of appeals for each of the country's 12 judicial circuits. Most cases are heard on appeal from district courts in the states under their jurisdiction by panels of three judges (rather than by a single judge, as at the district level). Only about one in ten federal cases makes it to this level.

District and appellate courts play important policy-making roles. Once the Supreme Court rules on a case, it often turns the issue back to the district court to implement the actual decision. The Supreme Court will generally

---

[6] Eric Schlosser, "The Prison-Industrial Complex," *Atlantic Monthly* (December 1988): 51–77.

Supreme Court
U.S. Supreme Court

Appellate Courts
U.S. Courts of Appeals
- 12 Regional Circuit Courts of Appeals
- 1 U.S. Court of Appeals for the Federal Circuit

Trial Courts
U.S. District Courts
- 94 judicial districts
- U.S. Bankruptcy Courts
U.S. Court of International Trade
U.S. Court of Federal Claims

Federal Courts and Other Entities outside the Judicial Branch
Military Courts (Trial and Appellate)
Court of Veterans Appeals
U.S. Tax Court
Federal administrative agencies and boards

restrict itself to articulating the general principle of law involved in the case, giving the district court a great deal of discretion in how to apply its ruling. For example, in *Brown v. Board of Education of Topeka, Kansas,* which outlawed state-sanctioned racial segregation, the Supreme Court did not fix a date for ending segregation but instead instructed the district courts to "act with all deliberate speed." But many district courts in the South reflected the region's opposition to *Brown* and used their discretion to forestall desegregation. They subsequently acted with "entirely too much deliberation and not enough speed," according to Justice Hugo Black, in requiring southern school districts to comply with the Court's ruling.[7]

Courts of Appeals also are important policymakers. Most of their decisions are final because the Supreme Court takes up so few cases that have been decided by these courts. Appellate courts hear 28,000 cases a year compared to the Supreme Court that normally hears less than 100. Consequently, in the real world, federal appeals courts have the final say in most matters of law. One important difference, however, between the Supreme Court and Courts of Appeals is that decisions by appellate courts apply only to the specific states covered by the deciding court, whereas Supreme Court decisions apply to the entire country. For example, in 1996, the Fifth Circuit Court of Appeals, covering Texas, Louisiana, and Mississippi, ruled that the University

---

[7] Quoted in David M. O'Brien, *Storm Center: The Supreme Court in American Politics* (New York: Norton, 1986), p. 290.

of Texas Law School discriminated against other applicants when it gave preference in admissions to Latinos and blacks. The court ruled that schools may not discriminate in admissions on the basis of race. This left the appeals court decision standing as the law in those states included within the Fifth Circuit's jurisdiction. Six years later, in 2002, the Sixth Circuit Court of Appeals, covering Michigan, Ohio, and Kentucky, ruled just the opposite to the Fifth Circuit on an identical question. It decided that the University of Michigan Law School could give preferential treatment to minority applicants. As a result of the two appeals court decisions, the law was different in one part of the country than it was in another. Schools were prohibited from giving preference in admissions to minorities in southern states covered by the Fifth Circuit but could do so in Midwestern states covered by the Sixth Circuit.

When federal appeals courts disagree, as occurred with regard to affirmative action in higher education, the Supreme Court will often take up the case and render a decision that applies nationally to all federal courts.[8] In 2003, the Supreme Court ruled in *Grutter v. Bollinger* that it was legal for colleges and universities to take race into account in their admissions decisions. The Supreme Court decision invalidated the previous ruling by the Fifth Circuit that had outlawed affirmative action programs by schools under that court's jurisdiction. (See Figure 8–1.)

Article II of the Constitution empowers the president to nominate federal judges, subject to the "advice and consent" of the Senate. This gives the Senate a veto over presidential appointments much like the veto power the president enjoys over bills passed by Congress. Appointments to the federal bench are especially consequential because federal judges have lifetime tenure. Unlike an administration's legislative successes that can be undone in the next Congress, the effect of a president's judicial appointments is long-term and enduring. Lifetime tenure of federal judges permits presidents to leave a legacy regarding how laws are interpreted through the judges they appoint to the federal bench. The impact of presidents on the court long after their terms expire was dramatically illustrated in *Bush v. Gore*. The five Justices who formed the majority in that case, which elevated George W. Bush to the presidency, were all appointed by previous Republican presidents who successfully nominated conservative justices during their terms in office.

Presidents generally appoint judges to federal courts who are from the same political party and share their values. With the exception of Franklin Roosevelt, who appointed more than 80 percent of federal judges over the course of his three full terms, no presidents have been more assiduous and successful in staffing the federal judiciary with like-minded judges than Ronald Reagan and his successor, George H. W. Bush. For the first time in American history, White House aides were involved in the process of

[8] Robert A. Carp and Ronald Stidham, *Judicial Process in America,* 4th ed. (Washington, DC: Congressional Quarterly Press, 1998), p. 43.

■ **FIGURE 8–1**

HOW CASES ASCEND TO THE SUPREME COURT

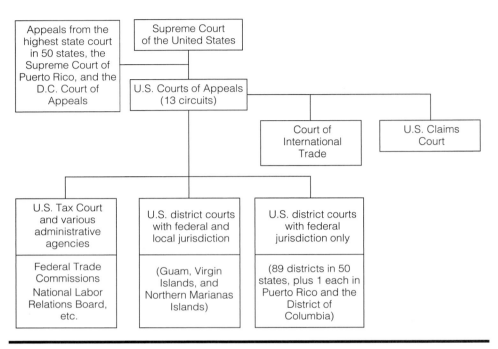

SOURCE: Administrative Office of the United States Courts.

reviewing the credentials of potential judges and screening them to confirm their conservative values.[9] These administrations did their job well, appointing a large number of conservative jurists to the federal bench.[10]

Under President Clinton, the White House did not participate in the selection of judges or screen them ideologically to the extent his predecessors had. Nor did Clinton try to counter the judicial legacies of the Reagan and Bush administrations by appointing liberal judges. Rather, he chose federal judges who reflected his centrist values. Their subsequent voting records were less liberal than those judges appointed by Jimmy Carter and more

[9] Gregory A. Caldiera and John R. Wright, "Lobbying for Justice: The Rise of Organized Conflict in the Politics of Federal Judgeships," in *Contemplating Courts*, ed. Lee Epstein (Washington, DC: Congressional Quarterly Press, 1995), p. 54.

[10] Kenneth Jost, "The Federal Judiciary," *CQ Researcher* (March 13, 1998): 230. It is not clear they voted more conservatively than other Republican appointments; rather, they now formed a significant majority. See also Timothy B. Tomasi and Jess A. Velona, "All the President's Men?: A Study of Ronald Reagan's Appointments to the U.S. Courts of Appeals," *Columbia Law Review* 87 (1987): 766–93.

comparable to those of Carter's Republican predecessor, Gerald Ford.[11] Clinton, however, did make his mark by stressing judicial diversity, by appointing more women and minorities to judgeships than any previous president.[12] One aide in the Clinton White House explained, "We don't see courts as a vehicle for social change. It's enough to put people of demonstrated quality on the bench. We've done this across gender, race, and national origin lines. And that is a legacy the president is proud of."[13]

The Clinton terms were also marked by a dramatic increase in Senate scrutiny of judicial nominations. Clinton's judicial nominations encountered unprecedented obstruction and delays once the Republicans gained control of the Senate in 1994.[14] One-third of Clinton's appointments to appellate courts were blocked by the Republican majority on the Senate Judiciary Committee, and the average time to confirmation for an appointment to federal district and appellate courts more than doubled. One Clinton nominee to the appeals court was confirmed more than four years after the date of his original nomination. The confirmation process under the Republicans broke down so much that it even drew the wrath of Chief Justice William Rehnquist. In his 1997 annual report on the state of the judiciary, Rehnquist warned that Senate delays posed a serious threat to the "nation's quality of justice." He urged Republicans on the Senate Judiciary Committee to relieve the burden on the courts and act more expeditiously in voting Clinton's appointments either up or down.[15]

George W. Bush moved quickly and aggressively to follow the same strategy that previous Republican administrations had adopted and from which he had benefited so much. First, Bush announced that he would no longer consult with the American Bar Association on judicial appointments, as past presidents had done. Rather, judicial appointments would be reviewed by a White House team, which would seek advice from members of the Federalist Society, a group of conservative legal jurists, lawyers, and academics. This resulted in Bush submitting a list of extraordinarily conservative and highly controversial judges for Senate confirmation. With Democrats in the majority at the time, the Senate Judiciary Committee rejected two of his nominations. But when Republicans reclaimed a majority in the Senate

[11] Tinsley E. Yarborough, *The Rehnquist Court and the Constitution* (New York: Oxford University Press, 2000), p. 39.

[12] David M. O'Brien, "Clinton's Legal Policy and the Courts: Rising from Disarray or Turning Around and Around?" in *The Clinton Presidency: First Appraisals*, eds. Colin A. Campbell and Bert A. Rothman (Chatham, NJ: Chatham House Publishers, 1996), pp. 126–63. See also Carp and Stidham, *Judicial Process in America*, pp. 243–45.

[13] White House Deputy Counsel Joel Klein, quoted in O'Brien, "Clinton's Legal Policy and the Courts," p. 139.

[14] Roger E. Hartley and Lisa M. Holmes, "The Increasing Senate Scrutiny of Lower Federal Court Nominees," *Political Science Quarterly* 117, no. 2 (Summer 2002): 259–78.

[15] Yarborough, *The Rehnquist Court and the Constitution*, pp. 38–41.

following the 2002 midterm elections, Bush renominated the two candidates who had been rejected previously. This was utterly unprecedented, the first time that a president had ever renominated defeated judicial candidates.[16] Conflict over another nomination led the Democrats to filibuster it on the Senate floor when the administration refused to turn over memoranda that would provide senators with information about the candidates' views. While Republicans complained that Democrats were obstructing the president improperly by holding up his appointments, Democrats viewed it as payback for the treatment Clinton's appointments had received when the Republicans controlled the Senate during his terms.

THE SUPREME COURT

At the top of the judicial system is the Supreme Court. It is the court of last resort; there is none higher. According to Justice Robert H. Jackson, judgments by members of the Supreme Court are "not final because we are infallible; we know that we are infallible only because we are final."[17] The Court receives the vast majority of its cases from the federal district and appellate courts. Many more cases are filed with the Court each year than it has the time or inclination to hear. Over time, the number of petitions to the Court has increased, while the number of cases on which the Court issues signed, written opinions has declined. In 2003, over 7,000 petitions were received by the Court, but it agreed to fully review only 71 of them. The Court carefully chooses which cases to hear, applying what is called "The Rule of Four." That is, the Court will decide only those cases that at least four justices want to hear.[18] In choosing which cases to hear, Chief Justice William Howard Taft explained the Court should devote its resources to cases "that involve principles, the application of which are of wide public importance or governmental interest, and which should be authoritatively declared by the Court."[19] In 1949, Justice Fred Vinson provided a fuller statement of the guidelines the Court has followed in selecting which cases to review:

> The Supreme Court is not, and never has been, primarily concerned with the correction of errors in lower court decisions. . . . The function of the Supreme Court is . . . to resolve conflicts of opinion on federal questions that have arisen

---

[16] President Bush then added to the unprecedented nature of the appointment process regarding these two judges when he appointed one of them to the bench when Congress was in recess, thereby temporarily overcoming a filibuster by Senate Democrats that had blocked his confirmation. This was the first time that a president had ever used a recess appointment to install a judge whom the Senate Judiciary Committee had voted to reject.

[17] *Brown v. Allen,* 344 U.S. 443, 540 (1953).

[18] Lee Epstein and Jack Knight, *The Choices Justices Make* (Washington, DC: Congressional Quarterly Press, 1998), p. 26.

[19] Taft is quoted in Epstein and Knight, *The Choices Justices Make,* p. 46.

among lower courts, to pass upon questions of wide import under the Constitution, laws and treaties of the United States, and to exercise supervisory power over lower courts. If we took every case in which an interesting legal question is raised, or our *prima facie* impression is that the decision below is erroneous, we could not fill the Constitutional and statutory responsibilities placed upon the Court. To remain effective, the Supreme Court must continue to decide only those cases which present questions whose resolution will have immediate importance far beyond the particular facts and parties involved.[20]

The Supreme Court has had as few as five justices, when it was first organized in 1789, and as many as ten. Its membership, set by Congress, has been fixed at nine since 1869. The head of the Court is the Chief Justice of the United States, who is appointed by the president—subject to confirmation by the Senate. Many chief justices toil in relative obscurity, which may explain why more Americans could name the judge of the television show *The People's Court* than could identify the Chief Justice of the United States.[21] The chief justice may be the official leader of the Court but is only first among equals in his relationship to the other eight justices. He cannot tell them what to do or how to decide a case. Chief Justice Charles Evan Hughes received a rude reminder of this when he sent a messenger to Justice James C. McReynold's chambers asking him to hurry as he was late for a Court conference. The messenger returned with McReynold's curt reply: "He said to tell you that he doesn't work for you."[22] The Chief Justice is, in effect, the leader of the orchestra, but he cannot tell the other justices what music to play. Some chief justices, however, are better conductors, getting the other justices to play the same tune, than others. For example, Chief Justice Earl Warren used every personal and political argument he could think of to convince two reluctant members of the Court to sign a unanimous opinion in the *Brown* decision. Other chief justices have not been so successful. The Court sometimes leads more than it is led by the chief justice.

Decision making on the Court begins after lawyers on each side plead their case. The justices then discuss the case in completely private sessions, without law clerks or secretaries attending. Confidentiality is designed to promote a frank and full exchange of views among the Justices. The chief justice leads the discussion at which the justices reveal how they would decide the case and the reasons for their position. According to Justice Antonin Scalia, "[N]ot much conferencing goes on" at conference anymore.[23] Views are stated rather than argued. There is less collective deliberation and

---

[20] Fred Vinson, "Work of the Federal Courts," *Supreme Court Reporter* (1949), cited in Emmette S. Redford and Alan F. Westin, *Politics and Government of the United States* (New York: Harcourt, Brace & World, 1968), p. 474.

[21] Epstein and Knight, *The Choices Justices Make*, p. 39.

[22] Jerome J. Shestack, "The Rehnquist Court and the Legal Profession," in *The Rehnquist Court: A Retrospective*, ed. Martin H. Belsky (New York: Oxford Univeristy Press, 2002), p. 167.

[23] Bernard Schwartz, *Decisions: How the Supreme Court Decides Cases* (New York: Oxford University Press, 1996), p. 43.

more expounding of individual views. After the conference reveals each justice's tentative vote on a case, the chief justice, if in the majority, assigns the writing of the Court's opinion to one of the justices who voted with the majority. (If the chief justice is not in the majority, the senior member of the majority assigns the opinion.) Here chief justices may use their power to assign a significant case to an ally who will write the decision in a way that conforms to their own views. The justice assigned to write the majority opinion then circulates a draft to the other justices, which elicits replies from them. Selecting who writes the majority opinion is regarded as so important that Chief Justice Warren Burger was suspected by the other justices of voting frequently with a majority he disagreed with so that he might select who would write the majority opinion. Whoever writes the majority opinion establishes the initial position to which the other justices react as the first draft circulates among them.

As a result of written exchanges among the justices, the rationale for the decision may be modified and votes may be switched, with a completely different decision emerging from the process. For example, the 1989 *Webster v. Reproductive Health Services* case threatened to overturn the 1973 *Roe v. Wade* decision establishing a woman's constitutional right to an abortion. A majority of five justices at conference voted to uphold a Missouri law that would have placed restrictive conditions on abortions. Chief Justice William H. Rehnquist assigned writing the majority opinion to himself. But as memos circulated among the justices in response to Rehnquist's draft, Justice Sandra Day O'Connor switched her vote. What once was a 5–4 majority at conference to effectively overturn *Roe* became in the course of an exchange of views among the justices a 5–4 majority to reaffirm *Roe* (while still upholding some of the restrictions in the Missouri law). The process leading to the *Webster* decision reveals that conference votes are tentative and not carved in stone. Indeed, Supreme Court scholars Lee Epstein and Jack Knight contend that justices change their minds frequently as to how they will rule as a case proceeds from conference to final decision.[24]

Presidents appoint members to the Supreme Court whom they believe will reflect their views. Sometimes they are spectacularly wrong in their predictions. President Harry Truman, for example, did not mince words over his disappointment with Justice Tom Clark: "Tom Clark was my biggest mistake. No question about it. . . . I don't know what got into me. He was no damn good as Attorney General, and on the Supreme Court . . . it doesn't seem possible, but he's even worse. He hasn't made one right decision that I can think of. . . ."[25] When asked what the biggest mistake was that he made while in office, President Dwight Eisenhower replied, "The appointment of . . . Earl Warren."[26] More recently, conservatives have been disappointed by the

---

[24] Lee Epstein and Jack Knight, *The Choices Justices Make*, p. 9.

[25] Quoted in O'Brien, *Storm Center*, p. 81.

[26] Schwartz, *Decisions*, p. 184.

liberal decisions of Justice David Souter, whom President Bush, a Republican, appointed to the Court in 1990. Sometimes presidents guess right, only to have their appointee change his or her views over time. Justice Harry Blackmun voted with his friend Chief Justice Warren Burger, another Nixon appointee, 90 percent of the time when he first came on the Court. But his views changed, and by the time he retired from the Court in 1994, he had become its most liberal member.[27] While these examples reveal that justices sometimes surprise a president, they are the exceptions that prove the rule. Most justices reflect pretty well the politics of the president who appoints them.

Presidential appointments to federal courts—and especially to the Supreme Court—are more contentious today than they were in the past. Prior to the Senate rejection of two of President Richard Nixon's Supreme Court nominees in 1969 and 1970, one had to go back to 1930 and the Hoover administration to find the last time the Senate rejected a presidential appointment to the Supreme Court. Pitched battles occurred in 1987 over President Reagan's appointment of Robert Bork and in 1991 over President George H. Bush's nomination of Clarence Thomas. The former was rejected as too conservative by a Democratic Senate, while the latter was confirmed by the Senate despite charges of sexual harassment against him. Part of the reason Supreme Court appointments have drawn increasing scrutiny is because more political issues are being placed at the Court's door. Groups are litigating what they cannot legislate. The Court increasingly is being called on to choose between competing policies in areas of profound disagreement. This, in turn, calls attention to the people appointed to the Court, who are increasingly perceived as making public policy when they decide cases. In addition, the frequency of divided government between Congress and the president, and the partisan and ideological polarization within Congress have also contributed to the frequent and contentious battles over judicial appointments.

THE SUPREME COURT IN HISTORY

We have seen how the Constitution established the Supreme Court and left it to Congress to create lower federal courts as they might be needed. But the Constitution did not stipulate the number of members of the Supreme Court or what its specific powers would be. For example, the power of judicial review, in which the courts can nullify any federal, state, or public law that they believe conflicts with the Constitution, is not explicitly granted by the Constitution and cannot be found within it. This power first was asserted by the Supreme Court in the case of *Marbury v. Madison* (1803), in which the

---

[27] O'Brien, *Storm Center,* p. 84.

Court ruled that Thomas Jefferson's secretary of state, James Madison, had failed to properly convey the commission appointing William Marbury to a government post as a last-minute act of President John Adams. In his *Marbury* decision, Chief Justice John Marshall wrote, "It is emphatically the province and duty of the judicial department to say what the law is. . . . A law repugnant to the Constitution is void; . . . courts as well as other departments are bound by that instrument."[28] Even after *Marbury*, however, judicial review was slow to institutionalize. The Court waited another 54 years before attempting to invalidate another act of Congress, in its infamous *Dred Scott* decision confirming black slavery, and it was not until the late 19th century that the principle was fully established.

The principle of judicial review is in tension with democratic theory inasmuch as it gives unelected judges the power to overrule laws made by a majority of elected officials. When courts overrule legislatures, it is regarded as an expression of judicial activism. Judicial restraint, its opposite, occurs when courts defer to the will of the people expressed through legislative majorities. Justice Oliver Wendell Holmes, for example, believed that democratic politics produced many bad laws that judges had no business changing. If his fellow citizens wanted to go to hell, Holmes once remarked, it was his job to help them on their way.

Most expressions of judicial activism, of courts failing to defer to elected officials, have preserved and protected property rights. The Supreme Court's 1905 *Lochner v. New York* decision, which struck down a state law that restricted working hours, and its initial rulings that much New Deal legislation was unconstitutional are examples where judicial review overturned progressive social and economic legislation. But there is no automatic identification of judicial activism with conservative results or, correspondingly, judicial restraint with liberal outcomes. *Brown v. Board of Education*, which overruled state laws governing school segregation, shattered any illusion that judicial activism cuts only one way. Law professor Philip B. Kurland has suggested that "[a]n 'activist' court is essentially one that is out of step with legislative or executive branches of the government" and that it is liberal or conservative "depending which role its prime antagonist has adopted."[29] While judicial activism may be hard to reconcile with democratic theory, there may be circumstances in which it actually enhances democracy, such as when legislation violates one of the provisions of the Bill of Rights or subjects minorities to the tyranny of the majority, as was the case in *Brown*.[30]

Marbury v. Madison settled a question that had divided the country along clear partisan lines. Judicial review was supported by the Federalist Party,

---

[28] *Marbury v. Madison*, 5 U.S. 137 (1803).

[29] Philip B. Kurland, *Politics, the Constitution and the Warren Court* (Chicago: University of Chicago Press, 1970), pp. 17–18.

[30] Morton Horwitz, *The Warren Court and the Pursuit of Justice* (New York: Hill & Wang, 1998), pp. 76–82.

which was dominated by northern manufacturing, finance, and mercantile interests. Southern and western agrarian, planter, and small landowning interests in the Republican Party who favored the principle of legislative supremacy opposed it. But Federalists and Republicans were also divided over the scope of national, as opposed to state, power. This question came before the court in the form of *McCulloch v. Maryland* (1819). In *McCulloch,* the Court ruled that federal law was supreme. State law would have to give way when federal and state laws were in conflict. But not until *McCulloch* did the Court decisively rule in this manner. Thus, the *Marbury* case confirmed the power of the Supreme Court, and the *McCulloch* case confirmed the power of the national government. Both marked a triumph of national industrial interests in the Federalist Party over local agrarian interests in the Democratic Party.

After Chief Justice John Marshall's death in 1835, President Andrew Jackson appointed Roger Taney to lead the Court. The Court over which he presided, in contrast to the Marshall Court, tilted toward states' rights and southern interests. This was particularly evident in its *Scott v. Sanford* (1857) decision, when the Court, by a 7–2 vote, ruled that no black could be an American citizen, that a black was "a person of an inferior order," that no individual of African descent was a "portion of this American people," and that blacks were slaves and possessions of their owners no matter whether they were in a slave or a free area of the country. The *Dred Scott* decision provoked an outcry in the North and hastened the onset of the Civil War.

Following the Civil War, the Court was in the hands of northern Republicans, who were chiefly concerned with safeguarding property and providing a legal environment for the development of capitalism. For example, the Fourteenth Amendment, adopted in 1868, was intended to protect black civil rights from hostile state actions. But its famous Due Process Clause—no state shall "deprive any person of life, liberty, or property, without due process of law"—served corporate interests more than it did blacks in the 19th century. The courts held that many laws regulating business were unconstitutional, precipitating a wave of judicial activism by the Court in which it repeatedly overturned state and federal laws designed to regulate business.[31] The Court used its laissez-faire interpretation of the Constitution to nullify so many laws that Justice Oliver Wendell Holmes complained there "was hardly any limit but the sky to the invalidating of [laws] if they happen to strike a majority of the Court as for any reason undesirable."[32] Not only did the courts protect business from most government regulation, but they limited the reach of antitrust laws and restricted the ability of unions to organize and to strike. In recognition of the Supreme Court's service to business, a New York bank president told an audience of

---

[31] James Q. Wilson and John J. Dilulio, Jr., *American Government,* 7th ed. (New York: Houghton Mifflin, 1998), p. 444.

[32] Quoted in Schwartz, *Decisions,* p. 79.

capitalists in 1895: "I give you, gentlemen, the Supreme Court of the United States—guardian of the dollar, defender of private property, enemy of spoliation, sheet anchor of the Republic!"[33]

But the Court's defense of property rights and freedom of contract could not withstand the popular momentum of Franklin Roosevelt's New Deal. Initially, the Court repeatedly struck down New Deal legislation. It outlawed the Agricultural Adjustment Act, a New York State minimum wage law, and the National Industrial Recovery Act. The outlook was grim for other New Deal legislation whose constitutionality was also being challenged, such as the Social Security Act and the National Labor Relations Act. The more the Court stood as a roadblock in the way of the New Deal, the more popular frustration with the Court's undemocratic character grew. Senator George Norris of Nebraska expressed this common complaint when he denounced the Court on the Senate floor, saying, "The members of the Supreme Court are not elected by anybody. They are responsible to nobody. Yet they hold dominion over everybody."[34]

Roosevelt had the misfortune in his first term to be the first president ever to serve a full four years and not appoint someone to the Supreme Court. Unable to change the Court through appointment, he proposed to reform the Court by appointing justices who were sympathetic to the New Deal. He proposed "court packing" legislation, which would have permitted the president to appoint a new justice, up to a total of 15, for each justice who reached 70 and did not retire. Since 6 of the 9 justices were over 70 at the time, this legislation would have let Roosevelt add 6 new like-minded justices to the Court. Roosevelt lost the battle to reform the Court in Congress, but he won the war. While Roosevelt was seeking acceptance for his plan to reform the Court and more court-curbing bills were proposed in Congress than ever before, Justice Owen Roberts, who had previously voted against New Deal legislation and had written some key opinions striking them down, now voted to uphold such legislation as constitutional.[35] One member of Congress noted that Justice Roberts had amended the Constitution and changed the lives of millions simply "by nodding his head instead of shaking it."[36] Justice Roberts's about-face is often referred to as the "switch in time that saved nine." This reversal provided Roosevelt with a majority on the Court, one he later expanded on. By the end of his presidency in 1945, he had filled more Court vacancies than any president since George Washington.

---

[33] Quoted in Redford and Westin, *Politics and Government*, pp. 498–99.

[34] Quoted in William E. Leuchtenburg, *The Supreme Court Reborn: The Constitutional Revolution in the Age of Roosevelt* (New York: Oxford University Press, 1995), p. 103.

[35] For example, Justice Roberts wrote the majority opinion in *United States v. Butler* (1936), striking down the New Deal's Agricultural Adjustment Act.

[36] Congressman Maury Maverick is quoted in Leuchtenburg, *Supreme Court Reborn*, p. 176.

This reform episode reveals much about the power and limits of the Supreme Court. The Court can nullify the will of the people, as it did initially, at least regarding New Deal legislation. But if the Court stands too hard and too long against public opinion, the Court's decisions risk losing legitimacy in the eyes of the public. The prestige and stature of the Court will suffer. This is particularly damaging because the Court does not derive legitimacy from democratic theory. Supreme Court justices are not elected and are not accountable to those affected by their decisions. Instead, the justices must depend on their eminence and prestige as the reasons why their decisions should be respected. The Court must constantly keep its reputation aloft, appearing above the political and partisan fray, since it cannot draw legitimacy for its decisions from democratic theory as other American political institutions claim to do.

After 1936, the Supreme Court upheld every New Deal statute whose constitutionality was challenged. Judicial supremacy gave way to deference to Congress and the president. Judicial activism was replaced with judicial restraint. In the course of confirming the New Deal, the Court initiated a constitutional revolution that greatly expanded the power of the federal government over business and the states. Previously, the Court had narrowly construed interstate commerce that was subject to federal law. But now the Court defined interstate commerce so broadly that federal law applied to virtually all business transactions. When lawyers for business argued, for example, that the federal government lacked the right to regulate working conditions, the Court ruled that Congress did have authority to legislate in this area, explaining, "When industries organize themselves on a national scale . . . how can it be maintained that their industrial relations constitute a forbidden field into which Congress may not enter. . . . ?"[37] The Court now interpreted the reach of the federal government so expansively that there were almost "no social welfare or regulatory statutes that the Courts would not validate."[38]

This constitutional revolution in 1937 replaced classical legal doctrines based on freedom of contract with a new jurisprudence that affirmed government regulation of business. Freedom of contract was just, according to the old classical legal theory, because it reflected the results arrived at in a neutral market among free and willing parties. But as legal scholar Roscoe Pound argued in 1903, the freedom of contract doctrine represented a conception of equal rights that was fraudulent to "everyone acquainted at first hand with actual industrial conditions."[39] Employers enjoyed much more market power than individual workers in bargaining, for example, over the

---

[37] *NLRB v. Jones and Laughlin Steel Corp* (1937).

[38] Leuchtenburg, *Supreme Court Reborn*, p. 154.

[39] Quoted in Morton Horwitz, *The Transformation of American Law, 1870–1960* (New York: Oxford University Press, 1992), p. 34.

■ FIGURE 8-2

ECONOMIC AND CIVIL LIBERTIES LAWS OVERTURNED BY
THE SUPREME COURT, 1900–1980

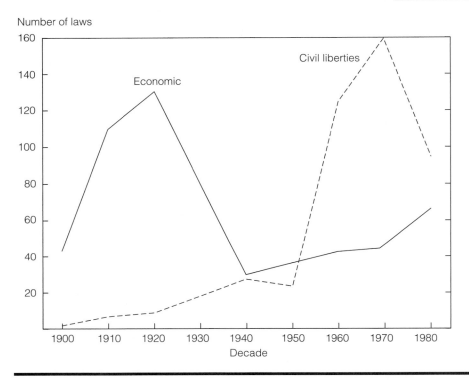

Number of laws

SOURCE: Lawrence Baum, *The Supreme Court* (Washington, D.C.: Congressional Quarterly Press, 1985), p. 188.

employment contract. Moreover, the Depression made it painfully clear that the interpretation of contractual freedom the Court wanted to protect rested on false assumptions about the ability of unregulated markets to satisfy people's needs. The formal, abstract, detached quality of classical legal doctrine was now replaced with one that was realistic and grounded in results. If the market was not neutral, if its results were harmful to society, then it was appropriate for government to intervene. The constitutional revolution of 1937 marked the rise of a new legal theory that could justify government interference in freedom of contract so as to require firms to pay minimum wages and bargain with their unionized workers, and prevent them from hiring child labor. The Court finally acknowledged what had long been recognized everywhere else: that laissez-faire capitalism was dead. (See Figure 8–2 for a graph of the number of economic and civil liberties laws overturned by the Supreme Court in the last century.)

THE MODERN COURT: FROM WARREN TO REHNQUIST

On March 16, 1948, twenty black citizens assisted by the National Association for the Advancement of Colored People (NAACP) filed suit in U.S. district court in Florence County, South Carolina. They claimed that racial segregation practiced by the Clarendon County Board of Education violated the Equal Protection Clause of the Constitution's Fourteenth Amendment. Simple justice, they believed, required the government to give black children the same educational opportunities it provided to whites. In Clarendon County, the local board of education maintained 12 schools for whites valued at $673,850 and 61 schools for blacks valued at a mere $194,575. White schoolchildren rode to school in buses, often passing black schoolchildren who had to walk because the school board provided no buses for them.

The suit was filed under the name of Henry Briggs, the first plaintiff in alphabetical order, who worked in a gas station. Before the litigation was over he would be fired from his job. Maisie Solomon, another plaintiff, also lost her job. John McDonald could not get a loan for his tractor, Lee Richardson could not secure credit for his farm, and no one would rent land to William Ragin on which he could grow cotton. The doors of justice may be open to everyone, but sometimes it requires uncommon courage to walk through them.

After two years of delay and defeat in the lower courts, this school segregation case reached the Supreme Court of the United States. There, the suit joined two other school segregation cases, from Delaware and Virginia, which the Court was also hearing on appeal. These cases were consolidated with a fourth school segregation case from Kansas called *Brown v. Board of Education of Topeka*. This case was listed first because the Justices did not want the issue of segregation to appear as purely a southern matter.

On May 17, 1954, Chief Justice Earl Warren read the Supreme Court's unanimous opinion in the group of school segregation cases known collectively as *Brown*. He told the assembled spectators and reporters that the Court had asked itself if racial segregation in public schools deprived black children of equal opportunity. "We believe that it does," he declared. His closing remarks left no doubt of where the Court stood: "We conclude that in the field of public education, the doctrine of 'separate but equal' has no place. Separate educational facilities are inherently unequal. Therefore the plaintiffs . . . have been . . . deprived of the equal protection of the laws guaranteed by the Fourteenth Amendment."[40]

The *Brown* decision was only one of many decisions the Warren Court made that created conflict and resonated across the country. Although the Warren Court is associated with the length of its Chief Justice's tenure from

---

[40] This material on *Brown* draws on Kluger, *Simple Justice*; and on Raymond Wolters, *The Burden of Brown: Thirty Years of School Desegregation* (Knoxville: University of Tennessee Press, 1984).

1954 to 1969, many of its decisions and principles still stand today. The issues with which the Warren Court wrestled were no longer those related to government regulation of business, as they had been for the New Deal Democratic coalition that preceded it. Since 1937, the Court had decisively settled such issues in favor of regulation. Now the Court reflected concern with civil rights and civil liberties.[41]

This focus entailed extending the promise of formal legal equality that most Americans took for granted to groups who had been excluded, such as blacks. The Warren Court proceeded to generate a more inclusive meaning of democracy, as was evident in its civil rights decisions, its rulings expanding freedom of speech and press protections, its voting rights decisions, and its application of the Bill of Rights to the states. These decisions provoked tremendous controversy. But the Warren Court prevailed because it was in tune with the activist, liberal wing of the Democratic Party, which was the governing coalition at the time.[42]

The Warren Court's effort to realize the promise of legal equality for all Americans was evident in a number of landmark decisions. *Brown,* of course, led the way in civil rights. But until Congress got serious about civil rights, the Court moved slowly, denying a hearing to many cases. Once Congress took the lead, the Court, in 1964, announced that the time for school districts to show deliberate speed in desegregating schools had run out *(Griffin v. County School Board of Prince Edward County).* Four years later, in *Green v. County School Board of New Kent County,* the Court required school districts that had practiced segregation in the past to not only stop discriminating but to take affirmative action to achieve racial balance in their schools. Nor did the civil rights legislation of the 1960s suffer the same fate at the hands of the Warren Court that the legislation passed by the Reconstruction Congress of the 1860s had suffered at the hands of earlier Supreme Courts. In the 1870s and 1880s, the Supreme Court had vitiated the intent of the Reconstruction Congress to protect the rights of newly freed slaves. A century later the Warren Court reinforced the will of Congress when it upheld the constitutionality of the Civil Rights Act of 1964 and the Voting Rights Act of 1965.

The Warren Court also acted to expand the notion of legal equality and ensure the effectiveness of each citizen's vote by requiring equally apportioned legislative districts. Some state legislative districts included many more voters than others. In *Baker v. Carr* (1962), the Court ruled that it was appropriate for federal courts to hear cases challenging malapportioned state election districts. Two years later, in *Reynolds v. Sims,* the Court took the next step on the road to making the promise of political equality a reality. It declared that the "one person,

---

[41] We might also add that the Warren Court reflected the Cold War consensus of the Democratic coalition as well as its domestic concern with rights. The Warren Court permitted the silencing of left-wing opinion with respect to admission to the bar and the conduct of congressional investigations.

[42] Mark Silverstein and Benjamin Ginsberg, "The Supreme Court and the New Politics of Judicial Power," *Political Science Quarterly* 102 (Fall 1987): 379.

one vote" principle, which governs congressional districting, also applies to state legislatures. Writing for the majority on the Court in requiring states to apportion their legislative districts fairly by population, Warren wrote, "Legislators represent people, not trees or acres."[43]

The Warren Court also was responsible for extending the boundaries of democracy by requiring states to abide by virtually every provision of the Bill of Rights. State law enforcement and criminal procedures would now have to meet federal due process requirements, giving defendants charged with crimes certain procedural rights and protections. In *Mapp v. Ohio* (1961), the Court ruled, in the words of two experienced reporters, "that evidence obtained in violation of the Fourth Amendment guarantee against unreasonable search and seizure must be excluded from use in state, as well as federal courts." Two years later in *Gideon v. Wainwright* (1963), the Court declared that states must provide legal counsel to all defendants charged with serious crimes. In 1966, the Court handed down its *Miranda* decision, which stated that a confession obtained from a criminal suspect during interrogation is not admissible as evidence in court unless the accused person has been informed of his or her rights to remain silent and to be represented by a lawyer. The Warren Court accelerated the process of creating a "second Bill of Rights" that now applied to the states, alongside the original document that applied to the federal government.[44]

Some of the Warren Court's decisions have become national standards. It is hard to imagine the law today tolerating government-sanctioned racial segregation, as it once did, or deviating from the principle of one person, one vote, as it once also did. While Supreme Court decisions have chipped away at the Warren Court's jurisprudence in recent years, its legacy lives on.

Conservatives attacked the Warren Court for coddling criminals, tying the hands of police and prosecutors, being irreligious, violating states' rights, and promoting civil unrest. Richard Nixon pledged to remold the Court in his 1968 presidential campaign, and within a year of his election, he had a chance to deliver on that promise. In 1969, Earl Warren retired, and President Nixon appointed Warren E. Burger, a known critic of many Warren Court decisions, to replace him as chief justice. By the end of Warren Burger's service as chief justice in 1986, Republican presidents had appointed six members to the Supreme Court. Only two members of the liberal bloc from the Warren Court, Justices William Brennan and Thurgood Marshall, remained on the bench, along with Byron White.

Circumstances were ripe for conservatives to undo the work of the Warren Court. But the counterrevolution many anticipated never happened. Indeed, it would be inaccurate even to describe the Supreme Court as the

---

[43] Quoted in Schwartz, *Decisions*, p. 105.

[44] This paragraph draws on the description of the "due process revolution" in Joan Biskopic and Elder Witt, *Guide to the U.S. Supreme Court*, 3rd ed. (Washington, DC: Congressional Quarterly Press, 1997), pp. 52–53. See also Leuchtenburg, *Supreme Court Reborn*, pp. 237–58.

Burger Court during the years he served as chief justice (1969–1986). Despite his title, Burger never led the Court intellectually or put his personal stamp on it to the extent that Earl Warren, his predecessor, had.

To the dismay and disappointment of conservatives, the Burger Court was caught in the backdraft of the Court it had succeeded. The power of judicial precedent, the lack of leadership provided by Burger, and the skill of liberal Justice William Brennan in coaxing a majority of justices to follow the Warren Court's rulings were enough to hold the line. Reviewing the Burger Court, political scientists Mark Silverstein and Benjamin Ginsberg concluded in 1987: "The most controversial decisions of the Warren era involving school prayer, reapportionment, desegregation, and criminal procedure remain the law of the land. The Burger Court nibbled at the edges of several Warren Court precedents, often seeking to confine their application, but overt attempts at overruling were either avoided or defeated."[45] Even though conservatives pilloried the Warren Court for judicial activism in invalidating state and federal laws as unconstitutional, the Burger Court was actually guiltier of this alleged sin than its predecessor, showing even less judicial restraint and less deference to elected officials than the Warren Court it followed.

Nowhere was the Burger Court more faithful to its predecessor than in the area of civil rights. In *Swann v. Charlotte-Mecklenberg County Board of Education* (1970), the Court made clear there would be no retreat from *Brown*. The Court unanimously upheld the use of busing to achieve racially balanced schools. The Court also gave constitutional approval to affirmative action plans as a way to remedy past discrimination against minorities and other protected groups. But the Burger Court's most famous decision, *Roe v. Wade* (1973), most clearly expresses the degree to which the Court drew on the legal reasoning of the Warren Court. The Warren Court first recognized a constitutional right to privacy in *Griswold v. Connecticut* (1965) when it stuck down a state law barring the use of contraceptives. In *Roe v. Wade,* the Burger Court applied the Warren Court's logic of a right to privacy in order to strike down state laws denying a woman's right to an abortion.[46]

But as the number of liberal holdovers from the Warren Court decreased and the decline of the Democratic governing coalition became more evident, the Burger Court, over time, became more conservative. The drift to the right was particularly apparent in criminal law, where the Burger Court began to chip away at the Warren Court's revolution in due process, reducing defendants' procedural rights and protections.

In 1986, Republicans pulled the equivalent of a double steal in baseball. Justice Burger retired and was replaced as chief justice by William Rehnquist, the most conservative member of the Court. Rehnquist was so at

---

[45] Silverstein and Ginsberg, "Supreme Court and the New Politics," p. 372.

[46] Many legal experts believe that there was less logic than invention involved in the Warren Court's holding that a constitutional right to privacy existed.

odds with the basically liberal thrust of the Burger Court that he wrote a record number of single dissents to its decisions, earning him the nickname "The Lone Ranger." Controversy over his nomination to chief justice erupted at his Senate confirmation hearings. Witnesses questioned the nominee's integrity, honesty, and respect for minority rights.[47] Rehnquist survived but only after one-third of the Senate voted against someone who had already served on the Court for more than 14 years. The controversy surrounding Rehnquist's confirmation to chief justice distracted attention from the appointment of Antonin Scalia to the seat formerly occupied by Rehnquist.

William Brennan, the most liberal member of the Court, stepped down in 1990. President George Bush replaced him with David H. Souter. Thurgood Marshall, the last liberal holdover from the Warren Court, resigned a year later in 1991. President Bush replaced him with another African American, Clarence Thomas. Skin color may have been the only thing that Marshall and Thomas had in common. Marshall opposed the death penalty and supported affirmative action and a woman's right to an abortion. Thomas, on the other hand, favored the death penalty and opposed abortion and government programs to remedy the effects of discrimination. While Marshall was esteemed within his profession, the American Bar Association's judiciary committee gave Thomas the lowest rating ever given a confirmed justice, with no member rating him well-qualified. His appointment was the last in an unbroken string of 11 Supreme Court appointments by Republican presidents (Republicans controlled the presidency for all but four years from 1968 through 1992).[48] They thus were able to use their power to transform the Court politically, appointing justices who would reflect their basically conservative values.

Scalia and Thomas are conservative firebrands who perceive their role as undoing the perfidious work of the Warren and Burger Courts. The other Supreme Court justices appointed by Republican presidents—Sandra Day O'Connor, David Souter, John Paul Stevens, and Anthony Kennedy—have resisted too great a turn away from the precedents built up by their predecessors. To simply discard the legal legacy of those Courts, this group believed, would damage the Supreme Court as an institution. Thus, in 1991, Justices O'Connor, Souter, and Kennedy wrote an unusual joint opinion upholding *Roe* in the abortion case *Planned Parenthood of Southeastern*

---

[47] For example, witnesses testified that Rehnquist had written a memorandum as a law clerk to Justice Robert H. Jackson in which he had defended the *Plessy* doctrine of separate but equal, had tried to intimidate black and Hispanic voters by challenging their qualifications, and had engaged in ethically questionable behavior by not removing himself from judging a case in which he had prior connections.

[48] The only Democratic president elected between 1968 and 1992 was President Jimmy Carter, who had the misfortune of never having the chance to appoint anyone to the Supreme Court.

AP/Wide World Photos

Members of the U.S. Supreme Court.

Pennsylvania v. Casey. Justice Anthony M. Kennedy signaled the intent of the group to Justice Blackmun, who had written the *Roe* decision, in a note that read: "Dear Harry, I need to see you as soon as you have a few free moments. I want to tell you about some developments in Planned Parenthood v. Casey, and, at least part of what I have to say should come as welcome news."[49] The trio of recent Republican appointees to the Court was aware that, if the Court overturned *Roe,* this would be perceived, quite accurately, as due simply to the fact that membership on the Court had changed. It would expose the Court to the charge that its decisions reflect election results, rather than the Constitution, and that the law mirrors the personal values of whomever the president appoints to the Court, rather than legal precedent or reasoning. The joint opinion of O'Connor, Souter, and Kennedy argued that, since *Roe* had been decided, people "had ordered their thinking and living around that case" and that no legal principle weakening *Roe*'s constitutional basis had occurred since 1973. "A decision to overrule *Roe*'s essential holding under the existing circumstances," their opinion continued, would be "at the cost of both profound and unnecessary damage to the Court's legitimacy and to the rule of law."[50] Thus, one survey that described the early terms of the Rehnquist Court was called *The Center Holds.*[51]

---

[49] *New York Times,* March 4, 2004.

[50] See James F. Simon, *The Center Holds: The Power Struggle inside the Rehnquist Court* (New York: Simon & Schuster, 1995), pp. 144–67, for the Rehnquist Court's process of decision making in *Casey.*

[51] Simon, *The Center Holds.*

President Bill Clinton was the first Democrat to appoint a justice to the Supreme Court in 26 years. In 1993, Byron White retired. President Clinton replaced him with Ruth Bader Ginsburg, the second woman appointed to the Court, following Sandra Day O'Connor. In 1994, Harry Blackmun retired, giving Clinton the chance to make another appointment. He chose Stephen Breyer.

The members of the current Rehnquist Court all share similar backgrounds, which distinguishes them from previous justices. In the past, many justices were career politicians who were acquainted with the president before joining the Court. Sandra Day O'Connor is the only current member of the Court who previously held elective office, and William Rehnquist is the only member of the Court to have even met the president before being nominated by him. Most of the current members of the Court are highly competent lawyers, with notable careers as lower court judges before being elevated to the Supreme Court.[52]

The Rehnquist Court is distinguished in other areas as well. Like the contemporary Senate, the current Court has become less collegial and more individualistic. The justices are reluctant to sign on to each other's opinions and insist on producing their own.[53] The result is such a confusing array of concurrences and dissents that it is sometimes hard to determine exactly how the Court ruled. In addition, the current Court is more activist in terms of asserting its power over the other branches of government and less active in terms of the number of legal issues it decides. On the one hand, it has struck down more federal laws per year than any Supreme Court in the last half century. An article in the *Washington Post* remarked that "not since the New Deal has the Supreme Court so consistently set itself against, and the Constitution, against Congress."[54] But at the same time the Supreme Court has been asserting itself against the other branches of government, its caseload has shrunk considerably. Whereas the Court decided 172 cases with 159 opinions in 1985–1986, the year before Rehnquist became Chief Justice, it issued just 71 opinions in 2003 (see Table 8–2). It is both a Court that asserts judicial supremacy in relation to the other parts of government and a Court that is reluctant to assert its power by deciding a large number of legal questions.

The Rehnquist Court's record has been a conservative one but not overly so. It has revived states' rights, it is suspicious of affirmative action, it likes the death penalty, it is willing to approve restrictions that states set on abortions, it is not sympathetic to the rights of defendants, and it is less vigilant

---

[52] Mark Silverstein, "Politics and the Rehnquist Court," in *Rehnquist Justice: Understanding the Court Dynamic,* ed. Earl. M. Maltz (Lawrence: University of Kansas Press, 2003), pp. 277–292.

[53] Lawrence Friedman, "The Rehnquist Court: Some More or Less Historical Comments," in *The Rehnquist Court: A Retrospective,* ed. Martin H. Belsky (New York: Oxford University Press, 2002), p. 145.

[54] Quoted in J. Mitchell Pickerill and Cornell W. Clayton, "The Rehnquist Court and the Political Dynamics of Federalism," *Perspectives on Politics,* no. 2 (June 2004): 233.

■ TABLE 8-2

U.S. SUPREME COURT CASES FILED AND DISPOSED:
1980–2000

Action	1980	1990	1994	1995	1996	1997	1998	1999	2000
Total cases on docket	5,144	6,316	8,100	7,565	7,602	7,692	8,083	8,445	8,965
Total cases available for argument	264	201	136	145	140	138	124	124	138
Cases argued	154	125	94	90	90	96	90	83	86
Number of signed opinions	123	112	82	75	80	91	75	74	77

SOURCE: From *Statistical Abstracts of the US, 2002* (Washington DC: U.S. Government Printing Office, 2002), p. 197.

of the separation of church and state. It has not overturned the Warren and Burger Court precedents but has instead hollowed them out, limited their application, or, in Justice Brennan's generous term, given them a "cramped interpretation."[55] For example, a woman's right to an abortion still stands, but the Court has permitted states to place more obstacles in the way of women who seek one. The principle of affirmative action is still intact, but the legal bar such programs must pass was raised higher. The due process rights of criminal defendants, such as access to a lawyer, still exist, but the Court is much more tolerant of the evasive ways that law enforcement officials apply them.

However, the Rehnquist Court did not stop at limiting the Warren Court's legacy. It also struck at legal doctrines regarding federalism that go back to the New Deal. After Rehnquist joined the Court in 1971, he issued lonely dissents on behalf of states' rights and limits to federal power. Now a majority on the Court agrees with him, reducing the authority of Congress over the states. In *United States v. Lopez* (1995), the Court struck down the Gun-Free School Zones Act of 1990, which prohibited possession of a gun within 1000 feet of a school. For the first time in 60 years the Court ruled a federal law was unconstitutional on the grounds that Congress had exceeded its authority because interstate commerce was not directly involved. Five years later in *United States v. Morrison* (2000), the same five justices, for the same reason, threw out the Violence Against Women Act of 1994, which permitted women

---

[55] Brennan is quoted in Jerome J. Shestack, "The Rehnquist Court and the Legal Profession," p. 171.

who are victims of gender-related violence to sue for damages in federal court. According to Edward P. Lazarus, who once clerked for Justice Harry Blackmun, "The Court today . . . is riven between those who see the federal government as the primary guarantor of constitutional rights and those who do not; between those Justices who still think the federal government must intervene to achieve racial equality and those who do not; and between those who for whom 'states' rights' still carries the taint of the slaveholder and those for whom it does not."[56]

On the other side of the ledger, the Court struck a blow for long-established legal rights when it rejected President Bush's arguments that he had the power as commander in chief to detain suspected terrorists indefinitely without knowledge of the charges against them or even access to a lawyer. The Court, in effect, ruled that the president was not above the law. The Rehnquist Court has also compiled a strong record on First Amendment cases. According to legal scholar Burt Neuborne, the Rehnquist Court has "echoed and deepened the powerful First Amendment doctrine [it] inherited . . . and has been among the strongest free speech courts in the nation's history."[57] Its most famous ruling in this arena was *Texas v. Johnson* (1989), which held that burning the flag is protected by the First Amendment. And in *Lawrence v. Texas* (2003), the Court strongly reaffirmed the right-to-privacy doctrine first enunciated in *Griswold* and culminating in *Roe* to strike down a Texas anti-sodomy law. The Court declared that gays are "entitled to respect for their private lives" by the government to the same degree as heterosexuals. This ruling was a constitutional watershed, providing a due process guarantee to gay men and women for their private sexual behavior, overruling the Court's previous 1986 *Bowers v. Hardwick* decision.

The Rehnquist Court has drawn the ire of liberals for undermining in practice, if not in principle, the Warren Court legacy. But it has also disappointed conservatives who expected it to make the counterrevolution that the Burger Court failed to produce. While pleased with the general drift of the Court to the right, conservatives condemn it for lacking the courage of its convictions.

Politically, the Court is defined by its members. On one side of the court are liberals, such as Ruth Bader Ginsburg and Stephen Breyer, who were appointed by Clinton; David Souter, who turned out to be surprisingly moderate in his opinions; and John Paul Stevens, perhaps the Court's most liberal member today. But these four Justices diverge enough in their decisions that they do not really comprise an identifiable bloc within the Court. The right wing was previously occupied by Rehnquist alone, but it became a consistent bloc and increasingly aggressive with the addition of Antonin Scalia and

---

[56] Edward P. Lazarus, *Closed Chambers: The First Eyewitness Account of the Epic Struggles inside the Supreme Court* (New York: Random House, 1998), p. 512.

[57] Burt Neuborne, "Free Expression and the Rehnquist Court", in *The Rehnquist Court: A Retrospective,* ed. Martin H. Belsky (New York: Oxford University Press, 2002), p. 15.

Clarence Thomas. The swing votes and the most important members of the Court in terms of deciding cases are Anthony Kennedy and especially Sandra Day O'Connor. For example in the 2003 Supreme Court term, Justice O'Connor was in the majority in all but 2 of the 14 five-to-four decisions issued by the Court. In 2004, O'Connor again led all Justices by being in the majority in 13 out of 18 of the Court's most closely decided cases. Both Kennedy and O'Connor are pragmatic conservatives who are sympathetic to Rehnquist's states' rights agenda but do not share Scalia and Thomas's desire to undo completely the last 100 years of constitutional law. Justice Brennan once said, "It takes five votes to do anything on the Supreme Court," meaning that the conservative bloc around Rehnquist, Scalia, and Thomas needs to pick up only two votes in order to prevail in cases.[58] But the price of victory for them has often undermined its significance and disappointed the three conservatives because Kennedy and O'Connor are not disposed to issue broad sweeping opinions. According to the judicial scholar Mark Silverstein, they work hard to avoid deciding too much. Thus, even when the conservative bloc wins, "their victory is undercut by a multiplicity of concurring opinions that strive to emphasize precisely how little new law is being created."[59]

That the Supreme Court follows the election returns is as true of the Rehnquist Court as it was of the Warren Court. The former reflected the shift in public opinion to the right and the Republican Party's resurgence, just as much as the Warren Court reflected Democratic Party dominance and popular demands to increase democratic rights. The Rehnquist Court, like its predecessors, confirms the thesis of the political scientist Robert Dahl, who found that "the main task of the Court is to confer legitimacy on the fundamental policies" of the dominant coalition of groups and interests in control of the government. "Except for short-lived transitional periods," he wrote, "when the old alliance is disintegrating and the new one is struggling to take control of political institutions, the Supreme Court is inevitably a part of the dominant national alliance. As an element in the political leadership of the dominant alliance, the Court, of course, supports the major policies of the alliance. By itself, the Court is almost powerless to affect the course of national policy."[60] But Dahl's thesis needs to be amended in two ways. First, Dahl, of course, could not anticipate that the Supreme Court would intervene to decide a presidential election, as it did in 2000. Thus, on the one hand, an amended version of Dahl's thesis would argue that the Supreme Court not only reflects and is part of the dominant constellation of forces but in some circumstances helps to create them as well. On the other hand, Dahl's thesis also needs to be softened because the Court sometimes tacks against the wind. There are moments

---

[58] Quoted in David Savage, *Turning Right: The Making of the Rehnquist Court* (New York: John Wiley & Sons, 1992), p. 12.

[59] Silverstein, "Politics and the Rehnquist Court," p. 287.

[60] Robert Dahl, "Decision Making in a Democracy: The Supreme Court as a National Policy-Maker," *Journal of Public Law* 6 (Fall 1957): 293.

when the other branches of government default and the Court provides political leadership, as it did in *Brown*, as well as times when the Court decides against what the dominant coalition would prefer, as the Rehnquist Court did in its *Lawrence* decision affirming gay rights.

THE LAW AND THE DEVELOPMENT
OF AMERICAN CAPITALISM

The Constitution and the law, guarded by an independent judiciary and a system of criminal law based on procedural rights and trial by jury, have underpinned popular sovereignty in the United States. Equally, the Constitution and the law have been fundamental to the development and success of the country's economic system. A capitalist economy that depends on economic exchanges via contracts cannot exist without the legitimacy, security, and stability that only a predictable legal system can provide. The first American government under the Articles of Confederation failed to provide these rudimentary conditions. By contrast, the new Constitution drafted by the Founders created an overarching legal framework for American capitalism. It created a national government that had powers of taxation, sole control over a national monetary system, and the right to regulate interstate and foreign commerce.

If the new Constitution provided the hardware to promote capitalist development, changes in common law provided the software. Prior to the 19th century, common law regarding commercial activity, property rights, and contracts had expressed the moral sense of a rural community. The law had a paternalistic, regulative, and protective quality. For example, judges regularly held that the inherent fairness of a contract determined its legality. Contracts were void if they were found to be inequitable and unfair to one of the parties.

But from the ratification of the new Constitution up through the Civil War, common law doctrine changed dramatically. A new "instrumental" conception of the law prevailed, in which the growth of the market and economic development were regarded as the ends of justice. Law became separated from morality, from any community sense of what is fair and equitable. In its place, judges substituted the values of the marketplace, which was regarded as neutral because it was governed by the impersonal principles of supply and demand. Contracts arrived at in the market were considered fair because the parties were regarded as free and willing and as equal in the eyes of the law. Whereas the courts previously protected weaker parties to prevent them from being taken advantage of, the courts now followed the new doctrine of *caveat emptor* (buyer beware), which left the weaker parties on their own.

The law limited the ability of legislatures and courts to impose their own moral judgment on commercial transactions. The allegedly neutral principles of supply and demand would replace the politically tainted moral judgments rendered by government institutions. The only role left for the law and political institutions would be to perfect the rules under which economic activity occurred. Consequently, the law became formal and technical, indifferent to the results. The formal conception of the law as concerned only with rules and indifferent to results masked its role in perpetuating the fiction of fair contracts among unequal parties.

The priority that judges now gave to economic development and the growth of the market over other competing values was reflected in how the law dealt with such issues as usury, property rights, liability, and juries. For example, usury laws no longer restrained creditors from charging high rates of interest in a society where capital was scarce. Usury laws remained on the books, but the penalties for usury were weakened, and the circumstances in which such laws applied were reduced. Judges moved to promote market values on other legal fronts as well. Previously, property rights were absolute and exclusive, giving an owner the power to prevent economic improvements that injured his or her property. Now the test of property rights was productive use, freeing property owners to develop their land without concern for the injury it might cause another's property. This, for example, meant that a landowner could obstruct the flow of water by building a mill on his or her property. This obstruction, of course, hurt others downstream, but the courts now held that possession of property implied the right to develop it for business purposes even if it might harm another's enjoyment of his or her property. Moreover, strict liability and nuisance laws that had made it easy for people to win damages when they were injured by business were relaxed. This new reading of the law shifted the cost of economic improvements to those who were injured by them.

According to legal historian Morton Horwitz, these changes in the law "enabled mercantile and entrepreneurial groups to broadly advance their own interests through a transformed system of private law."[61] By redefining property rights and other commercial laws, the courts promoted economic development and the interests of those who benefited from it. These changes in common law were uneven, even quirky, with some judges responding to the pressures of economic development, while others remained rooted in an older, more regulative jurisprudence. But as the forces promoting a free market advanced up through the Civil War, the law changed, albeit faster in some areas than others, to accommodate them.

POLITICS BY LAWSUIT

Americans are known to be litigious, settling their disputes in court rather than among themselves. The degree to which Americans engage in lawsuits is not a cultural trait but a reflection of the individual rights we enjoy and the openness of the judicial system to assertions of those rights. Recently, corporate

---

[61] Morton J. Horwitz, *The Transformation of American Law, 1780–1860* (Cambridge, MA: Harvard University Press, 1977), p. 211.

America has tried to reduce the prevalence of lawsuits, claiming they are frivolous and expensive and hamper innovation. It has tried to pass bills that would cap punitive damages awards by juries and discourage lawsuits by making plaintiffs pay if they lose. Its most telling example of a justice system that is out of control is the 1994 case of a woman who won a multimillion-dollar award from McDonald's after she spilled coffee on herself. But the common perception that her claim was trivial is a myth. In fact, McDonald's had received over 700 complaints about burns from their coffee, which was 20 degrees hotter than in most other restaurants, and the woman in question required skin grafts for the third-degree burns she suffered that took more than a year to heal. Moreover, the woman had offered to settle prior to the trial, and despite encouragement from the judge, McDonald's refused to do so. Only after it lost did McDonald's claim hypocritically to be the victim of a process that it chose to pursue. While the $2.9 million jury award received extensive coverage in the media, not many newspapers covered the story of how the woman later settled for $600,000 after the judge reduced the jury's punitive damages award. Corporations have mounted an effective public relations campaign against "frivolous" lawsuits, like that against McDonald's, which often are not frivolous at all. While the law may serve the interests of corporations, it can also be used to hold them accountable for unsafe cars, cancerous cigarettes, dangerous drugs, and risky products.

The same rush to the courts for judgment and restitution is occurring in politics as well as outside of it. More and more groups are looking to the courts to settle political issues. This is particularly so during extended periods of divided government when political actors look to the courts to settle issues in the absence of a stable political coalition to do so. At no time was this more evident than when Al Gore and George W. Bush appealed to the courts to settle questions surrounding the 2000 presidential election. Or take the example of how environmentalists shifted tactics once George W. Bush became president. They filed expensive lawsuits against polluters because they had little faith the Bush administration would enforce environmental regulations.[62] Environmentalists hoped to make policy through lawsuits in the courts as opposed to legislation by Congress or regulation by federal agencies. The courtroom has become simply another extension of the political battle once it moves past the electoral, legislative, and administrative arenas. More than a century and a half ago, Alexis de Tocqueville noted this peculiar trait when he observed, "There is hardly a political question in the United States that does not sooner or later turn into a judicial one."[63]

While the courts have always been a strategic political option, this has been particularly so since the 1960s. Supreme Court rulings made federal courts more open and inviting to those who wanted to bring suit. Previous restrictions regarding the kinds of cases that could be brought and the parties who could legally bring them in federal courts were relaxed. This

---

[62] *New York Times*, December 2, 2000.

[63] Alexis de Tocqueville, *Democracy in America* (New York: Knopf, 1946), p. 280.

change, according to two political scientists, Benjamin Ginsberg and Martin Shefter, has "given a wider range of litigants access to the courts, has rendered a broader range of issues subject to judicial settlement, and so has greatly increased the reach of the courts in American life."[64] As the courts have expanded their jurisdiction, making themselves open to a wider array of interests and issues, their power has increased. The federal courts have become more involved in policy issues that groups now bring to them in the form of litigation.

According to legal scholar Martin Shapiro, the new openness of the courts has contributed to a broader involvement of the courts in policy and politics. Nowhere is this more evident than in the growth of judicial activism. Nullifying laws as unconstitutional has become more frequent under both liberal and conservative Supreme Courts, from Warren to Rehnquist. Judge-made law substitutes for legislature-made law. Second, the courts have become more engaged in policy and politics through their greater role in implementing the law. For example, federal district courts have gone so far as to take over local school systems, constructing elaborate plans for their desegregation when local school boards have dragged their feet. Courts have become involved in such matters as what schools would close, where new ones would be constructed, and to which schools students would be assigned. In the 1970s, people in Alabama joked that the real executive leader of the state was Federal District Court Judge Frank M. Johnson, Jr., and not Governor George Wallace. Johnson earned such notoriety because his appointees oversaw Alabama schools, prisons, mental hospitals, and elections when state agencies failed to perform their constitutional duties.

Finally, the courts' growing involvement in policy and politics is evident in the lack of deference courts now show to federal administrative agencies. The courts, of course, have the final say over the meaning of legislation. They have, however, previously deferred to the expertise of administrative agencies in how legislation is to be interpreted and implemented. But courts today are more willing to invoke their authority, to have the final word on legislative meaning, and to overrule administrative agencies. For example, the U.S. Court of Appeals for the District of Columbia Circuit, which handles most challenges to federal regulations, recently prevented the Environmental Protection Agency (EPA) from implementing new, more stringent clean air standards. Such standards had been developed over two years in which interested parties had made their case to the EPA, an independent panel of scientists had confirmed the health effects of the new standard, and the new standard passed legislative scrutiny when Congress failed to overturn it. This did not prevent the American Trucking Association from challenging the stricter standards in court by bringing suit against the EPA. And it won![65]

---

[64] Benjamin Ginsberg and Martin Shefter, *Politics by Other Means: The Declining Importance of Elections in America* (New York: Basic Books, 1990), p. 150.

[65] John B. Judis, "Deregulation Run Riot," *American Prospect* (September–October 1999): 16–19. Later, in 2001, the Supreme Court reversed the Court of Appeals ruling that had overturned the EPA clean air standards.

Of course, the more courts substitute their judgment for that of administrative agencies, the more they invite litigation. Groups seeking vigorous enforcement of the law and groups resisting regulation now engage in politics by lawsuit in order to shape policy as much as they previously engaged in lobbying in order to influence agency rule making.[66]

The courts have grown in power. But so have the other branches of the government, Congress and the executive, with which they compete. Moreover, as we have already noted, the courts tend to reflect the politics of ruling coalitions. The courts are powerful so long as they blow with the prevailing wind and not against it. Consequently, while public interest advocacy groups have had some success in appealing to the courts and getting the law changed, what happens in the real world is often a different matter. Fifteen years after the *Brown* decision that began with a suit in Clarendon County, South Carolina, that district's public school system enrolled 3,000 black children and just a single white child. Twenty-five years after the *Brown* decision, in 1979, a new school desegregation suit was filed in Topeka, Kansas, by Linda Brown, the original plaintiff in the school desegregation case that bears her name, on behalf of her children! The same story is true with regard to abortion. Despite the victory in *Roe*, the number of abortions actually grew faster in the years preceding that landmark decision than they did in those afterward.[67] Legal victories can confirm changes that have occurred in the halls of Congress, at elections, and in the minds of citizens but are no substitute for them.

CONCLUSION

The courts are mostly conservative institutions that support the status quo. Their decisions usually follow and confirm reforms rather than cause them. On the basis of a study of civil rights, women's rights, and reapportionment, among other subjects, political scientist Gerald Rosenberg concluded that, in the United States, "courts can *almost never* be effective producers of significant social reform. At best, they can second the social reform acts of other branches of government."[68] The law usually follows politics, not the other way around.

Yet, as we argued in the introduction to this chapter, it would be a mistake to dismiss the significance of the courts or the degree to which the law can be a tool of social change. Legal change confers legitimacy on actions that

---

[66] Martin Shapiro, "The Juridicalization of Politics in the United States," *International Political Science Review* 15 (April 1994): 101–12.

[67] Gerald N. Rosenberg, *The Hollow Hope: Can Courts Bring About Social Change?* (Chicago: University of Chicago Press, 1991).

[68] Rosenberg, *Hollow Hope*, p. 338 (emphasis in original).

previously were outlawed. It removes blockages to change, as occurred when changes in the views, decisions, and membership of the Supreme Court overcame a constitutional impasse that threatened the New Deal in the 1930s. Finally, new legal principles, such as the right to privacy, can be applied in a different context to win new rights. The law confirms the powers that be, but it can also be a tool to change them.

PUBLIC POLICY

Trying to Resolve the Tension Between Capitalism and Democracy

Political participation is the motor that drives the machine of political institutions. Public policy charts the direction in which the machine moves. Some policies move government to the left, reducing inequalities, while others move it to the right, generating new and deeper inequalities. Nor do all policies fit neatly within a left–right continuum based upon whether they increase or decrease inequality. Policies regulate such mundane and relatively innocent issues as speed limits for drivers and licensing for pets. In Part IV we analyze three of the most important policy areas: foreign, social, and economic policy. We chose them because they connect closely with our central themes, they consume a large share of federal expenditures, and they heavily influence the practice of American politics.

Government policies are both a result and a cause. They result from struggles among private groups and public officials. They determine who gets what, where, and how. But policies also matter because they help shape future outcomes. They create the playing field that gives advantages to some political actors and disadvantages to others as they contend over new issues. Political actors come armed for new battles with the weapons that previous policies have given them.

Public policy is not made in a vacuum. In the United States, it occurs in a context of capitalist democracy, which we analyzed in Chapters 2 and 3, and within ideological and institutional settings, which we analyzed in Chapters 4 through 8. The democratic features of American politics mean that policies are widely debated and partially responsive to what mobilized groups demand. At the same time, however, the democratic features of American government are constrained and distorted by the mobilization of bias that capitalism creates and by social inequalities that are reflected in public opinion, political participation, and the operation of American political institutions. While there is considerable space for democratic debate and practice to alter the contours of policy, public policy choices are severely constrained by the capitalist organization of the economy and the design of political institutions. In sum, public policy reflects the changing ways American society attempts to resolve the tensions between capitalism and democracy.

9

FOREIGN POLICY

Two sets of statistics—military and economic—provide the context for understanding American foreign policy. The United States has a vast military establishment, the largest and most powerful in the world. It maintains 15 large military bases overseas and nearly 700 small ones.[1] Over one-quarter of a million troops are stationed abroad, not including those serving in Iraq.[2] The navy has patrols in every ocean; reconnaissance satellites circle the world; American warplanes enjoy uncontested supremacy in the skies; and the United States has the best trained, best equipped army in the world, ready to be dispatched at a moment's notice. Military treaties link the United States to the regimes of over 40 countries in Europe, Asia, and Latin America. The 2005 U.S. military budget of $500 billion is more than the GDP of most countries in the world and exceeds the military expenditures of the next 20 highest-spending nations put together.[3] These colossal expenditures seek to maintain American military superiority and a stable world in which the United States enjoys a preeminent situation.

Just how preeminent can be gleaned from statistics reflecting the U.S. economic position in the world. With less than five percent of the world's population, the United States accounts for over one-quarter of the world's gross domestic product (GDP). Income in the United States is about 4 times larger than the combined income of all the countries in East Asia and the Pacific (excluding Japan) and 14 times larger than the combined income of all the countries in the Middle East and North Africa. The United States consumes

---

[1] Department of Defense, "Base Structure Report: A Summary of DoD's Real Property Inventory" (June 2003), *http://www.defenselink.mil/news/Jun2003/basestructure2003.pdf.*

[2] Department of Defense, "Active Duty Military Personnel Strengths by Regional Area and by Country" (March 2004), *http://web1.whs.osd.mil/mmid/M05/hst0403.pdf.*

[3] Center for Defense Information (March 2003), *http://www.cdi.org/program/issue/document.cfm? DocumentID=1040&IssueID=34&StartRow=11&ListRows=10&appendURL=&Orderby= DateLastUpdated&ProgramID=15&issueID=34.* Also see Paul Kennedy, "The Greatest Superpower Ever," *New Perspective Quarterly* 19 (Spring 2002), for a good analysis and slightly different statistics.

■ TABLE 9-1

PER CAPITA INCOME, SELECTED COUNTRIES, 2003

Country	Per Capita Income (Constant 1995 US$)
Brazil	4,577
Canada	23,843
China	1,024
Dominican Republic	2,081
Ghana	447
Hungary	5,943
India	525
Italy	21,476
Mexico	3,717
Philippines	1,239
Russian Federation	3,528
Senegal	656
Sweden	34,081
United States	32,514

SOURCE: World Bank Group, Development Data, 2004 World Development Indicators, *http://www. worldbank.org/data.*

more oil than Germany, France, China, and India combined.[4] Overall, most Americans are wealthier (as can be seen in Table 9–1), enjoy better housing, suffer less from hunger, and receive more education and services than most people in the world. A note of caution: These figures are averages for all Americans and do not highlight the extensive inequalities *within* the United States, a subject analyzed in other chapters.

These statistics highlight the extensive economic disparity between American citizens and the vast majority of the world's population. When American political leaders talk of the need to maintain world order and stability, they are referring to the order and stability of a world in which the United States enjoys a vastly disproportionate share of the world's resources. The United States has not dictated that most of the world's inhabitants have

---

[4] Income estimate from the World Bank Group, "Development Data, 2000 World Development Indicators," p. 12, at *http://www.worldbank.org/data/wdi:2000/pdfs/tab_1.pdf.* See also *UNESCO Statistical Yearbook* (Paris: UNESCO Publishing and Bernan Press, 1999), sec. IV. On oil consumption, see *Key World Energy Statistics from the IEA,* 1999 ed. (Paris: International Energy Association, 1999), p. 10.

a lower standard of living than the average American. But it should be noted that the United States generally exerts its influence to maintain a stable world order in which it enjoys a highly privileged position. Much less priority is given to dealing with global poverty, disease, and economic inequality.

What explains the extraordinary fortune of the United States? Part of the explanation is that although Americans (both citizens and undocumented workers) are more productive than citizens in other industrialized countries—we work harder and longer on average—the United States also enjoys a favored geopolitical situation—abundant natural resources, fine climate, and a large internal market. Further, the United States benefited from a head start in the global economic race. Along with Britain, it was one of the first countries in the world to industrialize and therefore was not forced to compete with more economically and technologically advanced countries.

A key additional ingredient is the importance of politics and policy: Ever since the establishment of the United States in the 18th century, American political leaders have consciously crafted domestic and foreign policies to achieve and maintain a favorable position in the global political economy. In other words, American economic, military, and political dominance has not just happened; it has been *made* to happen. How that has occurred is the subject of the present chapter.

Immense changes have occurred in foreign policy following September 11, 2001, a watershed date in American history. On the morning of that dreadful day, militants of the Islamic fundamentalist movement al Qaeda hijacked four U.S. airliners, laden with jet fuel, and used them as missiles. Two planes were flown into the Twin Towers of the World Trade Center in New York City, causing the massive buildings to crumble and producing nearly 3000 deaths. The third plane crashed into the Pentagon, killing 184 people and causing extensive damage. The fourth plane never reached the hijackers' intended destination of the nation's capital. After learning by cell phones of the fate of the three other airliners, passengers courageously overpowered the hijackers, and the plane crashed in a field in Pennsylvania, killing all those aboard.

American foreign policy—as well as countless other features of American political, social, and cultural life—changed fundamentally after September 11. Yet alongside the significant changes that have occurred since that day, there are important continuities whose origins can be traced to the earliest years of the American republic. This chapter analyzes both continuities and changes in American foreign policy, key elements in understanding how the United States has achieved and maintained a position of global dominance.

AMERICAN FOREIGN POLICY BEFORE WORLD WAR II

How did the United States become the sole superpower in the world today? The question is especially puzzling because, throughout much of the 18th and 19th centuries, the United States was far removed from world power struggles. In his presidential farewell address, George Washington urged

Americans to profit from the good fortune that geography provided, in the form of an ocean separating it from Europe, and to avoid "entangling alliances" with other countries. For much of the 19th century, the United States chose to remain isolated from European intrigues. An important reason was a widespread concern that the United States might not be able to preserve its republican, and later democratic, political system if the government intervened actively abroad. The tension between democracy at home and intervention overseas has become more acute in the most recent period, when the United States adopted a far more activist foreign policy.

In the early years of American history, at the same time that the United States proclaimed a desire to remain distant from international conflicts, it engaged in an extraordinarily aggressive course of westward expansion. This included the decimation, conquest, and forced resettlement of native Indian populations, taking Florida from Spain in 1819, annexing Texas in 1845, and waging war with Mexico in 1846. (The Mexican-American War resulted in the United States forcibly incorporating a vast portion of Mexico: the area that is now California, New Mexico, Utah, Arizona, and Nevada.) Whereas European countries engaged in colonial expansion abroad, the United States expanded by annexing adjoining territory.

Furthermore, remaining distant from Europe did not mean abstaining from foreign intervention. The United States staked out its own sphere of influence in the Western Hemisphere. In 1823, President Monroe issued what came to be known as the Monroe Doctrine, in which he warned European powers not to intervene in Latin America. According to historian Richard Van Alstyne, "[I]t is not the negatives [in the Monroe Doctrine] that really count. It is the hidden positive to the effect that the United States shall be the only colonizing power and the sole directing power in both North and South America."[5]

The orientation of the United States began to change around 1900, as Britain's power waned. The Spanish-American War in 1898, when the United States gained control over the Philippines, Puerto Rico, and Guam, was the turning point, when the United States shifted from traditional isolationism to a more interventionist stance. The United States became more fully engaged abroad when it fully mobilized during the two world wars of the 20th century.

The United States was traditionally active in its own backyard. Political leaders practiced in Latin America what came to be called gunboat diplomacy, dispatching the navy to install and protect client regimes dependent on the United States and favorable to American business interests. President Theodore Roosevelt connived to build the Panama Canal, beginning in 1902, by carving out the client state of Panama from Colombia and pressuring Panama to grant the United States sovereignty over the land for the canal. (Nearly a century later, on December 31, 2000, the United States turned over control of the canal to Panama, finally closing the books on a flagrant instance of American imperialism.)

---

[5] Richard W. Van Alstyne, *The Rising American Empire* (Chicago: Quadrangle, 1965), p. 99.

Until the early 20th century, U.S. influence was mostly confined to the Western Hemisphere. But the two world wars enormously weakened the leading European nations. In particular, World War II brought the irrevocable decline of Great Britain as the dominant capitalist power and the hub of world manufacturing, commerce, and banking. The Soviet Union, Japan, Germany, Britain, and France—all the major industrialized countries other than the United States—suffered heavy war damage. By contrast, the war was not fought on American soil, and the U.S. economy received a powerful boost from the crash program of industrial expansion that occurred to support the war effort. The United States emerged from the war as the world's preeminent economic, military, and political power.

After World War II, the United States adopted a far more activist foreign policy, a response to the decline of the major European powers, the challenge to the United States posed by the Soviet Union—a political and ideological rival—and the fear of American officials that global instability might produce a resumption of the destructive 1930s economic depression. As Chapters 10 and 11 describe, new policies were devised to promote economic and social stability at home. In addition, policies were fashioned to deal with a rapidly changing global situation. Movements for independence of colonies in Asia and Africa formerly controlled by Western European countries, as well as demands for economic development and social justice throughout the world, encouraged the United States to seek a dominant role in shaping world order.

U.S. officials sought to create a peaceful, stable world open for international trade, where American industry would have easy access to raw materials and markets throughout the world. The United States helped sponsor international institutions to achieve these goals, including the United Nations, the International Monetary Fund, and the International Bank for Reconstruction and Development (popularly known as the World Bank). At the same time, the United States sought to achieve formal equality among nations, both for idealistic reasons and because leaders calculated that a world of independent nations was more likely to promote stability. Like President Woodrow Wilson after World War I, American leaders after World War II pressed the colonial powers (Great Britain, France, and the Netherlands) to dismantle their empires. Soon, the number of newly independent countries soared as former colonies in Africa and Asia gained independence. A key American goal was to ensure that those governments supported U.S. policies. Only one country posed a massive threat to the vision of an integrated capitalist world order: the USSR.

COLD WAR RIVALRY

Soon after the end of World War II, world politics became structured by the conflict between the United States and the Soviet Union. Each country was dominant in its sphere of influence: the United States in Western Europe,

North America, and Latin America; the Soviet Union in Eastern and Central Europe, Cuba, and the People's Republic of China. Each country also had client states in the less developed regions of the world: Africa, Asia, and Latin America—often referred to as the Third World, to distinguish these regions from the industrialized capitalist world (the First World) and the Soviet bloc (the Second World). During the Cold War, the United States devoted enormous political, military, and economic resources to checking the Soviet Union, maintaining regimes friendly to the United States throughout the world, and weakening movements and regimes allied with the Soviet Union.

An ideological chasm separated the liberal democratic, capitalist United States and the self-proclaimed communist Soviet Union, with a command economy and an authoritarian Communist Party. But historian David Callahan suggests, "Whether the Cold War had occurred or not, it is clear that the United States would still have played a much greater global leadership role after World War II than it did after World War I. . . . For quite apart from the problem of security, postwar U.S. economic growth was seen as requiring international economic order that could only be guaranteed if the United States took over the position of a declining Britain."[6]

The Cold War period was unique in one respect. Ever since the United States developed atomic weapons and unleashed two of them against Japan in the closing months of World War II, the world has faced the awful possibility of nuclear devastation. For decades (and to a lesser extent continuing into the present), the future of the world has hung by a thread. With thousands of nuclear-equipped intercontinental ballistic missiles targeted on opposing armed forces and civilian populations, there is the possibility that, by accident or irresponsible design, nuclear catastrophe could endanger the entire planet. Indeed, the two superpowers approached the brink of nuclear war on several occasions—most notably during the Cuban missile crisis of 1963. (Documents made public much later revealed just how close the two sides were to ordering their nuclear-tipped missiles to fly.)

Although the end of the Cold War has vastly reduced the risk that nuclear war will be initiated through conscious decision, Russia, the United States, and several other countries continue to maintain large nuclear arsenals. The risk of a nuclear device being detonated by accident remains significant. Further, nuclear proliferation has increased in recent years. India, Israel, North Korea, and Pakistan have developed nuclear weapons, and several other countries (notably, Iran) may soon join the nuclear club. Last but far from least, there is a significant chance that nonstatist terrorist groups like al Qaeda might obtain radioactive material or hijack a nuclear power facility and unleash a "dirty bomb."

The Cold War was in part misnamed. The United States and Soviet Union fought numerous deadly "proxy wars" in the Third World—including

---

[6] David Callahan, *Between Two Worlds: Realism, Idealism, and American Foreign Policy after the Cold War* (New York: HarperCollins, 1994), p. 30.

Angola, Mozambique, and Ethiopia, in Africa; and Nicaragua, El Salvador, and Guatemala, in Central America—that pitted client states against insurgent movements. The United States trained military, intelligence, and police officials of client regimes, and provided them with extensive military, political, and financial assistance to enlist in the anti-Soviet cause. In addition, since World War II the United States has dispatched troops or launched aerial attacks against Vietnam, Laos, the Dominican Republic, North Korea, Cambodia, Lebanon, Grenada, Panama, Libya, Iraq, Somalia, Yugoslavia, Afghanistan, and Iraq.[7] The two hottest wars in which the United States participated in the Cold War era were Korea (1950–1953) and Vietnam (mid-1960s–1973), where several hundred thousand U.S. troops fought communist forces. The Vietnam War in particular proved a nightmare for the United States. It cost over 50,000 American lives and many times more injured American troops (not to mention several million Vietnamese casualties).

Beginning in the late 1980s, momentous changes occurred on the Soviet side, culminating in the dissolution of the Soviet Union in 1991 and the emergence of a noncommunist Russia and a variety of independent states in East-Central Europe and Central Asia, regions formerly incorporated within the Soviet sphere of influence. The fact that the world was bipolar during the Cold War is why strategic analyst Richard Betts asserts, "Only the collapse of the Soviet pole [in the 1990s] . . . marked the real arrival of U.S. global dominance."[8]

Focusing on the Cold War rivalry between the United States and the Soviet Union—important as that issue is—may obscure the emergence of the United States during the postwar period as the dominant power in the world. In 1970, foreign policy analyst Graham Allison observed, in words that have proved remarkably accurate: "Historians in the year 2000, looking back with detachment on the Cold War, are apt to conclude that the main feature of international life in the period 1945–1970 was neither the expansion of the Soviet Union nor Communist China. Instead, it was the global expansion of American influence: military, economic, political and cultural."[9]

GLOBAL EXPANSION

Although American power grew steadily throughout the 19th and early 20th centuries, the United States became a dominant world power only after the ravages of the Second World War meant that no state had the resources

---

[7] Michael Parenti, "The Logic of U.S. Intervention," in *Masters of War: Militarism and Blowback in the Era of American Empire*, ed. Carl Boggs (New York: Routledge, 2002), ch. 1.

[8] Richard K. Betts, "The Soft Underbelly of Primacy: Tactical Advantages of Terror," *Political Science Quarterly* 117, no. 1 (Spring 2002), reprinted in *Conflict after the Cold War: Arguments on Causes of War and Peace*, 2nd edition, ed. Richard K. Betts (New York: Pearson, 2005), p. 522.

[9] Graham Allison, "Cool It: The Foreign Policy of Young America," *Foreign Policy* no. 1 (Winter 1970–1971): 144–45.

to challenge American supremacy. Given the shattered state of Europe's economy, American business was uniquely situated to expand into other regions of the world. U.S. policy sought to open up areas throughout the world to investment by American corporations and to prevent regimes that might challenge American commercial and political interests from reaching power.

American expansion abroad has taken two major forms: economic penetration by multinational corporations into Europe and the developing world, and political and military influence exercised by the American government. The two are distinct, yet intertwined, and each has contributed to advancing the other. According to political economist Robert Gilpin, the income generated by American business investments abroad in the postwar period was used "to finance America's global political and military position. The income from foreign investments, in other words, had become an important factor in American global hegemony."[10] Here again, we see important continuity from 1945 to the present.

Latin America had been largely under informal American control ever since the 19th century. In the postwar period, the United States expanded into other resource-rich areas. Particularly important was the Middle East, which contained the world's largest petroleum deposits. American oil companies soon gained control of this vital ingredient of an industrial economy. In 1940, Great Britain controlled 72 percent of Middle East oil reserves; the United States, 10 percent; and other countries, the rest. By 1967, Great Britain controlled 29 percent; the United States, 59 percent; and other countries, the remainder.[11] (As illustrated by the war in Iraq in 2003, the quest to dominate Middle East oil remains a high priority of American foreign policy.)

Although the decades following the Second World War II saw a drastic expansion of American influence abroad, the bulk of American production, investment, and sales were located within American borders. However, in the 1980s and 1990s, a steep increase occurred in cross-border economic flows. American-based firms sharply increased their operations abroad, including trade, investment, and finance. Americans began buying many more goods and services produced abroad. Foreign companies considerably increased their investments in the United States. These developments are often described as comprising a new era, commonly described as globalization. Yet some scholars, while agreeing that significant changes have occurred in the recent past, stress elements of continuity as well as highlight that the changes that have occurred are in considerable measure dependent on political choices.

---

[10] Robert Gilpin, *U.S. Power and the Multinational Corporation: The Political Economy of Direct Foreign Investment* (New York: Basic Books, 1975), p. 161.

[11] Harry Magdoff, *The Age of Imperialism: The Economics of U.S. Foreign Policy* (New York: Monthly Review Press, 1969), p. 43.

A NEW ERA OF GLOBALIZATION?

One can distinguish two opposing groups, which we will label globalists and skeptics, regarding the extent and character of globalization. Globalists claim that, in the title of one feisty account, we now live in "One World, Ready or Not."[12] According to globalists, for better or worse (and globalists debate whether or not globalization promotes progress), the world has entered a fundamentally new phase. Rapid means of transportation and communication enable people, commodities, capital, and information to circle the globe at vastly greater speeds. This results in exponential increases in linkages among citizens, groups, localities, companies, and governments throughout the world. The political consequences of globalization are similarly vast. States no longer can effectively police their borders, in part because physical borders pose no barrier to an electronically interconnected world. At best, states can try to devise policies that help position their economies at the cutting edge internationally, as well as help their citizens adjust to globalization; at worst, states refusing to accept the harsh realities of global competition can propel their economies into a downward spiral as domestic and foreign-based firms seek greener pastures elsewhere.

Although skeptics question some of the globalists' key claims and differ in their evaluation of the political consequences of globalization, the two camps do not totally disagree: Skeptics agree that qualitatively new developments have occurred within the global economy, especially the development of high-speed information processing and transportation, which have enormously increased cross-border communication. But they suggest that many changes are less dramatic than meet the eye, and they observe that the increase in transnational flows we designate as globalization refers to diverse changes that should not be considered a single unified process. Finally, they warn that one should not mistake description for cause. Many of the changes we associate with globalization may be the product of political decisions, not an automatic result of economic or technological forces.

The increase in some global flows is dramatic. Exports of the 24 members of the Organization for Economic Cooperation and Development (OECD), the most industrialized and richest countries in the world, increased from 11 percent of their GDP in 1960 to 21 percent in 2002. Foreign direct investment grew three times faster than international trade. Multinational corporations (MNCs, sometimes called Transnational Corporations, or TNCs)—firms with significant foreign operations—now control a third of the world's privately owned productive assets. However, the greatest increases in transnational economic flows are found in financial assets, including loans to foreign governments and firms, purchases of foreign government bonds,

---

[12] William Greider, *One World, Ready or Not: The Manic Logic of Global Capitalism* (New York: Simon & Schuster, 1997). For influential defenses of globalization, see Thomas L. Friedman, *The Lexus and the Olive Tree: Understanding Globalization* (New York: Farrar, Straus and Giroux, 1999), and Jagdish Bhagwati, *In Defense of Globalization* (New York: Oxford University Press, 2004).

and currency exchange. Increases in the volume of financial flows are truly astonishing: from several billion dollars daily in the 1970s to nearly $2 trillion a day today! In the 1990s alone, international bank loans rose from 4 percent to 44 percent of the GDP of the OECD countries.[13]

There is no disagreement between the two camps about these statistics. Where they disagree is how to evaluate the importance of these changes. For example, skeptics regard the current era of globalization as one phase in a much older story of capitalist development. They stress that the current period is not the first era of increased political and economic interdependence, that earlier ones were reversed by war or economic crisis—and that a reversal might occur in the future as well.

Consider foreign trade. As a proportion of the world's economic output, foreign trade was as high in the period before World War I—admittedly, an era when total production was much smaller—as in the 1970s. Indeed, the high point of international economic integration in the modern era may have occurred in the age of colonialism—when the imperialist powers of Western Europe, especially Britain, forged close (and exploitative) economic and political links among regions of the world. However, interdependence and integration were abruptly reversed from 1914 to 1945 by two world wars and the Great Depression. Military conflict and economic instability shattered the dense international political and trade networks constructed in the 19th century. When globalists stress the rapid increase in international trade since the 1970s, they often select the period just after World War II—a low point in international trade—as the baseline.

Another important qualification of the globalization argument is that the bulk of production in the world remains geared to domestic production. Consider the United States, a global economic leader. Guess what proportion of U.S. GDP is exported these days: less than one-fifth, about half, over half? The first answer is correct, and then some: Around 10 percent of GDP is exported. Most U.S. production is destined for domestic markets. Similarly, the vast bulk of what American consumers buy is produced at home. Nor should one assume that international investment and trade will perpetually expand. When a number of East Asian, East European, and Latin American countries experienced economic crises in the 1990s, international investment and trade stagnated. Rather than globalization exhibiting a pattern of steady expansion, it may proceed in waves and experience reversals.

Even granting that the world is highly integrated economically, the political implications of the change are complex. Globalists often explain globalization as a by-product of developments in technology and economics. In their view, political decisions cannot much alter the contours of globalization. Skeptics, on the other hand, tend to stress the importance of politics.

---

[13] Data presented by Robert Wade, "Globalization and Its Limits: Reports of the Death of the National Economy Are Greatly Exaggerated," in *National Diversity and Global Capitalism*, eds. Suzanne Berger and Ronald Dore (Ithaca, NY: Cornell University Press, 1996), ch. 2.

They claim that, just as political decisions have been necessary to construct the framework of international financial treaties and institutions that promote globalization, political decisions can alter the future direction and character of globalization.[14]

There is much merit to the skeptics' arguments. Globalization is not an impersonal, transhistorical, and irreversible force. It does not just happen; it results from the decisions of corporate and government leaders. We can gain a better understanding of this process by examining the strategies of U.S. corporations and the government that promote globalization. Past decisions and policies promoting globalization were a response to specific economic and political problems. No doubt globalization will be altered in the future by other political decisions and policies.

WHOSE GLOBALIZATION?

Globalization has been associated with enormous economic growth around the world. But the fruits of this expansion have often been distributed in ways that intensify political and economic inequalities within and across nations. And economic growth has often occurred in ways that have produced enormous social dislocations and environmental devastation. Social activists Robin Broad and John Cavanaugh provide a few illustrations of the economic consequences of globalization. According to annual United Nations Development Program Human Development Reports, in the 1960s, the richest fifth of the world's inhabitants had 30 times more assets than the poorest fifth; in 1997, the income gap was 74 times greater. In the 1960s, the richest fifth controlled 70 percent of the world's income; this rose to 85 percent of the world's total at the end of the century. During this period, the share of the poorest fifth declined from 2.3 percent of the world's income to 1.4 percent. *Forbes Magazine* reports that in 2004 the nearly $2 trillion owned by the 587 billionaires in the world exceeded the combined wealth of half the world's population.

The United States plays a leading role in the world order that generates these inequalities. For example, as will be described below, U.S.-based transnational corporations control vital sectors of many countries' economies. The U.S. government's financial agencies, including the Agency for International Development (AID) and the Export Import Bank, provide aid and loans to foreign governments and technical help and insurance to American businesses in an attempt to facilitate American business operations

---

[14] For several approaches to this issue, see Geoffrey Garrett, *Partisan Politics in the Global Economy* (Cambridge, MA: Cambridge University Press, 1998); David Held, Anthony McGrew, David Goldblatt, and Jonathan Perraton, *Global Transformations: Politics, Economics and Culture* (Stanford, CA: Stanford University Press, 1999); Dean Baker, Gerald Epstein, and Robert Pollin, eds., *Globalization and Progressive Economic Policy* (Cambridge, England: Cambridge University Press, 1998).

abroad and promote market-friendly policies. The United States' leading position in the North Atlantic Treaty Organization (NATO), the Organization of American States, the United Nations General Assembly, and the United Nations Security Council leverages U.S. influence. The United States uses its preponderant influence within international financial institutions, including the International Monetary Fund (IMF), the Organization for Economic Cooperation and Development (OECD), the World Trade Organization (WTO), and the World Bank, to regulate an international capitalist order and promote market-friendly policies that enable American business to prosper.

The global economic order is regulated by rules that favor the rights of property over democratic participation and human rights. For example, multinational pharmaceutical companies can patent herbs and traditional methods of medical treatment. Agribusiness firms can prevent governments from limiting imports of genetically modified seeds and food on the grounds that such regulation hinders free trade. WTO rules can prevent governments from subsidizing industries in their borders to enable them to compete with MNCs.

Yet this new world order is not unchallenged. For example, when trade ministers from governments around the world met in Seattle in 1999 to seek to expand the WTO's powers, 50,000 activists from unions, churches, environmental groups, and human rights organizations mobilized. The protest closed down the city and made the WTO a household name. Since then, protests have occurred in other sites of international economic negotiations, including Davos, Switzerland; Washington, D.C.; Prague, the Czech Republic; Québec, Canada; Genoa, Italy; and Cancun, Mexico. Indeed, virtually no international economic summit takes place nowadays without protestors challenging business as usual. (The exceptions are meetings held in locations, such as Doha, Qatar, the site of a WTO meeting in 2001, strictly off-limits to protestors.)

Globalization is not an inevitable historical tide. It is a consciously fashioned response to challenges. American corporate capitalism expanded outside the United States as a response by American business regarding four dilemmas: dependence on raw materials, dependence on open markets, dependence on foreign investment, and dependence on workers.

RAW MATERIALS

The United States is among the countries best endowed with natural resources. It has some of the world's largest deposits of coal, copper, natural gas, iron, petroleum, and aluminum. The United States is also among the world's leading food producers; for example, it is the largest producer of corn, soybeans, cotton, and oranges, and the largest exporter of wheat and rice. However, no country is fortunate enough to contain within its borders all the raw materials it needs for modern industrial production—and the United States is no exception. Moreover, the United States has begun to deplete many of the natural resources it once contained in abundance. Both factors produce a growing dependence on other countries for essential raw materials.

The speed with which the United States became dependent on other countries for raw materials can be seen from the following figures: Of the 13 minerals considered essential for a modern industrial economy, the United States had to import more than half its supplies of only 4 in 1950; two decades later that figure had climbed to 12.[15] Most of these raw materials come from less developed countries in Latin America, Asia, the Middle East, and Africa.

American corporations and the U.S. government seek to assure a cheap and adequate supply of minerals and other natural resources flowing to the United States. The most effective solution has been for American corporations to invest in the Third World and to gain direct control over foreign raw materials. For example, Kennecott and Anaconda control much of the world's copper deposits, located in Zambia, Chile, and elsewhere. And a handful of American petroleum corporations (along with a few foreign companies) control most of the world's petroleum supplies. Although gaining control over Iraq's petroleum reserves, the second largest in the world, was not the sole reason that the United States invaded Iraq in 2003, it is one important factor that explains the action.

FOREIGN TRADE

The United States is the largest exporter of agricultural products, industrial goods, and services in the world. Although, as we have seen, some of the rhetoric about the importance of globalization is overblown, global markets are essential to the prosperity of American business. Encouraged by government tax incentives, technical assistance, insurance against political difficulties, and, most important, a foreign policy that aims to open foreign markets to American exports, the expansion of America's foreign trade has been rapid. In 1960, U.S. exports were valued at $26 billion; by 1980, their value had increased to $272 billion; and by 2003, exports were valued at over $1 trillion—more than 38 times their value in 1960.[16] At the same time, imports of goods into the United States increased even faster: $22 billion in 1960, $291 billion in 1980, and $1.5 trillion by 2003. This two-way flow of goods highlights that globalization involves interdependence among countries. And the fact that imports have been significantly greater than exports for years highlights a weakness of the American economy.

OVERSEAS INVESTMENT

American corporations often find it more profitable to invest capital in building new plants abroad to produce and assemble products, or to outsource the production of goods and services, than to expand manufacturing at home. When food, services or manufactured goods are exported, the transaction

---

[15] *New York Times,* November 5, 1972; and December 22, 1973.

[16] *http://www.ita.doc.gov/td/industry/otea/usfth/aggregate/H03t01.html.*

ends with a purchase by foreign customers. However, when an American corporation creates a foreign subsidiary, the transaction only begins with the initial investment. The foreign subsidiary remains year after year, continuing to produce and sell goods that make a profit for the American home company. American corporations began investing heavily in foreign subsidiaries during the 1950s and have piled up substantial investments abroad since then. In 1979, U.S.-owned assets abroad were valued at $786 billion. Ten years later, as Table 9-2 shows, international assets of American companies had grown to over $2 trillion. By 2003, the market value of foreign assets of American companies was $7.8 trillion.[17]

Profits generated from foreign investments represent an increasingly significant proportion of total American corporate profits. The share of after-tax corporate profits accounted for by foreign investment rose from 7 percent of all corporate profits in 1950 to 18 percent in 1998.[18] The largest corporations, which are more likely to have foreign operations, obtain considerably more of their profits from overseas investment.

Conversely, the American economy has become vitally dependent on foreign investment and finance. MNCs operating in the United States employed 6.4 million American workers in 2004, slightly under 5 percent of the U.S. labor force. Over the last 15 years, the number of U.S. workers employed by foreign MNCs has doubled.[19]

The United States depends on a steady and substantial inward flow of foreign funds to maintain economic stability. The U.S. economy runs annual trade deficits exceeding $300 billion yearly with other countries, meaning that American consumers buy $300 billion more goods and services produced abroad than U.S. firms export. The United States has become the consumer of last resort for the world economy. Economic crisis would result if foreign governments and firms did not provide the U.S. economy with an equivalent flow of funds each year in the form of investments in plant, equipment, and corporate stock, as well as U.S. Treasury bonds and financial instruments.[20] The steady decline in the value of the dollar in the early years of this century reflects the reluctance of foreign investors and governments to underwrite the American trade deficit and reflects their falling confidence in the American economy.

---

[17] http://www.bea.gov/bea/newsrel/intinvnewsrelease.htm.

[18] Richard C. Edwards, Michael Reich, and Thomas E. Weisskopf, eds., *The Capitalist System: A Radical Analysis of American Society,* 2nd ed. (Englewood Cliffs, NJ Prentice-Hall., 1978), Table 13-B, p. 477; and for 1998, Department of Commerce, Bureau of Economic Analysis, *Survey of Current Business,* April 2000, p. 89.

[19] http://www.ofii.org/insourcing/.

[20] The fact that the United Sates is dependent on foreign investors highlights that U.S. dominance over other countries is not unlimited. Foreign investments in the United States highlight another tendency: interdependence within the global economy.

■ TABLE 9–2

U.S. INTERNATIONAL ASSETS, 1976–2003

Year	U.S. Owned Foreign Assets	Foreign-Owned U.S. Assets
1976	456,964	292,132
1977	512,278	340,838
1978	621,227	414,804
1979	786,701	469,775
1980	929,806	568,968
1981	1,001,667	661,900
1982	1,108,436	779,482
1983	1,210,974	912,670
1984	1,204,900	1,044,205
1985	1,287,396	1,233,053
1986	1,469,396	1,505,605
1987	1,646,527	1,726,534
1988	1,829,665	2,008,135
1989	2,070,868	2,330,374
1990	2,178,978	2,424,325
1991	2,286,456	2,595,715
1992	2,331,696	2,762,894
1993	2,753,648	3,060,604
1994	2,987,118	3,310,515
1995	3,486,272	3,944,734
1996	4,032,307	4,527,362
1997	4,567,906	5,388,588
1998	5,090,938	5,990,904
1999	5,965,143	6,740,631
2000	6,231,236	7,619,981
2001	6,270,408	8,160,088
2002	6,413,535	8,646,553
2003	7,202,692	9,633,374

NOTE: All figures are in millions of dollars.

SOURCE: Bureau of Economic Analysis, "International Investment Positions of the United States at Yearend, 1976–2003," *http://www.bea.gov/bea/di/intinv03_t2.xls.*

Any discussion of American foreign policy must deal with the immensely important role that MNCs play in the United States and abroad. According to economist Daniel R. Fusfeld, the emergence of multinational corporations "was made possible by advances in the technology of transportation and communication after World War II (jet aircraft and automatic data communication, for example). U.S. corporations were able to take advantage of the new technology much more readily than foreign corporations, in part because much of that technology was developed here but chiefly because of the predominance of the United States in world trade and international finance."[21] MNCs are the new Goliaths of the present era. The 500 largest MNCs controlled over one-third of the world's global assets in 1998. Most are headquartered in the United States: 15 of the 20 companies with the largest international profits in 2000 were U.S. companies.[22] By 2000, multinational corporations outnumbered countries on the list of the world's 100 largest entities. In 2002, the parent companies of American multinationals produced added value (the value of all goods and services) of $1.9 trillion.[23] This was more than the GNP of all the countries in the Middle East, Central and South Asia, and Africa.

WORKERS

Corporations may invest abroad to end-run American workers and recruit compliant and low-paid workers abroad. As two economists observed at the beginning of the period when production was starting to move offshore, "Production of the traditional industrial goods that have been the mainstay of the U.S. economy is being transferred from . . . factories in New England to . . . factories in the 'export platforms' of Hong Kong and Taiwan."[24] In one illustration among many, in 2000, the Zebco Corporation announced that it was relocating most of its fishing reel production from Tulsa, Oklahoma, to China. For some time, the company had threatened to pull out of Tulsa unless workers increased their output. A memorandum that management sent workers was blunt: "When we don't get quota, it is another day closer to China taking our jobs."[25] Although the plant's workers did increase their output, management decided that profits would be higher if the firm pulled up stakes in Tulsa and moved to China.

Improvements in worldwide communications enable firms nowadays to locate substantial parts of an integrated production and service chain abroad.

---

[21] Daniel R. Fusfeld, *The Rise of the Corporate State in America* (Andover, MA: Warner Modular Publishers, 1973), p. 3.

[22] Michael V. Gestrin, Rory F. Knight, and Alan M. Rugman, "Templeton Global Performance Index 2001," *http://www.templeton.ox.ac.uk/pdf/Briefings/13-TB.pdf.*

[23] Raymond J. Mataloni, Jr., "U.S. Multinational Companies: Operations in 2002," *Survey of Current Business,* July 2004.

[24] Richard J. Barnet and Ronald E. Muller, *Global Reach: The Power of Multinational Corporations* (New York: Simon & Schuster, 1974), p. 216.

[25] *New York Times,* July 7, 2000.

Typically, for these "hollow" corporations, the firm's headquarters, specialized research and development, and other strategic elements remain in the United States, while production, data preparation (keypunching), and other routine aspects are located in low-wage facilities abroad. A recent development is the farming out—that is, outsourcing—of service operations. One example is that many companies have been relocating to India in order to take advantage of the large numbers of Indians fluent in English and technically qualified. Of course, wages in India are a fraction of American pay scales.

Consider the Nike Corporation. About the only thing that Nike does in the United States is to design and direct the production of shoes, as well as market its products. Just about every other aspect of the firm's operations occurs overseas.

There is far less displacement of jobs to overseas locations than is commonly believed. Nonetheless, the movement of capital overseas heightens insecurity among all workers because of the potential threat that they may be next. As a result, plant closures and capital movements depress overall wage levels and weaken union bargaining power.

This was one reason why, even during the tight labor markets of the 1990s, workers did not press for higher wages and better working conditions. Although the result was to sustain the American economic boom, it provided meager benefits to millions of workers and their families. These developments make it understandable why the American labor movement has vigorously opposed agreements, such as the North American Free Trade Agreement [NAFTA], that promote international capital movement but fail to provide adequate protection—for example, the requirement of a living wage and the right to form independent labor unions—for American and foreign workers.

The bulk of MNC investment is located in other affluent countries of the North. The purpose is to gain access to skilled labor in these countries and to locate close to the markets where MNCs sell their products. But MNC investments in poor countries, such as Bangladesh, China, Indonesia, Malaysia, and the Philippines, probably have a more substantial impact on the host countries. MNCs in the South provide jobs where there are few adequate alternatives. Although pay scales in the South are much lower than in industrialized countries, MNCs may pay wages in these countries slightly above prevailing rates. Hence, MNCs can select from a large number of job applicants. Women, in particular, gain the opportunity to contribute to their family's income and to escape traditional constraints and isolation. Globalization can promote economic development as well as underdevelopment. South Korea, Taiwan, and China are among the countries whose integration into the global economy resulted in enormous economic expansion.

Is the result a win-win situation, in which multinationals gain access to motivated low-cost workers and workers gain the chance to improve their lives? Although this description highlights the favorable aspects of the situation, it overlooks other features, for example, the harsh restrictions on workers' freedom to organize in many developing countries, long hours and unsafe working conditions in many workplaces, and environmental damage caused by MNC operations.

Multinational investment in agriculture in Third World countries is transforming regions throughout the world. Agribusiness transforms patterns of land use in ways that often collide with local needs. Rather than land being devoted to raising staple foods for local consumption, it is converted to raising cash crops for export, with agribusiness taking the profits. Mechanized means of cultivation result in displacement of traditional farmers: One farm machine can do the work of several hundred small farmers.

Throughout the Third World, local farmers have become hired help for the United States and other Western nations' agribusiness or have been thrown off the land altogether. In some Third World countries, the rate of rural unemployment has reached 40 percent. The vicious cycle continues when the surplus agricultural population migrates to cities in search of jobs. The result is often that they swell the ranks of the urban unemployed and crowd into the shantytowns that ring most Third World cities.

MNC-fuelled economic development often promotes economic inequality and environmental damage in poor countries. Consider the burgeoning growth of aquaculture, the raising of seafood in coastal areas, much of which is controlled by multinational food processors. Indian environmental activist Vandana Shiva reports, "For every acre of an industrial shrimp farm, 200 acres of productive ecosystems are destroyed. For every dollar earned as foreign exchange from exports, six to ten dollars' worth of destruction takes place in the local economy. . . . In India, intensive shrimp cultivation has turned fertile coastal tracts into graveyards, destroying both fisheries and agriculture. . . . Shrimp cultivation destroys 15 jobs for each job it creates."[26]

THE MILITARY ESTABLISHMENT

The global economy that generates such tensions could not flourish without adequate protection. But diverse forms of resistance to the alliance between MNCs, the American government, and foreign allies have increased within the United States and overseas. We have described the opposition that has mobilized to protest meetings of international financial institutions. In countless countries, there have been strikes and demonstrations opposing cutting social spending and privatizing the provision of goods and services. The two targets chosen by al Qaeda militants on September 11, 2001, were the Pentagon, the U.S. military headquarters; and the World Trade Center, a nerve center of global capitalism.

---

[26] Vandana Shiva, *Stolen Harvest: The Hijacking of the Global Food Supply* (Boston: South End Press, 2000), p. 15.

In the post–Cold War era, following the demise of the Soviet Union, the military has been restructured to deal with new developments, including nuclear proliferation, possible aggression by small states, and threats by non-state-based networks of militants. After the end of the Cold War, resources were shifted from nuclear weaponry aimed at the Soviet Union to flexible, mobile forces able to counter local threats. The trend accelerated following the attacks of September 11, 2001.

According to journalist George Easterbrook, the American military is unique among the world's armed forces in that its "primary military mission is not defense. Practically the entire military is an expeditionary force, designed not to guard borders—a duty that ties down most units of other militaries, including China's—but to 'project power' elsewhere in the world."[27]

During the Cold War, the U.S. military establishment was geared to contain Soviet expansion and maintain peace. Both the United States and the Soviet Union possessed a staggering "overkill" capacity: The United States had a stockpile of over 9,000 strategic nuclear warheads (the Soviet Union had over 7,000) and several times that number of tactical nuclear weapons.

Although the Soviet Union has crumbled and Russia is not a hostile power, the United States retains an immense, if downsized, nuclear arsenal. It currently has 5,400 land- and sea-based intercontinental missiles equipped with multiple nuclear warheads, as well as 1,750 nuclear bombs and cruise missiles that can be launched from long-range bombers. An additional 10,000 nuclear warheads are stored in bunkers, potentially available to be deployed.[28] This stock of nuclear weapons could destroy the world many times over. Despite strong safeguards, the possibility of a catastrophic accident or sabotage cannot be ruled out. Moreover, Russia and newcomers to the nuclear club have a relatively low capacity to safeguard their nuclear arsenal and prevent nuclear proliferation. In 2004, it was revealed that a Pakistani nuclear scientist had been engaged for years in selling the secrets of nuclear weaponry to North Korea.

In the past decade, the U.S. military has sponsored "a substantial cutback in [its] strategic and forward-based forces, balanced by a move toward 'global reach'—the ability to project power around the world."[29] The shift toward long-range, mobile, rapid intervention forces has been achieved by developing aircraft based in the United States capable of flying long-range missions, thanks to aerial refueling. Thus, the United States Central Command that directed the war in Afghanistan and Iraq is based in Tampa, Florida, over 7,000 miles from Afghanistan. The reorganization is cheaper than stationing troops and equipment around the world and permits greater military mobility.

---

[27] George Easterbrook, "Apocryphal Now," *New Republic* (September 11, 2000): 24.

[28] Chalmers Johnson, "American Militarism and Blowback," in *Masters of War: Militarism and Blowback in the Era of American Empire*, ed. Boggs, ch. 5, op. cit.

[29] The quote and material in this and the following two paragraphs are from Paul Rogers, "The US Military Posture: 'A Uniquely Benign Imperialism'?" in *The New Imperial Challenge; Socialist Register 2004*, eds. Leo Panitch and Colin Leys (New York: Monthly Review Press, 2003).

The navy has also been restructured. The new organization is based on the concept of a carrier battle group, that is, a single large aircraft carrier, often nuclear powered, accompanied by cruisers, destroyers, support ships, and submarines. A single carrier battle group, of which there are many, ranks among the world's most powerful navies. The navy's combined forces exceed in tonnage and firepower that of all the other major world powers.

A newly created Special Operations Command (SOCOM), with 50,000 members and its own ships, aircraft, and weaponry, has been developed to deal with the drug trade as well as to assist compliant client regimes in the Third World to suppress insurgent forces.

Another important innovation has been "the development of precision-guided weapons, usually based on satellite or laser guidance, that could hit targets with great accuracy."[30] Political analyst Mary Kaldor observes, "Instead of ushering in a period of downsizing, disarmament and conversion (although some of that did take place . . .), the end of the Cold War led to a feverish technological effort to apply information technology to military purposes, known as the Revolution in Military Affairs (RMA)."[31] Kaldor describes the RMA as "the interaction between various systems for information collection, analysis, and transmission and weapons systems—the so-called 'system of systems.'"[32] These include unmanned guided offensive missile systems and sophisticated information systems for surveillance. The new weaponry, as well as the new flexible organization and sheer size of the American military establishment, gives the United States an enormous edge over all countries in the world.

What is the mission of this immensely powerful military force? At the broadest level, the goal is to maintain a stable, integrated world order consisting of states friendly to U.S. corporate capitalism. A particularly important aim is to assure U.S. access to the world's vital petroleum supply. Following the first Gulf War in 1991, the United States created military bases in Kuwait, Saudi Arabia, and Bahrain, the region with the world's largest petroleum reserves. Following the September 11 attacks, the United States established military bases in oil-rich Uzebekistan, Tajikistan, and Kyrgyzstan, in the Caspian area of Central Asia. Some critics charge that an important reason for the U.S. invasion of Iraq in 2003 was to gain control over the country with the world's second largest oil reserves. Political analyst Michael Klare goes further. He claims that the control of energy supplies, especially petroleum, constitutes one of the two pillars of American foreign policy: "What we have, therefore, is a two-pronged strategy that effectively governs US policy toward much of the world. Although arising from different sets of concerns—one

---

[30] Ibid., p. 149.

[31] Mary Kaldor, "Beyond Militarism, Arms Races, and Arms Control," in *Understanding September 11*, eds. Craig Calhoun, Paul Price, and Ashley Timmer (New York: The New Press, 2002), pp. 165–66.

[32] Ibid., p. 167.

energy-driven, the other security-driven—these two strategic principles have merged into a single integrated design for American world dominance in the 21st Century. One or the other of these policy concerns may play the lead role in any particular situation, but it is the combination of the two that increasingly will set the tone for America's international behaviour in the decades ahead."[33]

Is there a clash of civilizations in the world, with the United States and other regimes and people in the West pitted against "the rest" (of the world), a view popularized by political analyst Samuel Huntington?[34] In particular, is there a fundamental conflict between the Judeo-Christian United States and Islam? The apparently most persuasive piece of evidence in this respect is that the three most recent wars fought by the United States were with predominantly Muslim nations: two wars with Iraq (1991 and 2003) and one with Afghanistan (2001). And the current "war on terror" pits the United States against al Qaeda and other networks of militant Muslims. Yet the clash of civilizations seems a decidedly unhelpful template to understand the position of the United States in the world. For one thing, the vast majority of Muslims do not participate in movements launching violent attacks against the United States, and other Western countries and most Muslims are critical of such attacks. For another, the United States is closely allied with a host of Muslim nations in the world, such as Saudi Arabia, Egypt, and Kuwait—too closely allied, it might be argued, given these nations' autocratic regimes.

If there are clashes involving civilizations in the world today, it might be suggested that they involve clashes *within* rather than *between* civilizations. That is, one can discern strong conflicts within most religious communities today between more moderate, liberal elements versus those who claim to defend a traditional, orthodox understanding of religious practice.

THE SHIFT TO UNILATERALISM AND PREEMPTIVE WAR

The goal of American policymakers for well over half a century has been to maintain U.S. global superiority. Yet there have been extensive differences in how actively the United States has exercised power abroad in defense of this goal and the means different presidents have used. For example, during President Jimmy Carter's presidency in the 1970s, the United States displayed a more restrained stance. During Ronald Reagan's presidency in the 1980s, the United States was more assertive. The magnitude of these variations, however,

---

[33] Michael T. Klare, "Blood for Oil: The Bush–Cheney Energy Strategy," in *Socialist Register, 2004*, op. cit., p. 180. See the entire article, ibid., pp. 166–85, as well as Michael Klare, *Blood and Oil: The Dangers and Consequences of America's Growing Petroleum Dependency* (New York: Metropolitan Books, 2004).

[34] Samuel Huntington, "The Clash of Civilizations?" *Foreign Affairs* 72, no. 3 (1993).

was dwarfed by the change that occurred in the first years of the 21st century, when President George W. Bush sponsored the most aggressive expansion of American power in our history.

All postwar presidents until President Bush calculated that American interests would best be served by shaping and participating in multilateral economic, political, and military institutions. These are institutions, like the United Nations, in which many nations have a voice. President Bush represented a break in this tradition by championing a unilateral approach, that is, going it alone. The new orientation was evident from the beginning of the Bush presidency, well before September 11. Soon after taking office in 2001, President Bush announced that the United States would not comply with the Kyoto Protocol on global warming, which most nations of the world had ratified. The president also decided that the United States would reject a UN treaty banning land mines, despite its support by most nations of the world. Another example of unilateralism was the Bush administration's decision to reject the jurisdiction of the International Criminal Court, a tribunal created to try cases involving genocide, war crimes, and crimes against humanity. In every one of these cases, the United States bucked an international tide and parted company with its traditional allies in Western Europe and elsewhere.

The turn to unilateralism isolated the United States and produced a steep drop in U.S. popularity around the world. The situation was temporarily reversed following the attacks of September 11. The vast majority of governments and people were outraged by the attacks and expressed strong solidarity with the American people. When the United States formed a coalition to attack the Taliban government and the al Qaeda network based in Afghanistan that directed the attack, 19 nations participated and 22 countries contributed troops to the International Security Assistance Force.

However, support for the United States swiftly turned to opposition following the victory in Afghanistan. The reason was that, despite the lack of evidence that there was cooperation between al Qaeda and the Iraqi regime of Saddam Hussein, as well as the absence of evidence that Saddam's regime possessed weapons of mass destruction (WMDs), the Bush administration immediately turned from targeting al Qaeda to preparing for war against Iraq. When the United States attacked Iraq in 2003, its actions provoked protests around the world. Although the United States was joined by Britain, Spain, Australia, and several other countries, large majorities of citizens in these states opposed their leaders' decision to support the United States.

The United States became even more isolated following the war. On the one hand, no evidence was found that Iraq had stockpiles of WMDs or that Saddam's regime had links to al Qaeda, the major reasons that the Bush administration gave for going to war. On the other hand, the protracted fighting that followed Saddam's ouster produced large numbers of U.S. and Iraqi casualties, as well as widespread destruction in Iraq. According to former national security adviser Zbigniew Brzezinski, the result of the

Reuters/Staff Sgt. J. Knauth-USMC/Landov

American troops fighting in Iraq, 2004.

invasion was that "We're more unpopular in the world today than at any time in our history, and our policies are more unpopular than those of any country in the world."[35]

---

[35] Interview with Zbigniew Brzezinski, *The Charlie Rose Show,* PBS, September 14, 2004. Also see Zbigniew Brzezinski, *The Choice: Global Domination or Global Leadership* (New York: Basic Books, 2004).

Taking a step back from the immediate events, one can identify two important changes in American foreign and security policy sponsored by the Bush administration:

1. AN AGGRESSIVE ASSERTION OF U.S. POWER TO CONSOLIDATE ITS GLOBAL DOMINANCE. In 2002, the Bush administration described its foreign and military policy in a document entitled "National Security Strategy of the United States." In the plainest terms, the statement described the goal of U.S. foreign and military policy as maintaining American global dominance.[36] For the first time in American history, it asserted that the United States has the right to engage in preemptive action: "To forestall or prevent [potentially] hostile acts by our adversaries, the United States will, if necessary, act preemptively."

International law authorizes states to wage *preventive* war, that is, to attack an enemy demonstrably preparing to launch an attack. *Preemptive* war is very different and has no warrant in international law. It consists of launching an attack in the absence of clear evidence of the likelihood of an attack. Simply put, the United States has officially proclaimed the right to be judge and jury about when to launch war.

What might justify such a radical departure from international law and past U.S. doctrine? The administration pointed to the unprecedented threat posed by international terrorism and argued that the new situation requires preemptive action, rather than waiting until there is evidence of an imminent threat.

The announcement of the new doctrine was soon followed by action. Immediately after September 11, well before the United States attacked al Qaeda forces in Afghanistan, planning began to invade Iraq. Counterterrorism chief Richard Clarke describes his astonishment on September 12, 2001, when he attended several meetings in the White House. Rather than focusing on planning a response to al Qaeda and the Taliban regime in Afghanistan, much of the conversation was about Iraq. President Bush personally urged him to find evidence of Iraq's participation in the attacks despite the fact that Clarke stressed to the president that there was no evidence of cooperation between the secular regime of Saddam Hussein and the militantly Islamist al Qaeda network.[37] Moreover, despite what Secretary of State Colin Powell described at the UN before the invasion as "incontrovertible proof" that Iraq possessed WMDs, an official U.S. government report released in 2004 reported that a massive search had failed to produce evidence either of stockpiles of WMDs or an active program to produce them.

---

[36] "National Security Strategy of the United States," *http://www.whitehouse.gov/nsc/nss.html.*

[37] Richard A. Clarke, *Against All Enemies: Inside America's War on Terror* (New York: Free Press, 2004), pp. 30–32. Former Treasury Secretary Paul O'Neill reported that planning to remove Saddam Hussein began days after President Bush was inaugurated; several high-level meetings were devoted to the project well before September 11, 2001. Ron Suskind, *The Price of Loyalty: George W. Bush, the White House and the Education of Paul O'Neill* (New York: Simon & Schuster, 2004), pp. 72–75, 82–86, 129.

When the administration's case for going to war crumbled, another rationale was offered. The president claimed that the invasion was necessary to increase American security. Fighting terrorists abroad meant that the United States would not have to fight them within its borders. To this, former counterterrorism director Clarke replied, "Nothing America could have done would have provided al Qaeda and its new generation of cloned groups a better recruitment device than our unprovoked invasion of an oil-rich Arab country [Iraq]."[38]

2. IMMEDIATELY AFTER SEPTEMBER 11, THE BUSH ADMINISTRATION BEGAN TO EXPAND THE GOVERNMENT'S INTERNAL SECURITY APPARATUS. The justification offered was that new measures were needed to deal with the unprecedented situation of the war on terror at home and abroad. The administration claimed that the government needed to devise new measures to deal with the unprecedented threat represented by international terrorism. Yet the expanded security apparatus serve less to safeguard Americans against terrorism than to stifle political dissent.

According to constitutional scholar Ronald Dworkin, "Since September 11, the government has enacted legislation, adopted policies, and threatened procedures that are not consistent with our established laws and values and would have been unthinkable before."[39] For example, Dworkin observes, the USA Patriot Act, passed in 2001, "sets out a new, breathtakingly vague and broad definition of terrorism and of aiding terrorists: Someone may be guilty of aiding terrorism, for example, if he collects money or even contributes to a charity which supports the general aims of any organization abroad—the IRA, for example . . . —that uses violence among other means in an effort to oppose American policy or interests."[40]

The Patriot Act created a new crime called "domestic terrorism." The law outlaws activities that "involve acts dangerous to human life" if a person's intent is to "influence the policy of a government by intimidation or coercion." According to *New York Times* commentator Dahlia Lithwick, "If that sounds as if it's directed more toward effigy-burning, or Greenpeace activity, than international terror, it's because it is. International terror was already illegal."[41]

Executive power further expanded during the invasion of Afghanistan after September 11, when President Bush devised a new category, not recognized in international law, of "unlawful combatants." The administration declared that those resisting the invasion were not entitled to the rights and

---

[38] Clarke, *Against All Enemies: Inside America's War on Terror*, op. cit., p. 246. For evidence supporting Clarke's claim, see "U.S. officials See Signs of a Revived Al Qaeda in Several Nations," *New York Times*, May 17, 2003.

[39] Ronald Dworkin, "The Threat to Patriotism," in *Understanding September 11*, eds. Calhoun, Price, and Timmer, op. cit., p. 273.

[40] Ibid.

[41] Dahlia Lithwick, "Tyranny in the Name of Freedom," *New York Times*, August 12, 2004.

protections provided to prisoners of war by the Geneva Conventions—agreements ratified by the United States that require governments to treat prisoners of war humanely. The president further claimed the right to designate American citizens as enemy combatants and to imprison them indefinitely without legal counsel, trial, or review by civilian courts. Several hundred U.S. aliens and several American citizens were imprisoned under these procedures. The government even refused to reveal the identities of detainees. In 2004, the Supreme Court rejected some of the government's claims. One result, for example, was the release of a prisoner who had been held in solitary confinement for over two years without any formal charges ever being brought; the government admitted that it had no evidence of his having committed any wrongdoing.

An even uglier aspect of American power came to light in 2004, when photographs were made public depicting prisoners in U.S. custody being tortured at the Abu Ghraib prison in Iraq. Prisoners were stripped naked, hooded, and held in stressful positions in solitary confinement in darkened hot or cold rooms for long periods, deprived of sleep, photographed in sexually humiliating poses, submerged in water and led to believe they would be drowned, and attacked by vicious guard dogs. These practices were strictly outlawed by the Geneva Conventions requiring that prisoners of war be treated in a humane fashion. The army further violated the Geneva Conventions by holding countless "ghost detainees," that is, not providing prisoners' names to the International Red Cross. Practices that amounted to torture, devised for use in Afghanistan (and used against prisoners from that war who were held in a U.S. military facility at Guantanamo Bay, Cuba) were soon adopted in Iraq after the U.S. invasion in 2003. Yet there was even less reason to violate the Geneva Conventions in Iraq, following a war between the United States and the uniformed armed forces of the Iraqi regime.

The government tried to portray the abuses at Abu Ghraib as the regrettable excesses of a handful of low-level military personnel. However, official government inquiries, as well as independent investigations, found that the use of torture went far beyond a few poorly trained Army reservists; it was widespread, organized, and authorized by the chain of command. It emerged that, in order to extract useful intelligence information from detainees, dozens of career officers in the armed forces and intelligence agencies systematically engaged in torture.[42] An FBI memorandum made public as a result of a lawsuit described "abuse of prisoners by military personnel in Iraq that included detainees being beaten and choked, and having lit cigarettes placed in their ears."[43] The program was tolerated, and possibly organized, at the highest levels of government. At a congressional hearing on the abuses, Republican

---

[42] See, for example, the results of a high-level army investigation reported in the *New York Times*, September 10, 2004. Also see Seymour Hersh, *Chain of Command: The Road from 9/11 to Abu Ghraib* (New York: HarperCollins, 2004).

[43] *New York Times*, December 21, 2004.

Representative John Kline declared, "We had a gigantic failure of leadership—one that a year ago I would have said was impossible in the United States Army."[44] A panel appointed by Secretary of Defense Donald Rumsfeld identified "institutional and personal responsibility [for the abusive practices] at higher levels." Reflecting on the new developments, retired *New York Times* journalist Anthony Lewis observes that "[i]nstead of a country committed to law, the United States is now seen as a country that proclaims high legal ideals and then says that they should apply to all others but not to itself."[45]

CONCLUSION

A common term used to describe one country's domination of other countries and regions is *empire.* Until several years ago, to suggest that the United States exercised imperial power bordered on the unpatriotic. Political leaders proclaimed that, in contrast to past empires like those of France and Britain in the 19th century, the United States did not possess foreign colonies. This claim was only partially accurate. Although the United States never amassed colonies on a grand scale, its colonial possessions include Puerto Rico, Guam, the Marshall Islands, Samoa, and the Virgin Islands. Save for these significant exceptions, the United States is not an imperial power in the traditional sense. However, the United States has exercised enormous power on the international stage for generations—and never more so than in the post–Cold War period beginning in the 1990s. Today, American political, military, economic, and cultural power is evident in virtually every country of the world (save for a few exceptions, such as Iran, Cuba, and North Korea). There is intense scholarly and popular debate about whether the current American position of global dominance should be described as an informal or invisible empire. But less significant than the choice of terms to describe the relationship is the importance of highlighting the enormous disparity between the power of the United States and other countries throughout the world.[46]

---

[44] *New York Times*, September 10, 2004.

[45] Anthony Lewis, "A President Beyond the Law," *New York Times*, May 7, 2004.

[46] For an argument that the United States can be considered an empire, see Andrew Bacevich, *American Empire: The Realities and the Consequences of U.S. Diplomacy* (Cambridge, MA: Harvard University Press, 2002). For a strong defense of American empire, see Niall Ferguson, *Colossus: The Price of America's Empire* (New York: Penguin Press, 2004). Also see Ferguson's *Empire: The Rise and Demise of the British World Order and the Lessons for Global Power* (New York: Basic Books, 2003) and "The Empire Slinks Back," *The New York Times Magazine*, April 27, 2003. Also see contributions to a scholarly conference convened by the Social Science Research Council on "Lessons of Empire," which analyzed the relevance of European colonialism for understanding the United States' position today. In particular, Jack Snyder and George Steinmetz suggested a distinction between imperialism, involving intervention by a powerful state in weaker ones; and colonialism, which involved actually governing another territory. Social Science Research Council, "Lessons of Empire," *Items & Issues* 4, no. 4 (Fall/Winter 2003/2004). The contributions

The current posture of the United States points to a conflict between the claim of the United States to be a democracy and to support democracy throughout the world, versus the arrogant way the government has sought to impose its will on other countries. This conflict did not originate with the Bush administration. The United States has often practiced a double standard by ignoring human rights abuses and undemocratic practices of its allies. During the Cold War, this meant client states that suppressed radical insurgent movements. It has also included the oil-exporting regimes of the Middle East and elsewhere. However, in recent years the conflict became more pointed when the Bush administration proclaimed the goal of promoting democracy throughout the world yet condemned countries (including those with democratic regimes) that opposed U.S. policies.

Has the shift toward a more openly imperial and aggressive posture increased the security of Americans? September 11 demonstrated in the starkest terms that even the most powerful are vulnerable. More generally, foreign policy analyst Joseph Nye, Jr., suggests that security requires more than military strength: "Not all the important types of power come out of the barrel of a gun. . . . [M]any of the transnational issues, such as climate change, the spread of infectious diseases, international crime, and terrorism, cannot be resolved by military force alone. Representing the dark side of globalization, these issues are inherently multilateral and require cooperation for their solution."[47] The new unilateralism has complicated the attempt to deal with these challenges.

Tip O'Neill, Speaker of the House of Representatives in the 1970s and 1980s, famously remarked that all politics is local. He meant that people tend to judge the merits of a policy by its impact on their own lives. He might have added that all politics is also global, in that local and domestic political decisions affect the fate of the world while political decisions at the global level have an important effect on us all. This interdependence that links countries, as well as citizens, around the world, represents one of the most pressing reasons to promote fuller democracy within the United States.

---

by Snyder and Steinmetz are summarized by Frederick Cooper, "Modernizing Colonialism and the Limits of Empire," in ibid., p. 2, footnote 3. For analyses that criticize American imperialism in the current period, see David Harvey, *The New Imperialism* (New York: Oxford University Press, 2003), and *The New Imperial Challenge; Socialist Register 2004*, op. cit.

[47] Joseph S. Nye, Jr., "Soft Power and American Foreign Policy," *Political Science Quarterly* 119, no. 2 (Summer 2002): 263.

10

THE WELFARE STATE

"This isn't welfare reform," Senator Daniel Patrick Moynihan of New York thundered in dismay as an overhaul of the existing welfare system wound its way through Congress in 1996. "This is welfare repeal."[1] Republicans in Congress seized the initiative President Bill Clinton had given them when he promised "to end welfare as we know it" during the 1992 presidential campaign. Four years later, Congress sent the president a welfare bill that did what he pledged but in ways he never intended. Forced to choose between breaking his campaign promise to reform welfare and repudiating his own more generous welfare proposals, President Clinton chose the latter and signed the Personal Responsibility and Work Opportunity Reconciliation Act of 1996 (PRWORA). This legislation created a new welfare program, Temporary Assistance to Needy Families (TANF), to help impoverished children and their families.

TANF replaced the old welfare program, Aid to Families with Dependent Children (AFDC) and marked a radical shift in welfare policy. AFDC had been an entitlement program that required the federal government to provide income assistance to poor families for as long as they were eligible. The amount of federal money for welfare would adjust automatically to cover some of the money that states gave to poor families, regardless of the number of families on the rolls and regardless of how long they had been there.[2]

Under the new law, states now receive fixed lump sums of money from the federal government in the form of block grants to help pay for welfare. Federal money to pay for welfare no longer increases automatically with the welfare rolls. This means that if welfare rolls rise and states spend all of their federal money and choose not to supplement it, poor families that are eligible for income support may not receive any. Guarantees of cash assistance to poor families are now gone. The new law also gives states more discretion on how to spend the federal money they receive, to devise their own welfare

---

[1] Quoted in "Moynihan Turns Up the Heat," *Economist* 337 (November 11, 1995): 32.

[2] In *Goldberg v. Kelly* (1970), the Supreme Court ruled that beneficiaries, once eligible, could not lose their grants without a due process hearing.

policies, but with one important condition required by Congress. The new law set a limit of two years on welfare, after which recipients must work, and set a lifetime limit of five years during which recipients may receive welfare. The promise of a Democratic president and a Republican Congress to "end welfare as we know it" was redeemed. Welfare as an entitlement was eliminated by setting time limits on benefits and by removing the guarantee that the federal government would reimburse the states for each eligible recipient, regardless of how many there were.

The 1996 debate over welfare policy in Congress was as charged as any in recent memory. Conflict on the House Ways and Means Committee over eliminating the guarantee of welfare benefits to every eligible poor American was so furious that the sergeant at arms had to be called to restore order. When the bill reached the floor of the House, the debate reached uncommon levels of acrimony. Some Democrats compared Republican welfare proposals to Nazism, while some Republicans likened welfare recipients to wild animals.

The debate over welfare was overwrought because, more than most policy issues, personal values and public morality move close to the surface when considering welfare policy for the poor. Policymakers and social analysts are not shy about projecting their personal values onto the poor through welfare policy because the poor are often too weak, too vulnerable, and too outside the mainstream of political life to resist such impositions. Consequently, welfare policy often combines with other issues that are reflected through it. For example, the proper role of women in society has been projected through welfare policy. Some scholars argue that welfare policy in the past was used to reinforce the virtues of motherhood and to discourage women from entering the labor force.[3] Others argue that welfare policy has been about maintaining racial subordination.[4] From the start, welfare policy treated blacks differently, excluding them from programs and providing them with less when they were eligible. Some believe that welfare policy is just another terrain of class struggle between workers and capitalists.[5] Workers seek protection from the insecurity and rigor of the market through the welfare state, while employers try to use the welfare state to supplement and reinforce market discipline. Still others believe the welfare state is about federalism and which level of government works best.[6] Some prefer to locate authority with state governments, which can experiment with different

---

[3] Gwendolyn Mink, *The Wages of Motherhood: Inequality in the Welfare State, 1917–1942* (Ithaca, NY: Cornell University Press, 1995).

[4] Jill Quadagno, *The Color of Welfare: How Racism Undermined the War on Poverty* (New York: Oxford University Press, 1994).

[5] Charles Noble, *Welfare as We Knew It: A Political History of the American Welfare State* (New York: Oxford University Press, 1997).

[6] Sanford F. Schram and Samuel H. Beer, *Welfare Reform: A Race to the Bottom?* (Baltimore, MD: Johns Hopkins University, 1999).

approaches to welfare that reflect local conditions. Others prefer federal control, believing that citizens in every state should be treated equally. Finally, some argue that welfare is not about what level of government should respond to the problem of poverty but whether government should respond at all. Welfare policy is about the proper balance between the obligations citizens owe each other and the responsibility they should take for themselves.[7]

Cash assistance to the poor is emotionally charged and engenders so much conflict because it is freighted with so many meanings, from relationships between the sexes to relationships between the states. Since less than one percent of the federal budget is spent on income support for the poor, it is clear the symbolic significance attached to the issue is out of all proportion to the actual money spent on it.[8] Welfare policy has attracted so much attention not because we invest a significant amount of money to implement it but because it embodies our deepest public values.

THE THREE LEGS OF THE AMERICAN WELFARE STATE

But welfare policy extends beyond programs intended for poor families— what we have been referring to so far and is a distinctively modern American understanding of the term.[9] In the United States, the welfare state is divided into three parts, only one of which is oriented to the poor. Most welfare state spending goes to the working middle class through *social insurance programs*. These are programs based on contributions workers make in the form of payroll taxes to the government, which holds these funds in trust in the event of a worker's death, injury, unemployment, or retirement. The best known and most inclusive social insurance programs are Old Age and Survivors and Disability Insurance, under Social Security, and Medicare, which provides government health insurance for all elderly Americans. These programs, which enjoy widespread popular and bipartisan support, are universal, covering almost all those in the labor force and their families. Moreover, their benefit levels tend to keep up with the cost of living. Since the early 1970s, Social Security benefits have been indexed; that is, they

---

[7] Alan Wolfe, *Whose Keeper: Social Science and Moral Obligation* (Berkeley: University of California Press, 1989).

[8] Gary Bryner, *Politics and Public Morality: The Great American Welfare Reform Debate* (New York: Norton, 1998), p. xi.

[9] Welfare was once viewed favorably and referred to all sorts of programs that promoted economic security for everyone. However, once the welfare state was divided into social insurance programs for those who worked and public assistance programs for the poor, the term *welfare* came to be associated only with the latter. Welfare's original positive and inclusive meanings now turned into their opposites.

increase in step with the previous year's rate of inflation. Finally, clients of these welfare programs tend to be perceived as "deserving," since they worked and contributed toward their benefits through the payroll taxes they paid.

The second, smaller category of the welfare state is composed of *public assistance* programs directed to poor people, such as TANF, a part of the new welfare law we described earlier. These are programs for citizens whom social insurance programs miss. They include Medicaid, which offers health insurance to the needy, and Food Stamps, which offers coupons that the poor can redeem for food. In contrast to social insurance programs, these programs are selective, or means-tested. These programs are available only to Americans whose income or wealth is below the level set by law. Also, unlike Social Security, public assistance program benefits are not indexed nor is there a national standard of support. That is, benefit levels in public assistance programs can be eroded by inflation and are unequal across the states. Finally, unlike the aura surrounding recipients of social insurance programs, people receiving public assistance are viewed with suspicion, even as undeserving. Thus, the country's welfare state is split between social insurance programs, which have public approval, and public assistance programs, which offend dominant values regarding the work ethic and individual responsibility.[10] We can see this uneven history reflected in the spending patterns noted in Figure 10–1.

But the American welfare state stands on three legs, not two. Alongside social insurance and public assistance programs, Americans also depend on welfare benefits that flow through the private sector. Many Americans receive health insurance and a pension from their employer as part of the compensation package attached to their job. Indeed, the private welfare state dwarfs the public one. More people receive health insurance through work than from the government, and more money is distributed to pensioners from private retirement plans through their job than from social security. Jacob Hacker writes, "In no other nation do citizens rely so heavily on private benefits for protection against the fundamental risks of modern life."[11] But the private welfare state is not really so private. The government subsidizes the private welfare state through the tax code. Employer-sponsored health care and pension contributions are not taxed as income. Exempting income from taxation to support the private welfare state costs the government over $200 billion in revenue each year—about the cost of what the government spends on the Medicare program.

---

[10] Nathan Glazer, "Welfare and 'Welfare' in America," in *The Welfare State East and West,* eds. Richard Rose and Rei Shiratori (New York: Oxford University Press, 1986), pp. 41–63. See also Michael K. Brown, "The Segmented Welfare System: Distributive Conflict and Retrenchment in the United States, 1968–84," in *Remaking the Welfare State,* ed. Michael K. Brown (Philadelphia: Temple University Press, 1988), pp. 182–210.

[11] Jacob S. Hacker, *The Divided Welfare State: The Battle over Public and Private Social Benefits in the United States* (New York: Cambridge University Press, 2002), p. 6.

■ FIGURE 10–1

MEANS- VS. NON-MEANS-TESTED SPENDING AS A
PERCENTAGE OF GROSS DOMESTIC PRODUCT, 1962–1999

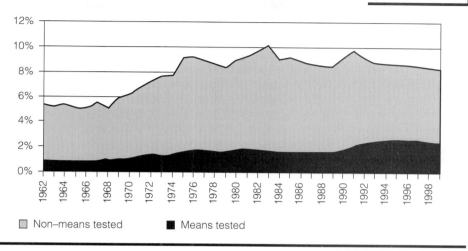

☐ Non–means tested   ■ Means tested

SOURCE: Department of Health and Human Services, 2000.

The private welfare state is a hallmark of the American welfare system; benefits that citizens in other rich democracies receive from the government are provided to Americans through their job. The difference between these two approaches, however, is substantial. When governments provide benefits, everyone is eligible for them. But when private firms are the source of benefits, only those workers who have the market power to make employers provide health insurance and private pensions ever receive them. Worse, most of the health care and pension benefits provided by employers go to those who are better off, while lower-paid employees receive less generous fringe-benefit packages. In other words, the private welfare state is more inequitable than government programs in terms of who benefits and how much they benefit.

AMERICA'S DISTINCTIVE WELFARE STATE

Spending on social insurance and public assistance programs, as well as state-subsidized private welfare programs, has expanded dramatically since World War II. Yet, the United States actually is near the bottom of the standings in terms of its welfare costs compared to European countries. Comparatively, the United States' welfare state is small, capturing a more limited share of tax revenues and national wealth than welfare spending in comparable advanced

■ TABLE 10-1

	WELFARE EFFORT
Country	**Public Social Expenditures as Percent of GDP**
Australia	18.7
Austria	28.5
Belgium	20.4
Canada	20.7
Denmark	35.9
Finland	33.3
Germany	29.2
Ireland	19.8
Italy	29.4
Japan	15.1
Netherlands	27.1
New Zealand	20.7
Norway	30.2
Sweden	35.7
U.K.	23.8
U.S.	15.8

SOURCE: Christopher Howard, "Is the American Welfare State Unusually Small?" *PS* 36 (2003): 413.

capitalist countries (see Table 10-1). In 1997, the United States devoted 15.8 percent of its GDP to public social expenditures. Most other rich democracies spend 25 to 30 percent of their GDP on welfare. They put "almost twice as much effort into their welfare states than the United States," according to the political scientist Christopher Howard. Even if we added to the spending totals the value of the tax breaks the United States provides to subsidize certain welfare activities, the United States still is a low spender. Among all affluent democracies, it only beats Japan in terms of welfare effort as measured by spending.[12]

But the American welfare state is distinctive in ways other than its low score on spending. Welfare states can also be compared by the degree to which they detach a person's well-being from dependence on the labor market. Some societies provide social rights, such as a right to health care, to all their citizens. Where a social right to health care exists, workers do not have to depend on employment in the labor market to afford or receive health

___

[12] Christopher Howard, "Is the American Welfare State Unusually Small?," *PS* 36 (2003): 411.

care; it is available automatically as a right of citizenship. Social rights may not relieve the whip of necessity that the market imposes on workers, but they do relieve the sting—and thereby the significance—of the blows. Americans, however, enjoy fewer and less generous social rights than can be found in other industrial societies. Government benefits tend to be low, stigmatizing, and of short duration. They hardly provide a reprieve from the market. Worse, where health insurance is attached to good jobs, American citizens are penalized heavily for failing in the labor market. Thus, the public and private welfare states each reinforce the discipline of the marketplace rather than offer an alternative to it.[13]

Today, welfare states are under tremendous pressure as a result of globalization and capital mobility. Employers are tempted to move their investments to locations where tax rates are relatively low and welfare states are relatively small. When they do so, they take jobs with them. Globalization thus can threaten a "race to the bottom," in which societies compete to reduce their welfare state costs in order to attract investment. Under this scenario, the American welfare state may be a model to which more extensive welfare states in Western Europe will conform. But there are counter trends. Globalization also creates pressures to maintain, even expand, the welfare state. Globalization increases the number of citizens who feel economically insecure, creating pressure on governments to respond to their unease. When economic insecurity is pervasive, voters pressure politicians to maintain the welfare state as an insurance against risk.

Welfare states also gain vitality from their economic role. It is far too simple to think of social policies merely as a drag on economic investment, productivity, and economic growth. To be sure, welfare states may require high taxes that discourage investment, but they can also increase the quality of the labor force, promote citizens' efficient integration into the labor market, and furnish essential services that cannot be obtained from the market. Extensive and generous welfare states can help promote economic competitiveness, increase labor productivity, and spur production. Large welfare states with an array of social rights that distribute benefits to all citizens can be an advantage in the global marketplace.[14]

THE HISTORICAL WELFARE STATE

The history of American social policy is not simply a story of slow and incomplete development. The perception that the American welfare state is a laggard, a late and stunted addition to the family of welfare states, is based

---

[13] Gosta Esping-Andersen, *The Three Worlds of Welfare Capitalism* (Princeton, NJ: Princeton University Press, 1990).

[14] Geoffrey Garrett, *Partisan Politics in the Global Economy* (New York: Cambridge University Press, 1998).

on when the "big four" welfare state programs—unemployment insurance, workers' compensation, disability insurance, and pensions—were first enacted. These welfare programs were first created at the federal level in the United States in 1935 with the passage of the Social Security Act, well after they were established in many European countries.

But this comparison gives a false impression that the federal government was not involved in social assistance prior to the enactment of Social Security. In fact, an unusual sort of welfare state, one that diverged from Europe, was present prior to 1935. The American welfare state appears as a laggard only if we use the "big four" as the standard of comparison. In other words, the American welfare state did not arrive late; it just did not develop along the same lines as those in Western Europe.

West European welfare states were aimed at workers, from unemployment insurance in the event of layoffs to workers' compensation in case of an industrial accident. A consequence of targeting workers was that these welfare programs predominantly covered men, who were far more likely to participate in the labor force than women. In the United States, on the other hand, the early American welfare state did not target working men but rather extended social protection to soldiers and mothers.

Between 1880 and 1910—well before the passage of Social Security in 1935—the federal government spent more than a quarter of its entire budget on pensions for Union Civil War veterans and their dependents. In fact, the federal government spent more money on pensions for former Union army soldiers and their dependents than on any other category, with the exception of interest payments on the national debt. By 1910, 28 percent of all men over age 65—more than 500,000 Americans—received federal benefits averaging $189 per year, a tidy sum at the time. An additional 30,000 orphans, widows, and dependants also received payments from the federal government.[15] Coverage rates were as high as those in some European old-age programs, and the benefits Americans received were more generous than those some pensioners received in Europe.

This unusual social assistance program in the form of veteran's pensions died of natural causes; the generation of Civil War veterans eligible to draw a pension passed away. As Civil War pensions faded away, a "maternalist" welfare state developed that promoted the cult of motherhood. During the Progressive era, the first two decades of the 20th century, a program of mother's pensions provided income assistance to single, poor, deserving mothers so they could stay home and raise their children. Providing income support to single mothers was perceived as preferable to a woman working outside the home or giving up her children to an orphanage or foster home because she could not provide for them. Each of these options would have undermined the mother's role, which advocates of mother's pensions sought to preserve.

---

[15] Theda Skocpol, *Protecting Soldiers and Mothers: The Political Origins of Social Policy in the United States* (Cambridge, MA: Harvard University Press, 1992), p. 65.

But not all mothers were treated alike. To qualify for assistance, they had to prove themselves worthy. Widows could easily do this, since they were not perceived as responsible for their plight, but unwed mothers were often excluded. Benefits, moreover, were made contingent on the behavior of mothers. They had to display moral character by showing "intelligence, willingness to learn English, piety, celibacy," compliance with directions from social workers, and dedication to "full-time child-centered domesticity."[16] The price of accepting mother's pensions was state regulation over the lives of women to ensure they conformed to traditional gender roles.

Mother's pensions are an example of how certain roles—in this case, roles based on gender—can be inscribed by social policy. According to the defenders of mother's pensions, mothers earned their benefits because caring for children was the natural, appropriate way for women to contribute to the well-being of society. Mother's pensions were defended as "the wages of motherhood" in Gwendolyn Mink's artful phrase. Society would profit from this investment in motherhood through the benefits that children derived from it.

THE NEW DEAL

When President Franklin D. Roosevelt declared in 1937 that "one-third of [the] nation" was "ill-housed, ill-clad, ill nourished," his estimate understated the problem. The proportion of the population that fit this description in the midst of the Depression, contemporaries agreed, was actually closer to one-half.[17] The main source of this distress was the staggering unemployment that afflicted the nation. In 1933, almost 13 million workers—a quarter of the workforce—were jobless, looking for work. Unemployment bred poverty and poverty bred despair. One man wrote relief officials in Washington, "Can you advise me as to which would be the most humane way to dispose of myself and family, as this is about the only thing that I can see left to do."[18]

Poverty, low wages, and unemployment led some to abstain from politics. But it led others to take political action. Thousands of workers sat down in factories to demand union recognition, the unemployed marched to demand food and shelter, and farmers dumped their produce to demand higher prices. The Roosevelt administration tried to blunt these challenges by offering federally funded jobs and social welfare programs to help the needy. The corporate community balked at these reforms, claiming they were a threat to private enterprise. But with the prospect of mass unrest growing, Roosevelt ignored their misgivings. The president recognized that concessions were necessary

[16] Mink, *The Wages of Motherhood*, p. 33.

[17] James T. Patterson, *America's Struggle Against Poverty, 1900–1994* (Cambridge, MA: Harvard University Press, 1994), p. 42.

[18] Quoted in ibid., p. 52.

to save capitalism, even if this meant opposing capitalists who urged thrift and passivity in the face of distress.

While conservatives strenuously opposed the New Deal, there was an element to it they could sympathize with, even if they could not appreciate it at the time. In 1935, *Fortune* magazine noted that "it was fairly evident to most disinterested critics" that the New Deal "had the preservation of capitalism at all times in view." Social reform was part of the administration's strategy to keep the market economy functioning. When the threat of civil disorder arose, the federal government expanded work relief programs. When the threat of disorder waned, federally funded jobs diminished. Some social welfare concessions were extended when the poor disrupted the status quo and were then retracted once the threat passed.[19]

But the New Deal also left an enduring liberal legacy in the form of the 1935 Social Security Act. This landmark legislation forms the basic legislative framework of the American welfare state even today. The Social Security Act offered pensions and unemployment compensation to qualified workers, provided public assistance to the elderly and the blind, and created a new national program for poor, single mothers, called Aid to Dependent Children (ADC). The protection and support the government provided through the Social Security program now made it possible for the blind, the unemployed, the elderly, and poor single mothers to live with a modicum of security and dignity. Moreover, as the government expanded its social welfare activities, people's expectations about the role and responsibility of government grew.

But even as the liberalism of the Social Security Act blazed new paths, it carried many conservative ideas about poverty from the previous period into the future with it. First, it continued the American tradition of localism. States were given the authority to set benefit levels and eligibility requirements for ADC and unemployment insurance. This discretion led to wide variations in benefits between states. Citizens in identical circumstances were treated differently, depending solely on the state in which they lived.

Second, benefits were set quite low. Benefit levels continued to follow the "least eligibility" principle, which held that no one should be better off on welfare than in work. Benefits should be set below the wage of the lowest paid worker so that the poor would rather offer themselves to any employer on any terms than accept relief.[20] Welfare should be made as undesirable as

---

[19] Francis Fox Piven and Richard Cloward, *Regulating the Poor: The Functions of Public Welfare* (New York: Pantheon, 1971).

[20] An example of the least eligibility principle can be found in the British *Poor Law Report of 1834*. For "able-bodied labourers who apply for relief," the *Poor Law Report* recommended "hard work at low wages by the piece, and extracting more work at a lower price than is paid for any other labour in the parish. . . . In short, . . . let the labourer find that the parish is the hardest taskmaster and the worst paymaster he can find, and thus induce him to make his application to the parish his last and not his first resort." Quoted in David Schmidtz and Robert E. Goodin, *Social Welfare and Individual Responsibility* (New York: Cambridge University Press, 1998), p. 173.

FDR signs the Social Security Act, August 14, 1935.

possible in order to reinforce the work ethic and ensure an abundant supply of cheap labor.

Third, the Social Security Act institutionalized the invidious distinction between deserving and undeserving welfare recipients. Programs organized on the principle of social insurance, like Social Security, were for workers who deserved them. These programs were financed through payroll taxes on employers and employees. Recipients "earned" their benefits through their contributions while they worked. Public assistance programs, on the other hand, were financed out of general tax revenues. These programs were means-tested and stigmatized the poor. While social insurance programs for workers enjoyed political support, public assistance programs for the poor were deplored as government handouts for the unworthy.

Finally, the Social Security Act reinforced racial and gender inequalities. The separation of the poor into public assistance programs and workers into social insurance programs segregated men from women and whites from blacks. For example, men were more likely to work than women and thus more likely to qualify for social insurance programs like Social Security and unemployment compensation. In addition, whites were more likely to work in occupations covered under Social Security, as opposed to disproportionately black occupations, such as agricultural workers and domestics, which were originally excluded. Consequently, many blacks and women did not qualify for pensions or unemployment compensation even though they were often the lowest paid and most irregularly employed groups in the entire nation.[21]

The New Deal, thus, had a liberal and conservative side: It extended new social protections to vulnerable groups but in a way that reinforced divisions between workers and the poor, whites and blacks, and men and women. The two sides of the New Deal, one liberal and one conservative, are present in every welfare state. On the one hand, the welfare state is conservative, stabilizing the corporate capitalist system. Welfare, British politician Joseph Chamberlain once said, is the ransom the rich must pay in order to sleep peacefully in their beds at night. The welfare state alleviates but does not correct the basic structural inequalities that are part and parcel of American capitalism. It reinforces the market by making the inequalities and insecurities of a capitalist economy tolerable.

On the other hand, the welfare state is a progressive force, offering an egalitarian alternative to the market. The welfare state can make workers' standards of living less dependent on the wages they receive, thus reducing the power that employers exercise over their employees. The welfare state can make workers less susceptible to the whip of necessity if they do not accept the terms that employers offer. For this reason, business generally has opposed extensions of the welfare state, while working-class and poor people's movements have supported it. In addition, where welfare states are extensive, as they are in Scandinavia, providing such benefits as health care and a modest income to all citizens, workers are less tolerant of inequality.[22] The egalitarian logic of the welfare state can spread to other activities, progressively infringing on areas that once operated according to market principles based on the ability to pay.[23]

Welfare states always are both conservative, reinforcing capitalism, and progressive, providing workers with an alternative to dependence on employers and the market. The mix of effects in different countries and at different historical moments depends on the precise kind of welfare state being offered. Some are quite limited, extending only the minimum required to maintain social peace and the status quo.[24] In this model, the welfare state functions as a safety net. Benefits are set low, below the lowest wage that workers could earn, in order to encourage the poor to work. The process of

---

[21] Charles Houston, a black lawyer, described the Social Security bill as a "sieve with holes just big enough for the majority of Negroes to fall through." Quoted in Michael K. Brown, *Race, Money and the American Welfare State* (Ithaca, NY: Cornell University Press, 1999), p. 61.

[22] Richard Scase, *Social Democracy in Capitalist Society* (Totowa, NJ: Rowman & Littlefield, 1977).

[23] John D. Stephens, *The Transition from Capitalism to Socialism* (Urbana: University of Illinois Press, 1986).

[24] Georg Simmel, "The Poor," in *Poverty: Power and Politics*, ed. Chaim I. Waxman (New York: Grosset & Dunlop, 1968), pp. 3–9.

applying for benefits is as demeaning and degrading as possible in order to discourage applications and stigmatize those who apply. Benefits are of short duration in order to force people back into the labor market as soon as possible on whatever terms are available. Government services are inferior to those available in the private sector so as not to compete with profit-making firms. Finally, benefits are targeted to the poor, segregating them from workers whose well-being is tied to the private economy.

More progressive welfare states, by contrast, provide more than a safety net for those unfortunate enough to fall out of the labor market. Such welfare states distribute more generous benefits to all citizens on a more equal basis, making it unnecessary for citizens to go to the market for their needs. Benefits are not targeted to the poor but are available as social rights to all citizens and long-term residents. Benefits are extensive and of long duration so that workers do not suffer a steep drop in living standards when they are out of the labor market. These programs enjoy broad political support because so many citizens are included within them.

Though there are liberal, even progressive, features of the U.S. welfare state, overall it is set apart by the degree to which it approaches the more conservative, safety net model. It is organized to provide the minimum necessary to support the market, stabilize capitalism, and ensure social peace. It does not go beyond this minimum to pose for workers an egalitarian alternative to dependence on employers and the market, like progressive welfare states do.[25]

Comparatively, the U.S. rate of poverty is higher than the rates in Western Europe, not because our economy produces more poverty but because our politics does.[26] Before government taxes and welfare programs are factored in, measures of relative poverty in the United States are approximately the same as those in Australia, Canada, Italy, the Netherlands, and Sweden, and they are lower than those in Britain, Ireland, France, and Denmark. But the United States diverges from all these countries, with more than twice and sometimes three times the rate of relative poverty, after government taxes and welfare programs are taken into account. Table 10-2 indicates that the United States eliminates less poverty through its government taxing and spending programs than does any other country to which it is compared. In other words, capitalism left to itself pretty much produces the same results everywhere. What matters in creating greater social equity is politics, and it is this that accounts for America's higher rate of relative poverty.[27]

---

[25] Ira Katznelson, "Considerations on Social Democracy in the United States," *Comparative Politics* (October 1978), 77–99.

[26] Relative poverty, which is the standard measure used in comparisons of poverty rates across countries, is the number of families with incomes 50 percent below the median family income.

[27] See L. Kenworthy, "Do Social Welfare Policies Reduce Poverty? A Cross-National Assessment," Working Paper No. 188, Luxembourg Income Study, 1998, in Robert M. Solow, "Review of *The Real Worlds of Welfare Capitalism*," *New York Review of Books* (March 23, 2000): 20–24.

■ TABLE 10-2

RELATIVE POVERTY RATES (PERCENT), 1991

	Post-tax/transfer Relative Poverty	Pre-tax/transfer Relative Poverty
Australia	6.4	21.3
Belgium	2.2	23.9
Canada	5.6	21.6
Denmark	3.5	23.9
Finland	2.3	9.8
France	4.8	27.5
Germany	2.4	14.1
Ireland	4.7	25.8
Italy	5.0	21.8
Netherlands	4.3	20.5
Norway	1.7	9.3
Sweden	3.1	20.4
Switzerland	4.1	12.1
United Kingdom	3.3	25.7
United States	11.7	21.0

SOURCE: L. Kenworthy, "Do Social Welfare Policies Reduce Poverty? A Cross-National Assessment," Working Paper No. 188, Luxembourg Income Study, 1998, in Robert M. Solow, "Review of *The Real Worlds of Welfare Capitalism*," *New York Review of Books*, March 23, 2000, 20–24.

BEYOND THE NEW DEAL

With the New Deal, the federal government took responsibility for social welfare, which it had never done before. But as much as the New Deal signi-fied a dramatic break with the past, it also contained traditional elements that reduced its progressive thrust. Conservatives in Congress and corporate opponents of the welfare state ensured that benefits were meager, that the poor were segregated in different programs from workers, that racial and gender hierarchies were not disturbed, and that the states would play a prominent role in administering social welfare programs.

The last major New Deal social policy initiative was the Fair Labor Standards Act of 1938, a law that established the first national minimum wage (25 cents per hour) and a 40-hour work week. Soon, World War II brought a halt to social reform, as the country's attention was fixed on defeating Germany, Italy, and Japan. When the war ended, liberals hoped to restore the momentum of the New Deal. But a politically resurgent business community in tandem with an increasingly conservative Congress resisted new social initiatives. Federal welfare programs were thrown on the defensive and effectively denounced in the early years of the Cold War as the opening wedge of communism and a threat to freedom. In 1946, conservatives in Congress weakened a bill that would have committed the government to a full-employment policy. In 1949, a national health insurance bill proposed by the Truman administration was defeated in Congress.[28] Other parts of President Harry Truman's Fair Deal met a similar fate.

Defeated politically, unions and other liberals who supported national health insurance tried to obtain from employers what they could not secure from Congress. Unions began to negotiate fringe benefits packages in collective bargaining with employers that included health insurance, employer-funded pensions, and supplementary unemployment benefits for their members. Between 1948 and 1959, the number of workers tripled who received health insurance and private pensions as part of their employment contracts. A private welfare system in which social protections such as health insurance and pensions were tied to the job, through the labor contract between employers and employees, began to develop. As we noted earlier, the United States is distinctive in the degree to which its mix of public- and private-sector welfare spending is weighted toward the latter. Approximately one-quarter of all welfare spending in the country comes from the private sector, compared to just five percent in France and Sweden. Welfare benefits, such as health insurance, that are provided by the government as a right of citizenship elsewhere are offered by American employers but only to those workers with enough economic clout to win them.

The private welfare system of employer-based benefits became a new form of welfare capitalism, reminiscent of what had existed in the 1920s— only now it was more generous and inclusive. Just as it was designed to do in the 1920s, modern welfare capitalism made workers dependent for their social protection—health insurance and pensions—on the firms that employed them.

This pattern of social provision not only tied workers to their employers but also divided workers from each other. Only workers employed in the corporate sector of the economy received extensive social protections from their employers. Workers who toiled for firms in the competitive sector of the economy often did not receive such fringe benefits because small firms could not afford to pay health insurance costs or contribute to private pensions for their workers. Consequently, workers in the corporate sector of the economy, who were receiving social protection from their employers, had less of a stake in improving, expanding, and adding new government programs that workers in the competitive sector and the poor depended on.

---

[28] Edmund F. Wehrle, "For a Healthy America: Labor's Struggle for National Health Insurance, 1943–1949," *Labor's Heritage* (Summer 1993): 28–44.

The private welfare system of employer-based benefits siphoned off political pressure from corporate-sector workers—the most organized and politically powerful section of the American working class—to increase the level of protection the American welfare state provided beyond the minimum necessary for social peace.

While the New Deal may not have gone forward under President Truman, a Democrat, neither did it go backward under his successor, President Dwight Eisenhower, a Republican. Under Eisenhower, conservatives did not try to revoke the Social Security Act or return to pre-Depression-style minimal government.[29] Corporations that had adamantly opposed Social Security in the 1930s now acknowledged that it could help stabilize the economy and was preferable to more radical, or conservative, alternatives. The issue for Republicans was striking the proper balance between private welfare plans run by employers and public welfare programs run by the government. Republicans were determined that the welfare state should not displace welfare capitalism in the form of private, employer-based welfare plans. According to Marion B. Folsom, an Eastman Kodak executive who became secretary of health, education, and welfare in Eisenhower's cabinet, government should provide only "basic minimum protection and it should not be intended to cover all the needs of everyone."[30] He argued that benefits in government programs should be low and that business should be offered tax incentives to subsidize their own employer-based welfare plans. Limited public benefits would encourage the need for and reliance on private, corporate welfare plans. These private, corporate plans, in turn, would act as a brake on the further extension of public welfare state programs.[31]

THE NEW POVERTY

The publication in 1962 of *The Other America: Poverty in the United States* by Michael Harrington, a democratic socialist, roused the nation's conscience, and the book became a bestseller. Using statistics that were widely available but had drawn little attention, Harrington bemoaned a disturbing truth: Despite unprecedented prosperity, 40 to 50 million people—one-quarter of all Americans—remained mired in poverty. In previous decades, full employment had reduced poverty. But by the mid-1960s, the traditional correlation between low unemployment and low AFDC welfare rates no longer applied. Throughout the 1960s, in the midst of one of the most prosperous decades in

---

[29] In fact, Social Security coverage expanded in the 1950s under President Eisenhower to include farm workers and maids, who initially had been left out of Social Security at the insistence of the segregated South.

[30] Quoted in Sanford M. Jacoby, "Employers and the Welfare State: The Role of Marion B. Folsom," *Journal of American History* 80, no. 2 (1993): 526.

[31] Ibid., p. 527.

the nation's history, the number of families needing income assistance grew by almost 10 percent per year.[32]

One reason that welfare caseloads grew even as the economy boomed was the changing color of poverty. A disproportionate and increasing number of the poor now were African Americans who lived in urban ghettos. Once blacks migrated from the South to join the modern industrial economy in northern cities like Cleveland, New York, and Chicago, they faced greater discrimination and larger obstacles to social mobility than did the immigrant groups, such as Italians, Poles, and Jews, who preceded them. Race proved a more visible and powerful marker of difference than ethnicity and nationality.[33]

Blacks, moreover, entered the modern industrial economy at the very moment it was passing from the scene. When previous immigrant groups had arrived with little education, the economy needed their unskilled labor to dig canals, lay railroad tracks, and work in the industrial plants of Detroit, Philadelphia, and Chicago. That was no longer true by the time blacks migrated north. Technology had reduced the need for labor in manufacturing. Capital had replaced labor in production. Economic restructuring now put a premium on education that many urban blacks lacked. In addition, factories no longer were located in cities accessible to blacks. Manufacturing plants were now located in the suburbs, where taxes and land were cheaper. This put many blue-collar manufacturing jobs beyond the reach of poor black residents located in center cities.[34]

At the same time postindustrial capitalism was producing well-compensated white-collar jobs requiring education, it was also creating service-sector jobs that failed to pay a living wage. As we showed in Chapter 2, both good and bad jobs in postindustrial capitalism have been growing at the expense of blue-collar jobs in the middle. The service-sector jobs available to unskilled workers, such as fast-food worker, maid, and security guard, are characterized by low wages, no fringe benefits, and irregular and temporary employment. A single parent with three children who worked steadily for 40 hours a week, 52 weeks a year at a minimum wage job would earn only 60 percent ($10,800) of what the government defined as the poverty line for such a family ($18,392) in 2003. Those who worked hard and played by the rules were consigned to poverty by a lack of skills, a lack of unions that could bargain up wages on their behalf, and a lack of government regulations that could assure them an adequate income.[35]

Not only was the color of welfare changing, becoming darker as job discrimination and economic changes conspired to restrain black mobility, but

---

[32] *Wall Street Journal*, April 24, 1969.

[33] Stanley Lieberson, *A Piece of the Pie* (Berkeley: University of California Press, 1980).

[34] William Julius Wilson, *The Declining Significance of Race: Blacks and Changing American Institutions* (Chicago: University of Chicago Press, 1978).

[35] Laurence E. Lynn, Jr., "Ending Welfare Reform as We Know It," *American Prospect* (Fall 1993): 83–90.

so was its sex. Women now increasingly filled the ranks of the poor. Poverty became feminized. Today, almost one-third of all female-headed households are poor. These families comprise more than one-half of all families in poverty, a significant increase from 30 years ago, when female-headed households accounted for only one-third of all poor families.[36] Single mothers are likely to be poor either because women earn lower wages when they work or because they need to stay home to care for their children and are unable to work.

Two factors contributed to the growth in the number of single mothers. One was economic. Men who were unemployed, underemployed, or unable to find jobs that paid adequate wages deserted their families, leaving single mothers to go on welfare in order to provide for their children. Divorce and abandonment deprived these families of a male breadwinner's income, leaving single mothers and their children in poverty. But if family breakup led to poverty, the reverse is also true: Poverty caused family breakup. According to the Census Bureau, two-parent families who were poor were twice as likely to break up within a few years as two-parent families who were not poor. The rise in the number of poor female-headed households was caused by poverty as much as poverty was its consequence.

The increase in the number of poor single mothers was also due to cultural factors. More women were willing to have babies out of wedlock. Illegitimacy no longer carried the stigma it once had. The proportion of babies born to unmarried women climbed not only among the poor but also among women in all social classes and racial groups.

Finally, the poor are younger—much younger than they once were. The great success of the American welfare state in reducing the poverty rate among the elderly has only underlined its greatest failure, the high and persistent poverty rate that remains among children. The poverty rate among those who are 65 years of age and older has declined by almost two-thirds in just 30 years, from 29.5 percent in 1967 to 10.5 percent in 1997. In the same period, the poverty rate among children has hovered stubbornly around 20 percent—almost twice the current poverty rate for the elderly.[37] The American poverty rate among children is three times the rate in Western Europe. Poverty among children in Europe is so much lower than in the United States because European countries spend more money on more programs for families with children, raising children above the poverty line who otherwise would be below it. No other developed welfare state is as generationally skewed as that of the United States, where benefits flow to the elderly through such relatively expensive programs as Medicare and Social Security, with no comparable effort made on behalf of children to insulate

---

[36] U.S. Bureau of the Census, *Measuring Fifty Years of Economic Change Using the March Current Population Survey,* Table C23, pp. C-40 to C-41.

[37] Ibid., Table C-21, p. C-37.

them from deprivation and its corrosive effects.[38] Indeed, after Congress enacted the new welfare law and repealed AFDC in 1996, the number of children living in deep poverty, defined as below half the poverty line, jumped by nearly 500,000, despite the country's strong economy at the time. This startling increase was directly related to cuts in public assistance and Food Stamps.

THE GREAT SOCIETY PROGRAM

The first great wave of social reform, the New Deal, was made possible by the sweeping Democratic electoral realignment spearheaded by President Roosevelt in the 1930s. The second wave of reform, the Great Society, was also the result of a thorough Democratic electoral victory. In 1964, 51 freshmen Democrats were elected to Congress on President Lyndon Johnson's coattails. Liberals now had enough votes to overcome the veto that the conservative coalition of Republicans and southern Democrats in Congress had exercised over social welfare legislation in the 1950s. A liberal Democratic president with concurring supermajorities in the Senate and the House could now overcome the obstacles that conservative opponents had used to stymie welfare state initiatives in the past.[39]

In his 1964 State of the Union address, President Johnson declared a War on Poverty that would result in a Great Society, free of hunger and privation. The AFL–CIO reflected the sentiment of other liberals when it crowed, "The New Deal proclaimed in 1933 has come to a belated maturity now under LBJ in 1965."[40] After a 30-year hiatus, the federal government was building on the legacy of the New Deal and assuming new responsibilities in almost every area of social welfare. Federally funded health insurance for the aged and the poor in the form of Medicare and Medicaid was passed. New educational opportunities for the disadvantaged, such as Head Start and Upward Bound, were enacted. Job-training programs, such as the Job Corps, were legislated. New initiatives in housing and urban development, such as the Model Cities program, followed suit. The thrust of these initiatives was to enhance the poor's opportunities, "to open up doors, not set down floors; to offer a hand up, not a handout," according to historian James T. Patterson.[41] Federal social welfare expenditures almost doubled from 1965 to 1975 in support of these efforts. Social welfare costs, which

---

[38] Barbara R. Bergmann, *Saving Our Children from Poverty: What the United States Can Learn from France* (New York: Russell Sage Foundation, 1996).

[39] James C. Sundquist, *Politics and Policy: The Eisenhower, Kennedy, and Johnson Years* (Washington, DC: Brookings, 1968).

[40] AFL–CIO Convention *Proceedings* (1965), pp. 2:1–6.

[41] Patterson, *America's Struggle Against Poverty*, p. 136.

amounted to one-third of the entire federal budget in 1965, accounted for more than one-half ten years later.[42]

But like the social reform period of the New Deal, the War on Poverty was short-lived. Initially, the War on Poverty drew its moral and political energy from the Civil Rights movement. But as the moral power of the civil rights declined amidst violence and internal strife, so did the impetus behind the Great Society. Equally important, the Johnson administration became distracted by the war in Vietnam. The more the war against communism in Asia escalated, the more the war against poverty at home lost momentum. A conservative backlash toward the Great Society first appeared in the 1966 congressional election, which restored the blocking power of the conservative coalition of Republicans and southern Democrats within Congress.[43] Two years later, in 1968, Richard Nixon, a Republican, was elected president, effectively bringing the moment of social reform to an end.

According to conservatives, the War on Poverty had failed; worse, the various poverty programs had been harmful. Welfare rolls continued to increase, not decrease; crime became worse, not better; more single mothers appeared, not fewer; and illegitimacy rates continued to rise, not decline. The country's cities burned as violent urban protests rocked the nation in the late 1960s. During his 1968 presidential campaign, Nixon captured this sense of disappointment when he charged, "For the past five years we have been deluged by government programs for the unemployed, programs for cities, programs for the poor, and we have reaped from these programs an ugly harvest of frustration, violence and failure across the land."[44]

Backlash toward the Great Society also developed because the War on Poverty had polarized the electorate along the fault lines of the dual welfare state. Workers covered by social insurance programs had little stake in the Great Society programs that aided the poor. As the prosperity of the 1960s turned into the stagflation of the 1970s, resentment over these expenditures and their tax burden grew. Race compounded this resentment. While many New Deal programs purposely had left blacks out, the War on Poverty purposely had targeted them for inclusion.[45] The political consequences of the Great Society program pitted taxpayers, who were part of the social insurance system, against tax recipients, who received public assistance; the private sector was set against the public sector, workers against the jobless, and whites against blacks.[46] Politicians in both parties exploited and exacerbated

[42] Sar A. Levitan and Robert Taggert, *The Promise of Greatness* (Cambridge, MA: Harvard University Press, 1976), p. 20.

[43] For the consequences of the 1966 election for the welfare state, see Alan Draper, "Labor and the 1966 Elections," *Labor History* (Winter 1989): 76–93.

[44] Quoted in Levitan and Taggert, *The Promise of Greatness*, pp. 3–4.

[45] Brown, *Race, Money and the American Welfare State*, p. 325.

[46] Thomas Byrne Edsall and Mary D. Edsall, *Chain Reaction: The Impact of Race, Rights, and Taxes on American Politics* (New York: Norton, 1991).

these tensions, using welfare as a code word to appeal to some voters' fears concerning crime, taxes, morality, and race.

The recoil against the Great Society reached its peak during the Reagan administration (1981–1989). President Ronald Reagan came to office pledging to shrink the federal government. His administration quickly aimed its fire at the poor and the Great Society programs on which they depended. Some federal programs, such as funding for public service jobs and revenue sharing for the states, were eliminated completely, while other poverty programs were cut back drastically.[47]

The Reagan attack on the welfare state overreached, however. Tax cuts for the rich and spending cuts for the poor exposed his administration to charges of unfairness, even meanness. As poverty became more visible due to government cutbacks and rising unemployment, the public became more upset with the results. As David Stockman, Reagan's budget director, observed, "The abortive Reagan revolution proved that the American electorate wants a moderate social democracy to shield it from capitalism's rough edges."[48]

Far from being a failure as conservative Republicans charged, the War on Poverty was a remarkable success in reducing the number of people living in poverty. The poverty rate dropped from 19 percent in 1964 to less than 12 percent in 1979. The number of people living below the poverty line was declining until President Reagan signaled retreat in a war we were winning. Government income-support programs, not economic growth, accounted for a large part of this decline in the poverty rate. Between 1965 and 1971, the number of households in poverty fell by only 900,000 before government income supports were factored in. However, when government income transfers to the poor were included, the number of poor families declined by 2.6 million, nearly three times the drop in the number of poor before receiving aid.[49] Government poverty programs not only lifted families out of poverty but also raised the quality of their lives, reducing malnutrition, increasing access to medical care, improving housing, and opening up educational opportunities that previously had not been available.[50]

Despite these dramatic changes, critics of the War on Poverty were suspicious of the type of difference such programs made in poor people's lives. Poverty programs, they argued, may have improved poor people's lives materially, but they did not change their behavior—welfare dependency, illegitimate babies, and family breakup. More of the poor's basic needs may have been met as a result of Great Society initiatives, but at the cost of their character. This seductive line of argument, however, does not

---

[47] James Midgeley, "Society, Social Policy and the Ideology of Reaganism," *Journal of Sociology and Social Welfare* (March 1992): 24–25.

[48] David Stockman, *The Triumph of Politics* (New York: Harper & Row, 1986), p. 394.

[49] Levitan and Taggert, *The Promise of Greatness*, pp. 200–201.

[50] John E. Schwarz, *America's Hidden Success: A Reassessment of Twenty Years of Public Policy* (New York: Norton, 1984).

hold up to close scrutiny. Larger cultural forces regarding sexuality and parenthood, not welfare policy, drove the trend toward more female-headed households. Moreover, poverty, low wages, and the growing insecurity of the market weakened the ties that bound families together. As noted economist Lester Thurow stated the point, "The traditional family is being destroyed not by misguided social welfare programs coming from Washington . . . but by a modern economic system that is not congruent with 'family values.'" [51]

Inaccurate impressions of welfare dependency also abound. In fact, there were many more people on welfare who received benefits episodically than people who were long-term users. Sociologist Mark Rank writes, "To be sure, some individuals do abuse the welfare system . . . [but] such cases constitute a very small fraction of the overall welfare population. Most welfare recipients want a better life for themselves and their children; they don't enjoy being on government assistance; and they persevere in the face of countless hardships and handicaps." [52] People moved in and out of the welfare rolls not because they wanted to be there but because personal and economic setbacks, such as divorce, abandonment, unemployment, lack of child care, or sickness, placed them there. And all the disadvantages of being poor that afflict one generation affect the next. What gets passed from one generation to the next among the poor is their poverty, not welfare dependency. [53] This was evident in the classic study of urban black men by anthropologist Eliot Liebow. Liebow found black street-corner men had followed in the failed footsteps of their fathers not because a culture of poverty had been handed down but because the same social and educational deficits of poverty that had prevented their fathers from succeeding were visited on their sons. Liebow wrote in 1967 in his classic work of ethnography:

> No doubt, each generation does provide role models for each succeeding one. . . .
> However . . . many similarities between the lower-class Negro father and son (or mother and daughter) do not result from 'cultural transmission' but from the fact that the son goes out and independently experiences the same failures, in the same areas, and for much the same reasons as his father. What appears as a dynamic, self-sustaining cultural process is, in part at least, a relatively simple piece of social machinery which turns out, in a rather mechanical fashion, independently produced look alikes. [54]

---

[51] *New York Times,* September 3, 1995.

[52] Mark Rank, *Living on the Edge: The Realities of Welfare in America* (New York: Columbia University Press, 1994), p. 5.

[53] Randy Albelda, Nancy Folbre, and the Center for Public Economics, *The War on the Poor: A Defense Manual* (New York: New Press, 1996), p. 82.

[54] Eliot Liebow, *Tally's Corner: A Study of Streetcorner Men* (New York: Little, Brown, 1967), p. 223.

THE CONTEMPORARY WELFARE STATE

The Reagan attack on the welfare state proved a partial success. Welfare state spending was slowed but not reversed. Great Society poverty programs took heavy cuts, mostly surviving in truncated form, while New Deal social insurance programs emerged relatively unscathed.[55] But the Reagan administration's impact on the welfare state was more profound than can be gleaned from looking at welfare state spending alone. Republicans succeeded in placing the welfare state on the defensive in two ways. Financially, Ronald Reagan and George Bush left massive budget deficits that would reach $4.3 trillion by the time President Clinton took office in 1993. According to political scientist Paul Pierson, oversized budget deficits are not neutral but favor "those who opposed an activist federal government."[56] The priority given to deficit reduction makes it hard to argue for new social programs or increases in social welfare spending. Quite the reverse: demands to reduce the deficit create fierce pressure to cut back social programs.

Second, conservatives now set the terms of debate over social policy. The problem of poverty was redefined from increasing the poor's resources to changing their behavior, from blaming their circumstances on the inadequacies of the economy to blaming it on the perverse incentives of the welfare state. The public mood changed so much that even Democrats were prepared to renounce their own New Deal and Great Society legacies. In March 1990, members of the Democratic Leadership Council (DLC), a group of moderate and conservative Democrats, announced they were ready to bury their party's past. Meeting in New Orleans, they dismissed the relevance of New Deal and Great Society programs, claiming that "the political ideas and passions of the 1930s and 1960s cannot guide us in the 1990s." At that meeting, the DLC selected a new president to present this view, putting a little-known governor from a small southern state on the national stage for the first time. His name was William Jefferson Clinton.[57]

President Clinton's social policy was shaped decisively by these two inheritances from previous Republican administrations: the need for deficit reduction and a conservative definition of the welfare problem. To reassure financial markets that he was serious about cutting the deficit, Clinton sacrificed his 1992 campaign promise to invest in domestic programs. His failed

---

[55] See Bawden and Levy, "Economic Well-Being of Families and Individuals," Table 16-5, p. 469.

[56] Paul Pierson, "The Deficit and the Politics of Domestic Reform," in *The Social Divide: Political Parties and the Future of Activist Government*, ed. Margaret Weir (Washington, DC: Brookings, 1998), p. 171.

[57] Howard Jacob Karger, "Responding to the Crisis: Liberal Prescriptions," in *Reconstructing the American Welfare State*, eds. David Stoesz and Howard Jacob Karger (Lanham, MD: Rowman & Littlefield, 1992), pp. 92–93.

health care plan also fell victim to fighting the deficit, relying on government regulation to control costs rather than new taxes and new spending to pay for it. Even as the budget began to run surpluses toward the end of the 1990s, the Clinton administration continued to give priority to reducing the deficit as opposed to restoring cuts to welfare state programs.

President Clinton's social policy was not simply mortgaged to deficit reduction but also conducted within a conservative definition of the welfare problem that the president adopted as his own—a view that public assistance programs undermined the character of the poor. From this perspective, the best way to build their character was to remove the welfare crutch on which they depended. This view was embodied in the Personal Responsibility and Work Opportunity Reconciliation Act (PRWORA), which President Clinton signed in 1996 and with which we began this chapter. Proponents of the new welfare law point to declining welfare rolls as a sign that the work deterrent in the new law is effective. Since welfare reform was enacted, welfare case-loads have dropped dramatically, down by more than half, with fewer people on welfare in 1999 than at any point in the last three decades.[58] But the welfare rolls had begun to decrease in 1993, well before the new welfare bill was signed. Moreover, most of the credit for lower welfare rolls belongs to the low unemployment and record job creation of the latter half of the 1990s. The surging economy pulled the most able people off the welfare rolls and into work. But the move from welfare to work that the new law was supposed to promote only applied to the most functional, employable individuals who had been on welfare. The hard core cases, composed of those who are ill, mentally or physically disabled, unskilled, not fluent in English, or unedu-cated, have not found work. And for them the welfare clock is ticking, their benefits running out now that welfare is time limited. Their situation has become even more desperate because of the new law, resulting in increased homelessness, deprivation, malnutrition, and child abandonment among the most vulnerable.[59]

All three legs of the American welfare state are under strain. The economic boom of the 1990s has been replaced with stubborn unemployment. Instead of creating jobs, the economy shed them. Budget surpluses have turned into budget deficits, and inequality continues to grow. For public assistance programs directed at the poor, the outlook appears grim. The recession that began in 2000 put tremendous fiscal pressure on state govern-ments. The recession reduced revenues, creating large budget deficits. Unlike the federal government, however, 49 states cannot run deficits because they must by law balance their budget. Raising taxes is politically unpalatable, so many have tried to reduce spending, which usually means

---

[58] *New York Times,* April 11, 1999.

[59] Demetrious James Caraley, "Ending Welfare As We Know It: A Reform Still in Progress," *Political Science Quarterly* 116, no. 4 (2001–2002): 525–60.

U.S. WELFARE RECIPIENTS, 1960–2002

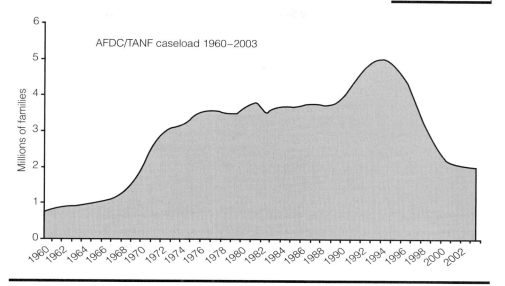

AFDC/TANF caseload 1960–2003

SOURCE: HHS. House Committee on Ways and Means. "1996 Welfare Reform Law Has Been a Success" (September 2004) p. 9.

cutting programs for the poor who are least able to resist or afford such reductions. For example, Medicaid, which funds health care for the poor and covers over 51 million Americans, is one of the largest expenses in state budgets and has suffered wholesale cuts as states try to meet their constitutional requirements. States have scaled back eligibility to receive Medicaid, cut benefits, increased co-payments, and reduced reimbursement rates to health providers to such an extent that doctors are refusing to treat Medicaid patients. Nor are states as willing to fund such useful work supports, such as child care, transportation, and job training, to help the indigent become self-sufficient. Quite the opposite, states are eliminating programs, making eligibility requirements stricter, cutting benefits, and enforcing administrative rules more strictly in an effort to reduce spending. Nor can states look to the federal government, which suffers its own deficit problems, to lighten their financial burden.

Many states set aside the deadlines for recipients who came up against time limits when the economy soured in 2001, but it is unclear that they will continue to do so as their own fiscal picture deteriorates. Now that welfare is no longer an entitlement, there is the prospect that needy families who qualify for welfare may be turned away because states do not have the money to pay them.

Social insurance programs, the second leg of the American welfare state, are as threatened as public assistance programs. Eligibility for unemployment insurance presumed that workers had full-time jobs. But this is less and less true for the growing number of service-sector jobs that use part-time or contingent workers. Many of the jobs created during the 1990 boom were of a type that left workers ineligible for unemployment insurance when workers were laid off in the 2000 recession. Less than 40 percent of the unemployed in 2001 were receiving unemployment benefits, and the value of those benefits has declined, replacing only 33 percent of workers' lost earnings, compared to 46 percent in 1985.

The long-term viability of the Medicare program is also in doubt as a result of legislation passed in 2003. This legislation created new prescription drug benefits for the elderly. But this new benefit, critics charged, was merely a Trojan horse designed to sneak in other elements that threaten to undermine the foundations of public health insurance for the elderly. The new law, for example, subsidizes private insurers to compete with Medicare. Younger, healthier seniors may now opt out of Medicare and choose private insurers that offer lower premiums, leaving older, sicker, and costlier seniors in the traditional program. The financial basis of Medicare will be jeopardized if fewer pay in and the costs per enrollee rise. In addition, the new legislation put a cap on money from general revenue to pay for Medicare. If costs go above a certain level, Congress now must either reduce benefits or increase payroll taxes. Thus, the effect of the new law was double-edged. At the same time the new law expanded the base of Medicare to include prescription drugs for seniors, it also made it less secure by allowing private companies to insure the most profitable seniors and by capping funding from general taxes for the program.

But the greatest threat to the social insurance portion of the welfare state is to the social security program. Social security benefits to retirees are paid mostly by current workers through payroll taxes. This worked well when the number of workers who contributed to social security was much greater than the number of people who received social security checks. Under these circumstances, social security accumulated a surplus. But the baby boom generation that swelled the workforce and created the surplus is about to retire and instead of contributing to social security will be drawing from it. This will drain the social security trust fund because the next generation of workers is not large enough to pay for all the benefits the preceding generation will receive. Projections show that at some point in the future, social security will pay out more in benefits than it collects in taxes. Worse, the surplus accumulated when baby boomers contributed to social security through their payroll taxes has already been spent to fund current government operating expenses. President Bush broke his 2000 campaign promise to not tap this surplus and instead used workers' social security contributions to finance the deficit created by his tax cuts. Unless benefits are cut or taxes increased, the social security system is threatened with insolvency as early as 2032.

Finally, the private welfare state, the third leg, is unraveling. Employers are less able to afford its escalating costs, and it is no longer appropriate to the way the labor market functions today. Regarding costs, employers complain that the expense of fringe benefits, of contributing to their workers' health insurance and pension, eats into profits and threatens competitiveness. As a result, employers are reneging on the promise of welfare capitalism—that their employees should look to them and not the government for insurance against social risks. The number of families without private health insurance reached 43.6 million in 2002, the highest it has been in five years and more than the total population of 24 states. Of these, almost 20 million were full-time workers without health insurance. Even those families lucky enough to be covered under employer-sponsored health care plans are under more financial stress as employers contribute less and workers pay more out of pocket in the form of higher premiums, deductibles, and co-payments.[60] Ten years ago, half of all companies with 500 or more employees offered a medical plan to retirees not yet eligible for Medicare; in 2004, just over one-third of those companies still offered such a plan to their former employees. The increasing number of uninsured citizens is a public health problem as people without coverage are less likely to get basic preventative care or to have their own personal physician familiar with their medical history, and are more likely to rate their own health as only poor or fair.

In addition, the private welfare state is out of step with the increasingly transient and mobile nature of the contemporary labor market. Firms increasingly hire part-time workers or outsource work to temps and subcontractors. As a result, only permanent, full-time core workers whose loyalty and satisfaction is important to the firm receive fringe benefits, while part-time and temporary workers, as well as employees hired by the subcontractor, receive none. This leaves a smaller percentage of the workforce covered by the private welfare state. In addition, workers are now more likely to work for many firms over the course of their career. But benefits accrued at one firm may not be portable to the next. Workers may not build up enough time with any particular firm to qualify for a pension, even though they have been working steadily.

CONCLUSION

By the end of the 1990s, when the stock market soared to new highs, when the American economy far outpaced that of any rival, when unemployment and inflation were at 40-year lows, and when the economy was creating 1 million jobs per year, more Americans were without health insurance than at the beginning of the decade, more children grew up in poor families than

---

[60] *New York Times*, September 10, 2003.

in any other Western industrialized nation, and the poverty rate hovered stubbornly around 12 percent. Thirty-four million Americans remained in poverty, more than at any point in the 1970s. At the end of the longest economic expansion in postwar history, little of the prosperity that the top fifth of income earners enjoyed over the course of the 1990s trickled down to the bottom fifth. These depressing trends were only accentuated when the business cycle turned and the prosperity of the 1990s gave way to the rising unemployment and job loss that marked the first term of the Bush presidency.

Economic growth alone cannot reduce poverty. Only government programs in tandem with a successful economy can do that. Poverty rates are sensitive to political choices governments make about the welfare state. Conservatives and liberals agree the welfare state is here to stay. Less clear is what kind of welfare state will emerge, that is, what the balance will be between the three legs of the welfare state: social insurance programs, public assistance for the poor, and benefits that are linked to the job.

11

ECONOMIC POLICY

Seymour Durst, a real estate magnate in New York City, created a clock that does not tell time. In 1989, Durst had the National Debt Clock installed on a building he owned on Sixth Avenue and 43rd Street in midtown Manhattan. It recorded the rise in the national debt, the total amount the federal government owes its creditors based upon figures from the U.S. Department of Treasury. Durst regarded the clock as an effective way to share his alarm about rising national debt with fellow citizens. The clock started at a mere $2.8 trillion and soon became a New York institution. Numbers on the clock moved so fast in trying to keep track of the mounting debt, sometimes at the rate of $10,000 per second, that at one point the mechanism powering the clock broke down. Numbers on the clock moved at such a speed that they were just a blur to those gazing up at it. Bemused native New Yorkers joked that tourists who stopped to look at the clock suffered from attention *deficit* disorder.

On September 7, 2000, the Durst family pulled the plug on the clock. The problem was the clock had started to go backwards, indicating the national debt was declining, not increasing. Budget surpluses under President Clinton were being used to pay down the government's debt, so the clock was now moving in the opposite direction at the rate of $30 per second. In its final moments, the clock read "Our National Debt: $5,676,989,904,887. Your family share: $73,733." The clock was covered with a red, white, and blue veil to mark its end.

But as deficits under President George W. Bush mounted and the national debt began to balloon again, Douglas Durst, president of his late father's real estate company, was inspired to restart the clock in 2002. The shroud was removed and the clock began flickering. The 500 bulbs on the 11-by-26 foot billboard came to life, showing a debt of $6.1 trillion, and immediately began calculating furiously. Then two years later, in 2004, the clock went dark again because the building on which it was located was slated for demolition to make way for a new high-rise apartment building. The clock's founders constructed a new clock on another Durst property just one block north of the original site. When the clock reappeared in May 2004 at its new location, it moved so fast trying to record the rising debt that the first seven numbers on

Stephen Chernin/Getty Images

National Debt Clock.

the clock—into the millions column—spun too quickly to be read by people staring at it.

The size of the national debt is almost too large to imagine. It is the result of accumulated deficits that the government runs each year when it spends more money than it collects in taxes. (See Table 11-1 for figures on the national debt and deficit.) Deficits require the government to borrow money to pay its bills. The government raises this money by selling assorted debt instruments, such as savings bonds and treasury bills, which it promises to pay back with interest to investors. Some of this debt is held by the government itself. For example, the social security trust fund invests surplus funds in treasury bills that are considered a safe and reliable investment. Other parts of the national debt are held by the public, which includes individuals, corporations, and even foreign governments.

The size of the national debt and of the annual deficits that contribute to it are of some concern because of the interest charges on the budget they create. Creditors must be paid or else they won't continue to finance the debt. These payments come out of current revenues, leaving less money in the budget to support vital services such as health care, environmental protection, and homeland security. In fiscal year 2003, the federal government took a charge of $153 billion in interest payments to holders of the national debt, to those from whom it borrowed money. This was 7.1 percent of all federal outlays, more than the federal government spent on any

■ TABLE 11–1

DEFICITS AND THE NATIONAL DEBT

(in millions of dollars)

	Gross Federal Debt	Annual Budget Surpluses and Deficits
1950	256,853	−3,119
1955	274,366	−2,993
1960	290,525	301
1965	322,318	−1,411
1970	380,921	−2,842
1975	541,925	−53,242
1980	909,041	−73,830
1985	1,817,423	−212,308
1990	3,206,290	−221,195
1995	4,920,586	−163,972
2000	5,628,700	236,445
2001	5,769,881	127,424
2002	6,198,401	−157,797
2003	6,760,014	−375,295

SOURCE: *Fiscal Year 2005 Historical Tables: Budget of the U.S. Government* (Washington, DC: U.S. Government Printing Office, 2004), pp. 22, 118–19.

agency or department with the exception of defense and health and human services.

On the other hand, deficits are not necessarily bad and are, at times, even appropriate. It depends on how well the economy is doing and what the government spends the money on. Governments can borrow money and invest in programs that contribute to social welfare and economic growth, or they can budget money for programs that have little payoff except to the special interests that receive it. Some investments yield a high social and economic return that makes borrowing money worthwhile, while others generate little value and only add to the debt burden of future generations. Whether deficits are good or bad depends not only on the state of the economy but on what the money is used for.

Deficits can powerfully affect the quality of social life, for better or for worse. So, too, can other aspects of economic policy: taxes, spending, regulation, trade policy, and setting interest rates. All of them have profound consequences on American citizens, and all of them help determine what Harold D. Lasswell once defined as the essence of politics: "who gets what when, how, and why."[1] Economic policy is concerned not only with the process by which the federal government makes policy but the outcome these decisions have on the welfare of citizens. This chapter will concentrate on just three arenas of economic policy: fiscal policy, which entails taxes and spending by the government; monetary policy, which involves setting interest rates; and regulation, which mandates or proscribes certain activities.

THE GOVERNMENT AND THE ECONOMY

In 2003, governments at all levels—state, local and federal governments taken together—collected $2.9 trillion in taxes and spent $3.3 trillion in outlays. When taxes and expenditures are combined, the total amount of money passing through the government was about 57 percent of GDP. These figures have given rise to the common belief that the government is too big, that it confiscates too much money in the form of taxes and spends too much in the form of wasteful programs. Indeed, government has grown dramatically since 1950, as Table 11-2 indicates. Government taxes and spending accounted for about 42 percent of the economy in 1950; fifty years later that figure had grown to 60 percent of the Gross Domestic Product—a more than 40 percent increase in the proportion of economic activity accounted for by government. As the responsibilities of government have increased, especially in terms of social welfare and defense, so have the expenses and taxes to pay for them.[2]

Despite these increases and frequent complaints about "big government," the size of the public sector in the United States is actually quite small when viewed comparatively, as indicated in Figures 11-1a and 11-1b. For example, the tax burden on American citizens is actually quite light compared to other advanced industrial countries.[3] No advanced industrialized country collects a lower proportion of its GDP in the form of taxes than the United States. The United States is also near the bottom when it comes to the proportion of its GDP that it allocates to government spending. Only Australia, Ireland, and Japan spend less through the public sector as a proportion of their economy than the United States.[4]

The smaller public sector in the United States, both in terms of tax revenue and government spending, is reflected in fewer public services available to

---

[1] Harold D. Lasswell, *Politics: Who Gets What, When, How* (New York: McGraw-Hill, 1936).

[2] *Historical Tables: Budget of the United States Government* (Washington DC: U.S. Government Printing Office, 2004), Tables 15.1–15.3, pp. 288–291.

[3] Christopher Heady, "The Truth About Tax Burdens," *OECD Observer* no. 230 (January 2002), p. 17.

[4] *OECD Economic Surveys 2001–2002: United States* (OECD 2002), Table "Basic Statistics: International Comparisons," p. 2.

■ TABLE 11-2

GOVERNMENT RECEIPTS AND OUTLAYS

(in billions of dollars)

	Total Government Receipts	Government Receipts % of GDP	Government Expenditures	Government Expenditures % of GDP
1950	56.6	20.7	58.5	21.4
1955	91.1	23.0	91.0	23.0
1960	131.3	25.3	126.8	24.4
1965	173.8	25.3	168.9	24.6
1970	288.9	28.5	283.6	28.0
1975	436.7	28.0	485.4	31.1
1980	776.1	28.5	841.2	30.9
1985	1,165.5	28.1	1,353.9	32.6
1990	1,646.9	28.7	1,858.5	32.4
1995	2,148.9	29.3	2,303.6	31.4
2000	3,084.9	31.8	2,793.6	28.8
2001	3,091.6	30.8	2,937.2	29.3
2002	2,964.5	28.6	3,126.2	30.1
2003	2,927.6	27.0	3,314.5	30.6

SOURCE: *Fiscal Year 2005 Historical Tables: Budget of the U.S. Government* (Washington, DC: U.S. Government Printing Office, 2004), pp. 288–91.

Americans. For example, other countries have public programs to either finance or provide directly such benefits as medical care to their citizens. In the United States, this and other services are not provided by the government. Citizens must instead purchase health care in the marketplace and pay for it out of their own pocket—if they can afford to.

The small size of the government in relation to the economy is also apparent when one measures it by jobs as well as by money. Public sector employees in the United States comprise about 15 percent of total employment, about 23 million government workers at all levels in 2003—state, local, and federal—out of a workforce of 145,000,000. Again, this places the United States near the bottom compared to other modern economies in terms of its share of public sector employment.

Not only is the government small, but it also lacks the power to manage the economy effectively and influence the behavior of private firms significantly. Corporate managers in the United States enjoy more autonomy to run their business without interference from the government than they do

■ **FIGURE 11–1A**

GENERAL GOVERNMENT DISBURSEMENTS, % GDP (2000)

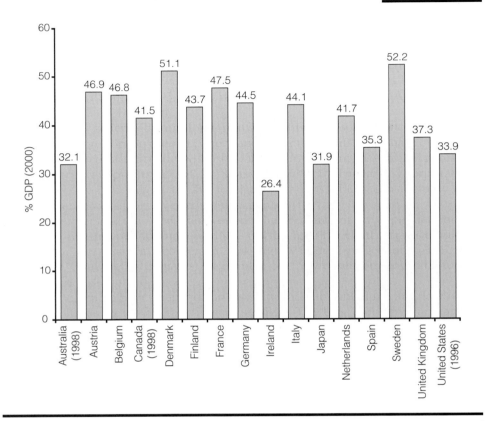

SOURCE: *OECD Economic Surveys: United States* (May 2004), Table: Basic Statistics: International Comparisons, Appendix, Unpaged.

elsewhere.[5] They are subject to fewer and less invasive government regulations that proscribe or require certain activities than their counterparts in other advanced economies. Nowhere else, for example, does the absence of government regulations give employers so much power to fire or lay off workers, leaving workers without protection from summary job loss. Alongside

[5] David Vogel, "Why Businessmen Distrust Their State: The Political Consciousness of American Corporate Executives," *British Journal of Political Science* no. 8 (January 1978): 45–79; Reeve Vanneman and Lynn Weber Cannon, *The American Perception of Class* (Philadelphia: Temple University Press, 1987), pp. 283–311; Howell John Harris, *Right to Manage: Industrial Relations Policies of American Business in the 1940s* (Madison: University of Wisconsin Press, 1982).

■ **FIGURE 11–1B**

TOTAL ESTIMATED TAX REVENUE IN 2000 AS % OF GDP

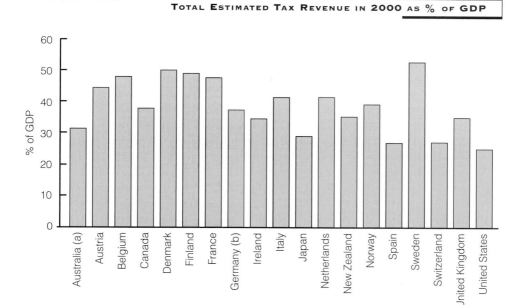

(a) 1999 figure
(b) Unified Germany beginning in 1991

SOURCE: Data from *OECD Revenue Statistics, 1965–2000.*

weak regulatory controls, the government also relies on indirect mechanisms, notably fiscal and monetary policy, to intervene in the economy. The government uses fiscal policy to try to manage the economy by adjusting the government's budget while it uses monetary policy to influence the economy by adjusting interest rates. But the ability of policymakers to effectively utilize even these tools is undermined by their institutional design. Control over fiscal policy is fragmented between Congress and the president, which invites conflict and often produces incoherence. Control over monetary policy is vested in the Federal Reserve Board (popularly known as the Fed), a fiercely independent agency insulated from democratic pressure and electoral control. Fiscal and monetary policies are assigned to different institutions that are independent of each other. Consequently, there is no assurance that fiscal and monetary policy will be coordinated—that is, that they will push in the same direction at the same time.[6]

---

[6] William Greider, *Secrets of the Temple: How the Federal Reserve Runs the Country* (New York: Simon & Schuster, 1987), pp. 351–405.

The restrained use of regulatory controls, the fragmentation of authority over fiscal policy between Congress and the president, the independence of the Federal Reserve Bank, and the lack of mechanisms to ensure coordination between fiscal and monetary policy deprive the elected government of the means to influence greatly the "private government" that owns and controls capital. The government's hand is restrained in its ability to determine who gets what, when, how, and why, leaving such issues to be decided largely by the market. But the American pattern of economic policy making is not simply arbitrary or illogical. If it were, it would be astonishing that the United States has been the world's preeminent economic power for the past century. Instead, the dependence upon markets is deliberate and designed to let corporate capitalism flourish, escape democratic accountability, and preserve inequality.

FISCAL POLICY

Fiscal policy manipulates the total amount of government taxing and spending so as to manage overall demand in the economy. Government can either stimulate the economy by running a budget deficit or restrain the economy by running a budget surplus. Budget deficits pump money into the economy, encouraging more spending, while surpluses take money out, discouraging investment and consumption. Fiscal policy envisions government budgets as thermostats, adjusting automatically to counteract the economy's ups and downs. But the budget is more than a fiscal tool. It also establishes the priorities and values of the government. For example, President George W. Bush declared: "The budget for 2003 is much more than a tabulation of numbers. It is a plan to fight a war we did not seek—but a war we are determined to win."[7] His 2003 budget called for the largest defense spending increase in 20 years in order to fund military interventions in Afghanistan and Iraq. The budget depicts in black and white what the priorities of the government are and who the winners and losers in society will be. It is a blueprint of how the government intends to distribute costs and benefits among different groups. Some groups will shoulder a larger share of the tax burden, while others will receive more in government benefits. The budget is a window through which relations of power in society are revealed.

The budget process is a long, difficult, and intensely political affair that involves partisan conflict between Democrats and Republicans, and institutional conflict between the legislative and executive branches, as well as conflict within each of these branches. The budget process begins within the Executive Office of the President (described in Chapter 6), where the Office of Management and Budget (OMB) formulates the president's budget. OMB negotiates with federal agencies to reconcile differences between their

---

[7] *New York Times*, February 6, 2002.

requests and the president's projections. It then submits a draft budget to the president for review and approval. Presidents then make whatever changes they think are necessary and present their budget proposal to Congress. The 2004 budget that President Bush submitted to Congress for approval weighed in at 13 pounds, consisting of five separate volumes with each volume over five inches thick.

The president's budget, reflecting the administration's preferences and priorities, becomes the point of departure for consideration by Congress. The Constitution gives Congress the power to make laws regarding taxing and spending, and it can reject or amend the president's budget. In recent years, Congress has displayed more budgetary independence, mainly as a result of "divided government," in which Congress and the presidency are controlled by different parties. For example, President Clinton's 1996 budget was submitted to Congress on February 1, 1995—and was promptly ignored. Republicans in the House and the Senate proceeded to develop and vote on their own budget that diverged sharply from the president's. It contained cuts in food stamps, school lunches, and Medicare at the same time that it included tax cuts for the rich. This prompted a veto from President Clinton. In the absence of a budget or continuing resolution to provide funding for current expenditures, the government could not legally pay its workers, and government offices and national parks were closed for 26 days. With Republicans dropping in the polls and being blamed for shutting down the government, Congress abandoned the fight and authorized the expenditure of funds to keep government open.[8]

Relations between Congress and the president do not often deteriorate to the extent of shutting down the federal government for lack of funds. Rather, the president's budget becomes the starting point for consideration by Congress, which begins when the Budget committees in both the House and the Senate adopt a Budget Resolution. This specifies the total amount of money the government intends to raise and spend, with expenditures distributed across 20 broad categories of government activity. The budget resolution is a general plan of spending and revenue targets. Committees within Congress are then charged with amending existing law to reflect tax and spending changes consistent with the totals called for in the joint Budget Resolution. "For example," Daniel J. Palazzolo writes, "it is one thing to agree that $35 billion in tax breaks will go towards tuition assistance for higher education; it is another thing to determine who is eligible, how much each person will be eligible for, how the tax credits will be structured and the like."[9] The Appropriations committees in both the House and the Senate review these changes and stipulate the actual funding levels for particular programs, with an eye to keeping total spending within the guidelines set by

---

[8] Elizabeth Drew, *Showdown* (New York: Simon & Schuster, 1996), p. 326.

[9] Daniel J. Palazzolo, *Done Deal? The Politics of the 1997 Budget Agreement* (Chappaqua, NY: Seven Bridges Press, 1999), p. 90.

the joint Budget Resolution. Appropriations bills are then submitted to presidents for their signature or veto.[10]

The final budget agreed to by the president and Congress is simply an estimate of what the government will spend and how much revenue it will collect. No one really knows for sure, for example, what the final cost of disaster relief will be in any given year, whether the United States will be in a war that it did not anticipate fighting when the budget was first drafted, or exactly how much revenue certain taxes will raise. Budgets are intentions that the future sometimes respects and at other times mocks.[11]

TAXES

Nobody likes taxes. Americans, like citizens in other countries, complain that they pay too much, that the tax system is too complicated and too difficult to enforce, and that it is unfair.[12] Yet, taxes are necessary to pay for government: for the services we receive from it, such as police protection; and for the benefits we collect from it, such as social security. They are the oil that keeps the machinery of government running. Just as no one likes paying money to fill up their car with gas, no one likes paying taxes. But cars won't run without gas, and government won't work without taxes. They provide the money for government to create and enforce the rules that permit us to live together. "Taxes," Chief Justice Oliver Wendell Holmes once wrote, are "the price we pay for civilized society."[13]

Tax policy is highly contentious as groups seek to influence what the overall level of taxation should be, how the total tax level should be divided among different types of taxes, and what share of these taxes different groups should pay. All of these aspects of tax policy have changed over time as a result of political conflict. For example, state, local, and federal taxes were a mere 7 percent of GDP in 1900. By 1969, the total tax bite from all levels of government was about 30 percent of GDP, where it hovered for the next 30 years. But the tax picture began to change considerably in 2001 as a result of recession and President Bush's tax cuts. Total government tax receipts that had risen to 31.8 percent of GDP in 2000 fell to 27.0 percent by 2003, a decline of 13 percent in just three years.[14] This was due almost entirely to falling federal tax revenue. Federal tax receipts that had been increasing

---

[10] The budgetary process is described in detail in Allen Schick, *The Federal Budget: Politics, Policy and Process* (Washington, DC: Brookings, 1995).

[11] Steven Waldman, *The Bill* (New York: Penguin, 1996), p. 74.

[12] Joel Slemrod and Jon Bakija, *Taxing Ourselves: A Citizen's Guide to the Great Debate Over Tax Reform* (Cambridge, MA: MIT Press, 1996), pp. 1–5.

[13] Holmes is quoted in Slemrod and Bakija, *Taxing Ourselves*, p. 1.

[14] *Historical Tables*, see Table 15.1, p. 288.

steadily since 1983 to 20 percent of GDP in 2000 declined to just 16.5 percent of GDP by 2003. The last time the share of federal taxes to the economy was that low was in 1955!

Declining federal tax revenue under President George W. Bush led to soaring budget deficits. A budget surplus of $236 billion in 2000 had turned into a budget deficit of $375 billion just three years later, an astonishing reversal of more than $600 billion in the national account. The National Debt Clock was whirring faster than ever trying to keep up as deficits escalated. Deficits are, of course, appropriate when fighting recession. Cutting taxes to create a deficit can have a stimulative effect on an economy that suffers from inadequate demand and feeble job creation. But as we argued in Chapter 3, the effort to revive the economy by reducing taxes was misdirected. President Bush offered the largest tax breaks to the rich and provided only modest relief to working and middle-class families who were most likely to spend it. Consequently, the benefits for the economy were not anywhere near proportionate to the size of the tax cuts enacted. The United States enjoyed little fiscal bang for the buck when it came to President Bush's tax cuts, leaving future generations to pay the bill.

Not only has the total level of taxation changed—rising to about 30 percent of GDP and then falling under President Bush—but so has its composition. There are different streams of tax revenue. State and local governments, for example, rely primarily upon sales and property taxes to raise revenue. The federal government, however, relies upon different kinds of taxes to raise money. As Table 11-3 indicates, the federal government raises more money from individual income taxes than it does from any other revenue source.[15] From 1950 to the present, it has collected between 40 and 50 percent of all its money from this one source. While the proportion of all federal revenues collected from income taxes has remained fairly steady, that cannot be said of other revenue streams. The contribution of corporate income taxes to total tax revenues has declined over time. Corporate income taxes accounted for one-quarter of all federal tax receipts in 1950. By 2003, they accounted for only 7.4 percent of federal revenue, contributing just $131 billion to federal coffers, the lowest annual total since 1993. The federal tax rate for big corporations is supposed to be 35 percent on profits, but loopholes, credits, and accounting gimmickry have cut the effective corporate tax rate to about 20 percent. Sometimes tax shelters permit corporations to avoid taxes altogether. Between 1996 and 2000, when profits were soaring, 60 percent of U.S. corporations did not pay any federal taxes at all.[16]

Along with corporate taxes, the proportion of taxes the federal government raises through excise taxes, which are federal sales taxes on such items

---

[15] *Historical Tables*, see Table 2.2, p. 29.

[16] "Many firms Avoided Taxes Even as Profits Soared in Boom" (April 6, 2004), *www.smartmoney. com/bn/ON/index.cfm?story.*

PERCENTAGE OF COMPOSITION OF TAX
RECEIPTS BY SOURCE

	Individual Income Tax	Corporate Income Tax	Social Insurance & Retirement Receipts	Excise Tax	Other
1950	39.9	26.5	11.0	19.1	3.4
1955	43.9	27.3	12.0	14.0	2.8
1960	44.0	23.2	15.9	12.6	4.2
1965	41.8	21.8	19.0	12.5	4.9
1970	46.9	17.0	23.0	8.1	4.9
1975	43.9	14.6	30.3	5.9	5.4
1980	47.2	12.5	30.5	4.7	5.1
1985	45.6	8.4	36.1	4.9	5.1
1990	45.2	9.1	36.8	3.4	5.4
1995	43.7	11.6	35.8	4.3	4.6
2000	49.6	10.2	32.2	3.4	4.5
2001	49.9	7.6	34.9	3.3	4.3
2002	46.3	8.0	37.8	3.6	4.3
2003	44.5	7.4	40.0	3.8	4.3

SOURCE: *Fiscal Year 2005 Historical Tables: Budget of the U.S. Government* (Washington DC: U.S. Government Printing Office, 2004), p. 31.

as alcohol, cigarettes, and gasoline, has also fallen. The federal government collected about one-fifth of its money through these kinds of consumption taxes in 1950. By 2003, they amounted to a negligible 3.6 percent of total revenue.

The decline in the proportion of federal revenue raised through corporate and excise taxes has been compensated for by a rise in the proportion of taxes collected by social insurance receipts. The Social Security payroll tax, which finances retirement and health benefits for the elderly and disabled, accounts for a large majority of these contributions. Social insurance contributions have replaced corporate income taxes as the second largest revenue stream to the federal government. Social insurance contributions amounted to about 10 percent of all taxes in 1950. Fifty years later, by 2000, they were about one-third of all tax receipts.

Taxes are collected from many different sources. They are also distributed among many different groups. Some pay more than others in taxes. Some argue that the tax system should be progressive, requiring the rich to pay a larger proportion of their income in the form of taxes. Others believe the tax system should be regressive, that tax rates should not increase as personal income rises. As Figure 11-2 reveals, when all types of state and federal taxes are considered together—federal and state income taxes, social security contributions, sales taxes, property taxes, and others—the distribution of the tax burden among the rich, poor, and middle class is pretty proportional; it is neither progressive nor regressive. That is, each quintile of income pays the same proportion of their income in the form of taxes. The bottom 20 percent of income earners paid $1,449 in taxes, or 18 percent of their average pretax income, while the top 20 percent paid $21,623 of their average pretax income in taxes, just one percent more than the bottom fifth. All income groups pay roughly the same proportion of their average pretax income in the form of taxes when all different kinds of taxes are lumped together.[17]

Finally, tax policy is not simply about how much money to raise, how to do it, and who should pay for it. It is also about creating incentives for certain types of behavior by offering tax exemptions, rebates, and deductions. For example, the government encourages home ownership by permitting homeowners to deduct the interest they pay on their mortgage from their taxes. It encourages investment by permitting businesses to deduct the cost of depreciation for equipment from their taxes. It encourages people to save for retirement by permitting citizens to shield income they contribute to a retirement account from taxation. That is, government often makes policy by subsidizing certain activities through the tax code. Policymakers often prefer to offer what are called tax expenditures—public subsidies through favored tax treatment—than to authorize expenditures for the same purpose. The cost may be the same to taxpayers in either case, whether it takes the form of direct spending or tax revenue that would otherwise be collected. But the political consequences are very different. Making policy through the tax code by giving favored tax treatment to certain activities is not as visible as new spending for programs. The costs of tax expenditures are diffuse and their effects not easily traceable. Policymakers prefer what Jacob Hacker called the "subterranean politics" of tax expenditures over appropriating money for new programs because it is less likely to arouse conflict.[18] As a result, the use of tax expenditures as a way to make policy has increased. This has resulted in a tax code that is very complex as it is now filled with an array of exemptions, deductions, and rebates in order to encourage citizens to act in certain ways. The tax code that was once perceived simply as a way to raise government revenue has now become a more concealed and more frequent means by which government makes policy.

---

[17] *New York Times*, January 21, 2003. Table from the *Times* is drawn from a Consumer Expenditure Survey of the Bureau of Labor Statistics.

[18] Jacob S. Hacker, *The Divided Welfare State: The Battle Over Public and Private Social Benefits in the United States* (New York: Cambridge University Press, 2002).

■ FIGURE 11-2

SPREADING THE TAX BITE AROUND

Taking all types of government taxes into consideration, the tax burden, as a percentage of pretax income, is roughly the same for all income groups.

Income group	Average pretax income	Total government tax receipts	As a percentage of income
Bottom 20%	$7,946	$1,449	18%
Second 20%	20,319	2,847	14
Middle 20%	35,536	5,622	16
Fourth 20%	56,891	9,835	17
Top 20%	116,666	21,623	19

Government receipts include federal and state income taxes. Social Security contributions (employee's share), property taxes, utility taxes, federal and state tobacco taxes, federal and state alcohol taxes, federal and state gasoline taxes and state sales tax.

SOURCE: From "Doubling up of Taxation Isn't Limited to Dividends" by Daniel Altman, *New York Times,* January 21, 2003, p. C1. Copyright © 2003 by the New York Times Co. Reprinted by permission. Data from Consumer Expenditure Survey of the Bureau of Labor Statistics; R. J. Reynolds Tobacco; Beer Institute; Wine America; Wine and Spirits Wholesalers of America; American Petroleum Institute; Tax Foundation.

SPENDING

Taxes are one side of the government budget. The other side is composed of spending. Political conflict is as pervasive and bitter over spending as it is over taxes. Groups struggle over how much money the government should spend and what it should be spent on. Evidence of these conflicts is apparent in how government expenditures have changed over time. Total state, local, and federal government outlays that were just $95.2 billion, or 25.5 percent of GDP in 1953, have increased 50 years later to $3.3 trillion, which was 30.6 percent of GDP in 2003. Governments at all levels spend more because they do more than they did 50 years ago. Social security coverage was not as broad as it is today, Medicare for seniors and Medicaid for the poor did not exist, multicampus state universities had not yet been built, and such offices as the Environmental Protection Agency had not yet been created.

The federal government accounts for about two-thirds of all government expenditures, with state and local governments spending the rest. Just as the taxing sources from which the federal government raises money have changed, so have the categories in which the national government spends it. Some federal activities that captured a large share of the federal budget now get less, while other activities now get more. Take, for instance, how spending

■ **TABLE 11–4**

FEDERAL OUTLAYS FOR DEFENSE
AND THE WELFARE STATE

(in millions of dollars)

	Defense	% of Federal Expenditures	Welfare State	% of Federal Expenditures
1954	49,266	69.5	13,076	18.5
1955	42,729	62.4	14,908	21.8
1960	48,130	52.2	26,184	28.4
1965	50,620	42.8	26,576	30.9
1970	81,692	41.8	75,349	38.5
1975	86,509	26.0	173,245	52.1
1980	133,995	22.7	313,374	53.0
1985	252,748	26.7	471,822	49.9
1990	299,331	23.9	619,329	49.4
1995	272,066	17.9	923,765	60.9
2000	294,495	16.5	1,115,481	62.4
2001	305,500	16.4	1,194,409	64.1
2002	348,555	17.3	1,317,437	65.5
2003	404,920	18.8	1,417,707	65.7

SOURCE: *Fiscal Year 2005 Historical Tables: Budget of the U.S. Government* (Washington DC: U.S. Government Printing Office, 2004), pp. 45–52.

for national defense and the welfare state, the two largest calls on the federal budget, have changed through the years as depicted in Table 11-4. Not only do defense and the welfare state together capture more of all federal money than they did in the past, but the balance between them has changed dramatically. In 1954, in the midst of the Cold War, 69 percent of all federal outlays were devoted to defense spending. From that peak, the share of federal spending committed to defense declined fairly consistently to 16.5 percent in 2000, until increases tied to the wars in Afghanistan and Iraq saw defense outlays increase to 18.8 percent of federal spending in 2003. In the interim, the percentage of the federal budget dedicated to welfare state spending, which includes federal expenses for health care, education, income support, social security, and veterans' benefits, has increased considerably. Welfare state expenses that comprised only 15.6 percent of the federal budget in 1954 accounted for nearly two-thirds of all federal spending by 2003.

Another way of looking at how federal money is distributed is to divide it between mandatory and discretionary accounts as opposed to separating expenditures by government activity or function. Two-thirds of all federal spending is mandatory. Spending for these programs is "governed by formulas or criteria set forth in authorizing legislation" passed by Congress "rather than by appropriations."[19] They are the result of previous commitments that Congress is obligated to meet. For example, mandatory spending includes payments on the national debt. In order to retain its access to credit, the government must pay off its debt when it comes due. But the most expensive form of mandatory spending takes the form of entitlement programs. Entitlement programs provide benefits to citizens as long as they meet certain eligibility requirements. Their cost is open-ended. The government will provide benefits to all those who qualify, regardless of how many there are or what the final cost may be. Social security, for example, is an entitlement program. Citizens who have contributed to the social security program receive social security checks from the government when they apply and become eligible. Food stamps and Medicare are other examples of entitlement programs.

Mandatory spending consumes so much money that not much is left over for discretionary spending. Unlike entitlement programs, discretionary spending is under the jurisdiction of the House and Senate Appropriations Committees, which provide authority for "federal agencies to incur obligations and make payments out of the treasury for specified purposes."[20] The largest expense of any discretionary program is defense. Defense spending consumes one-half of all discretionary spending by the federal government. The other half is composed of nondefense spending, which includes everything from highway maintenance, to grants and loans for those attending college, to paying the salaries of federal judges. The small share of federal outlays devoted to discretionary programs means that it is very hard for Congress to direct expenditures through its annual appropriations process. Only one-third of all federal spending is really up for grabs each year. It also means that it is very hard for Congress to control spending. Government outlays increase each year because the cost of entitlement programs grows each year. And that growth is automatic as more people qualify for such programs as social security and Medicare, the two largest and most expensive entitlement programs.

MONETARY POLICY

Along with fiscal policy, the government tries to manage the economy through monetary policy. Monetary policy attempts to fine-tune the economy by manipulating interest rates, the cost of money. High interest rates tend to slow down the economy by discouraging spending. Low interest

---

[19] Palazzolo, *Done Deal*, p. 230.
[20] Palazzolo, *Done Deal*, p. 229.

rates, on the other hand, encourage borrowing and spending by making credit cheap and easy to obtain. Like fiscal policy, monetary policy is used to counteract tendencies toward economic instability. If the economy is tending toward inflation or excessive demand, raising interest rates will cool it down. Conversely, if a recession occurs and demand is slack, reducing interest rates will help revive the economy by making loans more attractive for consumers who want to purchase new goods and for businesses that want to make new investments. For example, beginning in 2001, the Federal Reserve Bank cut interest rates 13 times in order to boost spending and investment. Interest rates dropped to their lowest level in 40 years, even lower than the rate of inflation, in order to revive the economy from recession.

But manipulating interest rates is not simply about trying to counteract tendencies toward inflation and recession. Like fiscal policy, monetary policy affects different groups in different ways. For example, the affluent generally benefit from higher interest rates, while the opposite is true for those without accumulated wealth. The affluent often have savings, and high interest rates—tight money—increase the value of these investments. On the other hand, middle- and lower-income groups are more likely to go into debt than to save. Lower interest rates on loans reduce the debt of this group. Thus, whether to err on the side of setting interest rates high or low is not simply a technical matter of managing the economy but a political one of rewarding some groups at the expense of others. A key question then is, who decides, and on what basis, if the economy needs higher or lower interest rates?

The chair of the Federal Reserve Board (along with other members of the Open Market Committee of the Federal Reserve Board) determines the rate of interest that the Federal Reserve System charges American banks to borrow funds. When the Federal Reserve Bank raises the rate it charges banks for loans, banks increase the rate they charge their customers to borrow money. Similarly, when the Federal Reserve lowers the interest rate it charges banks for loans, banks can give their customers easier credit terms, increasing the flow of money in the economy. In addition, the Fed affects the money supply via open market operations, in which the Federal Reserve Bank buys or sells government bonds. Buying government bonds puts more money into circulation while selling bonds withdraws money from the economy. Finally, the Fed influences the money supply by setting the reserve rate that banks must hold on deposits. The reserve rate is the proportion of money that banks must keep on hand in the event that depositors withdraw funds from their accounts. An increase in the reserve rate means that banks have to hold more of their funds in reserve and thereby have less money to lend out. This decreases the money supply. Lowering the reserve rate has the opposite effect. It permits banks to lend out a higher proportion of their deposits as loans to creditors, thereby increasing the money supply. These different methods the Fed uses to manipulate the money supply send ripples through the economy, affecting the direction of the stock and bond market, the rate of interest that banks charge on mortgages, and the rate of interest that credit card companies charge on unpaid balances. But the ripples continue far beyond, affecting whether companies hire more employees or prune their payrolls, whether wages and salaries go up or down, and, most generally, whether the economy expands or contracts. The fact that so little is known about the operation of the Federal Reserve Board is an extraordinary feature of American politics. Henry Ford, Sr., once observed, "It is well enough that the people of the nation do not understand our banking and monetary system for, if they did, I believe there would be a revolution before tomorrow morning."[21]

According to journalist William Greider, the Fed is "the crucial anomaly at the very core of representative government, an uncomfortable contradiction with the civic mythology of self-government."[22] When the Fed was created in 1913, it was deliberately insulated from democratic pressures and the influence of elected politicians. The Fed enjoys more political independence from both Congress and the president than any other government agency. It enjoys this enviable position because, ostensibly, monetary policy—adjusting interest rates—is a technical matter beyond politics. But as we have seen, nothing could be further from the truth. The Fed was deliberately given substantial autonomy in order to insulate monetary policy from democratic control.

The president and Congress are not completely without power over the Fed. Congress now requires the chair of the Fed to testify biannually before the House and Senate banking committees. The president can influence the Fed by appointing members to the Federal Reserve Board, subject to confirmation by the Senate. The president also appoints the chair of the Fed to a four-year term, and if the chair wishes to be reappointed, he or she must consider the president's priorities. While the Fed is anxious to appease the president, it is even more concerned with preserving its reputation for fiscal probity among bankers, who are its real constituency.

Banks and the financial community in general have inordinate influence over Fed policy. The Fed tends to adopt the perspective of banks because they are its primary constituency—over 2,000 banks are members of the Federal Reserve System; most Federal Reserve Board members either previously worked for banks or are economists trained in finance—and the Fed, after all, is a bank itself, the central bank of the United States. Moreover, representatives from the banking community participate and vote when the Fed deliberates over monetary policy. Interest rate targets are set by the Federal Open Market Committee (FOMC). The FOMC is comprised of the seven members who form the Federal Reserve Board, in addition to the presidents of the 12 District Federal Reserve Banks. Commercial banks in each district select the president of each Federal Reserve Bank, five of whom have voting privileges on the FOMC. In 1993, Representative Henry B. Gonzalez, chair of the House Committee on Banking, wrote an open letter to President Clinton

---

[21] Quoted in Greider, *Secrets of the Temple*, p. 55.

[22] Ibid., p. 12.

deploring the presence of bankers on the FOMC and the lack of influence the public has over its composition. Gonzalez wrote:

> In general, the Federal Reserve decision makers are bankers or friends of bankers. Decision makers representing the concerns of agriculture, small business, labor, and community groups are almost unheard of. . . . Last week, the Fed selected one of their [sic] own, William J. McDonough, as president of the New York Federal Reserve Bank. Mr. McDonough's qualifications and his views on monetary policy . . . will not be debated in public. His expertise in central bank monetary policy will not be questioned in Senate confirmation hearings. However, because he has been selected through the Fed's internal private mechanisms, he will manage our nation's money supply without ever going before the American people or their representatives.[23]

Banks influence the Fed in more subtle ways than the unusual practice just described of having representatives from the banking community actually participate and vote in policy-making discussions of the FOMC. The Fed tends to view the economy through the eyes of a bank because it adopts the financial markets as its frame of reference in setting policy. Nancy Teeter, a former Federal Reserve Board member, recalls how her own perspective changed once she began to serve on the Fed. She remembers telling Arthur Burns, the chair of the Federal Reserve Board who interviewed her for the position, "'Arthur, you don't want someone like me on the Board of Governors with my liberal background.' Arthur said, 'Don't worry, Nancy. Within six months, you will think just like a central banker.' Arthur was right. I think I'm very much like a central banker now."[24]

REGULATION

Fiscal and monetary policies affect economic actors indirectly by influencing the conditions in which they operate. Policymakers use fiscal and monetary policies to try to create a predictable environment in which price levels are stable and employment levels are high so that economic actors can plan with some certainty about the future. But government can also use more direct means to influence what economic actors do. The government can engage in regulation, setting explicit rules of behavior that firms and workers must follow. There is nothing indirect or incidental about regulation as a form of economic policy making by the government. Regulations dictate what economic actors can and cannot do. For example, regulations stipulate that firms cannot sell products that are unsafe, issue misleading financial statements, engage in deceptive advertising, or discriminate. Other regulations require

---

[23] Henry B. Gonzalez, "An Open Letter to the President," *Challenge* (September–October 1993): 30–31.

[24] Quoted in Greider, *Secrets of the Temple,* pp. 73–74.

firms to accurately label foods and drugs, post safety notices, and pay a minimum wage to their workers. Regulations seek to influence how firms behave in relation to each other, to workers, and to consumers by compelling them to do or not do something.

Complaints about "big government" extend to those about regulation. Conservatives and business grumble that the American economy is overregulated. They suggest that rules governing firms are proliferating, imposing unnecessary costs in terms of compliance, discouraging innovation with a maze of bureaucratic requirements, and promoting inefficiency by distorting the normal operation of the market. But, again, just as we saw previously with regard to the United States having a rather small public sector, when viewed comparatively the United States is one of the least regulated markets in the world. According to the Fraser Institute, a conservative Canadian think tank, the hand of regulation in the United States is not heavy but exceedingly light. The United States ranked second out of more than 100 countries surveyed in terms of having the freest credit, labor, and product markets.[25] Far from being overregulated, it appears the U.S. economy is one of the least regulated in the entire world!

The government issues regulations when markets don't work to protect the public interest and when markets fail to promote values that society treasures, such as clean air, safe workplaces, reliable products, and honest business practices. Unregulated markets where firms compete to maximize their profits will not produce these by themselves. Instead, regulations imposed by the government are necessary to create them.

The authority of the federal government to issue regulations governing economic actors stems from the power the Constitution gave Congress to regulate commerce among states and with foreign nations. But this power was largely dormant until the late 19th century when, under popular pressure, Congress created the Interstate Commerce Commission (ICC) to regulate railroad rates and routes. This was followed by a host of regulatory agencies created by Congress in response to popular outcries about the abuse of corporate power. In 1914, Congress established the Federal Trade Commission (FTC) to prevent firms from discouraging competition and to protect consumers from unfair business practices. The Food and Drug Administration (FDA) was created in 1931 to prevent firms from selling tainted food and harmful drugs, and the Securities and Exchange Commission (SEC) was created in 1934 to prevent investors from being defrauded by stock market manipulation. But these efforts often led to the opposite result of what reformers intended. Officials in government agencies developed close ties with the industries they were supposed to regulate as they engaged in day-to-day business with them, became familiar with industry executives, and were

---

[25] Fraser Institute, *Economic Freedom of the World: 2003 Annual Report.* See "Exhibit 3: Area Economic Freedom Ratings and Rankings, 2001," pp. 13–15.

hired away by them.[26] The FDA became responsive to the pharmaceutical industry and the SEC to Wall Street brokerage houses. In 1970, in a case involving the Civil Aeronautics Board (CAB), the U.S. Circuit Court of Appeals for the District of Columbia went so far as to accuse the agency of "being unduly oriented toward the interest of the industry it is designed to regulate, rather than the public interest it is designed to protect."[27] Watch dogs for the public had become guard dogs for industry.

The first wave of regulatory agencies created during the Progressive and New Deal eras, such as the aforementioned FDA, SEC, and CAB, were engaged in economic regulation. Congress created these agencies to regulate specific industries, which often involved managing competition and setting industry standards. In the 1960s, however, a new surge of popular protest emerged demanding social as opposed to economic regulation by the government. The civil rights movement pressed Congress to create agencies that would enforce new civil rights laws preventing discrimination. In 1970, environmentalists succeeded in getting Congress to establish the Environmental Protection Agency (EPA) to develop and enforce environmental quality standards. That same year, under pressure from the labor movement, Congress created the Occupational Safety and Health Administration (OSHA) to set and monitor workplace safety and health standards. And two years later, in 1972, the consumer movement successfully used its growing influence to get Congress to create the Consumer Products Safety Commission.

While the earlier and later waves of regulation both stemmed from popular dissatisfaction with free markets, economic and social regulation are very different from one another. The first wave of economic regulation fixed prices, managed competition, set standards, and issued licenses for specific industries. The FDA regulated the pharmaceutical industry, the ICC regulated trucking and the railroads, and the SEC regulated stock market brokerage firms. But the second wave of social regulation cut across industries to affect businesses in virtually all of them. All firms, regardless of the industry they were in, now had to abide by antidiscrimination laws, environmental regulations, and workplace safety rules. "The result," the political scientist David Vogel writes, "was a fundamental restructuring of both the politics and the administration of government regulation of corporate social conduct."[28] Public interest activists in the civil rights, women's, consumer, labor, and environmental movements successfully put business on the defensive. New government agencies created rules and enforced laws that now

---

[26] Marver H. Bernstein, *Regulating Business by Independent Regulatory Commission* (Westport, CT: Greenwood Press, 1955).

[27] Quoted in Barry D. Friedman, *Regulation in the Reagan-Bush Era: The Eruption of Presidential Influence* (Pittsburgh: University of Pittsburgh Press, 1995), p. 10.

[28] David Vogel, *Fluctuating Fortunes: The Political Power of Business in America* (New York: Basic Books, 1989), p. 59.

required certain courses of action by virtually all firms in terms of who they hired and fired (nondiscrimination employment laws), their process of production (workplace safety and health rules), and their environmental impact (environmental protection laws).

But the reach of these new agencies across industrial lines also helped forge a united front by business against them. The second wave of regulation had awakened a sleeping giant. Business mobilized to roll back what it perceived as new, intrusive, and costly social regulations. Campaign contributions from business soared. Lobbying increased as corporate executives pleaded their case personally with policymakers. New business organizations were formed and existing trade groups reinvigorated. Advertising campaigns to sway public opinion in favor of what was termed "regulatory reform" were launched. A counteroffensive by a mobilized and cohesive business community was moving across all fronts.

The deregulation movement prompted by business could not help but overshoot its mark. The same arguments that business raised against social regulations they found so objectionable—that such rules are costly, disturb efficient markets, and hamper innovation—could also be made against economic regulations that regulated industries found so congenial. These arguments were then used by consumer advocates from the left and by free market advocates from the right to criticize economic regulations for contributing to inflation, promoting complacency, and fostering inefficiency. In addition, business's arguments that regulations promoted big government and thwarted free enterprise created an atmosphere of distrust and antipathy toward all government agencies and activity, even those that protected their industries. Political leaders seized upon this broad antigovernment sentiment, which, ironically, business had done so much to promote, to make a popular case against entrenched regulated industries. The result was that regulatory reform even affected agencies that business had captured. For example, the Civil Aeronautics Board, which had been created in 1938 to prevent ruinous competition among airlines, was abolished in 1985. The deregulation of the railroad and trucking industries followed soon after. The grip of industries over the agencies that were supposed to regulate them may have been powerful, but it was not immutable. Political circumstances surrounding the agencies engaged in economic regulation had changed in such a way as to offset and neutralize the benefits previously offered by firms they regulated.[29]

The politics of economic policy is as evident in the tug of war over regulation as it is over fiscal and monetary policies. Business usually, but not always, decries government regulation, while others want the government to impose some values—fairness (nondiscrimination), honesty (fair trade practices), sustainability (environmental protection)—that the market cannot and will not create itself. But the politics of regulation are evident not

---

[29] Martha Derthick and Paul J. Quirk, *The Politics of Deregulation* (Washington, DC: Brookings Institution, 1985).

only in the presence or absence of rules but in the vigor with which they are enforced. Like fiscal and monetary policies that are adjustable in response to economic circumstances, the zealousness with which the government pursues regulation adjusts in response to political circumstances. There is regulatory slack in the system that can expand or contract depending on the political pressures brought to bear on it. The government can go out looking for environmental violations or wait for complaints to come to it; the government can issue large fines to those who violate labor laws or issue slaps on the wrist; the government can employ enough inspectors to ensure meat meets safety standards or just a few; and it can set high standards for car emissions or permit higher levels of pollution. Whether regulations are enforced energetically or negligently is as much a source of political conflict among advocates and opponents of regulation as the regulations themselves. Standard setting and enforcement by regulatory agencies stretch and bend in response to the political pressures applied to them.

CONCLUSION

In the United States, the production and allocation of goods and services is determined by the market. Yet, no economy, not even a capitalist one that operates according to the laws of supply and demand, can exist without government. Government is necessary to create a common currency that facilitates trade and exchange, to enforce contracts that promote security and predictability, and to supply public goods, such as police protection and highways, that society needs but the market won't provide because it is unprofitable to do so. As a congressman from Mississippi once acknowledged without a hint of irony, "The free enterprise system is too important to be left in the hands of private individuals."[30]

Economic policy sets the balance between markets and government. What is so remarkable about this in the United States is the degree to which markets are granted wide latitude at the expense of government to determine who gets what and how much. The Fraser Institute ranked the United States in third place, behind only Hong Kong and Singapore, as the most market-oriented economy in the world.[31] As this chapter has noted, the size of the government in relation to the economy is quite small, despite all the complaints about "big government." The government spends less and Americans are taxed less as a proportion of the economy than citizens in almost any other advanced industrial society. Not only does the government direct less of the flow of money

---

[30] Quoted in John McMillan, *Reinventing the Bazaar: A Natural History of Markets* (New York: Norton, 2002), p. 174.

[31] Fraser Institute, *Economic Freedom of the World: 2004 Annual Report. See* Exhibit 1.2 "Summary Economic Freedom Rankings, 2002," p. 11.

through the economy than is the case in many other countries, but it has weak levers with which to direct the economy. Fiscal and monetary policy can only influence the circumstances in which economic actors operate. They can only influence the behavior of firms indirectly. And the effectiveness of these tools of economic management is crippled by their institutional design. They are assigned to different institutions—Congress and the president in charge of fiscal policy, and the Federal Reserve Bank in charge of monetary policy—without any assurance that they will work in conjunction with one another. More direct means of governing what business does through regulation are not pursued with the vigor found in other countries. Firms must comply with fewer regulations, and those regulations that exist are not often vigorously enforced.

The wide latitude granted markets to determine the production and allocation of goods and services works to the advantage of those with market power, the large corporations who own and control the means of production. They can use their power in the marketplace to appropriate more of the national income in the form of profits for themselves as opposed to wages for their workers, and to reward their executives with unseemly pay packages as opposed to increasing compensation for their employees.

The pervasiveness and dependence on markets in the United States is due to the political power of business. But the latitude granted markets has to be defended constantly. Political conflict threatens continually to shift the border between markets and government. Social regulations of the 1960s and 1970s, which left a legacy of environmental, workplace, consumer, and civil rights protections, rolled back the private power of business. They were then the target of a deregulatory counteroffensive by employers to recover their prerogatives. But after giving some ground, the boundary between private and public power shifted back again as the excesses of deregulation prompted popular new demands for more regulatory initiatives. The same kinds of conflict that are evident in regulatory policy are also apparent in fiscal and monetary policy. The trench warfare of economic policy between those who advocate more market and those who support more government is never silent and never still.

12

DEMOCRACY'S FUTURE

The rules are the same for all the teams in baseball: Three strikes, you're out; three outs to a side; whoever scores the most runs, wins. The pitcher's mound is the same 60 feet 6 inches from home plate in Yankee Stadium as it is in Wrigley Field where the Chicago Cubs play. The distance between the bases is the same 90 feet for the home team as it is for the visitors. What we referred to as procedural equality exists in baseball. All the teams must abide by the same rules, which apply equally to all of them. No team is permitted four outs to an inning, a smaller strike zone for their batters, or ten players on the field.

And yet, the same teams continue to win. Some teams, like the Chicago Cubs, have not been in a World Series since 1945—and the last time the Cubs *won* a World Series was 1908. The New York Yankees, on the other hand, have been in 39 World Series—and have won 26 times. Indeed, the lack of competitive balance was regarded as such a problem that in 1999, Baseball Commissioner Bud Selig appointed a blue-ribbon panel to investigate. The panel found that inequality threatened the integrity of the nation's pastime. From 1995 to 1999, no team in the bottom half of payrolls ever won a divisional series or league championship game, and only teams in the top quartile of payrolls ever won a World Series game. Even worse, the gap between wealthy and low-budget teams was growing. Whereas the average payroll of clubs in the richest quartile grew by $28 million between 1995 and 1999, the average payroll of clubs in the lowest quintile increased by only $4 million. By 1999, the richest team had a payroll equal to the payroll of the five lowest teams *combined*. The rules are fair; the game is not.[1]

When baseball owners got hit where it hurt—in their pocketbooks because the obviously unfair system resulted in falling attendance, and therefore declining revenue—they took action. In 2002, they initiated a revenue-sharing plan that redistributed income from the wealthiest teams—those in large television markets with lucrative TV contracts—to the poorest teams. In 2004,

---

[1] Richard C. Levin, George J. Mitchell, Paul A. Volker, and George F. Will, "The Report of the Independent Members of the Commissioner's Blue Ribbon Panel on Baseball Economics," (July 2000).

$220 million was distributed from large- to smaller-market teams. For example, George Steinbrenner, owner of the New York Yankees, baseball's wealthiest team, paid $53 million into the revenue-sharing pool.[2] The plan went some distance toward leveling the steeply sloped playing field, but only some distance: The New York Yankees' payroll in 2004 of $184 million (the highest in Major League Baseball) was over six times larger than the payroll of the Milwaukee Brewers, the team with the lowest payroll. Compared to the situation in 1999 described previously, this represents progress. But, it can hardly be said to have resulted in a situation where all teams have an equal chance to compete for the best players.

And yet no matter how great the economic inequalities among teams, the game is not decided by whoever has the largest payroll or highest revenue. It still has to be played on the field where players must hit, run, pitch, and catch. In the end, high-spending teams are challenged to translate their higher payrolls into more runs. In 2002, the American League West Division finished in inverse order to their payrolls. The more money that teams spent on players, the lower the teams finished in the division standings.[3] In the 2003 World Series, the Florida Marlins, with a total payroll of $63 million—in the bottom third of all baseball teams—defeated the New York Yankees, whose payroll was almost three times more than that of the victorious Marlins. And the Yankees lost the American League Divisional playoffs in 2004 to the Boston Red Sox, a team with a significantly smaller payroll.

But the fact that money is not the only factor in determining the outcome does not mean its influence can be ignored. Low payroll baseball teams win—but only occasionally. High payroll teams may not win all the time, but the odds are in their favor that they'll win most of the time.

We trust that the point of this exercise is obvious: The politics of power, like baseball, offers structural advantages to players and teams with more assets. A mobilization of bias exists based on the inequality between baseball teams in large markets and those located in smaller markets, just as it does between large corporations that own and control the means of production and other, less advantaged political interests. Teams that enjoy this structural bias are able to accumulate higher revenues from television and other sources with which to purchase better players, just as corporations that enjoy a structural bias can utilize it to their political advantage to shape public opinion, lobby policymakers, contribute to candidates, and create supportive interest groups. The political conflict that ensues is unfair, similar to the way that the contest on the baseball diamond is unfair because of economic inequality, even though the rules are the same for everybody. But just as higher payrolls do not guarantee victories, so political advantages do not translate automatically into political success. The game still has to be played on the field. Politics still matters.

---

[2] Scott McCartney, "Leveling the Field," *Wall Street Journal*, October 18, 2004.

[3] Michael Lewis, *Moneyball* (New York: Norton, 2003), p. 270.

AMERICAN DEMOCRACY IN THEORY AND PRACTICE

We began this book by identifying the tension between democracy and capitalism, that is, the manner in which formal, legal equality and real, substantive inequality interact. Much of our analysis has described how American political institutions, processes, and policies can be better understood when this tension is placed at the front and center of analysis.

The Introduction of this book identified three elements that comprise a fuller approach to democracy than the usual standard requiring that all citizens have the right to participate in electing key political representatives. A more expansive definition goes beyond the guarantee of free and fair elections by requiring that citizens have the opportunity to participate in making political decisions, that citizens' interests be adequately represented, and that the political framework counter the advantages of class, race, and gender by promoting a more level playing field in the political, economic, and social spheres. When we judge the quality of American democracy by these measures, the political system comes up short. We analyze these three elements here in light of the material presented in this book.

First, consider whether the political system enables citizens to participate in deliberations that result in significant political decisions. For the most part, American politics is a spectator sport.[4] Even when political drama is at its most intense, such as during presidential elections, the great majority of those Americans who do "participate," do so by tuning into the presidential debates or writing a check to finance the campaign of their favored candidate or party.

The American political system also has a poor showing when judged by the second requirement of a more expansive democracy—that citizens' interests be adequately represented. The Introduction specified four criteria necessary to fulfill this requirement. The first is the need for procedures to ensure the full and fair expression of political views (especially unpopular ones) and strict adherence to procedures for electing representatives. As we discussed later in the book, the United States too often fails this test. Note the recent trend toward the enormous concentration of media control in a few giant corporations that makes it increasingly difficult for viewpoints outside the mainstream to be heard on network television or radio. (Granted, the centralization of the mainstream media has been partially offset by decentralized means of electronic communication—bloggers, cable television, and the like.) Note, too, the shocking violation of fair and honest electoral procedures. When dirty tricks are used to prevent citizens from registering to vote and votes are not counted—abuses practiced on a grand scale in the last two presidential elections—the United States fails an elementary test of democratic

---

[4] Robert D. Putnam, *Bowling Alone: The Collapse and Revival of American Community* (New York: Cambridge University Press, 2000), p. 41.

procedures. Consider other practices that systematically underrepresent substantial groups of citizens. For example, the Constitution specifies that every state elects two senators, a procedure that makes the votes of citizens of sparsely populated states worth several times as much as those of citizens from California, New York, Texas, Florida, and other large states. In another example, prohibiting convicted felons from exercising the right to vote disenfranchises millions of citizens (African American men are especially penalized).

The second criterion for adequately representing interests involves the need for political leaders to broadly reflect major social identities based on class, race, ethnicity, sex, and region. Congress is largely a club for affluent white men, although there has been some improvement in this respect in recent years. The mismatch between the demographics of Congress and the country at large means that Congress inadequately reflects the concerns of the diverse American electorate, especially African Americans, Hispanics, and women.

We discussed in the Introduction that a third dimension of political representation is responsiveness, the requirement that representatives seek to promote the interests of their constituents. In several chapters, we discussed how economic inequalities and political contributions by affluent citizens and organized interests powerfully influence the American political agenda. Chapter 10 analyzed important outcomes of this pattern of misrepresentation in that the American political system fails to meet basic social needs, such as housing and health care. More broadly, as in baseball, those who are wealthier and better organized are better able to compete in the great game of politics.

We also discussed in the Introduction that adequate representation can be fulfilled only when the political system is effective, which occurs when representatives can translate decisions into actual results. The American political system, with its multiple points of access and multiple opportunities for blocking reform, fails this test as well. Even when there is extensive mobilization for progressive reform, the cumbersome system of political decision making dilutes pressures for change.

The conclusion drawn from reviewing whether or not the American political system fulfills the promise of adequate representation is disquieting. And, following this failure—and closely connected to it—is the fact that the political system also fails the third major test of an expansive democracy: the narrowing of class, racial, ethnic, and sexual inequalities. As we have analyzed throughout this book, the American political system reflects, and even contributes, to these inequalities rather than narrowing them. As we stated in the Introduction, the fuller standard discussed here of substantive democracy represents a demanding yet realistic yardstick to assess the extent of democracy in America. Sadly, when we apply this yardstick, we find that America does not measure up in many key respects.

CAPITALISM AND DEMOCRACY

Our treatment of the politics of American power highlights what we identify as a tension at the very core of American politics, involving the tendency for capitalism to generate systematic inequalities as opposed to the tendency for democracy to promote equality. We have also stressed that the way this tension is structured and played out varies historically and from place to place. We provided concrete meaning to this claim throughout this book in our discussion of political institutions, public opinion and political culture, and public policy.

Our discussion of the way that capitalism is organized in the United States identified both generic features of a capitalist system of production—private ownership of capital, the principle of wage labor, and so on—as well as the ways in which American-style capitalism is distinctive. We termed this extreme market capitalism. One reason is that there is less public regulation in the United States compared to other advanced capitalist democracies. For example, consider the workplace rights that American workers enjoy. We referred to an account that describes how private employers in the United States "have more authority in deciding how to treat their workers than do employers in other advanced countries."[5] Another study reports, "By most international standards, American employers are still confronted with fewer direct regulations of employment conditions than employers in other countries."[6] More generally, the American model of extreme market capitalism has five parts: (1) deregulation—removing state restrictions on business, (2) privatization—shifting activities from the public to the private sector, where they will now be subject to the logic of the market, (3) labor flexibility—giving management a free hand in deploying labor by removing union work rules and government regulations from the workplace, (4) low taxes—letting the market and not the state direct the flow of society's income, and (5) a small safety net—reducing welfare state expenditures and making each citizen's welfare dependent on the market.

Thus, the United States is an outlier among advanced capitalist countries in terms of the balance between the two systems of organizing power (through private markets and through the public sphere). Moreover, the boundary between the two spheres varies not only among similar kinds of countries but historically within particular countries. Ever since the Reagan presidency in the 1980s, the scope of markets has increased and the scope of public regulation has declined. Since the boundaries between the private and public spheres vary rather than being determined once and for all, an obvious question is, "What determines changes in the relationship?"

---

[5] Richard B. Freeman and Joel Rogers, *What Workers Want* (Ithaca, NY: Cornell University Press, 1999), p. 1.

[6] Paul Osterman et al., *Working in America: A Blueprint for the New Labor Market* (Cambridge, MA: MIT Press, 2001), p. 47.

One can distinguish between two broad modes of change: structural and voluntaristic, meaning conscious political activity. Structural changes alter the basic framework within which politics is conducted, including political institutions, the broad distribution of economic, political, and social resources, and the composition and social identities of the citizenry. When the Department of Homeland Security was created in 2003, this reconfigured and expanded the size and power of executive agencies concerned with safeguarding the country from the threat of internal terrorism. Examples of structural economic changes are the concentration of economic resources by the mergers of giant corporations in recent years, the substantially increased extent of economic inequality, and changing demographic patterns (such as the growing proportion in the population of Hispanics and the elderly).

Structural change can be distinguished from voluntarist political activity aimed at changing the status quo. Elections are one means. Another is when citizens participate in social movements and other change-oriented organizations. Although the major emphasis in this book has been on the more enduring structural features of American politics, we discussed examples of voluntarist activity in Chapter 5.

Structural features and political activity are not independent of each other. When political activity is sufficiently powerful, it can alter structural features. Witness how the burgeoning environmental movement in the 1970s succeeded in introducing a host of public regulations to safeguard the environment, protect consumer safety, and increase occupational health and safety. Changes that affected the structure of the political and economic system ranged from fuel efficiency and safety standards in automobiles to a requirement that industries install technology minimizing pollution. More recently, determined citizens succeeded in partially reforming corporate accounting standards following the revelations of financial manipulation and fraud at Enron and WorldCom. Our intent is far from minimizing the importance of political activity. But the major focus of this book has been on how structural features of American political institutions and class structure misshape the playing field on which political struggles are waged. Attempts to reform face a steep uphill battle, especially when they involve challenges to structural features reflecting concentrations of wealth and power. Indeed, structural changes do not only reduce inequalities, as illustrated by the four major structural changes identified in the Introduction. We reexamine these changes here in light of the material analyzed in this book. We also seek to learn how political activity has affected these changes.

1. *THE UNITED STATES IS THE LONE SUPERPOWER IN A MORE INTERCONNECTED WORLD.* We described in Chapter 11 the position of the United States as the most powerful country in a world intensely interconnected as a result of technological, economic, and political changes. How the United States directs its vast power affects billions of people throughout the world. We suggested that a major aim of American foreign policy is to maintain the United States' unique advantage in order to reap the benefits of being number one.

The United States has been a superpower throughout the period since World War II. But only since the Soviet Union crumbled beginning in 1989 has it been the lone superpower. In the first years of the new era, under presidents George H.W. Bush and Bill Clinton, the United States sought to promote globalization and regional economic integration. For example, it was a sponsor of the North America Free Trade Association (NAFTA), designed to facilitate trade and investment among the United States, Canada, and Mexico. It sought to expand the regulatory power of the World Trade Organization (WTO). And the United States joined with other countries to promote humanitarian and peacekeeping operations in Somalia, the former Yugoslavia, and elsewhere.

Much changed following George W. Bush's election in 2000. In the first months of the Bush presidency, the United States shifted from supporting multilateralism to asserting power unilaterally in a more open display of dominance. From this perspective, U.S. actions following the attacks of September 11 on the World Trade Center and Pentagon mark not so much a break with the past as a sharp acceleration of the Bush administration's stance, initiated immediately after it took office, of asserting U.S. power unilaterally. The war on terrorism involved the U.S.-sponsored invasions of Afghanistan and Iraq to topple their regimes and attack al Qaeda, a substantial increase in U.S. military power abroad, and an expansion of government surveillance and control within the United States. The Bush administration made no secret of its intention to deal harshly with individuals, groups, or states who challenged U.S. global dominance.

2. MONEY HAS BECOME VASTLY MORE IMPORTANT TO POLITICAL DEBATE AND OUTCOMES. We documented at many points the vast amounts of money spent to shape election returns and political decisions. We also stressed that political contributions are highly concentrated, that is, a small number of private individuals and corporations give very large contributions to purchase political access and influence. We provided many examples in Chapter 5. Yet another example: The 2004 Republican National Convention held in New York City cost $154 million. Among the expenses: $11 million to renovate Madison Square Garden for the four-day affair, $300,000 for limousine services, $207,000 for the balloons that dropped from the ceiling after President Bush's acceptance speech, and about $100,000 to one of the hotels where delegates stayed. Most of these funds were provided by wealthy donors and corporations: New York mayor Michael R. Bloomberg and financier David Rockefeller gave $5 million apiece, and business firms, including Goldman Sachs (investment banking), Merrill Lynch (stockbrokers), and IBM, each contributed over $1 million.[7] Judging by the benefits these investments generate, it is money well spent. (Of course, the cost of the two nominating conventions pales in comparison with the more than $600 million that the two presidential candidates raised for the 2004 election.)

---

[7] *New York Times*, October 14, 2004, A-26.

Is it more than a coincidence that two recent trends have involved a substantial increase in economic inequality and an increase in political contributions by wealthy individuals and business interests? Trying to untangle cause and effect is like deciding whether the chicken or the egg comes first. That is, large political donations buy government action—or inaction—that in turn promotes further concentrations of wealth, while the newly accumulated wealth is a source of additional political contributions. In brief, round and round it goes, and where it stops, nobody knows.

The huge amounts of political money sloshing through the system, much of it provided by wealthy individual donors and large corporations, powerfully reinforces the status quo. The political marketplace is dominated by the two major parties and by political leaders who, whatever their beliefs, are painfully aware that they could not survive without the lifeline provided by political contributions. Outsiders may temporarily rock the ship, but without deep pockets to finance polls, advertising, and campaign organizations, they are unable to survive for long. The result of this situation is to fuel a widespread (and well-founded) belief among rank-and-file Americans that corporate money has corrupted our core democratic processes.

And yet, periodically in American history, this cycle has been stopped. Reform movements have mobilized to check the power of what was called, in the early 20th century, the "moneyed interests." Such movements exist today. But given the extent to which political institutions and policies have been reshaped by the power of political contributions, the fight to minimize the undue influence of private political contributions must be fought on an ever less level playing field.

3. Politics Has Become More Polarized in Terms Defined by the Interplay of Party, Class, Race, and Region. We analyzed in several chapters the fact that political parties have become more homogenous internally. As the South abandoned the Democratic party, in good measure because of the national Democratic party championing civil rights, the Democratic party became more liberal. Meanwhile, the Republican party became more conservative, as a result of the influx of conservative Southerners, rallying of business interests, and mobilization of the Christian right within the Republican party. Thus, as we discussed in Chapter 4, the atmosphere of bitter polarization is fueled by a partisan realignment in the electorate and Congress, in which the two parties are more homogenous internally and further apart externally. The intense partisan conflict has also been fueled by the close division between presidential candidates George W. Bush and Al Gore in 2000, and Bush and John Kerry in 2004. This ideological clash has become even more heated when electoral results are contested following charges of extensive fraud and corruption in regard to registering voters, intimidating voters, and counting votes, as occurred in the last two presidential elections.

4. Americans Demonstrate a Stronger Belief in the Virtue of Markets. We studied in various chapters how, as a result of ideological and partisan changes closely linked to the increased influence of political money, the balance has shifted from government to market forces. Compared to the situation in other capitalist countries, private enterprise has always enjoyed great freedom from government regulation in the United States. However, since the 1980s, market forces have obtained an even more secure position.

Many elements comprise the shift from public regulation, which tends to promote equality, to private markets, which tend to generate inequalities. Two important examples have occurred in the past several years. First, income and wealth have been redistributed upward, from Americans who work to those who control the economy. As a result of repeated tax cuts whose major benefits went to the wealthiest five percent of the population; stagnant wages at the bottom; steep increases in executive compensation at the top; and cutbacks in social spending, economic inequalities have sharply increased, the public sector is starved for funds, and the federal government runs annual deficits of hundreds of billions of dollars. Second, the impact of these changes has been compounded by changes in government tax policy and deregulation that have provided corporate America with greatly increased freedom, wealth, and power.

These shifts do not necessarily reflect changes in public opinion. On the one hand, public opinion has shifted toward the conservative end of the political spectrum; a majority of Americans now believe that government is too large, intrusive, and expensive. On the other hand, public opinion polls do not fully capture the widespread discontent about the results of market-based production, among groups ranging from elderly citizens who pay inflated prices for essential medicines to college students who challenge multinational corporations that violate human rights and labor rights in industrialized and less developed countries. Large majorities continue to favor vigorous government action in defense of the environment, better nutrition for poor children, and improved schooling.[8] A final point is that the media and corporate interests more generally have vigorously tried to shape public opinion. This has been apparent on specific issues, such as the successful advertising blitz in the early 1990s that blocked President Clinton's proposal to expand publicly financed health care. The media is often quite uncritical when presenting questionable official views. For example, more than a year after the U.S. invasion of Iraq in 2003, several newspapers and news magazines published articles apologizing for not having challenged the Administration's misleading justifications for going to war. (Of course, the apologies came too late to inform Americans during the public debate preceding the war.) At the most general level, the media and corporate sponsors help shape a climate of public opinion friendly to corporate capitalism. The campaign is waged by corporate sponsorship of sports events and stadiums, cultural institutions, public television, and

---

[8] Robert S. Erikson, Michael B. MacKuen, and James A. Stimson, *The Macro Polity* (New York: Cambridge University Press, 2002), pp. 203–210, 193–205.

conservative think tanks that convey the notion that private corporations are good public citizens.

CONCLUSION

We have analyzed in this book how political outcomes are a result of both the broad structural framework of American politics and the political struggles that occur within that framework. The two levels are analytically distinct but interrelated, for political struggles are affected by the structural framework and the outcome of political struggles affects the framework. Indeed, the structural framework is nothing more—although this is saying quite a lot—than the cumulative result of past political struggles. Why is this so important? Because however incomplete American democracy is, it provides ample space for political activism. Indeed, every one of the four important changes in American politics identified in Chapter 1 and restated in the preceding section has recently been challenged.

A central goal of this book has been to demonstrate that American democracy is flawed—and we have analyzed how structural factors are an important part of the explanation for the failings. One response to our description would be a cynical or resigned view that nothing much can be done to challenge the enormously powerful concentrations of wealth and power in the United States. Nothing could be further from the lesson that we hope students will take away from our account. Just as there have been momentous changes in the past, we can be confident that the future will be very different from the present.

But in what ways? The answer depends in large part on political participation—or nonparticipation. We urge students of American politics to be both critical and engaged: critical because, as this book has demonstrated, the promise of American democracy is far from being fulfilled; engaged because, without robust critical engagement, inequalities will intensify and produce an even more constricted form of democracy.

Critical engagement can be both politically effective and politically infectious. Ample opportunity exists to extend and deepen democratic possibilities. We hope that we have sufficiently informed readers about the politics of power for them to apply what they have learned in working to realize the thrilling promise of American democracy.

CREDITS